The Proportionality of State Intervention

Sebastian Weißschnur

The Proportionality of State Intervention

EU Responses to the Global Economic Crisis, 2008–2020

palgrave macmillan

Sebastian Weißschnur
Overath, Germany

ISBN 978-3-030-75675-8 ISBN 978-3-030-75676-5 (eBook)
https://doi.org/10.1007/978-3-030-75676-5

This Palgrave Macmillan imprint is published by the registered company Springer Nature Switzerland AG.
The registered company address is: Gewerbestrasse 11, 6330 Cham, Switzerland

This book is dedicated to those who believe that state intervention has a one-dimensional effect and that there is no need to question the current global economic and political science doctrine. The research underlying this text provides a rare opportunity to gain deep understanding of the European Union's financial policies and is therefore of particular relevance to lecturers and students of economic disciplines, the political advisors of EU Member States, and decision makers associated with the European Central Bank.

Preface

The research for this book commenced in 2015, initially as a potential thesis for a doctorate that would critically appraise the strategies and tactics taken by the European Union (EU) to recover from the global financial crisis, which began in 2007–2008. However, the project was gradually extended as a consequence of the diverse economic, political and social developments that occurred during that period culminating in EU responses to Brexit, and to the global COVID-19 pandemic. These two events represent the closing of an era of EU strategies and the commencement of a new one, which is likely to be shaped by changing global political order and the challenges of full integration of the former Central and Eastern European Member States. The series of unexpected events, which occurred during the thirteen years from 2008, meant that researching and writing the book were extremely interesting. The reader is provided with a brief history of the European Union, from the emergence of Council of Europe founded in 1949 to the signing of the Maastricht Treaty in 1992, which established it. In essence, the research confirmed German dominance in the group, and the widening political and social gap between powerful northern Member States and those in the south as a consequence of actions taken to mitigate the impact of the global financial crisis. The outcomes of those actions are shown to be contrary to the EU Principles of Proportionality and Subsidiarity that the populations of all Member States should be protected against the consequences of global financial instability. The stark differences between the outcomes of EU membership for different Member States are particularly evident from the three case studies focusing on Germany, Italy and the United Kingdom.

Overath, Germany Sebastian Weißschnur

Contents

List of Figures

List of Tables

CHAPTER 1

Introduction to the Research

Background

This research commenced in 2015 and began by tracing the origins of the European project in order to provide an understanding of how it developed and to determine its situation in 2008 at the time of the global financial crisis. The majority of the research and content of the chapters focus on the period from 2008 to 2015, but additions were made to reflect later important occurrences, and the present-day situation in 2020 is presented in the epilogue.

Origins of the European Union

The origins of the European Union are post 1945, the end of World War Two, and the underlying political philosophy for its formation was prevention of a recurrence of the conflict between major European nations that had occurred during that war, which had resulted in horrific events (OU, 2018). The Council of Europe (COE) was established in 1949 as an intergovernmental organisation with the purpose of preventing the previous social problems by promoting diversity and protecting individual human rights. This objective is embedded in Article 3 of the Statute of the Council of Europe which states that:

S. Weißschnur, *The Proportionality of State Intervention*,
https://doi.org/10.1007/978-3-030-75676-5_1

> every member of the Council of Europe must accept the principles of the rule of law and of the enjoyment by all persons within its jurisdiction of human rights and fundamental freedoms. (Council of Europe, 1949, p. 2)

The Council of Europe comprises 47 countries and has its headquarters in Strasbourg (Council of Europe, 2020); the European Convention on Human Rights became law in September 1953, such that all of the Member States committed to upholding human rights as a collective action.

By contrast the European Economic Community (EEC) was established in 1958, and created with the purpose of improving trade between the six initial member countries, making them interdependent, an additional intervention to minimise the conflict between them, which had been heightened during World War Two (EC, 2015). The original members were France, West Germany, Italy, Belgium, the Netherlands and Luxembourg. The European Union (EU) emerged as a political entity in 1993 from its economically based precursor.

The EU's key values are stated to be "respect for human dignity and human rights, freedom, democracy, equality and the rule of law" (European Parliament, 2015, p. 1), and any country that wishes to become an EU member must recognise these values, since they represent the source of member countries' unity. These values are set out by the Treaty of Lisbon, emphasising universal rights for all EU citizens and their political, economic and social rights. In addition, the Charter of Fundamental Rights forbids discrimination on the grounds of gender, race or skin colour. The European Parliament is the entity that passes legislation, which ensures that these values are upheld (European Parliament, 2015).

The 28 nations comprising the EU in 2008 developed from the initially small group of EEC countries, many of which also share a monetary union by means of the Euro (EC, 2015). The official European Council (EC) publication currently attributes over 50 years without conflict between the member nations to its presence. It also claims that members have experienced significant growth and stability, and that working and living in Europe have become easier (EC, 2015). However, the potential collapse of the Eurozone was imminent in 2015, owing to the conflict between the Greek government and European Central Bank (ECB), which refused to advance further funds to Greece unless it devised the appropriate austerity measures to reduce its national debt (Khan, 2015); this type of uncertainty continues to exist in the Eurozone as will become evident as this research progresses. The position of Greece and several other EU members, such as Italy and Portugal, does not reflect the prosperous growth and stability suggested by the EU, but instead demonstrate negative growth, labour issues owing to lack of economic stimulation to generate jobs and a falling standard of living (O'Leary, 2013). In 2014, Grillo Beppo, leader of the Italian Five Star Movement, cited the decline in the sovereign power of Member States to manage their own economics and finances, as the fundamental reason for requesting a national referendum on withdrawing from the Euro (BBC, 2014). New agreements with EU were sought by a newly elected Greek prime minister, Tsipras (Evans–Pritchard, 2015), and relations among the EU, ECB and the new Greek government became increasingly tense (Khan, 2015). The EU Principles of Proportionality and Subsidiarity are no longer regarded as reasonable or supportive by significant proportions of the public in the EU Member States.

Proportionality is generally based on the concept of justice and protection of the rights of human beings against political actions that could reduce or eliminate those rights. The core of the Proportionality Principle is the integration of "a liberal rights-based constitutional rationality with a strong commitment to a welfare state", according to Harbo (2010, p. 158). The EU's interpretation of the Principle of Proportionality is drawn from the associated traditional laws of the member countries, the influence of each country's law being dependent on its status within the group. This interpretation principally relies on the German concept of reasonableness and the French idea of balance of interests, according to Portuese (2013). The Principle pervades almost every aspect of EU community law. A key EU objective is to prevent market failure and therefore to reduce the number of public goods that would be needed to act as substitutes for those failures (Portuese, 2013). The EU employs Cost Benefit Analysis (CBA) to select a variety of public projects and to design regulation, so that the resulting benefits outweigh the costs met by public funding, and must represent the optimum selection against the available alternatives. The EU's description of the Principle of Proportionality is to limit the EU's power to specific actions necessary to accomplish the objectives of its Treaties (EU, 2014). The EUR-Lex (2020a p.1) provides the official definition as:

> The Principle Of Proportionality regulates the exercise of powers by the European Union (EU) as does the Principle Of Subsidiarity. It seeks to set actions taken by EU institutions within specified bounds. Under this rule,

> the action of the EU must be limited to what is necessary to achieve the objectives of the Treaties. In other words, the content and form of the action must be in keeping with the aim pursued. The principle of proportionality is laid down in Article 5 of the Treaty on European Union. The criteria for applying it are set out in the Protocol (No 2) on the application of the principles of subsidiarity and proportionality annexed to the Treaties.

The Treaty on European Union and the Treaty establishing the European Community were combined into the Treaty of Lisbon (European Parliament, 2020). The concept of proportionality is translated practically into EU legal activities in three ways: to eliminate an existing Act if it is no longer appropriate to EU treaty objectives; to enforce changes or elimination of Member State laws that do not align with treaty objectives; to restrict the EU Regulator's legislatorial discretion, which must be proportionate to the specified objective (Portuese, 2013).

The Principle of Subsidiarity embraces the idea of offering support to individuals or groups that may not have the skills or knowledge to accomplish an agreed goal or to solve a problem (Stoain, 2013). The EU interpretation of this Principle is regarded by Stoain (2013) as providing it with the capacity to support Member States in meeting any aspect of Treaty objectives, if it considers the Member States do not have the appropriate competencies and that the EU could achieve the objective more effectively (Stoain, 2013). The EU Principle of Subsidiarity is officially defined in EUR-Lex (2020b, p.1) as:

> The principle of subsidiarity is defined in Article 5 of the Treaty on European Union. It aims to ensure that decisions are taken as closely as possible to the citizen and that constant checks are made to verify that action at EU level is justified in light of the possibilities available at national, regional or local level.
>
> Specifically, it is the principle whereby the EU does not take action except in the areas that fall within its exclusive competence, unless it is more effective than action taken at national, regional or local level. It is closely bound up with the principle of proportionality, which requires that any action by the EU should not go beyond what is necessary to achieve the objectives of the Treaties.
>
> There are two Protocols annexed to the Treaty of Lisbon that are key:
>
> Protocol No 1 on the role of national Parliaments encourages national Parliaments' involvement in EU activities and requires EU documents

and proposals to be forwarded promptly to them so they can examine them before the Council takes a decision.

Protocol No 2 requires the Commission to take into account the regional and local dimension of all draft legislative acts and to make a detailed statement on how the principle of subsidiarity is respected. This Protocol allows national Parliaments to object to a proposal on the grounds that it breaches the principle, as a result of which the proposal must be reviewed and may be maintained, amended or withdrawn by the Commission, or blocked by the European Parliament or the Council.

In the case of a breach of the principle of subsidiarity, the Committee of the Regions or EU countries may refer an adopted act directly to the Court of Justice of the EU.

Therefore, the EU's definition of the Principle of Subsidiarity suggests that it will determine the degree of intervention required as relevant to the competencies shared between it and the Member State(s). This EU statement infers that the level of EU control will be determined on the basis of the EU's perceived capacity to be more effective than the state concerned, which suggests that tensions will arise when the Member State(s) does not agree that the EU to be more effective, and/or its interventions would be in conflict with its/their sovereign rights. Application of this Principle is exemplified by EU amendments to the Stability and Growth Pact (SGP), which forces Member States to agree to planning and implementing austerity budgets, monitored by the EU, so that their debt levels do not deter development of the EU as a whole. This is legislation that undermines the sovereign rights of states to manage their own finances (Lavdas et al., 2013). These principles are therefore important to this research, since the Principle of Proportionality should have protected the rights of EU member citizens as a result of the global crisis, and the actions taken by EU should have objectively considered the relative competencies of individual members; whether this was/is the case or not is a matter for appraisal in this study.

Hence, this period of EU history represents a particularly interesting opportunity to examine the proportionality of EU intervention in the market economies of member countries and what, how and why this has changed and resulted in the malicious state of affairs between the ECB and strong EU countries, particularly Germany and Greece. Hence, by tracing the origins of this position beyond the global economic crisis, which emerged in mid- to late-2007, this study seeks to critically appraise the policy measures instigated by the EU to manage the impact of macroeconomic conditions on its member countries and to consider their legitimacy, given the bloc's defined Principles of Proportionality and Subsidiarity. A study into the organisation of the EU conducted by Panico and Purificato (2013) sought to appraise how monetary and fiscal policies were managed before the global crisis and the impact this had on economic cycles within the member countries. The research found that the policies employed were inconsistent and unsound, leading to conflict with EU authorities and among Member States. The state interventions had not resulted in outcomes that aligned with EU Principles of Proportionality and Subsidiarity, since the populations of Member States had not been protected against the consequences of global financial instability. A crucial example related to the development of the Greek financial crisis and the manner that the EU and the ECB had managed it. Prior to the 2007 crisis, investor perceptions of Greek and German bonds were relatively equivalent, their 10-year bonds had similar interest rates. Prior to the bankruptcy of the Lehman Brothers in 2008, the interest rate difference between these bonds was only 0.79% but rose to 2.85% soon afterwards, and then fluctuated until Greece elected a new government. At this time, the revelation of financial mismanagement by the previous Greek government resulted in a 6.24% differential, which continued to grow and resulted in speculation on Greek debt. This situation was considered to have arisen owing to the lack of action by the ECB to intervene in the bond market and to buy Greek the bonds being sold by investors, which feared debt default by Greece (Panico & Purificato, 2013). In reality, the ECB was not willing to act as the lender of last resort by buying up the bonds as government debt, as had occurred in other countries, such as the UK and US. The reason for this omission was that acting as lender of last resort is not a mandated action in ECB rules (Winkler, 2014). The EC also failed to extend the credit to Greece, which should have been guaranteed by European Council of the Economic and Financial Ministers (ECOFIN). There were accusations that Greek government policies were responsible for its debt crisis, and that these policies had enabled Greek citizens to have a higher standard of living than could be provided for by their economic situation (Panico & Purificato, 2013). When ECOFIN eventually decided to act, loans for Greece were agreed but concurrently a new procedure, referred to as the European Financial Stabilisation Mechanism (EFSM), was instigated by the EU, which had the purpose of providing funds to Member States requesting financial assistance by means of a new private fund called the European Financial Stability Facility (ESFS). The conditions for granting such loans were based on the assumptions that government policies were not effective in managing the crisis. In Greece, the first recipient of the financial facility, the conditions of the loan were to effectively enforce considerably reduced public sector spending in the form of salary cuts of 22% for public sector employees, plus social service and local public service cuts. These restrictive measures, which were agreed and monitored by the EU, ECB and the International Monetary Fund (IMF), actually worsened the poor working conditions and inequality of income among individuals. However, the measures had little effect on redressing the issues; instead the country's gross domestic product (GDP) fell, and its debt-to-income ratio did not fall as was assumed by EU (Panico & Purificato, 2013). This type of approach had previously been ineffective in Latin American countries as research by Capraro and Perrotini (2013) confirmed; in other words, economic growth was found to be negatively impacted by austerity policies. The creation of the ESFS signalled a change of philosophy by the EC, since providing financial assistance to member countries by increasing the monetary base had previously been contrary to its policy principles (Panico & Purificato, 2013). This new approach to financial assistance is represented by the total amount of currency that is circulated either in the public sphere or in the commercial bank deposits held in the central bank reserves (Williams, 2012).

The research findings of Panico and Purificato (2013) and the apparent mismatch between EU founding principles and its austerity policies represent a fundamental rationale for this study. This research had the purpose of examining the long-term impact of the Principle of Proportionality of State Intervention on EU market economies more closely. It appraised the effects of the global financial crises on Member States, and considered the sustainability of the Euro as the common currency of Member States currently committed to it. The evolving nature of actions taken by the EU, their consequences on Member States and their citizens, and the shift in philosophy that may have occurred infer that this study of a contemporary issue will be of interest to a broad range of readers. Ultimately it acts as a reference guide to those individuals and groups wishing to gain more insight into how the EU functions and adheres to its founding principles. This project began as a research paper, so that its format has that theme, as implied by this first introductory chapter, research methodology and theoretical and empirical discussion of various themes.

Study Purpose and Objectives

This research was chosen for a variety of reasons but fundamentally to critically evaluate the position that the EC has taken to uphold the principles for which it was founded, whilst attempting to manage the effects of the global financial crisis on Member States; the EC is the body which represents the interests of the EU Member States and comprised representatives of them. The actions taken by the EC were made in an attempt to ensure that the impact on individual Member State development and EU collective development was minimised as much as possible. Previous academic study findings indicated that this has not been the case (Panico & Purificato, 2013) and that the policies implemented to manage Member State debt levels conflicted with the established theories. In countries that experience high debt levels, the interest payable on the debt reduced the economic growth rate, however, this could be mitigated if growth was stimulated, because the debt to GDP could be permanently stabilised when the economy grew faster than debt (Domar 1944 cited in Capraro & Perrotini, 2013). A study by Pasinetti (1997) also found that if the growth rate was greater than the interest rate on the debt, the latter would fall to zero. As the financial crisis developed and led to the Eurozone crisis, comparisons and contrasts can be made regarding the inconsistent impact the crisis had on the economies of different EU members, as well as the diverse relationships that have evolved between the EU and individual members.

Therefore, the overall purpose of this study is to critically appraise the proportionality of intervention of the EU in the market economies of EU Member States, according to the definition of development present in the Treaties, in the context of global financial crises. Consequently, it examines the public sector debt levels of some Member States, which were regarded as excessive and damaging to the development of the European Union. In order to accomplish this aim, the underpinning economic, political and financial reasons for the recession, which commenced in 2007, the subsequent credit crunch and debt crisis and interventions to mitigate their effects need to be evaluated, particularly those of the EU and individual member countries.

The key objectives of the research are to:

- Identify the underlying reasons for the global economic crisis that commenced in 2007

- Establish the meaning of global credit crunch and its major effects on states, economies, banks, capital flow and credit facilities
- Determine the causes of the global debt crisis and the effects globally and in the EU
- Identify the options governments generally have available for intervention in markets and those specifically employed in the EU
- Critically appraise EU responses to the economic crisis, the policies implemented, the rationale for them, their effects on individual countries and the EU as an economic/trading bloc
- Evaluate the methodology for supervising EU fiscal affairs
- Establish and evaluate EU policies on economic growth and employment
- Assess the positive and negative effects of EU intervention in the market economies of its member countries
- Suggest the future sustainability of EU

Therefore, the research sought to determine how the strategies taken by the EU in response to the global financial and external public debt crisis align with the Principle of the Proportionality of State Intervention in the market economies of European countries.

Two major research questions emerged from the problem statement integrated in this introduction:

RQ1: To what extent did the Principles of Proportionality and Subsidiarity protect the rights of EU Member States after the global economic crisis which began in 2007–2008?

RQ2: How effectively and objectively did the EU consider the relative competences of the Member States to manage the impact of the crisis on their economies and citizens?

These questions generate a third question relative to extension of this research to 2020 and beyond.

RQ3: What is the long-term impact of the application of the Principle of Proportionality of State Intervention on the individual EU market economies of original members of the single market?

The last research question provides the opportunity to identify trends in countries that have been members of the European Community for 30 years, similarities and differences in how the economies have evolved, as well as their relationships with EU institutions such as the European Commission (EC) and the European Central Bank (ECB).

The research undertaken is of ongoing and increasing significance, since it represents contemporary economic and financial issues managed by an institution instigated to maximise economic growth and prosperity as a consequence of political, economic and monetary union. The recent global financial crisis appears to have impacted inconsistently throughout the Member States; however, the EU, acting as a managing institution, has reacted by implementing a universal framework to rectify the government problems and/or private debt levels in all Member States, which currently appears to be ineffective and threatening to its existence and that of the Euro. These matters have serious global and European political implications for the EU, and trading blocs in other parts of the world, for world financial and economic stability and the capacity of institutions such as the International Monetary Fund (IMF) to continue operations in the context of multiple states defaulting on their public debt. Matters are complex and involve critically appraising the rationale behind EU strategies, legislation, interventions in Member States and their relative success in meeting their objectives, over a period of time extending beyond the 2007 crisis, as well as assessing the impact of globalisation and global trends on Europe during this period. The study also adds to published knowledge and seeks to reduce gaps regarding the successes and limitations of interventions by administrative bodies representing trading and/or currency blocs.

The author of this research report, who also conducted the research, is a citizen living in one of the Member States, and affected by the initial global crisis, but more recently by the Eurozone crisis. The Euro crisis threatens the sustainability of Europe as a viable trading bloc, since it was the complementary monetary system put in place to simplify and facilitate trade flows, and intended to leverage the prosperity and stability of member populations. Until the 2007 crisis, membership of the EU was regarded by non-members as a goal to aspire to, as a means of enhancing labour and financial flow, increasing standards of living and strengthening relationships between countries. However, opinions against retaining or gaining membership have become more noticeable (Braniff, 2011; AFP, 2015). Hence, undertaking this study enables the researcher to critically evaluate the extent of proportionality and subsidiarity within state intervention in these market economies, as well as the sustainability of the EU in its current form. As this research evolves and conclusions are drawn from the evidence gathered, new opportunities for research and further understanding of EU processes and their impact on Member States can be suggested.

Research Overview

The purpose of this study is ultimately to consider whether the EU is sustainable in its current form from the evidence gathered, by focusing on how it has interpreted and implemented its stated Principles of Proportionality and Subsidiarity, since the beginning of the global financial crisis. Therefore, the starting point is to critically appraise global economic principles before the crisis began, to set the scene and answer questions about what happened, how it developed and why the consequences were so far reaching. The EU's structure and functioning and the choices made for intervention from the options available are the foundation for understanding the selected EU strategy for dealing with the crisis, in a manner proposed as appropriate to limiting damage to the development and accomplishment of EU goals, and hence the prosperity of Member States. Interventions implemented by the EU to create financial stability, whilst encouraging economic growth and governance, employment prospects and monitor fiscal affairs, will each be appraised so that the impact made by Member State governments in meeting these goals can be assessed and future sustainability forecast.

The research framework is shown in Fig. 1.1.

Methodology

The research design for this thesis is based on the convergent model (Creswell, 2013), a combination of explanatory and exploratory approaches, which examines links between key variables and concurrently identifies new insights into existing issues, respectively; the results are then integrated. Hence, the study has theory testing, a deductive element, as well as theory building or an inductive element (Saunders et al., 2009). The research philosophy selected for this study is bridged-interpretivism with positivism, as perceived by Weber (1864–1920), cited in Ritchie and Lewis (2010), which is appropriate for this research because its purpose is to critically appraise objective facts and evaluate the subjective views and opinions of EU stakeholders. These stakeholders comprise those directly

Research Framework

- Introduction to Research: Purpose and Key Objectives
- State Intervention and Principle of Proportionality
- Global Credit Crisis/Recession
- Interventions by Governments, Including the EU government
- Research Methodology
- Discussion and Findings
- EU response to crisis
- EU initiatives
- Conclusions on the effect of government interventions, with regard to proportionality and subsidiarity and sustainability of EU in its present form
- **EU in 2020**

Case Studies: Italy, UK, Germany. Epilogue

Fig. 1.1 Research framework

affected, such as Member States and their citizens, and governments, institutions and people in other global locations.

The selected methodology is mixed methods since it is able to effectively integrate the two approaches to answer the research question with as considerable insight. Mixed methodology tests existing theories using a positive cause and effect approach that includes analysing quantitative data, but is also able to consider and appraise qualitative, open-ended subjective facts that impact on the issues leading to the current uncertainties about the EU's sustainability, at least in its current form. One methodology alone would not suffice for this study, since understanding statistical trends is vital, but so are social and behavioural factors. The mixed methodology approach is considered to minimise weaknesses in how both single methodologies are perceived by diverse academic and business groups (Creswell, 2013). Quantitative methods that examine links between variables in an objective manner, referred to as a close-ended approach, are considered restrictive because the underlying causes of the objective link driven by the values and experiences of participants are not explored. In contrast qualitative research is regarded as being limited in its generalisability to other contexts and too open to researcher misinterpretation, which is considered subjective (Ritchie & Lewis, 2010; Creswell, 2013). The research strategy uses a case study, which is appropriate because the research represents an in-depth appraisal of one organisation, scrutinises a real-life phenomenon, uses multiple information sources and considers the questions why, what and where of the research, fundamental to answering the research question (Yin, 2013). Case studies are often employed in research related to political science (Johnson & Reynolds, 2012), further justifying the strategy selected. This study is predominantly based on secondary research employing a range of highly reliable published documents available in the public domain; this researcher is aware that these documents were published for other purposes and data may have been manipulated (Johnson & Reynolds, 2012). However, potential weaknesses can be minimised by careful selection of sources (Saunders et al., 2009). A quantitative survey is also conducted to explore the perceptions of EU actions on citizens in three European states. Mixed methods data analysis requires numerical and textual data to be analysed separately so that quantitative data is analysed by means of statistical techniques and relationships between variables are represented by charts and graphs. In contrast, qualitative data gathered by carefully reading and searching source texts for key information is analysed by them for the meanings attached to words and phrases, so that the results can be organised into themes, presented in matrices and rechecking interpretations against original sources (Creswell, 2013; Ritchie and Lewis, 2010; Miles & Huberman, 1994).

Overview of State Structures

The major structures adopted by states are critically appraised so that the EU structure can be understood in the context of available choices. The European Union is considered to be based on the federal system of government (Stevens-Finlayson, 2019), in contrast to other contemporary forms of government such as federations and unitary systems. A federal system is described as comprising two co-existing levels of government, which are coordinated but have autonomous power (Riker, 1964). A different interpretation of federalism proposed by Filippov et al. (2004) is that federal government comprises policymakers operating at various levels, who are elected to those positions. The US, Australia, Russia, Mexico and the Federal Republic of Germany are further examples of federal systems (Stevens-Finlayson, 2019; Heslop, 2020). The main categories of governmental system are illustrated in Fig. 1.2.

A confederation system is characterised by a less formal agreement in which individual nations are bound to a central government and can choose to implement their laws or not; examples are Switzerland, which is composed of cantons, and the Commonwealth of Independents States that was previously the Soviet Union (Heslop, 2020).

In contrast a unitary state comprises local governments, which are subordinate to a central government, for instance the United Kingdom (UK) is regarded as unitary state that delegates some powers to Wales Scotland and Northern Ireland, as stated in the Internal Market Bill, which came into force in July 2020 (Deacon, 2020). The UK has a clearly defined list of responsibilities, and all other duties are devolved to the three countries; China is also a unitary state. The rationale for a unitary state being that too much centralisation of authority would demotivate local governments from contributing to the economic growth of the nation and to its stability (Kin, 2009).

The division of powers in a federalist approach is a strategy to reduce the degree of power held by one institution or individual and to enhance accountability; often the power and resources shared by the constituent bodies are defined by a written Constitution agreed by the parties (Auclair,

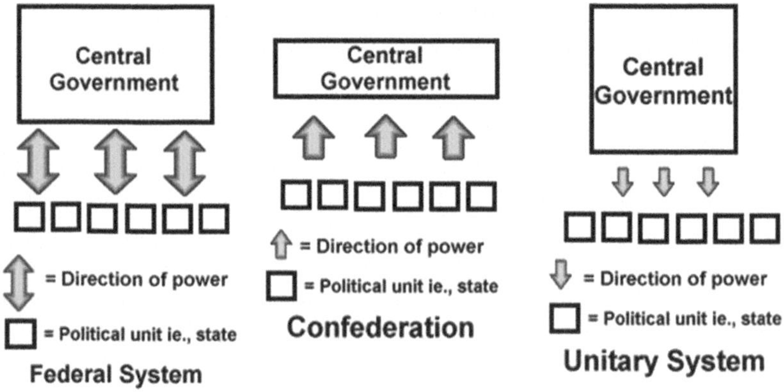

Fig. 1.2 Federal, confederation and unitary governmental systems. (Source: Britannica 2020 cited by Skyline College 2020)

2002). The Constitution stresses three government divisions: Legislative, which defines the laws; Executive that ensures laws are implemented and managed; Judicial that has the purpose of evaluating the law (Stevens-Finlayson, 2019). The meaning of federalism in the EU gives it precedence over the Member States and sub states in matters in which it is perceived the more competent body; Deacon (2020) notes that in recent years the range of matters in which the EU is considered to be more competent than its Member States has grown considerably, particularly those associated with the single market. However, Deacon (2020) emphasises that changes to EU law, and by association competence in specific matters, must be ratified by the European Parliament as complying with the Principles of Proportionality and Subsidiarity. If specific Member States consider that these Principles have not been followed, they can lodge an appeal with the EU Court of Justice (Deacon, 2020).

The major advantages of federalism are that there is free trade amongst members, freedom of movement within the entire geographical region, for example for educational, employment and tourism purposes, and channels for enabling citizens to voice their opinions and concerns to more than one government level. A common currency is often an additional advantage, which provides greater financial and economic security, and democracy is perceived as being stronger (Stevens-Finlayson, 2019).

Although many federalist arrangements operate globally, the EU interpretation is closest to that of the US; the EU federation comprises 27 states after Brexit and the continental US federation 50 states. In both cases the Member States share the powers stated in the respective Constitutions with the three federal government divisions. Similarly there is an institution that operates to enable discussion of matters relevant to the federal and member governments; the US House of Representatives and the Council of the European Union.

The political structures in both groups are similar in respect to many aspects of policy, although Table 1.1 demonstrates the more heterogeneous power sharing that operates in the EU.

The comparison table suggests that decisions regarding monetary, trade and agricultural policy are the only activities in which US and EU align; far more policymaking is delegated to Members States in EU than in US. Defence and fiscal policies, education, health, social and employment decisions, for instance, are taken mostly by specific, independent state ministries. However in the case of social and employment policy, shared decisions relate only to social welfare and employment in the Member

Table 1.1 Shared policymaking in EU compared with US

	European Union (EU)	*United States (US)*
Agricultural Policy	Power: Federal Institutions: Common Agricultural Policy	Power: Federal Institutions: US Department of Agriculture
Culture & Tourism	Power: Federal Institutions: State institutions vary across Member States	Power: Shared Institutions: Department of State and Department of Commerce (federal) and equivalent state agencies
Defence Policy	Power: Shared Institutions: Ministry of Defence or equivalent	Power: Federal Institutions: Department of Defense and Department of Homeland Security
Education Policy	Power: Shared Institutions: Ministry of Education or equivalent	Power: Shared Institutions: US Department of Education (federal) and equivalent state agencies
Energy Policy	Power: Shared Institutions: European Commission (federal level) state institutions vary across Member States	Power: Shared Institutions: US Department of Energy (federal) and equivalent state agencies
Environmental Policy	Power: Shared Institutions: European Commission, European Parliament and more (federal level) state institutions vary across Member States	Power: Federal Institutions: Environmental Protection Agency
Fiscal Policy	Power: Shared Institutions: Independent fiscal institutions vary across Member States	Power: Shared Institutions: President and Congress (federal) and state Department(s) of Revenue
Foreign Policy	Power: State Institutions: Ministry of Foreign Affairs or equivalent	Power: Federal Institutions: US Department of State
Health Policy	Power: State Institutions: Ministry of Health or equivalent	Power: Shared Institutions: Department of Health and Human Services (federal) and equivalent state agencies
Monetary Policy	Power: Federal Institutions: European Commission, European Parliament and more	Power: Federal Institutions: Federal Reserve

(*continued*)

Table 1.1 (continued)

	European Union (EU)	*United States (US)*
Social and Employment Policy	Power: State Institutions: Employment Social Policy, Health and Consumer Affairs Council (federal) state institutions vary across Member States	Power: Shared Institutions: Department of Labor, Security Administration and more (federal) and equivalent state agencies
Taxation	POWER:SHARED Institutions: State institutions vary across Member States	POWER:SHARED Institutions: Treasury Department (federal) and state Department(s) of Revenue
Trade Policy	Power: Federal Institutions: European Commission, European Parliament and more	Power: Federal Institutions: Department of Commerce

Source: Gold Mercury International/Stevens-Finlayson (2019, p. 7)

State, whilst the federal government devises policies related to labour rights and social security and coordinates the diverse national policies on these matters. Policy sharing for taxation and energy is common to both state structures, where the European Commission and the European Court of Justice collaborate with Member States. However in the EU, defining tax rates and collection of taxes remain the responsibility of the individual Member States and, whilst the EU has not harmonised them, it strongly influences decisions on tax reform and issues that would diminish cross-border economic activities (Stevens-Finlayson, 2019). The implication is that the EU federal government does not have either the authority or the capacity to manage its policies and cannot be compared on an equal basis to the US, according to Young (2018).

Two major differences between the EU and US federal governments are that the EU has no formal Constitution, instead it was formed by the Treaty of Rome, which was superseded by the Treaty of the Functioning of the European Union (Stevens-Finlayson, 2019); the concept of a Constitution was rejected by some Member States weakening its position (Young, 2018). This potential weakness is explained by Moravcsik (2006, pp. 219–220), who proposes that a Constitution is an important major federal government instrument for enhancing policy coordination and encouraging a national identity that generates unity between the Member States. A Constitution also enables clarification of the structure so that citizens gain a better understanding of the arrangement and subsequently increases the legitimacy of its actions (Moravcsik, 2006|). Identification of EU Member States with the EU has been weak in contrast with those forming the US, according to Cameron (2010) and Young (2018), potentially as a consequence of the lack of Constitution, but also the lower levels of power sharing illustrated. In essence Young (2018) emphasises that the EU is not totally federalist in nature but also resembles an intergovernmental model, in which the Member States tend to negotiate in their own interest in order to retain their rights. Hence the EU is perceived by Member States as undemocratic and complementary, and as following the liberal intergovernmentalist principle as being in existence owing to their agreement for its existence (Young, 2018). The individual EU and US Member States are also organised politically in diverse ways; the political structure of US Sates tends to be quite similar so that there is a greater perception of a shared identity than experienced by EU Member States (Stevens-Finlayson, 2019).

Overview of EU Institutions and Key Actors

The EU comprises seven institutions as defined in Article 13 of the Treaty of the European Union (EUR-Lex, 2020c); the interconnections between them are graphically represented in Fig. 1.3.

The purpose of these institutions is to implement EU values and objectives, protect and promote its interests and those of Member States and their citizens in a coherent and effective manner (EUR-Lex, 2020c). The European Commission established in 1958 is responsible for devising legislation, which is approved or rejected by the European Parliament and the Council of Ministers. The laws passed are implemented by the European Court of Justice, which ensures a standard interpretation of each EU law in all Member States. The Council of Ministers comprises representatives of all Member States, the number of representatives for each Member State being dependent on the population in each nation; it appoints the 27 Commissioners to the European Commission as representatives of their Member States, based on the approval of Parliament. The European Parliament also has the purpose of supervising the Commissioners and the unique authority to dismiss them. The Court of Auditors has responsibility for the EU Budget and monitors the efficiency of the expenditure (BBC, 2010; EU, 2020).

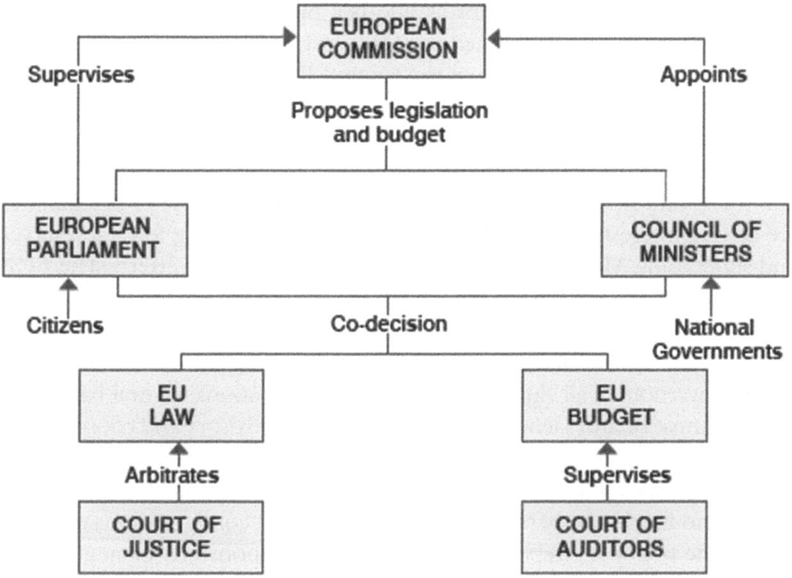

Fig. 1.3 The seven institutions of European Union. (Source: BBC (2010, p.1))

The European Parliament has three purposes: Legislative including passing EU laws, making decisions on accepting new Member States and on international agreements; Supervisory associated with ensuring all EU institutions operate in a democratic manner, electing the President of the European Commission and approving past budget expenditure, and discussing monetary policy with ECB assessing petitions presented by citizens and directing inquiries; and Budgetary comprising devising the EU budget and approving long-term budget plans. The Parliament is composed of MEPs from each Member State proportionate to population (EU, 2020). The EU Commission comprises a President and a Commissioner for each EU Member State; in addition to proposing new law, it enforces EU law, manages EU policies and allocates funding on the basis of priority and represents the EU in an international context (EU, 2020).

The Presidents of the European Parliament, the European Commission and the European Council are considered the most powerful in the EU. Their major responsibilities are summarised in Table 1.2.

The European Central Bank is another major contributor of the EU objectives, which was established in 1998, and key actors are the President, Vice-President and Governors of the Central Banks of Member States. The ECB President represents it at the most important EU and international conferences. Its main purpose is to manage the national currency, the Euro, and shape EU economic and monetary policies to enhance economic growth and job creation, which keep prices stable. Integral to these responsibilities are setting interest rates for Eurozone countries, managing foreign reserves and supervising Member State financial institutions (ECB, 2020). The ECB comprises three decision-making divisions: Executive Board that manages short-term activities and comprises President, Vice-President and four others elected by leaders of Eurozone countries; Governing Council which comprises Governors of all Eurozone Member States' national central banks and the Executive Board; General Council acting as an advisory and coordination body with the same composition as the Governing Council (ECB, 2020).

The European Council is a separate body from the Council of Ministers and has no fixed membership, but may meet in ten configurations depending on the policy matters to be discussed. It is responsible for negotiating and adopting EU laws in consultation with the European Parliament, where both bodies consider proposals presented by the European Commission. It also has the purpose of coordinating the policies of Member States, developing foreign and security policies, adopts the EU

Table 1.2 Priorities of EU Presidents

President	*European Parliament*	*European Commission*	*European Council*
appointed by	*Elected by members*	*Elected by heads of Member States; approved by EU Parliament*	*Elected by heads of Member States*
Major priorities	- Responsible for ensuring correct procedures are adhered to - Manages all activities - Approves the EU Budget - Represents Parliament in all legal matters and international relations	- Political guidance for the Commission - Initiates and chairs EU Commission meetings - Ensures EU policies are implemented - Participates in G7 meetings - Contributes to major debates in Parliament, between governments and in Council of EU	- Liaises with EU Commission to devise EU general political strategies and priorities - Promotes consensus and coherence - Represents EU in external foreign and security matters

Source: Author (EU, 2020)

budget in conjunction with the Parliament and reaches agreements with various other counties and institutions.

Structure of Research Report

This research comprises nine chapters. Chapter 1 is the introduction to the research and organisation of the chapters, which outlines the research problem, sets out the aims and objectives and indicates their importance and contribution to existing knowledge. Chapter 2 presents, discusses and justifies the research methods selected to answer the research question most effectively, including how reliability and validity of the research are enhanced and ethical considerations approached. The findings, analysis and discussion of the research are presented Chaps. 6 and 7. The literature review consists of three chapters: Chap. 3 critically appraises concepts of political science and philosophy most related to this thesis and outlines the impact of state intervention after 2008; Chap. 4 reviews the events leading up to the 2007 global financial crisis and how it developed globally and in various EU member countries; Chap. 5 evaluates the options that governments have for intervening in markets and specifically how EU intervenes in the market to accomplish its objectives, on behalf of the Member States. These three chapters represent a logical starting point for this research, since they provide the background to how the financial crisis shaped specific interventions ultimately taken by the EU to minimise the impact on its development objectives, as well as to examine major options governments employ to intervene in markets with focus on EU. Hence, it is possible to discover how key principles comprising EU intervention were adapted to do so, as becomes apparent as a consequence of the research. In Chap. 6, the responses to the global economic crisis employed by the EU are reported, including an overview of measures taken to ensure financial stability, growth and employment as well as improving corporate governance to provide greater protection against the risk of a future similar crisis. The overview then concentrates on governance, legal framework and creation of the ESFS. Chapter 7 is concerned with how the EU is organised to supervise its fiscal affairs, for instance, banking and banking supervision, insurance and occupational pensions, and systemic risk as a consequence of the crisis; it also includes some discussion of original methods and how these changed to meet new challenges. Chapter 8 is concerned with the support mechanisms put into place for economic growth and job creation, the common targets for growth, EU compact, EC Council to boost youth unemployment and appraisal of the single market as a driver for EU member growth. It draws conclusions on the effects of state intervention and the problems it has caused to Member States, exactly how this intervention relates to the Principles of Proportionality and Subsidiarity, and finally the implications of interventions taken for EU sustainability in its current form. The final chapter entitled 'Europe in 2020' appraises the European project 75 years after the end of World War Two by means of three case studies that compare and contrast their development as members of the single market and an epilogue that summarises the EU in July 2020.

Summary

This chapter set out the framework for the entire study, providing both the researcher and the reader with a snapshot of how the research developed and a robust framework to support focus on answering the research problem. The full details of the methodology are presented, discussed and justified in the next chapter.

Bibliography

AFP. (2015, March 12). Iceland Drops EU Membership Bid: 'Interests Better Served Outside' Union. *The Guardian*. http://www.theguardian.com/world/2015/mar/12/iceland-drops-european-union-membership-bid. Accessed 2 Apr 2015.

Auclair, C. (2002). Federalism: Its Principles, Flexibility, and Limitations. In *Forum of Federations, 2nd International Conference on Decentralization "Federalism: The Future of Decentralizing States?" July 25–27, 2002*; Manila, Philippines.

BBC. (2010, September 9). How EU Institutions Work: Overview. *BBC News*. https://www.bbc.com/news/world-europe-11710564. Accessed 22 Dec 2020.

BBC. (2014, November 24). Italy's Beppe Grillo Calls for Referendum on Leaving Euro. *BBC* [online]. https://www.bbc.com/news/av/world-europe-30031810. Accessed 2 April 2015.

Braniff, C. (2011). *Integrating the Balkans: Conflict Resolution and the Impact of EU Expansion*. I.B. Taurus.

Cameron, F. (2010). *The European Union as a Model for Regional Integration*. Council on Foreign Relations.

Capraro, S., & Perrotini, I. (2013). Revisiting Latin America's Debt Crisis: Some Lessons for the Periphery of the Eurozone. *Cambridge Journal of Economics, 37*, 627–651.

Council of Europe. (1949). *Statute of the Council of Europe* (European Treaty Series No. 1). Council of Europe.

Council of Europe. (2020). *Council of Europe*. Council of Europe. https://www.coe.int/en/web/about-us/do-not-get-confused. Accessed 27 Mar 2020.

Creswell, J. W. (2013). *Research Design: Qualitative, Quantitative, and Mixed Methods Approaches* (Kindle ed.). Sage Publications.

Deacon, M. (2020). *Back to the Unitary State?* University of Edinburgh Centre on Constitutional Change. https://www.centreonconstitutionalchange.ac.uk/news-and-opinion/back-unitary-state. Accessed 21 Dec 2020.

EC. (2015). *How the EU Works*. European Union. http://europa.eu/about-eu/index_en.htm. Accessed 2 Apr 2015.

ECB. (2020). *European Central Bank (ECB)*. ECB. https://europa.eu/european-union/about-eu/institutions-bodies/european-central-bank_en. Accessed 20 Dec 2020.

EU. (2014). *Proportionality Principle. Europa*. European Union. http://europa.eu/legislation_summaries/glossary/proportionality_en.htm. Accessed 27 Jan 2015.

EU. (2020). *Institutions and Bodies*. European Union. https://europa.eu/european-union/about-eu/institutions-bodies_en. Accessed 20 Dec 2020.

EUR-Lex. (2020a). *Glossary of Summaries: Proportionality Principle*. European Union. https://eur-lex.europa.eu/summary/glossary/proportionality.html. Accessed 21 Dec 2020.

EUR-Lex. (2020b). *Glossary of Summaries: Subsidiarity Principle*. European Union. https://eur-lex.europa.eu/summary/glossary/subsidiarity.html. Accessed 21 Dec 2020.

EUR-Lex. (2020c). *European Institutions*. European Union. https://eur-lex.europa.eu/summary/glossary/eu_institutions.html. Accessed 21 Dec 2020.

European Parliament. (2015). *Values*. European Parliament. http://europarlamentti.info/en/values-and-objectives/values. Accessed 12 Aug 2015.

European Parliament. (2020). *The Treaty of Lisbon*. European Parliament. https://www.europarl.europa.eu/factsheets/en/sheet/5/the-treaty-of-lisbon. Accessed 15 Jan 2021.

Evans-Pritchard, A. (2015, January 26). Greek Coalition Braces for Debt Showdown as Germany Rattles Sabre. *The Telegraph*. http://www.telegraph.co.uk/finance/economics/11370960/Greek-coalition-braces-for-debt-showdown-as-Germany-rattles-sabre.html. Accessed 15 July 2015.

Filippov, M., Ordeshook, P., & Shvetsova, O. (2004). *Designing Federalism: A theory of Self-Sustainable Federal Institutions*. Cambridge University Press.

Harbo, T. (2010). The Function of the Proportionality Principle in EU Law. *European Law Journal, 16*(2), 158–185.

Heslop, A. (2020). *Political System*. Britannica. https://www.britannica.com/topic/political-system. Accessed 21 Dec 2020.

Johnson, J. B., & Reynolds, H. T. (2012). *Political Science Research Methods* (7th ed.). Sage Publications.

Khan, M. (2015, April 1). Greece Threatens Default as Fresh Reform Bid Falters. *The Telegraph*. http://www.telegraph.co.uk/finance/economics/11509302/Greece-threatens-international-default-without-fresh-bailout-cash.html. accessed 2 Apr 2015.

Kin, L. (2009). The Relationship Between Central and Local Governments Under the Unitary State System of China. In J. Oliveira & P. Cardinal (Eds.), *One Country, Two Systems, Three Legal Orders: Perspectives of Evolution* (pp. 527–540). Springer-Verlag.

Lavdas, K. A., Litsas, S. N., & Skiadis, D. V. (2013). *Stateness and Sovereign Debt: Greece in the European Conundrum*. Kindle ed. Lexington Books.

Miles, M., & Huberman, M. (1994). *Qualitative Data Analysis: An Expanded Sourcebook* (2nd ed.). Sage.

Moravcsik, A. (2006). What Can We Learn from the Collapse of the European Constitutional Project? *Politische Vierteljahresschrift, 47*, 219–241.

O'Leary, N. (2013, October 19). *Italian Anti-austerity Protesters Clash with Police*. Reuters [online]. http://www.reuters.com/article/2013/10/19/us-italy-demonstration-idUSBRE99I06B20131019. Accessed 2 April 2015.

Open University. (2018). *Europe and the Law*. The Open University. https://www.open.edu/openlearn/society-politics-law/europe-and-the-law/content-section-0?intro=1. Accessed 12 July 2018.

Panico, C., & Purificato, F. (2013). Policy Coordination, Conflicting National Interests and the European Debt Crisis. *Cambridge Journal of Economics, 37*, 585–608.

Pasinetti, L. (1997). The Social Burden of High Interest Rates. In P. Arestis, G. Palma, & M. Sawyer (Eds.), *Capital Controversy, Post Keynesian Economics and the History of Economic Thought: Essays in Honour of Geoff Harcourt* (Vol. I, pp. 149–172). Routledge.

Portuese, A. (2013). Principle of Proportionality as Principle of Economic Efficiency. *European Law Journal, 19*(5), 612–635.

Riker, W. (1964). *Federalism: Origins, Operation, Significance*. Little, Brown.

Ritchie, J., & Lewis, J. (2010). *Qualitative Research Practice*. Sage Publications.

Saunders, M., Lewis, P., & Thornhill, A. (2009). *Research Methods for Business Students* (5th ed.). Pearson.

Skyline College. (2020). Federal, Unitary & Confederate Government Systems: Home. *Skyline College* [online]. https://guides.skylinecollege.edu/c.php?g=279117. Accessed 2 April 2020.

Stevens-Finlayson, B. (2019). *EU vs US: Comparing the EU and US Federal Systems*. Gold Mercury International.

Stoain, A. (2013). Influences of the Principle of Subsidiarity in the Activity of the Public Administration. *Social-Behavioural Sciences, 4*(72), 383–482.

Williams, J. C. (2012). *Monetary Policy, Money, and Inflation*. FRBSF Economic Letter Federal, Unitary & Confederate Government Systems: Home.

Winkler, A. (2014). *The ECB as Lender of Last Resort: Banks Versus Governments*. Frankfurt School of Finance & Management.

Yin, R. (2013). *Case Study Research: Design and Methods* (Kindle ed.). Sage Publications.

Young, E. (2018). The European Union: A Comparative Perspective. In R. Schutze & T. Tridimas (Eds.), *Oxford Principles of European Union Law Volume 1: The European Union Legal Order* (pp. 142–190). Oxford University Press.

CHAPTER 2

Research Methods

Introduction

The purpose of this chapter is to document the methodology used for this research and to justify it as being most appropriate to assessing how the strategies taken by the EU to respond to the global financial and Member State public debt crises align with the principles of the Proportionality of State intervention in the Market Economies of European Countries.

The publicly available data on the trends in the global economies prior to the 2007–2008 financial crisis, the interventions that governments generally make in their market economies and the reasons underpinning the interventions are appraised in Chaps. 4 and 5; substantial focus is given to those of the EC specifically. The main objective is to appraise the concepts concerned and the theoretical basis for government market intervention, so that the actions taken by the EC, as the crisis developed into a longer recessionary period, could be evaluated, in terms of the Principle of Proportionality on which the EC was founded. This chapter will focus on the research design, the research philosophy and research strategy selected for the study. The data gathering and analysis methodology, which complement the research philosophy and strategy, are documented and discussed, as well as the interventions taken to ensure that the study has high reliability and validity. Ethical considerations and limitations are the final section of this chapter.

S. Weißschnur, *The Proportionality of State Intervention*,
https://doi.org/10.1007/978-3-030-75676-5_2

Research Design, Research Philosophy and Research Strategy

Research Design

A variety of research designs were available to the researchers, including explanatory, exploratory, descriptive and evaluative, and their main features are summarised in Table 2.1.

Evaluative research design is therefore selected for this study, since it is an appraisal of EC policy and aims to examine which policies are associated with the Principle of Proportionality and how the policies operate. The study also seeks to create greater understanding of the outcomes of such

Table 2.1 Research designs

Design approach	*Application*
Exploratory research	Generation of fundamental data, particularly on new or poorly understood issues, for instance, uncertainty as to precisely the nature of the problem, so that the problem needs clarification or discovery of new insights. Flexible, open-ended process in which focus can change as the study proceeds, will start broad and then narrow. The design is frequently associated with qualitative methodology.
Descriptive	Designed to provide further insight into the research problem by describing events, people or situations. Employed for profiling, defining, segmenting, estimating, predicting and examining relationships between variables. Conclusions are not drawn from this design, and it often is the precursor to explanatory design, when the combination may be referred to as descripto-explanatory. Descriptive design can be associated with qualitative, quantitative or mixed methodology.
Explanatory	Provides explanations in a cause and effect manner, the relationship between variables. It is used to explain why phenomenon occurs, the forces that influence the event happening. This type of research design is most often associated with quantitative methods but is also frequently used with qualitative methodology.
Evaluative	This design is a combination of descriptive, explanatory and exploratory, often employed to evaluate existing practices and/or theories, as well as in policy-related investigations. Hence, it examines how policies operate and their effects or consequences. All three methodologies may be employed with this design.

Sources: Richey and Klein (2007); Saunders et al. (2012); Rubin and Babbie (2014); Ritchie and Lewis (2010)

policies by identifying their effect and consequences on market economies of the EC and Eurozone Member States, as well as the various ways they are achieved or occur. According to Ritchie and Lewis (2010) evaluative research design is an established design for studies with these characteristics. The purpose of choosing this design is to appraise five key factors: identifying factors that contribute to successful or unsuccessful implementation of the policies; evaluating the effects of policy on participants and how these occur; determining specific requirements of different groups affected by the policies; specifying the range of features or organisational aspects involved in implementing the interventions; identifying the context in which interventions are received and the impact it has on their effectiveness (Ritchie & Lewis, 2010, pp. 29–30).

This description of the employment of evaluative design provides a framework for answering the research question, and therefore fully justifies its selection. In the exploratory focus, the research will seek to uncover new insights into this live phenomenon and to appraise it from different perspectives, to uncover new data, which is also emerging on a daily basis as the research proceeds. This unique live phenomenon means changing focus and direction constantly throughout development of the research, which is enabled by the evaluative design, as is the gradual narrowing of the emphasis of the investigation. Hence, the collection of data is perceived as also being initially relatively unstructured owing to the changing nature of the phenomenon, since how individual EC Member States responded to policy interventions could determine adaptations or changes in direction (Ritchie & Lewis, 2010). The descriptive research methodology, which initiates the study, precedes the exploratory approach, since it helps to build a profile of the phenomenon. In this study, for instance, profiles prior to the 2007–2008 crisis were needed to account for reactions of the Member States to the EC interventions, which were implemented in an effort to regenerate progress towards meeting its core goals after the crisis. However, the effect of the policies applied also needs to be considered in a cause and effect way; in other words, what the EC considered each intervention would accomplish and the extent to which this occurred or not, which might also be influenced by subjective factors (Saunders et al., 2012). The explanatory design was particularly important for the case studies developed for Germany, Italy and UK.

Research Philosophy

The two extremes of research philosophy are the interpretivist and the positivist approaches (Collis & Hussey, 2014). Interpretivist is generally associated with qualitative studies and positivist with quantitative studies. The major aspects of each type of philosophy are provided in Table 2.2.

However, there is a requirement to appraise objective facts with subjective factors in this research, such as how the Member State governments and populations respond to interventionist policies prescribed by the EC. According to Collis and Hussey (2014), there has been an increasing trend to move away from the two extreme philosophies, so that a continuum has been developed between them representing different relative emphases on the two extremes, integrated into one study. This is also reflected in the research philosophy or paradigm referred to as bridged-interpretivism with positivism proposed by Weber (1864–1920) and cited by Ritchie and Lewis (2010). This version of interpretivism allows an objective approach to the findings, so that relationships between variables can be determined concurrently with considering the beliefs and values of humans, regarding their perceptions of EC policies and their impact on their communities. A purely objective approach, represented by a positivist philosophy, would mean that the rich insights concerning the

Table 2.2 Positivist and interpretivist research philosophies compared

	Positivism	*Interpretivism*
The researcher	Independent of the study	Recognised part of the study
Human interests	Should be relevant	Key drivers
Explanations	Objective, cause and effect	Enhance general understanding of the phenomenon
Research based	Generation of hypotheses and deductions	Gathering rich data from which new ideas emerge
Concepts	Operationalised in order for measurement to occur	Incorporates stakeholder perspectives
Unit of analysis	Reduced to simplest terms	May include the complexity of entire phenomenon
Generalisation	By means of statistical probability	Theoretical notions
Sampling	Large number selected randomly	Small numbers of cases selected on the basis of the subject matter expertise

Sources: Saunders et al. (2012); Easterby-Smith et al. (2002)

real environmental setting for the research, and the manner in which the individuals interacted with their environment and made choices regarding acceptance or rejection of EC policies, would be lost, and render the validity of the findings questionable (Saunders et al., 2012). The interpretivist philosophy was generated by Kant (1781), who argued that knowing about the environment as perceived by others was not merely a matter of direct observation of the same event, but needed to be combined with the way that others interpreted it; human interpretation of the same event differed according to the individual's value set. Hence, the interpretivist philosophy relies on the freedom of each individual to make moral judgements and decisions, which is important to answering the research question but also leads to uncertainty regarding the nature of the answer, as a consequence of the unpredictability of the human factor. Qualitative research tends to focus on similar principles in which human interpretation of knowing about the social world is valued and emphasised; therefore this researcher is cognisant of own interpretation of the research findings having some impact on the outcomes. Whilst this potential bias in interpretation is an acknowledged feature of interpretivism, a positivist approach considers that the researcher is detached from the research and has no influence on the findings, a concept that Creswell (2013) suggests is totally unrealistic.

Consequently, the approach to the research is a combination of both induction or theory building and deduction, which is theory testing (Saunders et al., 2012); the two approaches are compared in Table 2.3.

There is significant emphasis on induction in this research, since the phenomenon under study is not well understood and there is also a high degree of uncertainty because of the focus on how the Principle of Proportionality has been applied over the period since 2008, how this has impacted on Member States and what the consequences for their populations are. However, the policies are defined and the desired impact is documented, so that the relationships between variables can be tested to some degree, for instance by the numerical data emerging from the EC on economic growth, including employment trends and changes in GDP. Theory testing or deduction could reveal the degree of success of EC actions taken, particularly in relation to the three single Member State case studies. This research employs both approaches, referred to by Saunders et al. (2012) as the abductive approach, offering several advantages. Since the deductive approach is perceived as preferable when substantial previous research had been conducted, and the inductive

Table 2.3 Features of deduction and induction compared

Emphasis of deduction	*Emphasis of induction*
Scientific principles	Understanding the meanings humans associate with events
Theory testing	Building theory
Quantitative data collection	Qualitative data collection
Controls to validate data	Flexible allows change of emphasis
Operationalises concepts to define them clearly	Researcher participates in study
Structured approach	Sample size not important and generalisation not a key factor in study quality
Research independent of study	
Sample size important to generalise findings/conclusions to whole population	

Source: Adapted from Saunders, Lewis and Thornhill (2012)

approach more appropriate to phenomenon that is poorly understood, a holistic approach is implemented to appraise the issue from demand and the supply perspectives. The demand side relies significantly on existing theories and the supply side addresses subject matter that lacks useful theories or frameworks. Creswell (2013) suggests that the specific research study should inform the approach, and that by using both approaches, the advantages or disadvantages of the single approach are minimised. In addition, the familiarity of those assessing the study with the deductive approach is a major advantage, since the inductive approach is less widely accepted; adoption of the two approaches also enables triangulation of the data (Saunders et al., 2012). Hence, the use of both approaches is justified.

Research Strategy

The commonly used research strategies are experiment, survey, case study, action research, grounded theory, ethnography and archival research. However, conducting primary research covering 27 countries was much too prohibitive meaning that observation, action research and experiment were not options for this study. Ethnography is concerned with a descriptive design, which is not suitable for answering the research problem and, while grounded theory can be combined with the abductive approach, it usually employs a particular line of enquiry rather than taking a broader approach, as needed in this case. Case studies rely on multiple data sources and in-depth analyses and are not a realistic option (Saunders et al., 2012; Ritchie & Lewis, 2010).

Initially archival research is selected because it enables the researcher to review what has happened in the past, to appraise changes that have occurred over time, and the strategy can be used with all three research designs or in combination as evaluative design, as has been selected for this research. However, the degree of documentation relating to the core subject of the study can be restrictive, data may be missing or confidential and therefore unpublished, which are potential disadvantages according to Saunders et al. 2012. Nevertheless, Corti (2011) suggests that archived data represents an unexploited source of research material, which has been gathered across a wide range of social science subject areas, and which enables rich, unique insights into the actual experiences of individuals. It also captures the interpretations they give to real live phenomenon and data that can be analysed many times to provide new insights into the issues, since this data is collected in the course of day-to-day activities of those participating in the reported events. Archival data provides reality to what is being researched, even if the original purpose for collecting the data was different, according to Hakim (2000). Corti (2011) emphasises that much archival data becomes a historical account over time, and that researchers can gain insight into the historic attitudes and behaviour of groups, individuals and organisations, as well as obtaining these in a more contemporary context. The fact that data from various sources can be compared across different social and cultural groups, and over a period of time, provides substantial power to answer research questions more accurately. Other significant advantages of using archival data are the capacity to apply scientific rigour to the data, as well as to challenge its findings, but also the ease with which other researchers can replicate the study, which Corti (2011) proposes encourages greater transparency in the research findings reported.

Towards the end of the research period, important differences were identified in the development of EU Member States since the initiation of the single market idea following World War Two; these differences motivated the addition of three case studies. The countries chosen were Germany, Italy and France because they best represented the diverse impact of EU policies on three member countries over the past 50 years. A decision was made to invite citizens in these states to participate in a survey to gather their opinions of the impact that EU policies had on them and to identify similarities and differences. Therefore, limited primary research complemented the secondary research and focused long-term effects from 1950s to 2020.

Research Methodology

Data Gathering

Single data gathering methodologies are referred to as qualitative and quantitative methods, the former being predominantly focused on non-numerical data and the latter on numerical data. A basic comparison is given in Table 2.4, which demonstrates the alignment of each with the complementary research design and approach.

In qualitative research, the term reflexivity refers to the researcher acknowledging own influence on the process and outcomes, in other words, the interpretation, since the researcher is integrally involved in the study; the perspective adopted by the researcher influences the entire research process (Creswell, 2013).

The processes under which the research is conducted also have significant differences, as summarised in Table 2.5.

These single research methodologies have strengths and weaknesses regarding answering a research question, therefore the selection of an appropriate method is related to the data to be collected (Saunders et al., 2012). Traditional researchers perceive that qualitative methods are inferior to quantitative methods, on the basis that no objective data is gathered on which to construct a logical answer, merely human interpretation of words and phrases. However, qualitative methods have become more acceptable over time, as researchers have recognised that the

Table 2.4 Qualitative and quantitative research methods overview

Methodology	*Quantitative*	*Qualitative*
Aim	Discovery	Invention
Initiated by	Hypothesis	Meanings
Design	Experiment	Reflexivity
Technique	Measurement	Conversation
Analysis/interpretation	Testing: Verification/contradiction	Significance of words
Outcomes	Cause and effect	Insight

Sources: Saunders et al. (2012); Bryman and Bell (2011)

Table 2.5 Qualitative and quantitative research methods

Qualitative research	*Quantitative research*
Often exploratory.	Usually explanatory.
Open ended and participants offer diverse views.	Frequently closed; for example, in questionnaire surveys, respondents are usually required to select one response from a restricted number of options.
Involves establishing patterns and themes from the text or recordings made.	Statistical analysis employed.
Hypotheses not normally used. A general statement or question that needs to be qualified or answered by the study findings; need to discover what is happening in a specific context.	Generation of hypotheses at the start of the study.
Objective is to gather rich, in-depth data, which needs to be analysed, which can be challenging and may lead to ambiguous findings. Generalisation is usually limited to the context researched.	Data generated is substantial, readily analysed by established statistical methods. Generalisation possible but provides fewer insights into the issue.
Data collection employs direct research tools, time and resource intensive, so that limited data is gathered frequently.	Often indirect data gathering tools such as questionnaire surveys are used, consuming relatively large resources, particularly cost and time. Large amounts of data can be gathered.

Sources: Johnson and Onwuegbuzie (2004); Bryman and Bell (2011); Creswell (2013)

researcher cannot be inseparable from the study and that interpretation of participant words and phrases can be accomplished without substantial bias. Quantitative studies use passive, formal language, whereas qualitative research employs more informal words and phrases to provide 'thick description' or insight into what participants have contributed (Creswell, 2013; Johnson & Onwuegbuzie, 2004). Pragmatists suggest that the extreme views of the relative worth of qualitative and quantitative methodology are illogical, just as quantitative methods cannot be purely positivist, qualitative techniques cannot be wholly interpretative (Onwuegbuzie & Daniel, 2002; Onwuegbuzie & Leech, 2005). These comments reflect the growing emergence of an approach to data gathering and analysis in which various proportions of each research stance are combined to optimise the solution for a specific research problem (Collis & Hussey, 2014). Therefore, Creswell (2013) proposes that combining the two methodologies provides a more credible outcome, providing that this approach is appropriate to the research question and the design.

Mixed methodology was chosen for this study, as the design infers that an objective or quantitative approach needs to be taken to facts relating to policies based on the Principle of Proportionality, whilst also gaining insight into the values and beliefs of the recipients of those policies in the 27 Member States, that requires the qualitative methodology (Creswell, 2013). The quantitative element enables the effects caused by the EC interventions to be appraised in objective terms, for instance from a survey questionnaire completed by EU citizens in Germany, Italy and UK and the numerical economic and social data contained in the secondary sources. The qualitative data supplies the words and phrases communicated in official reports and other published works, which are vital to exploring how and why the interventions were interpreted in specific ways. A key weakness of the qualitative method is regarded as inherent researcher bias, owing to own values and beliefs influencing the interpretation of those words and data. The researcher intends to minimise this by continually checking back to the original text, as recommended by Creswell (2013), and employing the bracketing technique, in an attempt to focus on the text and distance own thoughts whilst scrutinising it (Tufford & Newman, 2012). The time horizon for the research is associated with the time allocated to complete it; if the time period is relatively short, it is referred to often as a snapshot, or cross-sectional, which was originally the case with this research (Saunders et al., 2012). However, in July 2019, diverse developments currently impacting on EU were appraised as important to answering the research question such as: the unresolved situation between the UK and EU regarding the terms of Brexit; the threat to the EU and the Euro from Italy; the divisions between Member States on how to manage continuing immigration particularly from Syria and Africa, particularly since Italy had eventually banned all rescue ships from entry to its main ports owing to the high burden on its resources relative to all other EU countries (BBC, 2018). Therefore, the time horizon for the study was adapted to take an even more longitudinal perspective.

Primary data is collected from EU citizens in Germany, Italy and France by means of quantitative survey that has the purpose of gathering perspectives on the advantages and disadvantages of EU membership; the questions being shaped by the content of the case studies that demonstrated highly diverse experiences. Although good questionnaires are considered to be difficult to design, the advice of research methods' practitioners is followed (Saunders et al., 2012; Creswell, 2013). The questionnaire comprises a logical flow of questions, commencing with category questions, which provide a profile of the participants. The remainder of the survey relies on rating questions characterised by a Likert approach, in which participants are provided with statements and asked to indicate their degree of agreement with them, by selecting one of five options. The participants are also asked to comment on their choice of response, in order to gather the reasons for the level of agreement chosen. The questionnaires are translated into the national language, tested by a native speaker in each case and then distributed and collected online using Survey Monkey. The online service also provided assurance that participant selection bias was eliminated (Creswell, 2013).

Secondary sources are employed to gather data for the main part of the research, and the researcher is aware that the purpose of collecting the original secondary data employed in this research was for a different reason from the objective of this study, as well as the fact that some data gathered could have been combined and/or manipulated (Ritchie & Lewis, 2010). However, the most reliable sources are gathered from different bodies, so that convergence of the facts, known as triangulation, will support the need to validate the data (Saunders et al., 2012; Bryman & Bell, 2011). The secondary sources include peer-reviewed academic journals, other academic journals, possibly with studies generated from Member States and not entered into the top journals, studies by global and European institutions, quality newspapers, institution websites and other reliable sources. Databases such as EBSCO and Google Scholar, supplemented by Google searches, are employed to locate appropriate reports using search terms, exemplified by EC strategies for growth and monetary policies for EMU (Saunders et al., 2012).

Data Analysis

The quantitative case study surveys are analysed using spss analysis, which provides a variety of descriptive statistics and the results of hypothesis testing. The analytical method employed was correlation and t tests to compare the differences in means between groups (Saunders et al., 2012). Qualitative data analysis is usually conducted by means of frameworks suggested by various qualitative research experts, such as Ritchie and Lewis (2010); there are no single rules or procedures but creativity and systematic scrutiny of the data gathered are vital to finding the meanings associated with the words and phrases used by the originator (Ritchie & Lewis, 2010; Creswell, 2013). In this study, qualitative content analysis, as described by Ritchie and Lewis (2010) and Mayring (2014), is employed; conflicting views and opinions can be extracted from the sources and the frequency of each view can be documented. This is a particularly important technique that highlights issues to which solutions are not easily found. The first stage in this analysis is to read the text carefully and then to organise the content, the words and phrases into categories on the basis of themes, concepts or similar features; in other words, conduct thematic analysis (Miles & Huberman, 1994; Creswell, 2013; Mayring, 2014). Each theme is initially given a code as the text is read, and then all the words and phrases with the same code are transferred to a separate document, to read over the content again and to interpret the meanings that the originator of these words/phrases gave to them. Hence, the researcher attempts to identify and devise new concepts, and to scrutinise the relationships between the concepts that comprise the article or study. Since the researcher is interpreting the words and phrases used by others, personal interpretation bias is reduced by constant reference back to the original text (Creswell, 2013).

The quantitative data is analysed for trends and presented by use of statistical charts that directly indicate relationships to the reader, for instance, pie and bar charts (Saunders et al., 2012).

Reliability and Validity

The quantitative measure of a study's reliability or rigour is the ease with which the study could be repeated by another researcher using identical methodology to generate similar findings. It can also be measured by the value of a statistical constant. In qualitative research, reliability is associated with the consistency with which the research instrument measures what it was designed to measure; other perceptions of reliability are similar, relating to the trustworthiness of the findings. The lack of a single accepted definition of reliability in qualitative research and no objective method of measuring it mean that qualitative studies are perceived as weak traditional researchers. However, the reliability of qualitative studies is strengthened by regularly retesting data against the original text (Creswell, 2013) and by the researcher bracketing own thoughts away from the text studied, and fully focusing attention on the actual words and phrases it contains (Tufford & Newman, 2012).

Validity is measured by the extent to which the research findings measure what they were intended to measure, as stated in the study objectives. Therefore, validity focuses on how well the research question has been answered but this is only one aspect of validity, referred to as the internal validity. External validity concerns confirming findings by external means, such as triangulation or convergence among the different data sources employed. In this study, internal validity should be high, since the theories and concepts in the Literature Review chapters directly relate to the study objectives. External validity is also expected to be relatively high, as the secondary sources should show a relatively high degree of convergence, and in the quantitative analysis the survey findings should be generalisable (Ritchie & Lewis, 2010).

Ethics

This study involves the collection of primary and secondary data, so that ethical principles regarding protecting potential participants from harm are applied. The participants choose to contribute to the research, are informed of its purpose and assured that any information they provide remains confidential. In relation to the use of secondary data, the researcher is aware of the possibility of bias in the selection of secondary sources for both the literature reviews and the reported findings; s/he also appreciates his/her responsibility to produce credible findings and attempts to minimise bias by using keyword searches, and a wide range of sources including conflicting views on aspects of the subject matter (Saunders et al., 2012).

Limitations

The major limitations of this research are time and the predominant use of secondary research. The time factor limits the number of documents that can be sourced, selected for inclusion or not, and therefore may fail to gather certain opinions that could add another dimension to the findings. The researcher attempted to source material from a wide range of documents generated globally, in order to lower the impact of the potential limitations. Conducting primary research for this study is limited to three EU Member States, selected on the basis of their diversity, and representative of those which joined the single market prior to 1992 when the Euro was first promoted. No attempt is made to include former communist states in Eastern Europe as only two joined the Eurozone from 2007 onwards so that the relevance of their membership is considered relatively very minor to this study.

Summary

The research methodology selected in this chapter is justified as appropriate to answer the research question; the non-inclusion of alternatives that might have been employed is explained. The detail included in this section enables another researcher to easily replicate the study using the same methodology. The research findings are reported in Chaps. 6, 7 and 8: in Chap. 6 the EC responses to the global economic crisis is concerned with an overview of the measures taken to ensure fiscal stability, growth and employment; Chap. 7 focuses on how the EU is currently organised to supervise its fiscal affairs; Chap. 8 appraises the support mechanisms planned and implemented for economic growth and job creation.

Bibliography

BBC. (2018). *Migrant Crisis: Italy Minister Salvini Closes Ports to NGO Boats*. BBC. https://www.bbc.com/news/wo. Accessed 2018 Aug 18.

Bryman, A., & Bell, E. (2011). *Business Research Methods* (3rd ed.). Oxford University Press.

Collis, J., & Hussey, R. (2014). *Business Research: A Practical Guide for Undergraduate and Postgraduate Students* (4th ed.). Palgrave Macmillan.

Corti, L. (2011). The European Landscape of Qualitative Social Research Archives: Methodological and Practical Issues. *FQS*, *12*(3), 1–25.

Creswell, J. W. (2013). *Research Design: Qualitative, Quantitative, and Mixed Methods Approaches* (Kindle ed.). Sage Publications.

Easterby-Smith, M., Thorpe, R., & Lowe, A. (2002). *Management Research: An Introduction* (2nd ed.). Sage Publications.

Hakim, C. (2000). *Research Design: Successful Designs for Social and Economic Research* (2nd ed.). Routledge.

Johnson, J. B., & Reynolds, H. T. (2012). *Political Science Research Methods* (7th ed.). Sage Publications.

Johnson, R. B., & Onwuegbuzie, A. J. (2004). Mixed Methods Research: A Research Paradigm Whose Time Has Come. *Educational Researcher*, *33*(7), 14–26.

Mayring, P. (2014). *Qualitative Content Analysis. Theoretical Foundation, Basic Procedures and Software Solution*. Klagenfurt [online]. Available at: http://nbn-resolving.de/urn:nbn:de:0168-ssoar-395173. Accessed 15 June 2015.

Miles, M., & Huberman, M. (1994). *Qualitative Data Analysis: An Expanded Sourcebook* (2nd ed.). Sage Publications.

Onwuegbuzie, A. J., & Daniel, L. G. (2002). A Framework for Reporting and Interpreting Internal Consistency Reliability Estimates. *Measurement and Evaluation in Counseling and Development, 35*, 89–103.

Onwuegbuzie, A. J., & Leech, N. L. (2005). On Becoming a Pragmatic Researcher: The Importance of Combining Quantitative and Qualitative Research Methodologies. *International Journal of Social Research Methodology, 8*(5), 375–387.

Richey, R., & Klein, J. (2007). *Design and Development Research: Methods, Strategies and Issues*. Lawrence Erlbaum Associates Publishers.

Ritchie, J., & Lewis, J. (2010). *Qualitative Research Practice*. Sage Publications.

Rubin, A., & Babbie, E. R. (2014). *Research Methods for Social Work* (8th ed.). Cengage Learning.

Saunders, M., Lewis, P., & Thornhill, A. (2009). *Research Methods for Business Students* (5th ed.). Pearson.

Saunders, M., Lewis, P., & Thornhill, A. (2012). *Research Methods for Business Students* (6th ed.). Pearson.

Tufford, L., & Newman, P. (2012). Bracketing in Qualitative Research. *Qualitative Social Work, 11*(1), 80–96.

Yin, R. (2013). *Case Study Research: Design and Methods* (Kindle ed.). Sage Publications.

CHAPTER 3

State Intervention and Principle of Proportionality

Theories of European Integration

The major theories relating to European Integration are outlined in this section because they have relevance to the Euro crisis that commenced in 2008 (Hooghe & Marks, 2019), and therefore associated with the nature of the interventions adopted by the EU to recover economic growth, and with the reactions of specific Member States to the measures taken.

Neofunctionalism

Neofunctionalism refers to a theory of regional political and market integration by countries that have decided to integrate, and which involved authority passing from the individual states to a regional power, such as the European Union (Sandholtz & Sweet, 2014). Neofunctionalism is based on pluralism and functionalism, where pluralists consider that two or more states or bodies can exist together, and functionalists suggest that the sovereignty of states can only be avoided by their functions being performed by specialist supranational agencies (Hooghe & Marks, 2019). In neofunctionalism, the regional power creates, implements and enforces rules as a supranational governance body (Sandholtz & Sweet, 2014). Neofunctionalism is, therefore, characterised by the processes of technocratic decision making, incremental change and learning (Niemann & Schmitter, 2009, p. 45). Neofunctionalism increased significantly in the

S. Weißschnur, *The Proportionality of State Intervention*,
https://doi.org/10.1007/978-3-030-75676-5_3

EU as it developed its capacity to make rules, its responsibility for policy-making has expanded and policies have become more substantive (Sandholtz & Sweet, 2014) as have elite attitudes of the constituent EU bodies (Niemann & Schmitter, 2009). Integration developed as a result of transactions occurring across country boundaries, setting up European institutions and developing policies. Supranational governance would facilitate ways to reduce the defence of national interests by national government political parties, industry associations and trade unions (TUs), and to replace it by diverting attention to the economic gains nations could acquire by transnational activities and the associated negative externalities that they could minimise. In addition, regional solutions to issues that the individual countries shared could be made by European bodies, private individuals and companies rather than national ones, by means of rules created by the supranational governance body. Over time, change can be observed in how the members of the group behave and the type of objectives that develop, such that they are willing to devote resources and policy efforts to supporting the supranational body, a new political arena with different types of interest groups that have the purpose of influencing its policies (Sandholtz & Sweet, 2014). However, integration as defined by Lindberg (1963) occurs when the constituent nations belonging to the group no longer have the aspiration or the capability of developing independent national domestic and foreign policies, because they delegated it to the supranational body. This assumption is not the case in the EU post-2008 crisis (Nicoli, 2019) as this thesis demonstrates. However, the consequence of this type of action by interest groups is to generate new opportunities for the supranational government to expand its reach in terms of policy making into new domains; the feedback from interest groups is referred to as spillover. In terms of the EU internal market, spillover from its policies is associated with the necessity to remove a range of obstacles to trade between countries, such as tariffs, duties and different sets of health and safety regulations and technical specifications (Sandholtz & Sweet, 2014). This is an example of functional spillover and associated with another important EU example of the need for home affairs and justice, where there would be a strong need for functional spillover and supranational agents to resolve them. In home affairs, for instance the demand for free movement of people creates requirement for legal policy making on visas, asylum, immigration and collaboration between police forces (Niemann & Schmitter, 2009).

This process of a developing supranational body also allows nationals, individuals or groups, that have the objective of furthering integration, to lobby the supranational governance body directly instead of the national one, as would have happened prior to integration (Sandholtz & Sweet, 2014). This type of action is considered to be characteristic of a political spillover by Niemann and Schmitter (2009), integrative pressure particularly by non-governmental national elites, who perceive that some important issues of general interest cannot be effectively resolved by national governments. The rationale underlying this perception is that integration allows high gains, the interest groups are able to observe the advantages of the EU action, there are international incentives for the supranational solution to take place, the subject is already being dealt with by EU and the interested parties are aware of procedures. A fourth type of spillover demonitated cultivated occurs when supranational institutions have the objective of enhancing their power. In that case, they act as agents of integration so that the body that created them tends to lose control of them. In effect, they position themselves as policy entrepreneurs or enhancers (Bergmann & Niemann, 2015).

Geographical spillover explains the expansion in the number of member countries and why increasing numbers were incentivised to join, for example, the UK joined owing to its fear of being isolated (Niemann & Schmitter, 2009); integration is a gradual process. Initially the EU demonstrated the economic and political success of integration, the post war peace between countries that had been achieved over a long period, which also underpinned economic success. The group was also quite dynamic, for instance the monetary union project in 1992, an initial stage of EU political union, which was not merely trade based as before that date. The consequence was that other countries such as those in Eastern Europe wanted to join owing to the advantages that they could not afford to ignore. The overall effect of neofunctionalism is that the national governments adopt policies that they would not have considered without the creation of the intergovernmental body (Sandholtz & Sweet, 2014). Neofunctionalism was not envisaged as applicable to military or defence issues, nor has it been applied to development of a common European Foreign Policy (Bergmann & Niemann, 2015). Neofunctionalism theory is particularly important to this thesis because it explains how the EU was able to develop many new institutions, policies and projects to drive reform in the Eurozone countries, and integration is deepened by crisis according to Nicoli (2019).

Intergovernmentalist Theory

Intergovernmentalist theory of European integration proposes that it will only occur in cases in which there are more permanent joint advantages than joint disadvantages for the countries seeking membership. In this context the integration would be conducted on each country's rules, such that the supranational body's power and involvement are less stressed than with neofunctionalism theories. Therefore, the supranational body does not have independent control to innovate and implement any suggested changes but depends on the agreement of the national governments (Bergmann & Niemann, 2015). A liberal intergovernmentalist theory was developed by Moravcsik (1993), in which a potential national Member State makes its decision to join based on its national preferences, its relative position to other nations in the system and therefore the amount of power it has to negotiate its interests; further integration occurs when the current members judge a potential entrant to have qualities that improve the status quo. Liberal intergovernmentalists propose that Member States delegate a limited degree of authority to the supranational body that is sufficient to make sure they will agree with the outcomes decided for them. The level of that authority is dependent on the nature of the shared national challenge, and national governments dispense with the supranational body when they consider that they can make decisions alone (Hooghe & Marks, 2019). Hence in this theory, some convergence of national interest is necessary for integration and expansion and, as with neofunctionalism, intergovernmentalist theories were not usually applied to foreign policy but remain economic or issue specific (Hooghe & Marks, 2019). Some intergovernmentalist foreign policy related to security and defence is indicated by the close collaboration of Germany, France and the UK after the liberation of East European countries in 1991, as US protection declined considerably at that time and had been perceived as necessary prior to that date (Hoffmann, 2000). If the economic and/or welfare interests of potential state governments are not affected, they are likely to integrate on foreign policy regarding security and defence only when they do not have their own credible alternatives (Moravcsik, 1993). This idea was exemplified by Britain and France rejecting this kind of supranational foreign policy when the Maastricht and Amsterdam Treaties were being formulated, because they had strong national policy alternatives, whereas Germany preferred it because it had no suitable alternative. Hence, in the liberal governmentalist theory, EU Member States decide which areas of policy they will delegate to a supranational body to increase their credibility or to prevent them from evading commitments that they have made. In this perspective, the original Treaties, such as the Treaty of Rome and the 1999 Treaty of the European Union, were not imposed by supranational bodies, instead they were a consequence of the convergence of preferences of the most powerful Member States that awarded limited powers to the supranational bodies (Pollack, 2014).

Intergovernmentalist theory related to EU enlargement is limited to Britain's attempt to join the EEC in 1960, when it was rejected on the basis of gaining more from membership than the EEC obtained from its inclusion (Hooghe & Marks, 2019; Moravcsik, 1998). In regard to more recent Eastern European membership, their bargaining power was so relatively weak that the EU could demand they agreed to the proposed rules or accept rejection (Bergmann & Niemann, 2015). The liberal intergovernmentalist theory is criticised as being unrealistic since it inferred that EU institutions had little influence on the outcomes of the EU policies.

State Intervention by EU

Governments may adopt two extreme approaches to market economics, a planned or a free market approach; in the planned economy they make all economic decisions and in the free market individuals and firms decide how to participate (Sloman et al., 2018). The free market was promoted by Adam Smith (Smith, 1776) as being a collaborative relationship between producers and consumers that had social benefits, whilst government intervention in the market often led to excessive production of goods or shortages. In practice most economies combine the planned and free economies to various extents, for instance China has a predominantly planned economy but uses limited free market principles to grow its economy and trade with the West (Morrison, 2019). In contrast, the US is characterised by a high proportion of free market principles, regarded as a capitalist economy (WPR, 2020). Therefore, government or state intervention refers to any direct and deliberate interference by a government or a public body that impacts on the market economy or how industries conduct their operations, which goes beyond contract regulation and providing public goods that commercial bodies may not produce (Sloman et al., 2018). Groups that favour state intervention propose that specific economic policies are required to minimise the imperfections in the system that would create substantial economic unpredictability, since the law of supply and demand is too weak to do so. Hence a range of fiscal and monetary economic policies are established as possible solutions to providing a more balanced economy, for example Keynesian, New Keynesian and Monetarism. The alternative approach of non-intervention is referred to as laissez-faire, and based on the market economy balancing automatically; minimal or non-interventionist approaches include liberalism, the Austrian school and New Classical Macroeconomics. The US, UK and Australia are considered to be liberal free market economies and characterised by decentralised industrial relations, in which individual firms make decisions that impact on the market.

Good governance, economic performance and political performance are closely allied and are a characteristic of global and regional organisational policies (Stivachtis, 2015), for instance the European Union's development of the single market, a liberal economy (Wolf, 1995). Any state wishing to become an EU member is tasked with reforming its national political and economic policies to align with its free market, democratic approach as occurred with the former USSR nations such as Hungary, Poland and Romania, for instance (Bowden & Seabrooke, 2007).

The form of liberal economy represented by the EU is not a laissez-faire approach but neoliberalism, which Phelan and Dawes (2018) describe as a specific combination of liberalism, capitalism and democracy that has its origins in the 1970s and in which the state actively promotes principles relating to the market and to competition between firms that are considered by opponents of the intervention as anti-democratic. Classic liberalism is associated with the economics of Adam Smith, which rejected mercantilism, an economic approach that was essentially protectionism promoting the export of as many goods as possible but restricting imports to a minimum, so that national wealth is accumulated. Instead, liberalism was focused on generating profitable trade and a social contract that involved society, governments and economies enhancing human health and welfare.

Neoliberalism is linked to monetary interventionist policies (Phelan & Dawes, 2018). It comprises theories that would enable governments, companies, economies and global trade to operate under perfect market conditions, under market equilibrium and based on a set of mathematical models. Therefore, the fundamental principles on which neoliberalism are based are highly relevant to this research. Neoliberalism was perceived as releasing businesses from the control of the state, government and trade unions and allowing free market competition as encapsulated in the 1993

Washington Consensus attributed to Williamson (Phelan & Dawes, 2018), comprising ten concepts that were designed to improve economic growth and development in Latin America (Williamson, 2004). These concepts are described by Williamson (2004) as:

- Controlling state budget deficits to a maximum value that could be financed without inflation tax, since excessive deficits drive up inflation.
- Focusing public expenditure on areas that can provide high economic return, for instance public health, education and state infrastructure with the objective of enhancing the distribution of income.
- Reform of the tax systems so that there were less tax bands as income rose.
- Deregulating financial markets in order that interest rates were determined by the market; six types of deregulation were identified. These were financial factors that were controlled by government; credit, interest rates, new entrants to the financial sector, government bank ownership, bank operations, international capital flows.
- An exchange rate, which was competitive enough to generate rapid growth in non-traditional exports, goods originally intended for internal consumption, such as agricultural products.
- Replacement of monetary trade restriction by low-rate tariffs, existing high tariffs being gradually lowered. The objective was to provide the government with income rather than specific importers, to stimulate imports as necessary.
- Foreign direct investment (FDI) should no longer be restricted, and that large foreign firms were motivated to operate outside their headquarters base and expose the population of other nations to new products, consequently contributing to their development. Prior to 1989 foreign investment was not generally welcomed including FDI.
- Privatise state-owned industries.
- Allow new firms to enter the market and abolish restrictions on competition.
- Allow the formal and informal sector to obtain legal property rights at an affordable cost, allow the informal sector to access credit from the formal financial services sector, which would simultaneously generate tax income for government and reduce poverty.

Consequentially policies developed by global institutions such as the World Trade Organisation (WTO), the International Monetary Fund (IMF) and World Bank were highly influenced by these principles. The neoliberal influence on government policies intensified into the twenty-first-century, free markets and corporate rationality (Phelan & Dawes, 2018) rather than state intervention with Keynesian type fiscal policy to shape market forces. Neoliberalism in late 1990s and early 2000s was described by Western political leaders as a third way, part socialism and part capitalism, although Foucault (2010) suggests this description was a ploy to gain favour with the trade unions, which had lost their powerful position.

Neoliberalism is described with a different emphasis by Foucault (2010) as covert administrative state intervention and associated with "permanent vigilance, activity and intervention" (Foucault, 2010, p. 132); it must interfere on society so that competitive forces exert a regulatory effect and as a result markets will control society, in other words economic government but a societal government. Neoliberal policies sought to dispense with worker protection rights, such as employee social insurance costs, to reduce trade union power to set working hours and conditions, for instance collective bargaining, and to eliminate government protection of specific industries (Crouch, 2011).

The OECD began to favour reduction of employment rights from 1994 but EU did not adopt the neoliberal approach until the early twenty-first century, preferring to balance supporting competitive market economics with social rights. Whilst neoliberals did not have the power to eliminate trade unions, as this is non-democratic and does not align with basic liberalism, government/politicians with neoliberal objectives could ensure that TUs were not mandatory and employers could choose to work with them or not (Crouch, 2011).

The term neoliberalism is not frequently used by strong advocates of the politico-economic philosophy but typically referred to as monetarism (Thorne, 2010), rational choice theory (Blakely, 2019), supply-side economics (Sloman et al., 2018), sharing economy (Martin, 2016) and therefore difficult to define owing to the various forms it can take or integrate, but enabling the concept to fit a specific context. Neoliberalism is described by Rosenzvaig and Munck (1997, p. 57) as "messianic, authoritarian and exclusionary, mathematic modelling" that enables national disintegration and can replace it with the integration of a number of countries. Two types of neoliberalism are described by Walton (2004): movement from planned economy to a somewhat greater reliance on free market forces and associated lower social services support from the state; change to predominantly free market economy and withdrawal of state welfare and social support systems. The second type of neoliberalism is portrayed as a type of colonialism that creates huge inequalities between the transnational group, a few individuals forcing many to adhere to new policies relating to finance, taxation, privatisation, new state systems, income (Rosenzvaig & Munck, 1997) and austerity (Blakely, 2019). Neoliberalism was planned for underdeveloped countries in the 1980s and 1990s; their welfare social structures were removed in the process of imposing late capitalism (Rosenzvaig & Munck, 1997), and Walton (2004) suggests both types have been imposed at times by different government regimes in Latin America.

The ten concepts in the 1993 Washington Consensus are perceived differently by opponents of neoliberalism and described critically by economists such as Stiglitz (2002). Amongst the criticisms are the stress on personal responsibility rather than on state provision, which ignores the social, political and economic instability that results, whilst eliminating capital controls between nations allows illegal transfer of money that creates market volatility and facilitates companies and investors to exploit arbitrage opportunities such as cheaper labour, natural resources and lower tax regimes. The concept of personal responsibility is considered to be hypocritical when nations/banks are provided with monetary bailouts, which are required owing to poor fiscal control and negligent risk management, also driven partly by allowing many new non-sector entrants into the financial sector and enabling new high-risk financial instruments to be sold at high profit. Institutions aligning with these free market principles also strongly advise privatisation even when the nation has immature and/or non-mature private markets and lacks the regulatory competence to ensure the former public assets are managed appropriately. The IMF and World Bank are particularly criticised for imposing their narrow ideological perspective of the need for rapid privatisation globally on unsuitable countries (Stiglitz, 2002). Other practices are also fostered by such policies as reducing taxes for top earners whatever the level of economic development in the country, and the equal treatment of foreign and domestic investors in a nation despite the lower interest of foreign investors in the social and economic needs of the country. The notion of a natural rate of employment and unemployment are not natural phenomena because employment is affected by policies that encourage offshoring and outsourcing, and lack of trade union representation suppresses employee rights, wage rates and working conditions. There is a general promotion of free trade, meaning that developing countries are unable to defend their economies owing to lack of human skills/knowledge and physical resources, whilst neoliberal developed countries use a range of means to protect theirs.

Governments operating market economies attempt to control them by devising regulations for their efficient functioning, these rules impact on the rights and behaviours of the population, businesses and government. However, the regulations do not always achieve the desired goals, for example changes in the external environment render them ineffective, but regulation makes it possible to implement desired reforms on industry by imposing sanctions, for instance (OECD, 2011; van Cise, 1996). Devising and implementing the regulatory framework consume financial resources in the form of government and public administration operations; its existence hinders business competitiveness and irritates citizens who consider that too much time is taken to complete the required document (OECD, 2011). The stance taken by industries regarding competition trade policies is resentment of government regulation as interference and that self-regulation is preferable because governments lack the funds and the industry knowledge to be effective (van Cise, 1996). However, Beales et al. (2017) support government intervention by regulation, proposing that it has an important purpose in generating free market competition if it is founded on sense-making evidence, and enhances the provision and quality of crucial public benefits, for instance health and safety, investors, environmental protection and civil rights. The challenge for regulators is selecting the appropriate technologies and companies because failure to do so induces negative outcomes, such as low growth, lack of job creation and public confidence. Regulatory mistakes often generate demands for more regulation, whereas policies created at local level might allow for trial and error and observation of how different policies impacted on behaviour and outcomes. In contrast, universal governance structures impede learning by eliminating diverse approaches that stimulate it (Beales et al., 2017).

The alternative to the free market approach adopted by neoliberals is government control, predominantly based on the ideas of John Maynard Keynes and a macroeconomic concept founded on controlling large fluctuations in the economy. The intervention is applied by investment in times of low or no economic growth, referred to as recession, and, when there is an economic boom raise taxes as one way of reducing demand- and potential-associated inflation. Although monetarist policies are applied in periods of market failure, there is often more confidence that government investment in the economy has a superior outcome in periods of recession, and is characterised by investment in projects that benefit society, for example building road infrastructure, housing and other public sector works (Sloman et al., 2018). Demand in the economy was a consequence of the combined spending power of households, businesses and government but when full employment does not exist, there is no automatic mechanism to restore spending to previous levels, or to prevent failing prices and therefore to move back from recession to a boom situation. The extent of economic output was dependent on four factors: investment; consumption of goods and services produced; the difference in value between imports and exports; government purchases. Consumers buy less goods when there is fear of downturn in the economy and demand falls, companies also invest less so that redressing the balance depends on government purchases and investment (Jahan et al., 2014; Skidelsky, 2016). Therefore, the economy would be dependent on changes in aggregate demand, and associated prices and wages; aggregate demand was influenced by company decisions to reduce investment, which meant that the market failed and must be supported by government intervention. However, Keynes believed that mixed private and public economy would create a more stable solution. As the balance of supply and demand in the economy changed, wages adapted slowly so that labour shortages or unemployment resulted depending on whether demand increased or fell but prices changed less. Government investment to restore demand in a falling market could create a multiplier effect, where each pound sterling spent generated a proportionally larger increase in output, if the increase in spending was the only component of demand to alter. Government intervention increased public spending and public debt levels but, in contrast to monetarism/neoliberalism, budget deficits were not considered to be a major issue in Keynesian economics because spending focused on government investment in public sector projects that increased employment and provided the households with a stable income, which enabled demand to rise again. When demand was restored, there was overheating in the economy; too much demand was moderated by raising taxes so that households had less disposable income and demand for goods/services reduced. An alternative approach for stimulating the economy was to effectively control the money supply by lowering interest rates during a recession, a strategy to encourage investment. Keynes believed this option was less dependable, because borrowers might speculate on paper assets rather than buy goods/services. Keynes perceived that rather than leaving the market to adjust itself in the long term, short-term interventions were preferable because long-term unemployment in recession or high inflation in boom periods would be the consequences (Sloman et al., 2018). Governments and economists have favoured both approaches over time, Keynesian economics being relatively abandoned in developed countries from the 1970s until the 2008 financial crisis, when it was adapted to integrate more recent financial theory.

Postfunctionalism

The main difference between postfunctionalism and neofunctionalism and intergovernmentalism is that it focuses on the disruptive outcomes from tension between functional pressure and national identity, whereas the other two theories perceive integration as enabling the Member States to be more economically efficient (Hooghe & Marks, 2019). Postfunctionalism appraises the causes and effects of exerting governance over groups, politicising them and relevant to European integration. The initial reason for postfunctional policies is non-alignment between the current national situation and the pressure for interdependence between states, which might require multi-level governance. In Europe, postfunctionalism was applied to obtain higher benefits from the provision of public goods as a group compared with those achieved by the individual countries. Once an issue is identified for potential shared action, an evaluation of which group should make the associated decisions is undertaken by government leaders, civil servants, interest groups, society generally or European supranational bodies. The drivers underlying the elite group selected include the gravity of the issue, the competence of specific groups in that context and/or the nature of conflict that could arise from the issue. Integration tends to be constrained by the strength of national sovereignty as is demonstrated by referendums and national elections. Therefore, European integration has a significant impact on the type of political conflict that could result in potential Member States, as different interest groups appraise how much the national systems will be altered. The opposition also instigates new political configurations, and old political parties may decline whilst radical new left- and right-wing national parties evolve to limit the supranational's influence on the country, and are referred to as Eurosceptics. Therefore, in contrast to neofunctionalism and intergovernmentalism, which emphasise the benefits of cooperative action, postfunctionalism highlights the potential for economic stagnation, and incapacity to change the status quo to accomplish higher economic outcomes. In this sense postfunctionalism presents European integration as a conflict situation in which cultural divide and diverse beliefs are a source of a range of outcomes including disintegration (Hooghe & Marks, 2019).

Theories Underlying Rise of Neoliberalism

Public Choice Theory

Public Choice Theory is concerned with the behaviour of voters, the decisions taken by politicians, government bureaucracy and the role of the state, and relies on economic theory (Pressman, 2004). Therefore, it is important to this thesis since the Principle of Proportionality is predominantly employed to protect human rights in a variety of contexts, but the decisions reached are most influenced by senior politicians, civil servants and the state (Möller, 2012; Vadi, 2016). Politicians obtain power by competing for votes in the same way as businesses compete for consumers to buy their products, but their purpose is to remain in power by implementing the policies that will gain the maximum number of votes whilst creating minimum voter dissatisfaction (Schumpeter, 1954). This type of approach was forecast to generate disproportionate government spending and high taxes, whilst the majority imposed their political ideals on the minority (Wicksell, 1958). Therefore, Public Choice Theory is employed by neoliberalists as a rationale for reducing intervention in markets.

Cost benefit analysis and associated opportunity cost are tools developed by economists and used by political scientists to analyse decisions made by politicians, which focus on the cost of abandoning one option in order to accomplish another outcome that is perceived as being more valuable. Political decisions may benefit certain groups whilst others experience the costs, for instance governments imposing austerity measures that impact negatively on employment and social service levels experienced by the citizens; the minority being subject to control by the majority despite political decisions being posed as democratic (Shaw, 2020; Farnsworth & Irving, 2015|). Economists are often employed by politicians to evaluate the costs and benefits of a proposed project/strategy, before politicians decide on how to proceed, and Butler (2018) suggests that the self-interest of politicians, the public who elect them and who may be influenced by the stances taken by pressure groups, and the officials who implement the decisions, all influence the shape of the decision made. The outcome is that democratic choices are not always the optimum solution. Politicians also agree to support measures that certain groups prefer so as to gain their support for their favoured projects, such that a bad initial project is supplemented with many provisions to retain support of minority groups (Samuelson and Nordhaus, 1985). Civil servants, who are not expected to consider profit but generally have other objectives, also pressure government for higher budgets and bigger departments that also provide them with job security; these goals can be attained by encouraging the legislators, usually parliament, to pass more laws than are needed. Public voice is not considered even though the costs are born by the public rather than the decision makers (Butler, 2018; Shaw, 2020). Therefore, Public Choice theorists propose that the political process is dominated by powerful vested interest groups that form coalitions of these types to make decisions that are not in the public interest and to exploit minority groups that are poorly represented (Pressman, 2004). Consequently government intervention is not considered as a rational answer to market failure because government failure to make appropriate decisions to correct it can be even worse (Samuelson and Nordhaus, 1985; Butler, 2018.). The failure of Keynesian interventions to correct market failure in the 1960s and 1970s was linked with application of Public Choice theories and the public service bureaucratic culture, and led to the adoptions of monetarist policies and neoliberalism (Shaw, 2020; Thompson, 2008).

Rational Choice Theory

The alternative to a Public Choice Theory approach was adherence to rational choice theory, which is associated in economics with neoliberalism, with market like mechanisms. The argument is that rational actors are able to examine options, and rank them is order of preference, in the same way as a consumer would rate products available in the market. Economists and other groups proposed that rational choice was similar to a natural science and offered them better forecasting power in terms of predicting GDP growth, inflation rates, unemployment levels and the merits of free trade agreements. However, the expected outcomes from it have not been realised because the assumption of its scientific nature has not been proven (Blakely, 2019).

The Concept and Definition of Proportionality, Theoretical Roots and Practical Applications

Proportionality is defined as a tool used for conflict resolution, which compares the human rights or interest of competing parties (Cottier et al., 2012; Möller, 2012). Proportionality is a concept with origins attributed to Aristotle and refers to a rational permissible action taken by a state that does not encroach on fundamental human rights (Engle, 2012). It is used as a test to evaluate the extent of administrative and constitutional legislative restrictions and to measure their impact on human rights and, therefore, whether implementing them is in the public interest (Cottier et al., 2012). Proportionality is promoted as representing a universal principle that can be applied to resolve conflicting norms, and a means of justice that is relevant to common and civil laws in existence throughout the world (Engle, 2012). Therefore, proportionality is the means to develop global laws by merging national laws, an intervention that has the purpose of supporting better communication between nations, higher trade levels and lower transaction costs. Consequently, proportionality is expressed as a way of generating trade between nations as an alternative to the undesirable armed conflict that results from poor communication and no mutual benefit (Engle, 2012). The Principle of Proportionality is defined by the Federal German Constitutional Court as comprising the elements of suitability, necessity and proportionality; suitability for accomplishing the objective required, necessity meaning that the most effective, least restrictive means should be employed, and proportionality that the measure taken should align with the objective concerned and not exceed it. The Principle of Proportionality is defined with a somewhat different emphasis by Alexy (2014), who explains that principles differ from rules/laws because the purpose of principles is to optimise an issue as much as is possible factually and legally, whereas laws are definitive commands. The factual and legal optimisations are applied to the three associated factors of constitutional review; suitability and necessity are focused on what is factually possible and proportionality stresses the optimisation of the legal possibilities. The suitability factor is exemplified by a new law being passed that affects two groups, whilst the associated facts are suitable for one group, they are excessive in regard to the actions of another, and therefore the condition of suitability is not met. In the same case the necessity condition is that the interference of the law to both groups must be the least intrusive, meaning that if the law improves the previous position for group one, there is no additional burden on group two (Alexy, 2014). In relation to EU Member States therefore, it is evident from this explanation of the principle that considering the constitutional positions of a growing number of Member States is a very complex task. The third principle, proportionality in its narrower sense, is related to making the optimum legal judgement in the specific case and guided by

> the greater the degree of non-satisfaction of, or detriment to, one principle, the greater must be the importance of satisfying the other. (Alexy, 2002, p. 102)

Hence the solution must be optimum for both groups (Alexy, 2014). When these three sub-principles are taken into consideration in terms of the principles applied to a punitive settlement, for instance, they direct that the sentence awarded should fit the crime committed (Focus, 2013), in other words, in general, justice should be proportional to the circumstances of a case (Portuese, 2013). Therefore, proportionality is associated with justice and equity being exercised by the law; disproportionate legal sentences and actions contravening proportionality (Portuese, 2013).

EU law substantially relies on the Principle of Proportionality, a means employed by government to accomplish a specific goal (Cottier et al., 2012), for instance Article 5.4 of the Treaty on the European Union states that the content and form of any action taken by EU must not go beyond that required to accomplish its goals, and that all EU institutions must apply both the Principles of Proportionality and Subsidiarity (Wolf, 2001). The Principle of Subsidiarity is concerned with balancing historic, nationalist sovereignty-driven actions of Member States with EU objectives of integrating them (Barton, 2014, p. 83). In general, the Principle of Subsidiarity links authority with responsibility, and suggests that decisions should be made by those responsible for their outcomes, and as close as possible to the location in which actions are implemented (Barton, 2014; Wolf, 2001), the rationale being that the relevant information regarding the decision is based on accurate knowledge of the actual situation. Localisation is vital for EU Member States to respond with self-determination and accountability, to defend the consequent decisions that undergo close media scrutiny, and which direct the voting preferences of the electorate (Barton, 2014). Therefore, in the context of the public sector, and in relation to most strategic decisions, which require decision makers to have a wide, deep knowledge of an issue, top executives at the apex of the organisation should apply the principle. The recommendation is made on the basis that senior managers are the most capable of evaluating and balancing competing goals regarding their appropriateness to accomplish the overall organisational goal; individuals at lower status levels are then tasked with implementing them (Wolf, 2001).

The Principle of Proportionality is also described as being concerned with obtaining the means to accomplish certain outcomes, whilst the Principle of Subsidiarity relates to the advisability of the existence of different centres of power that control making decisions about society. It states that power to make decisions that impact on society should not be vested in a single central authority, political or otherwise. The inference is that power should not be exercised or transferred without justification at any level of a social body, from private individual to the largest group, which may not be the highest, in alignment with democratic principles (Buxbaum et al., 2011, p. 14). In the case of the EU, the Principle of Subsidiarity means that power should be shared between the central EU authority, Member States and associated regional governments; concisely EU should not intervene when its contribution would add no value, instead interventions should be concentrated on issues that concern all European countries (Lopatka, 2019). The Treaty of Union Article B, final paragraph, States that:

> the objectives of the Union shall be achieved as provided in this Treaty in accordance with the conditions and the timetable set out herein whilst respecting the principle of subsidiary as defined in Article 3b of the Treaty establishing the European Community. (Buxbaum et al., 2011, p. 14)

The Principle of Subsidiarity was not included in the original European Economic Treaty in 1957 but formally included by means of the Single European Act in 1986, Article 130R, in relation to environmental matters being more competently managed by the EU than by individual Member States. Subsidiarity is also mentioned in relation to Justice and Home Affairs, proposing that joint action in these matters is more effective owing to the extent and/or the effects of the interventions required. The wording also states that it may be necessary for decisions to be made by a qualified majority (Buxbaum et al., 2011, p. 14). The Maastricht Treaty 1992 substantially increased integration of EU Member States, and insertion of subsidiarity effectively meant that escalating integration of the Member States would not result in the eventual creation of a superstate. This fact reduced tensions between those states that opposed integration considered to be development and those that favoured it (Buxbaum et al., 2011). The basic terms of the Maastricht Treaty are therefore an important inclusion in this research because they not only increased collaboration between member countries but initiated the plans for creating the Euro and European citizenship, which allowed individuals from Member States to move between them and to reside in any of them without restrictions: 12 states signed the Treaty. In order to progress with the single currency, the European Central Bank (ECB) and the European System of Central Banks were established with the objective of protecting the value of the Euro and maintaining stable prices in the Eurozone countries (ECB, 2020). The Maastricht Treaty provided subsidiarity with a horizontal and a vertical aspect: the horizontal aspect is that subsidiarity applies only when both Member States and the EU have competence, and not in areas in which only EU is competent, stated as external trade and fisheries policies, creating and managing the internal market; the vertical dimension relates to both the areas of joint competence and its exclusive competence, and is that the EU must state why it is taking an action and explaining the extent of that action. Therefore, in the vertical dimension, EU must explain why it is necessary to create a detailed regulation rather than provide guidelines that each nation can incorporate into a national or regional law, referred to as harmonising. In the horizontal dimension the EU can gradually acquire exclusive competence in aspects that were originally joint competences, but it must justify doing so (Buxbaum et al., 2011). Tax and exports are one example for which countries had been able to set their own rates and implement sustainability policies, for instance, whereas the case of product packaging was associated with an exclusive EU competence. This EU claimed that the variation in packaging policies between member countries could be perceived as a barrier to internal EU trade and lack of conformity for exports from EU. Whilst Member States could contest such a change, they would have to invoke the ECJ stating that it was illegal because there had been a violation of Article 3b. Conflicts tend to arise most often when the Maastricht Treaty provides no clear guidelines as to when exclusive or joint competence is appropriate. However, the power vested in the ECJ suggests that it can control the EU's capacity for political power, which it accomplishes by extending its areas of exclusive competence (Buxbaum et al., 2011); allowing the EU to dominate is to infantilise Member States, according to Davies (2006). The Member States and lawyers are uncertain of the ECJ's neutrality (Davies, 2006). An additional issue for Member States is the short eight week period they have to examine proposals for new regulation or directives, in order to check whether the Principle of Subsidiarity applies (Lopatka, 2019). Proposed new regulations must be reviewed from three perspectives according to Barton (2014): whether they are theoretically fair and meaningful; if the way they have been integrated into the Treaty framework is logical and consistent; deciding whether implementation and monitoring throughout the EU have been effective (Barton, 2014). However, Lopatka (2019) comments that new regulation associated with subsidiarity would be more effective if it focused more on what was realistic, rather than idealistic, and eradicated excessive regulation (Lopatka, 2019).

Therefore, it is evident that the EU Member States do not always agree with the legislation that the EU attempts to impose on them (Kumm & Cornella, 2008) and this has resulted in conflict in applying the changes to national laws since the 1970s. This position by EU members is important because it demonstrates that, despite the rhetoric of a single united market, underlying contradictions have been common and heightened by the events imposed by the EU since the 2008 financial crisis. According to the European Court of Justice, the Principle of Proportionality infers that EU law takes precedence over the national laws in the Member States, it necessitates that national authorities alter or annul their laws otherwise the Member State could risk being accused of acting illegally within EU law. Although Member States assign more importance to EU law than its Treaties, considerable resistance has continued, and they pronounce that national constitutional laws are more valid under specified circumstances. However, when there is conflict, Member States generally accept EU law as most appropriate. Three aspects of the National Constitution for Europe have met substantial resistance, although others remain, and the issue underlying resistance varies by |state. The first concerned fundamental rights and has been a conflict since the 1970s and, whilst still contended, less attention has been given to it recently because the probability of serious conflict is relatively low. The second related to the Principle of Subsidiarity referred to which body or Member State(s) would make a decision about the validity of the EU enacting legislation, a decision as to whether the proposed legislation was considered beyond the EU competence and conflicted with jurisdiction in national Member States. The European Court of Justice has the power to act in such conflicts but, since it is appointed by the EU, the highest courts in Germany and Denmark, amongst others, proposed that they had the right to decide on such matters. In the third major conflict concerning constitutional identity, one example concerned elections, the rights of EU citizens to stand as a political candidate in any EU Member State and/or to vote for a political candidate within all EU countries. This law was in direct conflict with Spanish Constitutional Law which allows solely Spanish Citizens to stand for election and to vote in Spanish elections. Other examples of resistance referred to the extent of female participation in the armed forces that was contrary to German law and the legal position of degrees awarded by private universities in some Member States (Kumm & Cornella, 2008).

In the EU the test of proportionality is applied to any potential intervention that is proposed, which might violate its Treaties; therefore they are permissible only if four conditions apply: the objective underlying the intervention aligns with the objectives of the Treaty, it is justifiable for the prevailing public interest; appropriate for accomplishing its objective; no alternative measures could achieve the same outcome with lower restrictions; and does not exceed the actions needed to do so (Bendor & Sela, 2015; Portuese, 2013). This structure does not fully align with the German federal government's definition (Focus, 2013) as it has an initial stage of establishing whether the objective is legitimate in regard to EU Treaties; this action of deciding whether the objective is legitimate is also stressed as an initial consideration in the process by Möller (2012). The Principle of Proportionality is integrated into the justice systems of all EU Member States and the measure has the purpose of manipulating human behaviour to reflect that of a reasonable person. Over the past fifty years it has been integrated into national constitutional law globally (Bendor & Sela, 2015; Portuese, 2013).

The word reasonable is extremely contentious, as is evident from the opinion of the International Court of Justice in 1982 in the case of Tunisia v Arab Jamahiriya on its usage, because the circumstances of the individual case render its reasonableness and equity (Corten, 1999). Hence, reasonableness is a subjective concept, judgements in proportionality are dependent on the facts and the reasonable interpretation of them by participants and the predispositions of the decision makers, and should be the result of "balance, symmetry, effectiveness, humanity" (Newton & May, 2014, p. 300). The subjectivity of proportionality is emphasised in the case of making a decision under pressure and stated to rely on reasonableness of what might be expected in the circumstance, military action being used as the example by Newton and May (2014). These authors also stress that, although subjective, the concept of reasonableness is not totally manoeuvrable and that a rigorous assessment should be made but decision makers should also acknowledge their power in the matter and ensure that they evaluate all the perceivable consequences.

Therefore, whilst there is substantial consensus that the Principle of Proportionality is valuable, its effectiveness has been questioned more recently by constitutional rights theorists. If proportionality is considered in the context of conflict between an existing right and a competing right or interest, the latter is likely to hold much less weight. The first condition for testing proportionality is that the intervention must have a legitimate goal, but Möller (2012) argues that policies are devised by people, for instance civil servants and politicians, and that policies cannot have goals, what is important is that consideration is given to each goal as being legitimate based on moral arguments, rather than the subjective preferences of the policy makers. An example of an unsuitable legitimate goals is one cited in the legal case of human rights of homosexuals who wished to join the armed forces, *Smith and Grady v UK*, where policymakers' personal beliefs were applied to ban their participation; legitimacy must be determined by moral argument (Möller, 2012).

The main reasons for the success of the Principle of Proportionality are restricting the exercise of public authority by reviewing conduct as associated with good governance, influencing the nature of judicial review and directing the expectations of private citizens, according to Vadi (2016). The application represents a calculated, intentional methodology in which all relevant facts are considered and balanced according to the context and the importance of the relevant interests. This process implies that a government's actions must be justified in terms of their rationality and reasonableness, in order to be proven as legitimate. In this way, the power of the decision-making state officials is limited because the actions it has taken can be subjected to a judicial review by courts and tribunals. Simultaneously the principle can set the limits or define the legitimate rights/expectancies of individuals in relation to government or regulatory interference with their vested rights. However, in reality, there are five issues associated with it: institutional competences, scales of values, cultural arguments, inability to judge some issues by the same standards, overprotection of property rights. The inference of balancing competing interests negates the concept of separation of legal powers between different parts of the legislature, the civil service, the judiciary and the executive, which is contrary to the principle that each part is monitored by another independent body for the benefit of society. Therefore, political and legal boundaries are not well characterised, and democracy is negatively impacted. No value scales have been defined that indicate how to balance values in the third stage of the process, meaning that the adjudicator can apply own values to the decision, which are based on personal preferences and ingrained culture. This situation infers that the decision made lacks an objective, logical rationale and has not taken the cultural context of competing interests into account. However, Portuese (2013) suggests that EU assumes that divergent values can be balanced by applying the principle of cost benefit analysis in an attempt to compare the administrative costs of the options considered on society with the net benefits of the alternatives, a procedure that the EU refers to as economic efficiency. The issue of individual/national values is particularly relevant because the principle was applied after World War Two to ensure each nation's constitution reflected its unique cultural identity, and that constitutional courts defended the people against infringement of those rights. Hence the additional weakness in relation to evaluating cultural values in context is that some values cannot be judged by the same standards, which infers that any judgement made is liable to legal redress since it cannot be justified logically by the cost benefit methods that are often applied. The Principle of Proportionality has also been criticised as providing those with most power with a means to transfer the democratic process to the courts, meaning that local/national constitutional values are ignored. This has been the case in the EU application to accomplish its goal of European integration according to Vadi (2016). The European Court has been accused of adopting a much stricter approach to the proportionality test in the context of national interests and a weaker one towards the interests of European integration. Whilst the European Court has held for national constitutional rights in some judgements, it has more often made decisions that align with the integrated Europe goal (Vadi, 2016).

Justice Theory

The Theory of Justice is associated with fairness in a non-interventionist society and is a suitable framework for the use of political power in a justifiable and moral manner, meaning that each member of the population is considered equal and free within a democratic society (Rawls, 2001). Justice is linked to fairness and to the Principle of Proportionality, in the legal sense of criminal law, for example it is fairness when the judicial responses to crime are publicised and applied on a similar basis to all cases, and to proportionality when no person should be awarded a punishment that is not commensurate with the crime, and equivalent for all offences of that level (Tonry, 2017). Justice as fairness is therefore an important underlying theory relating to proportionality in relation to EU principles and actions, because the major political and social institutions, the national constitution, the legal system and the economy should be founded on justice as fairness (Rawls, 2001). The concept of justice as fairness relies on two principles, the first of which takes priority: every individual has a right to basic freedoms that cannot be removed; social and economic equalities satisfy two conditions, the offices and positions that enable them are open to everyone on the principle of equal opportunities, which should be integrated into national constitutions, and that they should be of most advantage to the least advantaged individuals in society, referred to as the Difference Principle, and applicable to economic institutions (Rawls, 2001). The Difference Principle is subject to the Maximin rule that no member of society becomes more disadvantaged, these individuals must become better off than they were previously so that there is no opposition to the equality gap increasing (Barata & Cabrita, 2019). Citizens are free and equal but also reasonable and rational under Rawls' (2001) concept of justice and fairness: being reasonable they are able to agree to cooperate when the terms are fair if others are also willing to do so, even if cooperating is against their own interests; citizens' rationality implies that they have the capacity to change their viewpoint after revaluating what is most important to them. In order to foster reasonableness and rationality, citizens require certain conditions, primary conditions, and political institutions measure social and economic progress, political impact, by the number of these primary conditions that citizens accumulate. The primary goods comprise fundamental rights and liberties, supplemented by a free choice of occupations, freedom of movement, income and wealth, status of occupation and associated responsibilities which provide self-respect and feelings of self-esteem.

The Nature of State Intervention in the Post-crisis Developed World

The global financial crisis impacted more negatively on the EU than other regions or countries, for instance bank write-downs amounted to 3.6% in Eurozone countries and 5.1.% in EU countries that had not joined the

Euro (IMF, 2009). The southern EU countries were particularly vulnerable because many had taken advantage of low interest rates when they joined the Eurozone, and by 2011 had accumulated excessive debt partly generated by interest rate rises from 2008; in France, Italy and Spain debt levels were greater than 300% of GDP (Eposito, 2014). The low-interest loans were often not used to make long-term investment that would enhance competitive advantage but to improve GDP in the short term, and southern nations with weaker economies were most badly affected when the 2008 crisis happened.

The EU interventions after 2008 can be divided into two categories that were shaped to: ensure financial stability in terms of economic growth and employment; measures that would protect the bloc for a recurrence of the crisis. The strategies to accomplish these two objectives comprised financial reforms, establishing a financial stabilisation programme, strengthening economic governance and implementing measures that would drive economic growth and associated employment prospects (Barnard, 2012; Table 3.1).

Financial Reforms

The ECB was not authorised to be the lender of last resort or to supervise national banks by the terms of the Maastricht Treaty, and could not compel them to provide confidential information; therefore, the EU had no treasury function or capacity to assist Member States with potential lack of solvency. Consequently, financial reforms comprised a new European banking authority, recapitalisation of banks, reducing risk of bank failure

Table 3.1 Strategies for financial reform

Strategy	*Key aspects*
Financial reforms	Monitor banking sector Legislate on the capital retained by bank as a risk-mitigation method Increase in the level of deposit guarantees
Financial stabilisation	Support grants to Member States based on issuing debt instruments in capital markets
Strengthen governance	Supervise Member State budgets especially Eurozone countries
Economic growth and employment	Fiscal stimulus

by increasing the capital amounts the banks were forced to retain, standardising and enhancing the amount of deposit guarantees to a maximum of €100,000 for all Member States, replacing the diverse existing guarantees in addition to guaranteeing speedy pay out. Commission and reward for employees, which had resulted in poor financial advice prior to the crisis, were subject to review (Barnard, 2012; Pisani-Ferry & Sapir, E). In order to effect these changes, the European Parliament had amended the Capital Requirements Directive (CRD) in 2019 and instructed the EU to devise measures for cross-country integrated financial supervision embracing all Member States. The European System of Financial Supervision (ESFS) was the solution proposed, the supervisory framework came into force in January 2011 (NCA, 2015), and European Systemic Risk Council (ESRC), later renamed as the European Systemic Risk Board (ESRB), was created as an integral part of the ESFS in December 2010, to ensure that integration was achieved and that it was supervised by the ECB. The strategy effectively increased EU integration and the degree of control that the EU had over Member States, but also created severe tensions for them owing to the disruption it caused to their markets (Schmieding, 2012). In November 2013, another reform, the Single Supervisory Mechanism (SSM) regulation, became law as part of the EU's plan to create a banking union, and its capability to supervise all banks and implement common financial services regulations across Member States. This was followed by ECB employing its new supervisory responsibilities to establish what risks could threaten banks within the banking union with balance sheet asset values of greater than or equal to €30 billion; these banks were forced to implement ECB rules (NCA, 2015). The Bank Recovery and Resolution Directive (BRRD) was integrated into the SSM as a measure to: force banks to be fully prepared for a future crisis; to change legal and company structures to facilitate quick resolution of crises without taxpayer funding them, for instance by selling assets or being subject to a merger; for the ECB to intervene and even to replace staff and existing strategies if capital requirements were not retained; to have funds for restructuring as necessary. Hence bank bail-in became possible and would avoid ECB providing bailout funds (EC, 2014).

Financial Stabilisation

Although the EU applied fiscal policies to stimulate economic growth and generate demand so that companies would recover from the downturn and employment levels improve as a consequence, Member States were instructed that they must continue to reduce their public debt and their support of financial institutions (EC, 2009). The incentive for Member States to agree to funding the stimulus package was the promise that those which did would gain permission to breach the 3% GDP rule on deficits (Tait, 2008). In 2010 a further measure was taken to stabilise the financial situation in Greece, Ireland and Portugal, which were described as being in exceptional difficulties, it was denominated the European Financial Stability Facility (EFSF), which comprised the European Financial Stabilisation Mechanism (EFSM), and the European Stability Mechanism (ESM) (Barnard, 2012). The funds had been raised from the private sector by issuing debt on the capital markets, an intervention allowed under ESM rules. The debt-based instruments used were similar to SUVs that had caused the original crisis, which began in the US, although this was denied by the CEO of EFSF (Olivares-Caminel, 2011). Germany and France were particularly opposed to this development suggesting that the recipient countries were not subject to exceptional difficulties, and there was uncertainty amongst the other Eurozone Member States that one country supporting another financially was contrary to the meaning of Article 125 of the *Treaty on the Functioning of the European Union* (TFEU) (De Witte, 2011). Hence an amendment was made to Article 48(6) that concerned internal policies, and later to Article 136 to allow the Eurozone Member States to operate this type of stability measure (De Witte, 2011; EUI, 2015). This revision was far more constitutionally important than realised at the time and is further discussed in Chap. 6. Whilst all other Eurozone Member States in difficulty after 2012 received funds from the ESM, a permanent measure to help countries in financial difficulties (Schoenbaum, 2012), Greece continued to be subject to the rules of EFSM until June 2015 (EFSF, 2015). The Member States wishing to raise funding by means of ESM were obliged to follow a procedure devised by the EU and IMF resulting in signing a Memorandum of Understanding (MoU) (Olivares-Caminel, 2011). The conditions for funding, including the interest rate, were based on the perceived weakness of the individual state's policies, for instance over-generous healthcare systems and other social services, and the Member State was compelled to reform those identified (Touri & Touri, 2014). In addition, it was compulsory to make loan payments on time as loans had to be paid in full at the end of the term (Schoenbaum, 2012).

Enhancing Economic Governance

The EU's main objective in developing and implementing economic governance reform was to gain market confidence that it had the economy under control, and that it was no longer at risk from a recurrence of the crisis (Barnard, 2012). The SGP was amended to focus on Member State debt levels, imposing debt limits, stronger enforcement of procedures (Arroyo, 2011) and much greater accuracy in financial reporting, such that EUROSTAT use was made more widespread because it was able to generate higher quality fiscal data. EUROSTAT also allowed EU bodies to identify imbalances more quickly owing to automatic signals resulting from identification of non-compliance with the agreed procedures (Arroyo, 2011). Gradually a group of measures, referred to as the Six Pack that strengthened the SGP, were devised and became law in 2011; the Six Pack comprised fiscal monitoring of all Member States budgets, regardless of whether they had deficits and/or sovereign debt, over or under the 3% deficit limit, and 60% GDP maximum sovereign debt (Barnard, 2012; EC, 2019a). Hence, EU controls over Member State financial matters were increased again. The legislation integrated into the Six Pack also represented a change in voting rules regarding the recommendations or proposals that the EC presented to the Member States; any sanctions proposed would be adopted unless a majority of Member States voted against them (Barnard, 2012). On ratification of the Six Pack, the Treaty on Stability, Coordination and Governance (TSCG), which included several of its objectives, would run parallel. TSCG came into force in June 2013 (Cramme & Hobolt, 2014) with the purpose of enforcing permanent fiscal union between EU Member States, especially those comprising the Eurozone (Schoenbaum, 2012); the part of the TSCG relating to fiscal matters was subsequently referred to as the Fiscal Compact. The Article relating to balanced budgets, Article 3, and known as the debt-brake mechanism imposed severe restrictions on annual budget deficit levels of 0.5% nominal GDP and annual reduction of sovereign debt of 5% for those Member States that had debt in excess of 60% (Cramme & Hobolt, 2014; Schoenbaum, 2012). In addition, these terms were enforceable by EU instigating legal action in the ECJ, and Member States refusing to sign the Treaty could receive no loans from ESM. The declared rationale was that EC would predict whether a Member State was in danger of crisis (Barnard, 2012, but Schoenbaum (2012) regarded it as a form of austerity and even more limiting on Member State freedom than previous measures.

In 2010, the EU instigated the EU Semester Process into Economic Governance as an initiative to ensure that the Member States were able to harmonise their economic policies, which inferred that public finance policies aimed at minimising debt, investment was increased and structural changes implemented, with the purpose of generating jobs and economic growth, and preventing excessive macroeconomic imbalances in the EU (EU 2020a). The unchecked large imbalances in EU are stated to be the main reasons for the 2008 economic crisis in the EU (Hume, 2018). Macroeconomic balances are defined by the EU as

> any trend giving rise to macroeconomic developments which are adversely affecting, or have the potential to adversely affect, the proper functioning of the economy of a Member State or of the Economic and Monetary Union, or of the Union as a whole. (Hume, 2018, p. 2)

The reason for this description is that prior to the crisis the EU considered external asymmetric shocks would cause temporary imbalances in national economies, which would gradually self-correct over time, owing to the economic measures it had implemented, therefore, policies to remedy them were neglected. Consequently, the focus of the EU definition is that macroeconomic change generates macroeconomic financial risk associated with current account deficits, competitiveness, higher borrowing by the private sector and rapidly increasing asset values; imbalance in the external environment is stressed since internal imbalance in the Eurozone was considered to be much less likely to be damaging (Hume, 2018).

The EC is involved in the European Semester Programme as the major analyst of national budget plans and their associated macroeconomic and structural reforms, the generator of advice for each national government for a future period of 12–18 months, and monitors each nation's progress in meeting its Europe 2020 targets. Individual governments decide on what action they will take regarding EC recommendations (EC, 2020a).

Generating Economic Growth

The method of generating economic growth was to inject a fiscal stimulus equivalent of €200 billion or 2% EU GDP to support business and employment expansion. The Euro Plus Pact (EPP), devised by the French and German governments, was introduced to enhance the competitiveness of Eurozone Member States and involved some of them agreeing to political reforms as the perceived means to achieve it, particularly to labour law. The terms could be imposed on holders of an MoU under EFSM and ESM, and the rules prevented Member States from making investments to reach the growth targets assigned to them by the EU; they were unable to devalue currency to increase their competitiveness either, since their prices were based on the value of the Euro in international markets (Barnard, 2012). The IMF (Banerji et al., 2015) review of these measures aligns with the evidence in this section regarding the complexity of these policies as they developed. The economic governance framework is identified as being stronger than before 2008 but complicated because of the range of enforcement tools and overlapping processes that it comprises. It overlaps with the SGP, which is presented as separate framework, and its development described as increasing intricacy as the Six Pack and two pack legislation were integrated, and then EPP and Fiscal Compact as rule-based intergovernmental framework structures. The effectiveness of the economic governance framework was negatively impacted by this complexity, primarily because Member States did not fully understand the underlying reasons for the reforms or what function the EU performed. According to IMF (Banerji et al., 2015) accountability and responsibility for the required reforms were lacking; the EU was perceived as becoming too controlling in national government matters and failed to treat all Member States equitably. The reforms were limited by the Principle of Subsidiarity, although legislation had supported the effectiveness of some, but dissatisfaction of some Member States with the degree of EU interference had weakened their application, because the individual states decide how to shape the implementation of the change (Banerji et al., 2015). This criticism may have induced the EC to introduce the Structural Reform Support Service (SRSS) in 2015, which was effectively a customised training and development initiative for each of the EU Member States to support them in the preparation, design and implementation of the reforms and in monitoring progress; SRSS also included strategic and legal advice. The coverage was extensive in each of the five areas of: governance and public administration; revenue administration and public financial management; growth and business environment; labour market, education, health and social services; financial sector and access to finance (EC, 2019a). In relation to the Subsidiarity Principle, the huge amount of detail that was provided for Member States indicates an initiative that could be extremely intrusive regarding national policies, without appearing to be compulsory, such that common practices were starting to be used across all countries. In May

2017 the Structural Reform Support Programme was introduced as funding support for EU members wishing to become part of the Eurozone; €222.8 million budgeted for the period 2017–2020 (EC, 2019a). Initially the budget had been inadequate, exemplified by the fact that requests received in 2018 amounted to five times the budget allocated; 26 countries asked for support for more than 260 projects related to joining the Euro in 2019. The plans for expansion of SRSS after 2020 were allocated a €25 billion budget and associated with a stronger economic and monetary union are described as comprising Reform Delivery Tool, a financial incentive for Member States to implement reforms that had resulted from the European Semester Process; technical support to assist with reform design and implementation as well as improving administrative skills; convergence facility intended for EU members progressing their application to join the Euro. The Reform Delivery Tool takes precedence with a budget allocation of €22 billion (EC, 2019a) indicating its importance to further EU integration.

National Productivity Boards were introduced in 2016 as a recommended initiative for all Eurozone Member States but all EU countries were invited to implement them; they are described by EC (2020b) as independent institutions. The rationale was that they could conduct 'high-quality' (EC, 2020b, p. 1) economic and statistical analysis that would be published and available to the public. The EC envisaged their influence in generating public debate on policies, and support for policies that were drivers of sustainable economic growth and convergence. In relation to non-Eurozone members they were envisaged as demonstrating price stability, secure public finances, exchange rate stability and convergence in long-term interest rates. Member States implementing National Productivity Boards are able to use the data produced as part of the European Semester Process. The EC rationale was another intervention to force Member States to follow its economic and fiscal policies, because it stated that productivity had slowed considerably since the year 2000, owing to low investment, imbalances and associated labour and product market rigidity, as well as failure to develop skills. By 2019, ten Eurozone countries had established the Boards, and EC stated they were already generating discussion on productivity issues, and that all others had committed to doing so soon (EC, 2019b).

The EC continued to monitor all states in 2018, in order to prescribe budgets for 2019, 2020 and beyond; despite the long period from the 2008 economic downturn, some Member States were not meeting their

Medium Term Budgetary Objectives (MTO). The analysis of the preventative aspect of the SGP identifies those Member States that worsened their structural position and those continue to "make a negative effort" (EC, 2019a, p. 13) to reduce their expenditure. Debt-to-GDP ratios had generally declined since the peak at 2014, but reductions were greater in the non-Euro Member States than in Eurozone, owing to non-Euro states' GDP growth and associated financial capacity to pay off public debt. However, debt ratio in Italy, the third largest economy and Eurozone member, continued to rise (EC, 2019a).

The Economic Recovery Plan (ERR)

The Economic Recovery Plan, which was published in November 2008 and agreed by the Member States before it could be officially implemented in 2009, comprised common targets for all member countries. Member States were encouraged to take joint action to restrict the impact of economic downturn, inspire confidence that would generate demand, take measures to ensure business continuation and to preserve jobs until the economic upturn. Therefore, the ERR targets were designed to promote growth, investment for growth and employment, and EU proposed that Member States could exploit EU strengths to accomplish these goals. These strengths were cited as: effective coordination, strong frameworks, for instance the Stability and Growth Pact and the Lisbon Strategy, in addition to the huge advantages that the Euro provided along with the EU Single Market, which was the world's largest (EC 2009). The Lisbon Strategy was devised by the European Council as the economic and social means to accomplish EU competitiveness by means of the knowledge economy and the associated innovation-based growth model. In the economic sense this inferred increasing investment in continuous research and development to exploit changes in the external environment, whilst the social dimension focused on investing in human capital development and striving for social inclusion. In 2001 an environmental strategy was integrated to meet the need for sustainable development, and the consequent focus on careful consumption of resources, reuse and recycling. The Lisbon Treaty is also based on the Principle of Subsidiarity (Bongardt & Torres, 2012), the EU's exclusive competences are only relevant when the competences of individual Member States can be demonstrated as inadequate (Devuyst, 2012). The Lisbon Treaty was replaced by the 2020 Strategy in 2010, since the former had been devised in a period in which sustainable growth was expected. However, the 2020 strategy has similar goals even though those stated in the Lisbon Strategy were never accomplished (Leschke et al., 2012).

The strength of the SGP was envisaged by Schuknecht et al. (2011) as providing the rationale that would avoid Member States accumulating excessive budget deficits. Therefore, the SGP had two strands: a preventative measure that demanded Member States retain budgets that were in surplus, balanced or almost balanced, with the purpose of sustainable debt management that would mitigate risk of large debts arising when there was an economic downturn; a corrective mechanism represented by a procedure to correct deficits that reached the equivalent of more than 3% of GDP, a process that required stricter monitoring but sanctions could be imposed for failure to conform. However, the weakness was that EU enforcement was challenging, since European Commissioners had to agree before proceedings could be taken against any Member State, the Commission might also be too lenient. A qualified majority of the ECOFIN Council was also required to agree to proceedings and a sufficient number of countries might vote against a penalty if many were in similar deficit situations (Schuknecht et al., 2011). The SGP is a concept that has substantial relevance in terms of EU interventions after 2008, justifying a fundamental description of it at the beginning of the discussion on post-2008 EU interventions.

The ERR stated that recovery was based on solidarity and social justice (EC, 2009), but as it developed it was associated with austerity measures, most affecting the poorest groups in Member States (Oxfam, 2013a, 2013b, 2013c, 2013d, 2013e). The ERR comprised two interventions, financial injection and monetary policy intended to support recovery. The financial injection was part funded by the EU and the individual Member States, €3 billion and €170 billion respectively, amounting to approximately 1.5% GDP. The amount was referred to as smart investment and an integrated part of the SGP. The terms of the smart investment that Member States were to undertake were narrowly defined:

- Investment in the most vital skills for future growth and productivity
- Developing as a knowledge economy
- Specific focus on energy efficiency and clean technologies and infrastructure

The purpose was to enhance growth in the auto manufacturing and construction industries in particular, to reduce reliance on energy imports and become self-sufficient, whilst also reducing domestic and commercial energy costs. In the infrastructure aspect, the emphasis was on becoming more connected by leveraging internet skills and use of internet to improve innovation and productivity. The associated monetary policy was characterised by low interest rates, overhauling the banking system and ensuring banks made loans at low rates to businesses participating in the smart investment initiatives. The European Investment Bank (EIB) was the major institution for delivering the plan, with an additional €7.5 billion of funding for over two years plus funds sourced externally. The European Bank for Reconstruction and Development (EBRD) received funding of €500 million a year specifically to support new EU Member States. Member States were instructed to devise their individual plans based on the ERR, including monitoring their fiscal imbalances and rectifying them. These plans should integrate measures to:

- Boost employment and economic growth by discretionary spending on specific projects to create demand, for instance by instigating projects related to climate change, in alignment with the smart investment objective, tax reductions were not to be used for generating growth and employment
- Restrict social benefits to the poorest households and extend the length of unemployment benefit temporarily to those who had just completed full time education or had lost their job in the past four weeks
- Make loans available for companies experiencing temporary financial difficulties

Hence the EU attempted to use fundamental monetary policy and government control of the money supply and interest rates to recover from the recession; interest rates were decreased to encourage companies to borrow, and money supply increased by injecting the extra funds into the economy for companies and people, to create confidence and demand. However, other recommended incentives were to lower employment taxes and social contributions and to temporarily lower value-added tax and measure the increased disposable income for households as an additional means of boosting demand, fiscal policy (Sloman et al., 2018). The fiscal policy was stated as aligning with the Lisbon Treaty which focused on people, research and innovation, business and infrastructure (European Parliament, 2020), and therefore also with supporting accomplishment of ERR.

Outline of the Impact of State Intervention After 2008

This section provides a brief overview of how some interventions impacted on specific nations, in order to emphasise the wide variation; these aspects are discussed in detail in later chapters.

Economic Impact

In the initial period after the 2008 financial crisis, Keynesian economics were applied in many countries globally as a means to prevent further recession. Whilst the approach prevented further decline, the budget deficits that it created were perceived as preventing economic recovery, so that economists returned to their neoliberal monetarist policies (Skidelsky, 2016), which resulted in many years of recession for some EU Member States (Hall, 2012). A major factor in the differences between the impact of EU monetary policy on the Eurozone members in the northern EU countries and those in the south was the cultural preferences for managing economic cycles. Germany had adopted a balanced budget approach to economic management, with government guiding society only as necessary and focusing on exports as their growth strategy, whereas France and Italy had traditionally preferred a Keynesian approach of intervention and a demand-led approach to growth (Hall, 2012).

The policies adopted by the EU were generally founded on monetary policies to keep inflation low, as had been the historic preferences of many northern Eurozone countries particularly Germany; this policy has enabled growth in northern Member States and continued to do so until quite recently. However, southern European countries had traditionally used inflation as a means to increase their export competitiveness and consequently to fund public sector spending, in other words, to pay off debt. When the EU imposed its monetary policy, the southern nations no longer had any control over their national monetary policy and their industrial base shrank, whilst GDP became more reliant on service industries such as tourism, and the countries required EU bailouts to service their debt interest. In contrast to the northern states, the southern countries' GDP fell and was worsened by leading consumers purchasing goods made outside the EU rather than those from the southern nations, because they were cheaper, lower quality imports. A common monetary policy without the implementation of a common economic and fiscal policy meant that trade balances became unstable; inflation could not be used as means to balance the system (Eposito, 2014). The northern states' economies were capital and knowledge based, for instance specialist manufacturing, finance and product design, whilst the Southern European countries relied on agriculture, tourism and low-skilled manufacturing, which makes them less able to recover from economic downturns. The EU never made any serious effort to ensure that there was equalisation of competitiveness and/or sustainable interdependence in an economic region characterised by high diversity. Systemic imbalances were not controlled, and therefore they increased causing the rift between north and south. Consequently, the impact of the financial measures taken to return to economic growth on the population living in EU countries was possibly more damaging than the direct interventions (Eposito, 2014). The levels of unemployment in most EU countries between 2012 and 2014 were the highest in the world and had greatest impact on youth employment. As a consequence, the most affected Member State citizens had very low confidence in the EU, and their governments seemed unable to resolve the increasing debt and unemployment (Eposito, 2014). The various financial interventions undertaken by the EU were associated with its stated economic and political goals that all Europeans would gain sustainable benefit from the huge collective resources it represented, but that systemic change, involving human and financial capital issues, needed to be applied to accomplish these outcomes. The EU aimed to become a unified superstate, a sustainable economic model based on peace, cooperation, prosperity for all, by whatever means were required (Eposito, 2014), and using the Proportionality Principle as its basis (Engle, 2012).

Social Impact

After the 2007/2008 financial crisis, social welfare initiatives that remained in states or groups of states such as the EU, were diminished under the austerity programmes designed for economic recovery. Austerity is described as a process typically involving activities such as reducing wages, prices and public sector spending as a means to return to economic growth, but instead of generating public confidence that it will do so, austerity often results in further weakening of an already weak economy (Blyth, 2013). The effects of austerity measures imposed by the EU on the PIIGS group of countries, Portugal, Italy, Ireland, Greece and Spain, served as a good example, according to Blyth (2013). Although these interventions were intended to reduce their high public debt and restore confidence, they generated low or negative economic group, higher debt levels and the associated interest payments increased (Blyth, 2013).

Bibliography

Alexy, R. (2002). *A Theory of Constitutional Rights*. Oxford University Press.

Alexy, R. (2014). Constitutional rights and proportionality. *Revus, 22*(2), 51–65.

Arroyo, H. T. (2011). *The EU's fiscal crisis and policy response: Reforming economic governance in the EU*. European Commission.

Banerji, A., Barkbu, B., John, J., Kinda, T., Saksonovs, S., Schoelermann, H., & Wu, T. (2015). *Building a better union: Incentivizing structural reforms in the Euro area* (IMF working paper WP/15/201).

Barata, A., & Cabrita, M. (2019). What principle of difference for a truly egalitarian social democracy? Rereading Rawls after social democracy's failures. *Palgrave Communications, 5*(69), 1–9.

Barnard, C. (2012). The financial crisis and the euro plus pact: A labour Lawyer's perspective. *Industrial Law Journal, 41*(1), 98–114.

Barton, O. (2014). An analysis of the principle of subsidiarity in European Union law. *North East Law Review, 2014*, 83.

Beales, H., Brito, J., Davis, J.K., Devine, D., Dudley, S., Mannix, B., & McGinnis, J. (2017). *Government regulation: The good, the bad, & the ugly*. The Regulatory Transparency Project of the Federalist Society. https://regproject.org/wp-content/uploads/RTP-Regulatory-Process-Working-Group-Paper.pdf. Accessed 20 Jan 2020.

Bendor, A., & Sela, T. (2015). How proportional is proportionality? *I•CON, 13*(2), 530–544.

Bergmann, J., & Niemann, A. (2015). Theories of European integration. In E. Knud, A. Jorgensen, A. Kalland, E. Drieskens, K. Laatikainen, & B. Tonra (Eds.), *The SAGE handbook of European foreign policy* (pp. 166–182). Sage Publications.

Blakely, J. (2019). How economics becomes ideology: The uses and abuses of rational choice theory. In P. Rona & L. Zsolnai (Eds.), *Agency and Causal Explanation in Economics* (pp. 37–52). Springer.

Blyth, M. (2013). *Austerity: The history of a dangerous idea*. Oxford University Press.

Bongardt, A., & Torres, F. (2012). Lisbon strategy. In E. Jones, A. Menon, & S. Weatherall (Eds.), *The Oxford Handbook of the European Union* (pp. 469–483). Oxford University Press.

Bowden, B., & Seabrooke, L. (2007). *Global standards of market civilization.* Routledge.

Butler E. (2018 September 13*). Public choice theory – The economics of government failure. Institute of economic Affairs.* https://iea.org.uk/the-economics-of-government-failure/. Accessed 23 Jan 2020.

Buxbaum, R., Hertig, G., Hirsch, A., & Hopt, K. (2011). *European economic and business law: Legal and economic analyses on integration and harmonization.* De Gruyter.

Corten, O. (1999). The notion of "reasonable" in international law: Legal discourse, reason and contradictions. *The International and Comparative Law Quarterly, 48*(3), 613–625.

Cottier, T., Echandi, R., Leal-Arcas, R., Liechti, R., Payosova, T., & Sieber-Gasser, C. (2012). *The principle of proportionality in international law* (NCCR Trade Regulation Working Papers, No. 2012/38).

Cramme, O., & Hobolt, S. B. (2014). *Democratic politics in a European Union under stress.* Oxford University Press.

Crouch, C. (2011). *The strange non-death of neoliberalism.* Polity Press.

Davies, G. (2006). Subsidiarity: The wrong idea, in the wrong place, at the wrong time. *Common Market Law Review, 43*(1), 63–84.

De Witte, B. (2011). The European treaty amendment for the creation of a financial stability mechanism. *European Policy Analysis, 6*, 1–8.

Devuyst, Y. (2012). The constitutional and Lisbon treaties. In E. Jones, A. Menon, & S. Weatherall (Eds.), *The Oxford Handbook of the European Union* (pp. 163–180). Oxford University Press.

EC. (2009). *Economic Crisis in Europe: Causes, Consequences and Responses: European Economy 7/2009.* Brussels: European Commission.

EC. (2014). *EU Bank Recovery and Resolution Directive (BRRD): Frequently Asked Questions.* Brussels: European Commission.

EC. (2019a). *Factsheet: Structural reform support service.* European Commission.

EC. (2019b). *European semester winter package: Assessing member States' progress on economic and social priorities.* European Commission.

EC. (2020a). *The European semester: Why and how.* European Commission. https://ec.europa.eu/info/business-economy-euro/economic-and-fiscal-policy-coordination/eu-economic-governance-monitoring-prevention-correction/european-semester/framework/european-semester-why-and-how_en. Accessed 8 Feb 2020.

EC. (2020b). *National productivity boards.* European Commission. https://ec.europa.eu/info/business-economy-euro/economic-and-fiscal-policy-coordination/national-productivity-boards_en. Accessed 8 Feb 2020.

ECB. (2020). *Five things you need to know about the Maastricht treaty*. European Central Bank. https://www.ecb.europa.eu/explainers/tell-me-more/html/25_years_maastricht.en.html. Accessed 2020 Jan 31.

EFSF. (2015). *About EFSF. European Financial Stability Facility Commission* [online]. http://www.efsf.europa.eu/about/index.htm. Accessed 17 June 2015.

Engle, E. (2012). The history of the general principle of proportionality. *Dartmouth Law Journal, 10*(1), 1–11.

Eposito, M. (2014). *The European financial crisis: Analysis and a novel intervention*. Harvard University. https://scholar.harvard.edu/files/markesposito/files/eurocrisis.pdf. Accessed 31 Jan 2020.

EUI. (2015). *Constitutional Change Through Euro Crisis Law*. EUI. http://euro-crisislaw.eui.eu/topic/tfeu/. Accessed 14 July 2015.

European Parliament. (2020). *The treaty of Lisbon*. European Parliament. https://www.europarl.europa.eu/factsheets/en/sheet/5/the-treaty-of-lisbon. Accessed 15 Jan 2021.

Farnsworth, K., & Irving, Z. (2015). *Social policy in times of austerity: Global economic crisis and the new politics of welfare*. Polity Press.

Focus. (2013). The principle of proportionality and the concept of margin of appreciation in human rights law. *Basic Law Bulletin, 15*, 1–9.

Foucault, M. (2010). *The birth of biopolitics*. Palgrave Macmillan.

Hall, P. (2012). The economics and politics of the euro crisis. *German Politics, 21*(4), 355–371.

Hoffmann, S. (2000). Towards a common European foreign and security policy? *Journal of Common Market Studies, 38*(2), 189–198.

Hooghe, L., & Marks, G. (2019). Grand theories of European integration in the twenty-first century. *Journal of European Public Policy, 26*(8), 1113–1133.

Hume, M. (2018). *Managing macroeconomic imbalances*. European Union. http://www.structural-reforms.eu/workshops/programme/Hume_Imbalances_April_27_2018.pdf. Accessed 8 Feb 2020.

IMF. (2009). *Global financial security report: Navigating the financial challenges ahead*. International Monetary Fund.

Jahan, S., Mahmud, A., & Papageorgiou, C. (2014). *What is Keynesian economics?* International Monetary Fund.

Kumm, M., & Cornella, V. (2008). The primacy clause of the constitutional treaty and the future of constitutional conflict in the European Union. *International Journal of Constitutional Law, 3*(2–3), 473–492.

Leschke, J., Theodoropoulou, S., & Watt, A. (2012). How do economic governance reforms and austerity measures affect inclusive growth as formulated in the Europe 2020 strategy? In S. Lehndorff (Ed.), *A triumph of failed ideas: European models of capitalism in the crisis* (pp. 243–281). Brussels.

Lindberg, L. N. (1963). *The political dynamics of European economic integration*. Stanford University Press.

Lopatka, R. (2019). Subsidiarity: Bridging the gap between the ideal and reality. *European View, 18*(1), 26–36.
Martin, J. (2016). The sharing economy: A pathway to sustainability or a nightmarish form of neoliberal capitalism? *Ecological Economics, 121*, 149–159.
Möller, K. (2012). Proportionality challenging the critics. *I • CON, 10*(3), 709–731.
Moravcsik, A. (1993). Preferences and power in the European Community. A liberal intergovernmentalist approach. *Journal of Common Market Studies, 31*(4), 473–524.
Moravcsik, A. (1998). *The choice for Europe. Social purpose and state power from Messina to Maastricht.* Cornell University Press.
Morrison, W. (2019). *China's Economic Rise: History, Trends, Challenges, and Implications for the United States.* Washington: Congressional Research Service.
NCA. (2015). *The European system of financial supervision.* Netherlands Court of Audit. http://www.courtofaudit.nl/english/Publications/Topics/EU_governance_to_combat_the_economic_and_financial_crisis/The_European_system_of_financial_supervision. Accessed 24 June 2015.
Newton, M., & May, N. (2014). *Proportionality in international law.* Oxford University Press.
Nicoli, F. (2019). Integration through crises? A quantitative assessment of the effect of the Eurocrisis on preferences for fiscal integration. *Comparative European Politics, 17*, 397–425.
Niemann, A., & Schmitter, P. (2009). Neo-functionalism. In A. Wiener & T. Diez (Eds.), *Theories of European integration* (2nd ed., pp. 45–66). Oxford University Press.
OECD. (2011). *Regulatory policy and governance: Supporting economic growth and serving the public interest.* OECD Publishing.
Olivares-Caminel, R. (2011). The EU architecture to avert a sovereign debt crisis. *OECD Journal, 2011*(2), 1–32.
Oxfam. (2013a). *The true cost of austerity and inequality; Portugal case study.* Oxfam.
Oxfam. (2013b). *The true cost of austerity and inequality: Italy case study.* Oxfam.
Oxfam. (2013c). *The true cost of austerity and inequality; Germany case study.* Oxfam.
Oxfam. (2013d). *The true cost of austerity and inequality; Greece case study.* Oxfam.
Oxfam. (2013e). *The true cost of austerity and inequality; France case study.* Oxfam.
Phelan, S., & Dawes, S. (2018). *Liberalism and neoliberalism. Oxford research encyclopedia, communication.* Oxford University Press. https://oxfordre.com/communication/view/10.1093/acrefore/9780190228613.001.0001/acrefore-9780190228613-e-176?print=pdf. Accessed 24 Jan 2020.
Pisani-Ferry, J., & Sapir, A. (2009). *Banking crisis management in the EU: An interim assessment* (p. 2009/07). Bruegel Working Paper.
Pollack, M. (2014). Realist, intergovernmentalist and institutionalist approaches. In E. Jones, A. Menon, & S. Weatherill (Eds.), *The Oxford Handbook of the European Union* (pp. 3–17). Oxford University Press.

Portuese, A. (2013). Principle of proportionality as principle of economic efficiency. *European Law Journal, 19*(5), 612–635.
Pressman, S. (2004). What is wrong with public choice? *Journal of Post Keynesian Economics, 27*(1), 3–18.
Rawls, J. (2001). *Justice as fairness: A restatement.* Harvard Business Review Press.
Rosenzvaig, E., & Munck, R. (1997). Neoliberalism: Economic philosophy of postmodern demolition. *Latin American Perspectives, 24*(6), 56–62.
Samuelson, P., & Nordhaus, W. (1985). *Economics.* New York, NY: McGraw-Hill.
Sandholtz, W., & Sweet, A. (2014). Neo-functionalism and supranational governance. In E. Jones, A. Menon, & S. Weatherill (Eds.), *The Oxford handbook of the European Union* (pp. 18–33). Oxford University Press.
Schmieding, H. (2012). Tough love: The true nature of the Eurozone crisis. *Business Economics, 47*(3), 177–189.
Schoenbaum, T. J. (2012). *The age of austerity: The global financial crisis and the return to economic growth.* Edward Elgar Publishing.
Schuknecht, L., Moutot, P., Rotherm, P., & Stark, J. (2011). *The stability and growth pact crisis and reform* (p. 129). European Central Bank. Occasional Paper Series No.
Schumpeter, J. A. (1954). *History of economic analysis.* Oxford University Press.
Shaw, J. (2020). *Public choice theory.* https://www.econlib.org/library/Enc1/PublicChoiceTheory.html. Accessed 25 Jan 2020.
Skidelsky, R. (2016, March 24). *Does Keynes's theory still hold up?* World economic forum. weforum.org/agenda/2016/02/does-keynes-s-theory-still-hold-up/. Accessed 27 Jan 2020.
Sloman, J., Garrett, D., & Guest, J. (2018). *Economics* (10th ed.). Pearson.
Smith, A. (1776). *The wealth of nations.* http://political-economy.com/wealth-of-nations-adam-smith. Accessed 24 Jan 2020.
Stiglitz, J. (2002). *Globalization and its discontents.* Penguin.
Stivachtis, Y. A. (2015). Liberal democracy, market economy, and international conduct as standards of 'civilization' in contemporary international society: The case of Russia's entry into the 'community of civilized states'. *Journal of Eurasian Studies, 6*, 130–142.
Tait, N. (2008, November 26). EU's stimulus plan met with doubts. *Financial Times* [online]. http://www.ft.com/cms/s/0/0b216d84-bba6-11dd-ae97-0000779fd18c.html#ixzz3dEYyxmuW. Accessed 16 June 2015.
Thompson, N. (2008). Hollowing out the state: Public choice theory and the critique of Keynesian social democracy. *Contemporary British History, 22*(3), 355–382.
Thorne, K. (2010). Does history repeat? The multiple faces of Keynesianism, monetarism, and the global financial crisis. *Administrative Theory & Praxis, 32*(3), 304–326.

Tonry, M. (2017). Fairness, equality, proportionality, and parsimony: Towards a comprehensive jurisprudence of just punishment. In A. Bois-Pedain & A. Bottoms (Eds.), *Penal censure: Engagements within and beyond desert theory*. Hart Publishing. Chapter 14.

Touri, K., & Touri, K. (2014). *The Eurozone crisis: A constitutional analysis*. Cambridge University Press.

Vadi, V. (2016). A history of success? Proportionality in international economic law. In A. S. Serano (Ed.), *The reform of international economic governance* (pp. 171–192). Routledge.

van Cise, J. (1996, March). Regulation—By business or government? *Harvard Business Review*. https://hbr.org/1966/03/regulation-by-business-or-government. Accessed 25 Jan 2020.

Walton, M. (2004). Neoliberalism in Latin America: Good, bad, or incomplete? *Latin American Research Review*, *39*(3), 165–183.

Wicksell, K. (1958). New principle of just taxation. In R. Musgrave & N. Peacock (Eds.), *Classics in the theory of public finance* (pp. 72–118). New York (NY).

Williamson, J. (2004, January 13). The Washington consensus as policy prescription for development. In *Practitioners of development*. World Bank. https://www.piie.com/publications/papers/williamson0204.pdf. Accessed 24 Jan 2020.

Wolf, M. (1995). Cooperation or conflict? The European Union in a Liberal global economy. *International Affairs* (Royal Institute of International Affairs 1944–), *71*(2), 325–337.

Wolf, M. (2001). Authority: Delegation. In N. Snelser & P. Bates (Eds.), *International encyclopedia of the social & behavioral sciences* (pp. 972–978). Elsevier.

WPR. (2020). Capitalist countries 2020. *World Population Review*. http://worldpopulationreview.com/countries/capitalist-countries/. Accessed 24 Jan 2020.

CHAPTER 4

Literature Review: Global Economics Before and After the 2007 Economic Crisis

Events Leading to the 2007 Global Recession

Origins of the Factors and Initial Symptoms

The volatility of the UK stock market in July 2007 was one of the initial signals of an impending financial crisis in the UK. The sudden cessation of UK inter-bank lending was an additional signal, which resulted from fears of losses related to high-risk mortgages, a trend that had its origins in the US housing market (Telegraph, 2009). However, the announcement made by the largest French bank, BNP Paribas SA, on 9 August 2007 that withdrawals could no longer be made from three of its investment funds created panic in financial markets; these funds were linked to high-risk mortgages referred to as sub-prime mortgages. The reason BNP Paribus gave for this announcement was that the value of the funds' assets had declined by 20% within less than two weeks, and that these comprised one-third of sub-prime securities, which were rated as AA or above. The value of these securities was stated to be €1.6 billion on 7 August but it was impossible to value the funds accurately, owing to the extent of default on the mortgages associated with them. The consequence of this pronouncement was that investors ceased buying these debt-based investments, which were secured by home loans (Boyd, 2007). A month earlier in July 2007, the Bear Stearns Company had applied for bankruptcy protection in the Cayman Islands, owing to sub-prime investment losses

S. Weißschnur, *The Proportionality of State Intervention*,
https://doi.org/10.1007/978-3-030-75676-5_4

related to two hedge funds, and had prevented investors from redeeming their investments in a third hedge fund (Boyd, 2007). In the UK, the Northern Rock Building Society, which was considered a lender of last resort for mortgages, approached the Bank of England (BOE) for emergency funding. However, when the BOE publicly stated that Northern Rock was solvent, the announcement induced a run on the bank as investors withdrew their funds. This type of investor behaviour had not been observed since the 1930s' depression and resulted in Northern Rock being nationalised by the UK government in February 2008 (Llewellyn, 2009). The American government was forced to support its two largest mortgage lenders in July 2008, Freddie Mae and Freddie Mac, which owned or guaranteed $US 5 trillion in home loans, and it is estimated that the largest US and European banks, which were bailed out by governments during the crisis, cost taxpayers $US 23.7 trillion (Marshall & Concha, 2012; Telegraph, 2009; Kopechi & Dodge, 2009). These events had origins in the developments, which occurred in financial markets in the years immediately preceding the emergence of these warning signs, and eventually led to the discovery of major flaws in the global financial systems initiated several decades earlier.

Historical Influences

The boom in the housing market and the associated over-exposure of mortgage lenders, which immediately preceded the 2007 crisis, were not the first such incident. The origins of his housing bubble and previous booms were fuelled by fundamental changes made to mortgage lending regulations in the US in the 1970s and subsequent regulation changes. The cumulative effect generated the worst global recession observed since the 1930s (Morris, 2008). The promotion of home ownership by the US government in the 1970s was realised by changes it made to savings and loan regulations. Home ownership loans had traditionally been funded by the limited deposits made by consumers to savings and loan companies (Morris, 2008), but the creation of government-backed agencies, which purchased the mortgage loans from the savings and loans companies, enabled them to sell more mortgage loans and to increase US homeownership. The government agencies, which acquired the mortgage loans, resold them as debt packages to investors, referred to as mortgage-backed securities. The main agency was Freddy Mae, previously a state bank created in 1938, but privatised in 1968 as nationalisation had become unfashionable. The second agency, Freddie Mac, was a similar institution established in 1970 and privatised in 1989 (Marshall & Concha, 2012). The savings and loan companies had no liability to their original customers or to the government agency once they sold their mortgage loans (Morris, 2008) and were able to use the incoming funds to grant further home loan/mortgages (Klimechi & Wilmott, 2009). The study of the government-sponsored agencies Freddie Mae and Freddie Mac conducted by Marshall and Concha (2012) reveals that the government extended credit facilities of $US 2.5 billion to enable them to purchase mortgage debts. The consequence of the increased availability of home loan funding was that underwriting standards became much more lenient, and loans were frequently granted to those whose incomes and/or credit ratings would previously have excluded them from home ownership. This trend was particularly evident in the US from 2006 onwards (Rudd, 2009; Mishkin, 2008).

From the mid-1980s onwards both major US political parties devised financial regulation policies aligned with the interests of Wall Street (Marshall & Concha, 2012) so that as share values rose, confidence in taking on higher risks also increased (Morris, 2008). This change was illustrated by Morris (2008) in the description of the Payment in Kind Bond (PIK) financial vehicle for which missed debt payments were resolved by the debtor effectively increasing the number of debt bonds to the creditor, hence creating a debt spiral and encouraging higher borrowing. The growing competition between large companies, underpinned by government policies for enhancing GDP, also resulted in huge increases in corporate acquisitions, so that the bid prices made by acquirers rose so rapidly that banks stopped financing them, and acquisition finance had to be procured by other means. In many cases, the creditor defaulted on the acquisition loan within a period of months after the acquisition took place, but the firm which had arranged the finance had earned huge fees, for instance $80 million for one transaction (Morris, 2008). These examples demonstrate the interrelationship between government actions in pursuit of economic growth, which also led to looser regulation of financial organisations and to increasing fixation on generating higher profits, as well as to the investor pursuing higher returns (Baker, 2010). These developments all contributed to the financial crisis in 2007 and Morris (2008) demonstrated that it was basically a consequence of increasing investor greed; the individuals who bought equity and debt securities were professional investors, whose sole purpose was profit maximisation, which led to an incapacity to consider the risks.

Securitisation

Mortgage-backed securities were created by combining a group of mortgages into a trust in which investors bought shares, for instance, a trust with a value equivalent to $100 million in mortgage debt and a specified percentage interest yield. The investor received an annual yield proportionate to the share of trust purchased but the total interest paid to the investor was a share of the total interest accrued, minus any default in payments by the original mortgagees; for instance, 6% interest would yield $US 6 million annually, if all the original mortgagees continued to make all payments (Morris, 2008). The financial process of converting illiquid assets, such as mortgage debt and other types of debt and risk, into a specific instrument is referred to as securitisation, illustrated by the trust example. The originator, which converted the illiquid assets into the security, receives the proceeds from selling the debt(s) to others (Gorton & Souleles, 2005). The securitisation process is represented in Fig. 4.1.

The specific instrument was later referred to as an SPV, a special purpose vehicle, which was a legal entity, for instance a limited company or a trust. SPVs had additional advantages for companies, for instance they could remove liabilities from their balance sheets, which enabled their financial situation to appear more positive (Gorton & Souleles, 2005). Investment banks were able to create bonds by purchasing debts or risk from the original lenders to customers A, B, C. The bonds created in the securitisation process were sold to investors represented by D and E; the original assets purchased by ABC formed the SPV collateral (Juhas, 2013). The banks created a significant variety of SPVs for loan securitisation (Fabozzi & Choudry, 2004), which were Asset-backed Securities (ABS),

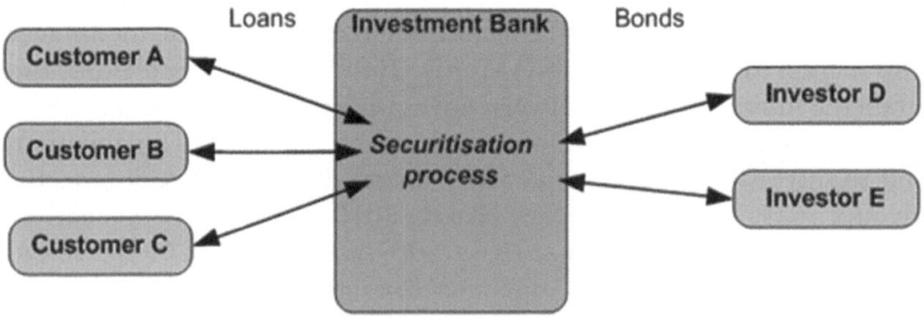

Fig. 4.1 The securitisation process. (Source: KunalFintech.com)

Mortgage-backed Securities (MBS) both commercial (CMBS) and residential (RMBS), Collateralised Debt Obligations (CDO) and Repackaged Securities.

Mortgage-Backed Securities

Two SPV instruments, which were related to mortgage loans, are particularly important to understanding the sub-prime crisis that initiated the 2007 global financial crisis, and ultimately led to the housing bubble and signalled the instability of global financial markets. These are explored later in this chapter and relevant to this study. The Collateralised Mortgage Option (CMO) and Credit Default Swaps (CDS) represented the SPV for packaging mortgage loans and then for insuring the investor against losses, which might be generated by the original mortgagee failing to make its mortgage payments (Morris, 2008; Noeth & Sengupta, 2012). The creation of the CMO was possible by dividing the mortgage loan package into three segments with different credit ratings, so that the risk level of each segment aligned with the expected return; the lower the credit rating the higher the return (Morris, 2008). As CMOs increased in popularity financial institutions competed fiercely, with the consequence that CMO complexity increased, especially as technology advanced in the late 1990s and early 2000s. The technology developments enabled very fast financial modelling and consequent lack of understanding of the risks of the financial instrument devised especially as the number of segments in the trust or other financial vehicles also grew; the segment with the lowest rating and highest risk later referred to as being 'toxic' (Morris, 2008). The collapse of the bond market in 1994 was attributed to computer-generated securitised bonds of lower complexity than those in 2007, and this event had been labelled the worst market loss since the introduction of securities. It was also caused by the increasing competition to acquire securitised bonds, which had driven huge growth in the bond market from $96 billion in 1981 to £1.27 trillion by 1994 (Ehrbar, 2013).

The CDS were SPVs, which covered investors against losses on CMOs, caused by the original debtor/mortgagee defaulting on loan repayments. However, the CDS market was very large and unregulated, its size attributed to very large investors, exemplified by hedge and pension funds, purchasing CDSs as insurance against losses (Noeth & Sengupta, 2012). CDSs made the CMO much more attractive because it insured against losses. However, unlike standard insurance, there was no insurable interest clause, and the CDS could be sold to investors, who had no link to the original CMO (Morris, 2008) and who paid a spread fee based on the perceived degree of risk of default on the original SPV, of which CDOs were one example. The higher the CDS spread, the greater the implied risk, and Noeth and Sengupta (2012) proposed that the spread provided valuable information regarding the level of default risk related to corporate and sovereign debt; CDS instruments were also in common use in EU countries for some time before 2007, but spreads on sovereign debt tended to be low, inferring low risk of default (Noeth & Sengupta, 2012).

Advantages of SPVs

SPVs were stated to be worth trillions of dollars by banks and were sold to individuals and corporate investors, concurrently reducing debt on the banks' balance sheets. This action made banks appear more solvent than was actually the case and enabled them to comply with their regulatory capital requirements (Kenins et al., 2013). The substantial fees, which banks also earned for SPV generation and management, formed a significant proportion of their revenues. In the UK, this process was initiated in 1987 (Fabozzi & Choudry, 2004) and was recognised by the taxation body, Her Majesty's Revenue and Customs (HMRC), as representing three major advantages for the SPV originator: to raise finances at a competitive rate, with lower interest payable than is the case with traditional lending mechanisms; in cases in which the SPV originator is subject to compliance with a regulatory capital structure, it is possible to comply with regulation by moving SPVs off balance sheets, so that working capital can be made available for other projects; additional funding could be obtained by diverse means, since credit rating is enhanced (HMRC, 2015). The UK was the first European country to generate special purpose vehicles (SPVs), initially as mortgage-based securities. The development of SPVs varied in Europe, significant volumes appearing by 1996 and then gradually increasing and CDOs first appeared in Europe in 1998. Portugal first issued SPVs in 2000 and Greece and Poland issued them on becoming EU members in 2003 (Fabozzi & Choudry, 2004).

Bank strategies to implement and increase the range of SPVs demonstrate they changed attitude towards lending; they generated more income generated from selling their loans to other bodies, and fees for creating the instruments. The looser regulations also allowed banks to borrow funds from international financial markets, whilst simultaneously enhancing the apparent state of their solvency through off-balance sheet entries. These factors all interrelate and explain the serious financial consequences of the 2007 crisis. The next section appraises the trends in interest rates, credit availability and changes in financial regulations prior to the 2007 financial crisis and their role in it.

Financial Markets Immediately Prior to the 2007 Crisis

The trends in financial markets prior to the first announcement that there were issues with SPVs in mid-2007 provide insight into the initial symptoms that later revealed the deeper issues, which had been the fundamental cause of the market collapse; the underlying weaknesses in global financial systems became apparent (Elliott, 2011). Those who were considered experts in analysing financial markets made statements regarding the flaws they had discovered, for instance, George Soros proposed that the crisis was not caused by an unexpected external shock but by the characteristics of the financial system, which had developed owing to personal agendas and the greed of those who worked in and shaped the financial sector. These individuals and groups had been able to manipulate the situation of low interest rates and loose regulations to create a domestic and commercial property boom, which had quickly and sharply resulted in soaring asset values. Governments were blamed for allowing the crisis to develop because they had continuously failed to concentrate on the public good by allowing private parties to shape global financial markets. The lack of government regulation of the markets and intervention in them resulted in their financial unsustainability (Baker, 2010, p. 1). The behaviour leading to these market conditions was referred to as 'generalised and aggressive risk taking' (Borio, 2008, p. iii), and the sub-prime collapse was merely indicative of the issue, which was related to financial instability resulting from financial imbalances, typical of positive economic conditions, and individuals and companies overstretching their borrowing to income/asset ratios (Borio, 2008). This stance was supported by Borio and Zhu (2008) with regard to the change in risk behaviour demonstrated by Central Banks, which had increased their risk because there had been a long period of financial stability, and consequently had poor understanding of how to respond to the unexpected financial trauma that emerged in 2007.

In 2003, the Chairman of the US conglomerate Hathaway Incorporated, Warren Buffett, made a comment about new financial instruments in the company's annual report describing them as similar to "financial weapons of mass destruction, carrying dangers that, whilst currently now latent, are potentially lethal" (Buffett, 2003, p. 14). The report by Rudd (2009) referred to the consequences of the use of such instruments as driving an asset bubble of a size never previously encountered, which fulfilled that forecast. The term 'bubble', as associated with asset price increases, refers to a debt bubble rather than an equity situation and was dangerous, because an environment of imperfect information existed and therefore monitoring also provided inaccurate data on which to base decisions, according to Rudd (2009). In addition, rather than being the more usual demand bubble, it was a supply-driven bubble caused by mortgage originators with seemingly endless funding because they were able to transfer debt and responsibility, neglect underwriting and create a 'moral hazard' (Coffee, 2009 p. 5). Changes in asset values in the US and UK, which resulted from the housing boom, are shown in Fig. 4.2.

As a consequence of the increasingly deregulated financial sector and low interest rates, credit became accessible to large numbers of people who would have been previously unable to obtain it, and the US government ignored three key factors, according to Rudd (2009): the fourfold rise in mortgages backed by securities from 2001 to 2006; rapidly rising residential property prices generated by growing demand for housing and lower supply available, an environment of affordability, owing to low repayment levels based on low interest rates; a huge increase in sub-prime lending (Rudd, 2009; Coffee, 2009).

At the same time, domestic debt was rising and comprised a variety of loans; credit cards, home loans and other debt, which was increasing at the highest rate, as shown in Fig. 4.3.

In the domestic sector, debt was rising at a higher rate than incomes, as shown in Fig. 4.4, secured debt being the higher proportion. In the UK, a £700 billion gap existed between customer bank deposits and lending by 2008, which the banks filled by borrowing from overseas financial institutions (Farlow, 2009).

However, cheap exports from countries such as China made domestic purchases less expensive and inflation low. Global economic trade was in a growth phase, creating confidence in a secure future, with no apparent signs of financial burden, owing to the strength of asset prices that more than covered the credit levels (Borio, 2008).

Fig. 4.2 Soaring asset values. (Source: Bank of England)

Changing Regulation

The gradual changes in global financial regulation led to new practices, new financial institutions and integration of global financial markets, which had resulted in the development of derivative instruments, for instance, hedge funds, a new financial paradigm, referred to by Crotty (2008) as the New Financial Architecture (NAF), an attempt at creating efficient capital markets. Financial innovation driven by regulation changes relied heavily on the development of instruments that transferred credit risk, and led to a new asset class (Borio, 2008). The changes in financial intermediation transferred risk away from the original lender because rather than the originator of the loan bearing the risk until the loan was

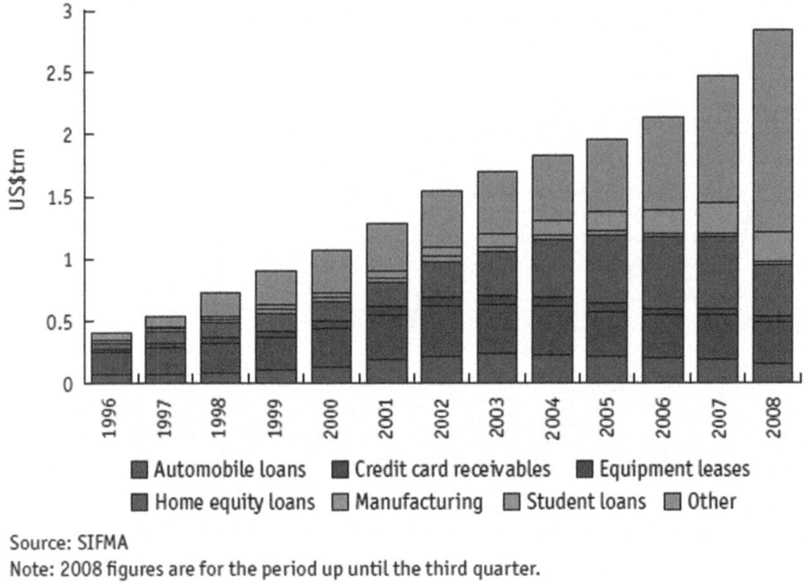

Fig. 4.3 Domestic debt trends 1996–2008. (Source: SIMFA)

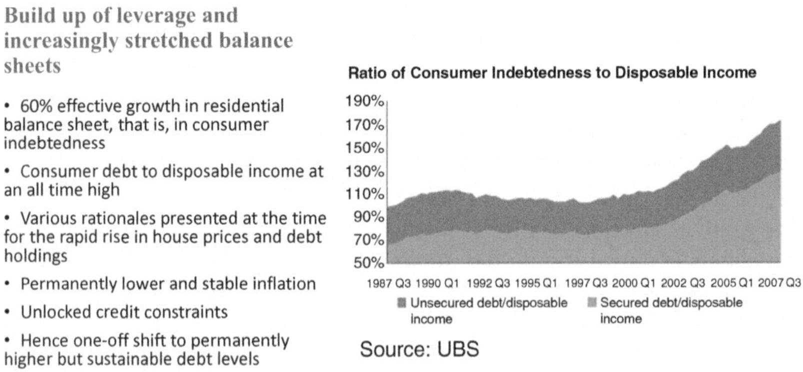

Fig. 4.4 Gap between income and debts. (Source: Farlow (2009, p. 15); SIMFA)

paid off, the new process was characterised by the originator selling a package of loans to another entity, which then distributed them (Borio, 2008; Mishkin, 2008). The growth of banks into conglomerates, which were able to conduct retail and investment banking, also allowed them to develop hedge funds and other similar intricate instruments and deal in them. The NAF was described as complex, excessively risky and without the types of transparent practice that had been typical in earlier periods. These factors hindered accurate valuation of investments, so that when the crisis occurred, values dropped sharply (Crotty, 2008; Avgouleas, 2009). The development of the unregulated financial sector, referred to as shadow banking, also emerged in this period, partly owing to high liquidity levels; these were organisations that conducted banking operations but were not banks (Kodres, 2013). These shadow banking firms were not bound by the same rules as banks, for example by capital structure requirements, and they did not possess the consumer protection afforded to banks by the National Central Bank, the potential guarantee that the investor's investment is repaid. The huge growth of banking institutions during the pre-2007 period represented a major contribution to the crisis, owing to the number of high-risk instruments traded (Avgouleas, 2009). This NFA exhibited very serious structural weaknesses that could be categorised into five major flaws, according to Crotty (2008). The first weakness was engagement with the theory of efficient capital markets, which fundamentally proposes that securities prices will reflect their risk–return ratio, and not considered to be a strong model, as well as the positive manner in which it was perceived by the regulator, which was misleading. Crotty (2008) argues that models such as the Capital Asset Pricing Model (CAPM) and Options Pricing Theory make numerous assumptions, such as possession of perfect information relating to pricing assets, including generating future cash flows, and that competition ensures that the optimum equilibrium security pricing decisions maximise agent preference functions. Hence, the assumption is that risk is priced accurately (Mishkin, 2008; Crotty, 2008). Therefore, if investors and financial institutions are able to price risk, they will hold just as much risk as is considered safe, and consequently government regulation is unnecessary, despite the contrary evidence emanating from the 1930s' recession. This view of efficient markets is also reinforced by Avgouleas (2009), who states that studies by financial experts have demonstrated that financial markets are complex, evolving and characterised by investor behaviour, which is irrational as well as rational. The second factor was that unreasonable and irrational incentives created an environment in which extraordinary levels of risk emerged, in combination with the third aspect, the complexity of instruments that could not be accurately valued but lost considerable value after the boom. The irrational incentives related to the transfer of liability for the loan away from the lender, the large fee earned for selling the loan as well as the potential to earn additional fees by packaging the loans in SPVs and offering them to investors were serious flaws. The huge new incentives created were exemplified by investment bank incomes becoming less reliant on traditional mergers and acquisition fees and more reliant on securitisation. New York Traders and Dealers earned $21 billion from underwriting securities and $35 billion from trading them, in 2006 alone; huge bonuses were also paid to associated financial executives and employees, according to Crotty (2008). Credit rating agencies were blamed for providing unrealistic credit ratings to the complex debt instruments, by for instance CDOs, which could not be accurately valued (Avgouleas, 2009), and the product risk was so difficult to assess that without the agencies, no products trading could have occurred (Crotty, 2008). Credit rating agencies gave 80% AAA ratings to the securities that inferred that securities were as low risk as corporate bonds, a rating that was accepted by regulators and analysts. The underlying reason for the actions of rating agencies may have been their reliance on investment banks for income. Capital market demand for these securitised instruments was the underlying reason for the mortgage bubble and the demand for sub-prime mortgages (Coffee, 2009); this factor related back to the profit motive of banks ignoring risk, as stated by Crotty (2008). The fourth factor was that, in stark contrast to what was reported about the high success rate and profitability of the banks, their risk levels were dangerous, and the fifth factor was the new structure generated high gearing and systemic risk that diffused globally. The 1930s' recession had resulted from the type of loose regulation that characterised the NFA, and stricter government-led regulation of the sector after this period had been the norm, including separation of retail and investment banking (Crotty, 2008).

The on-balance sheet assets grew so rapidly from 2000 to 2007, from $10 trillion to $23 trillion, that the Bank of England was commented on their increase; however, the value of securitised instruments was part of this figure. One part of the banking sector's rationale for holding securities was either to convince investors to purchase them, or because they could not sell them. In addition, Crotty (2008) states that the banks retained the riskiest instruments, which substantially reduced total bank asset values, when their asset value fell. However, just because the loans were sold for the purpose of securitisation did not mean that there would be no residual liability in case of a default of the original lender.

Another major regulatory change that occurred with NFA was that banks set and managed their own risk levels, as well as their capital requirements, and were allowed to take risky assets off balance sheets. All of these factors led the banks to take excessive risks and ultimately to create high risks throughout the whole financial system, according to Crotty (2008). The dangerous behaviour associated with modern financial markets was exemplified by all of them adopting the same strategies, and highlighted by Avgouleas (2009), who stated that this behaviour represented the very highest risk to policy reforms, and unless altered the 2007 situation would recur. Therefore, gaining an understanding of the NFA was vital to devising new, more robust financial markets and institutions that reduced the capacity of financial institutions to generate future crises (Crotty, 2008; Avgouleas, 2009). These remarks are important to this study as a means of evaluating the actions taken by the EU to redress financial risk issues in Member States.

The 2007 failure is also considered to be a consequence of poor regulation (Coffee, 2009), and the key change that underpinned it was the action of the Securities and Exchange Commission (SEC) virtually removing the limit on gearing for financial institutions as a result of fear that these institutions would lose their global competitiveness. This approach was implemented by other major economies for the same reason, using the rationale that stricter regulations would mean business being transacted elsewhere rather than in their countries. Press notifications in the early months of 2007 based on extracts from the Bank for International Settlements (BIS) 78th Annual Report suggested the beginning of a new financial crisis for instance:

> years of loose monetary policy have fuelled a giant global credit bubble, leaving us vulnerable to another 1930s style slum. (Evans-Pritchard, 2007, p. 1)

This BIS report included remarks on the consequences of loose monetary policy derived from the regulatory changes, commenting on mass selling of new credit instruments, excessive risk-taking by investors, highly established imbalances in global currency systems and fast rising domestic debt. The US Federal Reserve, specifically its Chairman Alan Greenspan, was considered to be the driver of these regulatory changes, and the concept that it was possible to eliminate asset bubbles without negative consequences.

Despite the warnings in early 2007 and the fact that there had been three financial crises within ten years, no systematic remedial plan was implemented, but rather those who had constructed the NFA continued to believe in the neo-liberalism approach and self-correcting theory of efficient financial markets (Manne & Knight, 2010).

Liquidity

The liquidity, which facilitated the increase in lending levels that led to the crisis, was considered to be supported by the imbalance of the current national account levels of countries in different parts of the world. The countries with negative current account balances borrowed from nations with positive balances at low interest rates for several years before 2007, for instance oil-producing countries and Asia had current account surpluses of $1 trillion in 2007, and China alone had currency reserves of $2 trillion. This situation led to confidence that the financial boom would continue (Farlow, 2009). The demand for liquidity was therefore satisfied by these conditions, and investor need for higher investment yield by the development of increasingly complex derivatives (Borio, 2008). However, Liang (2012) questions this theory as an explanation for the global financial crisis, arguing that both global financial imbalances in current accounts and financial instability are consequences of financial globalisation, within the global and financial monetary systems. Additionally, using imbalances as the rationale for 2007 merely conceals global financing patterns, which are the fundamental reason for financial fragility. Imbalances in current accounts were explained as being partly a result of countries, which had policies of high export-led strategies, whilst concurrently suppressing domestic demand in order to drive up surpluses, as well as countries at the financial core attracting large financial inflows. Financial fragility, as a result of globalisation, was attributed to deregulation and innovation driving large capital flows, and recurrent bust and boom cycles, as well as the lack of any international clearing body to provide liquidity and clear international payments. However, the US was described as acting as a clearing body and as a consumer and provider of these two actions, but without the capacity to provide the services required; this added to the fragility (Caballero & Krishnamurthy, 2009).

However, Merrouche and Nier (2010), whilst acknowledging the theories that high global capital flows, looser monetary policy and weaker regulation were the cause of the 2007 crisis, stated that three years later, there remained no general agreement regarding the main reasons for the sudden financial shock. Therefore they conducted a further study on behalf of the IMF, to test each of the potential theories associated with the crisis and concluded that increasing capital flows were the fundamental reason for it. The basis of this proposal was that capital flows, in combination with global regulatory systems that were both inadequately designed and regulated, underpinned the eventual collapse. The increase of global imbalances was not linked to looser monetary policy, which was stated to be a coincidental factor rather than the root cause of them. This conclusion was based on comparison of Organisation for Economic Co-operation and Development (OECD) countries' current balances which showed that those nations with tighter monetary policies than the US had stronger accumulation of current account imbalances than those with weaker policies. In addition, investors tended to look for high yield on their investments, and private capital was likely to flow to countries with higher interest rates, so that loose monetary policy in the US could not explain the high exposure to US securitised sub-prime assets of banks, financial intermediaries and individuals in other parts of the world. However, OECD (2009) stated that, despite the convergence of academic/financial reports on the reasons for the crisis, the core reasons were not well understood and that the latest one was caused by the financial sector, unlike other global crises.

Consequences of the Crisis

In 2008 the OECD predicted that global trade would shrink by 13% in the coming year so that McKibbin and Stoeckel (2009) proposed that there would be a crisis transition from financial to economic crisis. The change in the focus of the crisis was nevertheless a consequence of the failure of Lehman Brothers and similar banks, which would make it almost impossible to obtain credit facilities. The initial impact of the financial crisis and the sequential economic impact are outlined in this section so that they can be compared later with the European situation. The interventions taken by various governments to attempt to rectify the consequences of the financial crisis are also explored and contrasted because these factors and the results of the interventions are relevant and important to answering the fundamental research problem.

Outline of the Financial Effects

In the initial months after the first signs of a crisis, the US and UK governments prevented banks from entering bankruptcy by nationalising them. This was a direct attempt to deter a global financial melt-down, which had caused a huge shock to financial markets and was a consequence of the impact of the Lehmann Brothers failure. Investors had previously assumed that famous established banks could not fail, they were too big for failure to be possible, and that governments would rescue them if they experienced difficulties (Elliott, 2011; Stanford, 2009). Lehmann Brothers, a Wall Street-based investment bank, became insolvent after 150 years of trading; it sought a merger with several banks and support from the central bank, the Bank of America, but none of these pleas was successful, and the bank was advised to file for bankruptcy by the US Government (Nicholas & Chen, 2010). Therefore, the fall of Lehman Brothers seriously impacted on global confidence, owing to its previously exalted reputation, and the closure underpinned the movement into deep recession, which governments failed to stem with their bank rescue packages. Initially it was assumed that the Bank's high-risk involvement in sub-prime and commercial property was the reason for Lehmann's severe liquidity problems, but Bris (2010) reported that a consequent enquiry attributed the failure to poor corporate governance. Creative Balance Sheet accounting, referred to as repo 105 transactions, had been used by the bank to hide loss and risk since 2001, and hence to inflate its asset value; repos 105 activity doubled from US $25bn to US $50bn from 2007 to 2008, and leverage/gearing stated as 12.1 in June 2008 was 13.9 in reality, a difference of 1.8, where 0.1 difference was considered a cause for concern. The auditors Ernst and Young were implicated as they were a party to the published inaccuracies. In contrast, Lehmann's competitors had not employed the repos 105 technique (Farrell, 2010).

The social effects of the crisis, driven by media reports, were manifested in the lack of consumer trust in banks, particularly as they were rescued by national governments, a factor which Vaskova and Vaskova (2010) suggest had made the banks more willing to take risks. Since the government rescue, bank charges had risen and large bonuses remained, so that taxpayers have become cynical about the management of banks, and pay more attention to the extent to which the money injected has created a new culture, particularly as banks were perceived as less stable than had previously been the case.

The extent and growth of national debt by up to 86% was a major characteristic of the 2007 crisis, a typical occurrence for government debt, and lasting for up to three years after a banking crisis, according to Reinhart and Rogoff (2009). At the beginning of 2009, US and UK were reported to have budget deficits of 12.5% and 11.6% GDP respectively, the UK deficit forecasts to rise to 13.2% within a year. Projections for the coming five years were US 84.9% and UK 91.8%; other countries had higher debt levels before the crisis, exemplified by Greece, Italy and Japan. Since economic growth was not likely to return quickly, these debt levels were forecast to be considerably problematic for governments, since public sector spending would simultaneously increase in supporting an ageing population in many countries (Verick & Islam, 2010). The changes that occurred in the financial performance of 148 global banks after the 2007–2008 financial crisis, 103 in developed countries and 45 in developing countries were investigated in a quantitative study by Fang et al. (2013). The findings indicated that banks in developed countries suffered a much greater decline in performance, and that larger commercial banks with high capitalisation were better able to recover from the negative effects of the crisis. A well-established US financial rating system referred to as CAMELS (Capital adequacy, loan Asset quality, Management performance Earning, Liquidity and Sensitivity) was used to assess and compare the banks. The findings included evidence that the capital adequacy of banks in developing countries was much higher, and there were greater restrictions on capital. Bank profitability was negatively affected by the crisis in developed and developing markets, and the risks related to managerial capability and growth increased as a consequence. However developed country banks also had increased issues with liquidity, and hence capital adequacy and asset quality, owing to the nature of the loan portfolio. The lower overall negative impact on banks in developing countries was found to relate to their higher capitalisation and the lack of involvement in the sub-prime market, in other words their lower maturity stage. The financial effects of the crisis were still having an effect in 2019, for example in Italy the government rescued Banca Monte Paschi di Siena and liquidated Banca Populare di Vicenza and Veneto Banca, and four banks that had been previously put into resolution in 2015 were sold in 2018 (Panetta, 2018). In April 2019 the Italian Depositor Protector Fund initiated a €900 million rescue procedure for the Carige bank based in Genova; part of the solution was to convert €313 million bonds into shares. The bank's failure was attributed to a long period of poor management and the quantity of bad loans that had origins in the post financial crisis recession in Italy (Piovacarri, 2019). The ECB had rejected to previous bailout plans presented by Carige and demanded a solution to the loans issue by 25 July, which appears to have generated the rescue plan (Piovacarri, 2019). This would not have been possible before the 2008 financial crisis, since the lack of any procedure for insolvent banks to exit the market had not existed. It was not until January 2015 that the EU had instigated an exit procedure to prevent taxpayers from being responsible for the bail-out of troubled banks. Therefore, the Banking Recovery and Resolution Directive (BRRD) was designed to allow the banks to exit the sector without government funding and comprised four actions: bail-in that means losses were taken up by shareholders and creditors; permission to sell part or all of the bank to a private entity; bridging, which involved moving good assets and essential operations of the bank to another bank and then attempting to sell them; asset separation, involving identifying the negative assets and administering them in a rational manner if immediate liquidation is not considered a better action (Waiglein, 2017). EU members outside the Eurozone, for instance Royal Bank of Scotland (RBS), were rescued by the government at the outset of the crisis and remained partly government owned in 2019. In the initial bailout, £24 billion of the original £45 billion bailout funded by the taxpayer represented 70% public ownership and several additional poor governance practices emerged over the period (Warner, 2018), for instance LIBOR interest rate manipulation in collaboration with other banks operating globally (McBride, 2016). The UK government has begun to sell its shares to the public but was criticised in October 2018 for the effective loss to the British taxpayer, owing to the fall in share price compared with the time of acquisition. The UK government still retained 62.4% ownership of RBS and is forecast to have sold it to private investors by 2024 (Rumney, 2018), 16 years after the original rescue in 2008. An academic study on EU banks by Macchiarelli et al. (2019) found that although the overall level of non-performing loans had declined sharply by 2019, there was still substantial EU concern about those held by banks in Italy, Spain, Portugal for instance. This uneven resolution of the bad loan issue throughout the Eurozone countries has so far prevented the implementation of a European Common Deposit Scheme and ultimately delayed the full European Banking Union to which the EU is committed and considered a solution to prevent further non-performing loans, from becoming a reality.

A report by Desjardins (2019) showed that global debt had risen to more than $US 63 trillion by 2017, which represents the latest figure available from the IMF, and that government debt was now regarded as a normal situation, with the levels gradually rising. Amongst EU countries, Italy and France occupied fourth and fifth ranking at 3.9% and 3.8% of total global debt and Greece, Italy and Portugal held second, third and fifth positions in the level of debt to GDP at 181.6%, 132.6% and 130.3%. In contrast Eurostat (2018) data showed that Portugal, Austria and Spain had reduced their debt to GDP ratio by 15%. Overall debt in EU countries decreased from 83.3% in December 2016 to 81.6% in December 2017 but it emphasised the fact that 15 countries continued to have debt levels that exceeded the membership level of 60% GDP, Greece and Italy being highest.

Economic Effects

In the initial period after Lehman Brothers collapsed and the crisis emerged, the decline in economic activity was described by McKibbin and Stoeckel (2009) as the worst in modern history, and a very serious recession was in progress; the impact was predicted to be greater than the 1930s' recession. In 2009 there were huge rises in unemployment, and signs that governments might initiate protectionism to protect domestic economies (McKibbin & Stoeckel, 2009; Stanford, 2009). The study conducted by McKibbin and Stoeckel (2009) appraised the impact of three shocks on the global economy, which derived from the financial crisis: the effects of the bubble bursting, the business response and household response. The findings suggested that, had the economic and fiscal policies of many global nations not been similar, referred to as contagion, the crisis would have been less severe. However, the effect of the bubble bursting was that investors, including nations, reappraised risk as a consequence of the crisis and there seemed to be nowhere safe to invest, so that investment levels fell sharply. Developing countries, such as India, were affected by this trend, since Foreign Direct Investment was much lower, with the result that employment prospects in such countries were worsened (Bramble, 2009). Interest rates for borrowing capital for projects were raised significantly by the uncertain financial conditions, causing low demand for funds by business, and poor motivation for households to save rather than spend, exacerbating the situation and leading to negative or flat economic growth, especially if businesses and householders expected these effects to be permanent. The OECD (2009) report reinforced these economic effects, which were stated to have been experienced by the majority of industrialised and non-industrialised countries, and across whole sectors. Hence firms were subjected to higher credit scoring for loans, as well as higher interest rates than pre-2007, and demand fell dramatically in some sectors, for example car manufacturing and construction. In the US, for example, car sales fell by 38% from 2008 to 2009 and the construction industry almost collapsed, with the industries in the supply chains of these key sectors also being badly affected (Barker, 2011). The impact of employment across all sectors in the US was far more serious than the previous two recessions, as indicated by Fig. 4.5; between December 2007 and December 2009, manufacturing jobs fell by 2 million or 17% of total workforce, the lowest recorded level since 1941 (OECD, 2009a: Stanford, 2009). In addition, those remaining employed were subject to lower wage rates than prior to recession, collective agreements on working conditions were not adhered to and were benefits reduced (Bramble, 2009).

Owing to these economic effects and banks refusing to lend to companies for fear they would go bankrupt (Bramble, 2009), national governments were lobbied to support industries by means of subsidies and the introduction of trade protection policies (OECD, 2009), as stated by

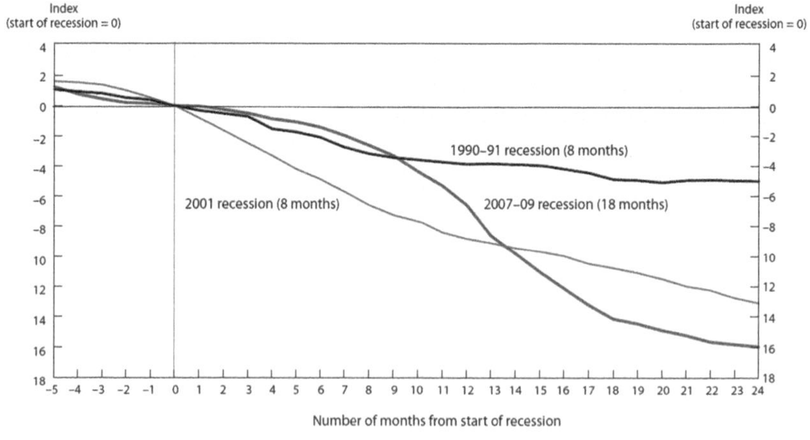

Fig. 4.5 Effect of 2008 recession on employment compared to previous two recessions. (Source: US Bureau of Labour Statistics; Barker (2011, p. 29))

McKibbin and Stoeckel (2009). The excess capacity within many industrial sectors in 2009 suggested many would not survive in the longer term without support, a factor also highlighted by Barker (2011). Hence agencies designed to enforce competition laws were urged by governments, in an attempt to reduce the effect of competition policies and support recovery, whilst concurrently making sure that competition was sufficiently stimulated to encourage innovation and productivity, and to produce sufficient choice for consumers. The relaxations of competition policies that included control of merger-acquisitions to prevent monopolies had been employed in other recessions to protect the domestic market (OECD, 2009). The large drop in national imports, in the year ending at second quarter of 2009, ranged from 15% to 45% across countries; Fig. 4.6 demonstrates the change in trade driven by the recession and suggests that changes in trade laws were responsible (Bramble, 2009).

The lack of direct governmental intervention in industrial sectors other than the financial sector highlighted its importance to national economies,

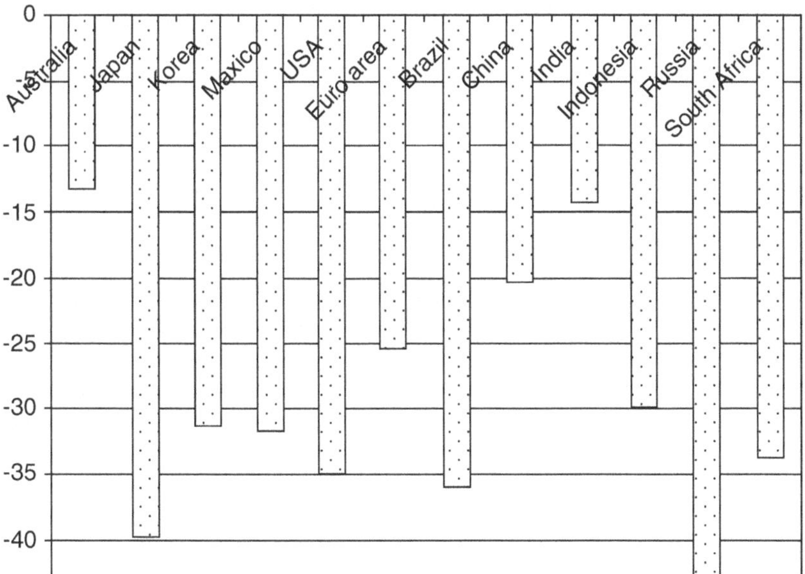

Fig. 4.6 Drop in imports 2008–2009. (Source: OECD Date in Bramble (2009, p.40))

as noted by the huge sums provided by governments to prevent bank failure; the financial sector was also perceived differently by governments in terms of the competition model. Economic growth in the Eurozone has been stagnant and below the 2005 level (World Bank, 2018) with some countries continuing to experience low growth or negative growth: Germany had GDP growth of 3% in 2008 and 8.2% in 2013, whilst UK growth was -4.6% in 2008 rising to 0.5% by 2013, and Italy -6.1% rising to -3.1% by 2013 (Balcerowicz, 2014). The EU economy has experienced less growth than US economy, both economies had approximately -1% growth in 2008–2009 but by 2012, the US economy had risen to 0% whilst EU remained at -1% (Balcerowicz, 2014). The research report by MGM (2018) demonstrates that US growth has always exceeded that of the EU, but the gap has widened since 1980, so that US GDP was 1.7 times that of EU in 2018. In the EU, five countries represent 70% of its GDP, Germany, UK, France, Italy and Spain in order of contribution; for instance, Germany had GDP $US 4029 billion and Spain $US 1437 billion. In terms of real GDP growth, the EU has lower overall growth than US, whereas US GDP growth in 2018 was 2.9%, Austria had the highest GDP growth of 2.8% whilst Italy was lowest at 1.5% (MGM, 2018).

These economic differences from 2008 to 2012 were considered to be partly a consequence of high investment in new machinery in US and employment, and labour productivity data for 2008 and 2012 show US rising from -1.9% to 6.9% whilst EU rose from -2.2% to 1.5% (Balcerowicz, 2014). Official unemployment in EU averaged 6.3% in July 2019 decreasing from 6.6% in December 2018, for instance Germany 3.1% and Italy 9.9%, whereas US rate was 3.7%. The average EU youth unemployment rate was 14.3% in 2019 declining from a high of 24%, but contrasts are highly visible, Germany 5.1%, Italy 30.5% and Spain 31.7% (TE, 2019a). The trends in GDP per capita, which is related to productivity, show that from 1980 to 2018, the figure had increased sevenfold in the US compared with a multiple of five in the EU (MGM, 2018). This data suggests that the EU has failed to manage the economy in a manner that has supported all members to recover, southern European countries continuing with recessionary environments and, in contrast to its purpose, the gap in GDP growth and productivity between the US and EU has considerably widened. The decision by the UK population to leave the EU by 2019, referred to as Brexit, is likely to impact negatively on EU economic growth as it is the second highest contributor after Germany (MGM, 2018; Macchiarelli et al., 2019), and German GDP is also currently falling, its growth forecast revised from 1.6% to 0.6% as industrial production fell by 1.9%, partly attributed to the continuing uncertainty regarding Brexit (Jolly, 2019).

Home ownership has declined significantly, for instance in the UK (Partington, 2018) and US (Garber, 2018), where ownership rates have been traditionally high; the fall attributed initially to repossessions but more recently because lending criteria have been severely tightened since 2008 and have not relaxed substantially. In the EU the average rate has declined from 73.1% in 2010 to 69.3% in January 2018 (TE, 2019b), the implication being that this is a reflection of economic stagnation, unemployment and tighter bank lending norms.

Financial Sector Competition

The pressures for governments to alter competition policy rules are noted in the previous section. However, an OECD (2009) report appraised a range of actions taken by governments attempting to apply initial remedies to stem the crisis, especially those relating to preventing the failure of banks, and the consequent effect these had on competition within the financial sector. Measures taken by governments included the following: acting as brokers for mergers between large banks, an example of which was Lloyds being asked to rescue Halifax Bank of Scotland (HBOS) by UK government (McConnell, 2014); quantitative easing to increase liquidity, as well as stimulus packages, for instance US US$ 787billion (bn), China $US 585bn and Japan $US 270 billion (OECD, 2009; Bramble, 2009); decreases in bank interest rates to zero, in comparison to the 1930s' recession in which the US rate never reached less than 3% (Bramble, 2009). A major indicator of the lack of competition after the crisis was the low proportion of consumers switching accounts in the previous year, an activity that generally stimulated better benefits for the retail customer as banks tried to attract the custom from their rivals (OECD, 2009). Whilst changing the nature of market competition (OECD, 2009), the interventions failed to revive economic growth to pre-2007 levels (Bramble, 2009). The OECD (2009) report highlighted the difficulty that governments would have as a result of their interventions in the sector, for instance how to withdraw from providing liquidity and guarantees and divesting the government share in banks currently in the public sector would be a challenge. OECD (2009) suggested that competition was likely to be altered substantially by the removal of guarantees and sale of bank shares to the private sector.

The 2007 crisis had resulted in future competition policy being difficult to define, owing to various other factors, which created substantial market and individual consumer uncertainty: volatility of exchange rates globally; fluctuation in commodity prices including oil, with prices dipping from their peak value after recession hit; unknown individual wealth levels; lack of reliable data for firms to forecast production and/or investment levels. The findings of these studies imply a situation of considerable governmental uncertainty regarding how to intervene in the markets to rectify the issues, especially as research had demonstrated that apparently attractive policies relaxing competition laws to end recession had not been successful, had lengthened the recession period, suppressed wealth creation derived from international trading and had led to high government spending to compete on subsidies (Fingleton, 2009). The competition situation and ownership of banks by governments have receded somewhat since 2015 but for instance, the Italian government rescued the world's oldest bank, Monte Paschi di Siena, in 2018, and in 2019 the UK still retains almost two-thirds ownership in RBS. Interest rates have remained near zero, for example Eurozone refinancing rate is currently 0.0%, and deposit rate -0.4% a downward trend from 0.3% in 2015, whilst the UK interest rate at 0.75% and the US at 2.5% demonstrate a change of rate from their lowest level of 0.25% (GR., 2018; Rumney, 2018; TE, 2019c, 2019d). In July 2019, the ECB announced that it was considering cutting interest rates owing to the slowdown in economic growth (BBC, 2019).

These concepts are important to this study, when examining the alternatives governments have in Chap. 5 and the effects of the choices made by the European Union (EU) in Chap. 8.

Crisis Severity

Overview

Crisis severity can be measured as the impact of GDP on private consumption (Krishnamurthy & Muir, 2015), and when considered in the context of growth rates for G7 nations from 2008 to 2009 (Fig. 4.7), the worst affected nations were not those associated most with the sources of the crisis, which were the UK and US (Bramble, 2009).

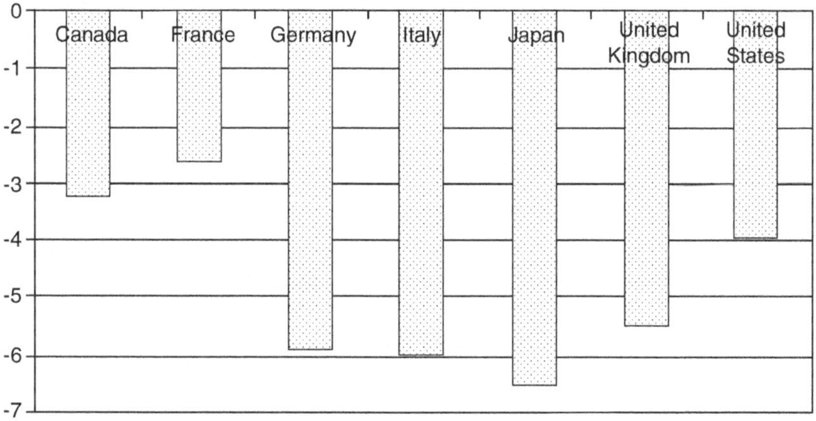

Fig. 4.7 Changes in GDP globally 2008–2009. (Source: OECD Data Bramble (2009 p. 39))

In the US, investment in business fell by the annual equivalent of 40% in quarter 1 of 2009 (Bramble, 2009), and whereas in 1929 the time between the stock market peak and lowest point prior to recovery was 35 months, in 2008 the low had been reached in 10 months after the first shocks, and the value had plunged by 50% (Bramble, 2009).

The Crisis in Europe

The crisis began in Europe as a financial crisis, and then developed into an economic downturn (Cukurcayir & Tezcan, 2013), as with the US and UK. Prior to the beginning of the crisis, sovereign debt securities of the various EU countries were subject to relatively little fluctuation and attracted similar interest rates for investors, in other words there was little spread. However, Fig. 4.8 shows the manner in which that changed from 2009 onwards, with those of Greece rising more sharply than any other country, contrasting with the German and French rates, which declined.

The reasons for the emerging spread were a consequence of unbalanced macroeconomic conditions according to Panico and Purificato (2013), as these trends emerged tensions increased between the EU member states. Even prior to 2007 there had been concern about a lack of policy coordination between the EU Member States, with national fiscal bodies taking

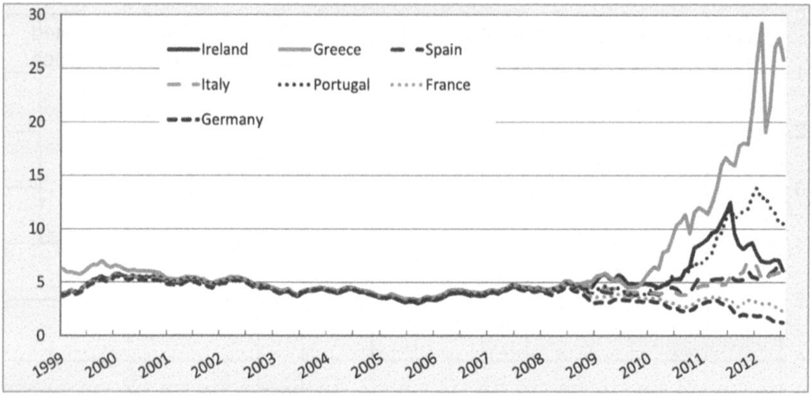

Fig. 4.8 Interest changes on sovereign debt securities. (Source: Oxford University Press: Panico and Purificato (2013, p. 589))

independent decisions on fiscal policy, whereas the European Monetary Union (EMU) had sovereignty in decisions on monetary policy (Panico & Purificato, 2013). In other words, national governments could follow their internally created fiscal policies, that is, change tax rates and dictate the level of government spending to create demand in their economies, even though there was an EU body, ECOFIN (European Council of Financial and Economic Ministers), which made fiscal policy decisions for the whole EU. In contrast, the EMU was responsible for monetary policies on behalf of all EU countries, the interest rates and money supply (Pilbeam, 2005; Panico & Purificato, 2013; Slay, 2011). The EU was therefore characterised by strong financial integration and the single currency, and Europe was promoted politically as a unified, strong trading zone (Slay, 2011). In general, membership of EU required countries to commit to joining the Euro and the only non-members of the single currency were UK and Denmark. On joining the EU, all Eurozone countries are committed to meeting convergence criteria for financial stability, referred to as the Stability and Growth Pact; these criteria are fiscal deficits of no more that 3% GDP and public debt of no more than 60% GDP (Slay, 2011). However, there are additional criteria for acceding to the monetary union including price stability demonstrated by consumer-based inflation rates within 1.5 points and long-term interest rates within 2 percentage points of the three best performing member nations, proving that the exchange of rate of the potential member's sovereign currency has been stable for the previous two years (EC, 2015). The UK and Denmark opted not to join the Euro at the time it was introduced, using reasons of economic sovereignty to opt out, according to EC (2021); many other countries which joined the EU after 2004 are still not members since they do not meet the full criteria, for example Croatia, Poland Czech Republic (EC, 2021).

One major motivation for joining the EU and hence the Euro was to provide members with macroeconomic stability, especially new smaller member countries such as Montenegro (Slay, 2011). Any member wishing to withdraw from the Euro has severe legal issues, since there is no provision for any withdrawal from the European Union, of which the single currency is a part. Therefore, a member country cannot opt out of the Euro and has no mechanism for leaving the trading bloc (Slay, 2011).

The study by Rivera (2012) examined the way in which the 2007 crisis had specifically affected different EU regions, the impact experienced by appraisal of the trends in productivity and per capita income. At initiation and since then, the EU has comprised nations/regions with varying economic development but has attempted to compete globally as a block, whilst integrating territories, economies and social attributes. In the seven years up to 2007, the regional differences in the two factors, productivity and per capita income, had reduced, EU rationalisation goals were being met, but from 2007 onwards the gap reopened. The GDP per capita figures demonstrate huge disparities ranging from a 14 factor gap between Inner London and north-east Romania showing a GDP per capita of 335.0 compared with 24.7, and 72 of the 275 regions having less than 75% purchasing parity with EU average. In addition, a similar trend was observed in the coefficient of variation of employment rates in the 27 Member States, with greater dispersion after the 2007 period than before it, variation moved from 11.3 to 11.9 compared with 11.9 to 11.1 respectively. The decline in employment rates from 2007 to 2011 was greatest for Greece, Finland and Hungary (Rivera, 2012). The recent trends confirm that these anomalies remain, although official figures suggest that unemployment, for example, has declined somewhat it remains very high in some countries, especially youth unemployment. The variation in GDP has not been resolved, in 2018, Ireland had the highest GDP of $US 75,192, 6th highest globally, compared with Romania generating GDP of $US 12,189, in 64th position, according to IMF data (ST, 2019).

Public finance sector debt or budget deficit and public debt levels provide an accurate assessment of the involvement of the state in the economy and in the EMU. Member States are not able to shape their own monetary policy, merely their fiscal policy, and to a degree that is limited by EU rules, representing a significant challenge to those whose traditional preference is fiscal. The graph (Fig. 4.9) illustrates that in 2007, 10 out of the 12 countries in the Euro met the criteria for budget deficits and 6 out of the 10 had budget surpluses.

The two Member States that did not meet the EU criteria were Greece and Portugal, but when the economic crisis was at its peak in Europe, all countries registered a deficit of more than 3% GDP, except for Finland and Luxembourg, Ireland having the worst deficit. However, debt consolidation and an upturn in the economy in most Eurozone countries in 2010-2011 improved their deficit position, except for that of Greece, which was on the trajectory for bankruptcy. There had been an

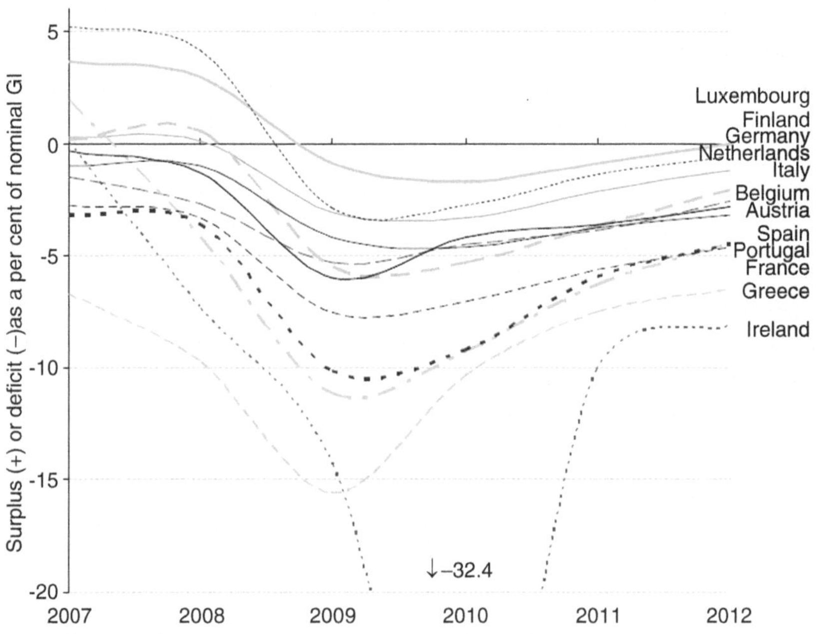

Fig. 4.9 Public sector debt EU countries 2007–2012. (Source: Kowalski (2012, p. 13))

over-reaction to the transitional financial issues initiated by the global financial crisis, according to Kowalski (2012), and the weaker EMU members were most affected; the EMU's decision-making process partly stimulated and spread the situation, which affected the financial intermediation sector most adversely (Fig. 4.9; Kowalski, 2012). The major example was Ireland, which had developed its banking sector to be a core part of its economy, adopting an international presence, and consequently most affected by the crisis and EMU actions (Kowalski, 2012).

The budget deficits of just 5 of the 12 EMU members were within the required limit of lower than 60% GDP in 2007, including Ireland and Spain at 25% and 36.1%, respectively, whereas Italy had 103.6% and Greece 105.4% GDP but by 2010, the three with the lowest increases in debt were Italy, Belgium and Austria, others with soaring debt levels especially Spain and Ireland, when comparison was made with 2007 levels (Fig. 4.10).

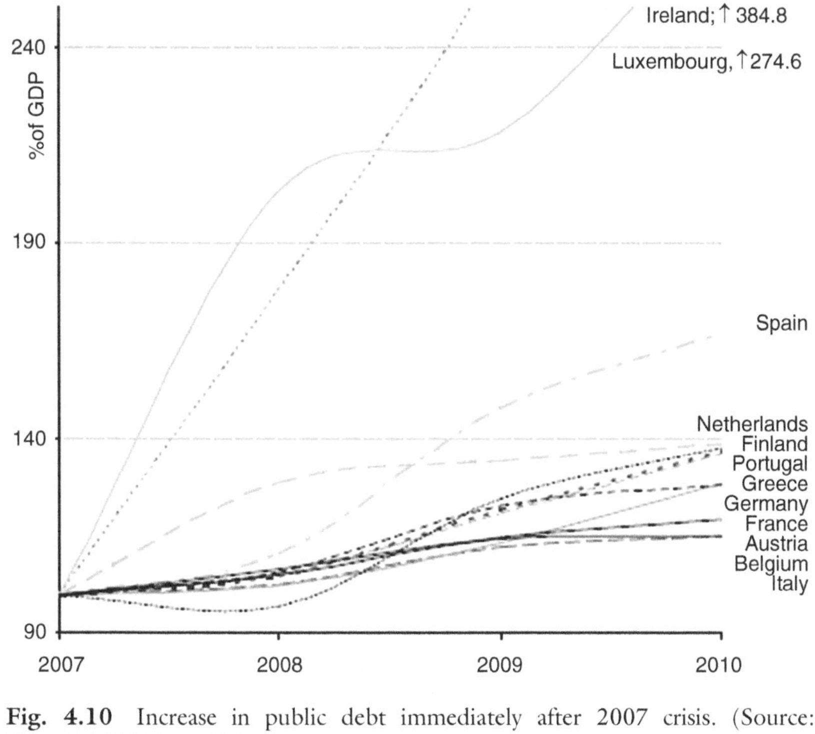

Fig. 4.10 Increase in public debt immediately after 2007 crisis. (Source: Kowalski (2012, p. 15))

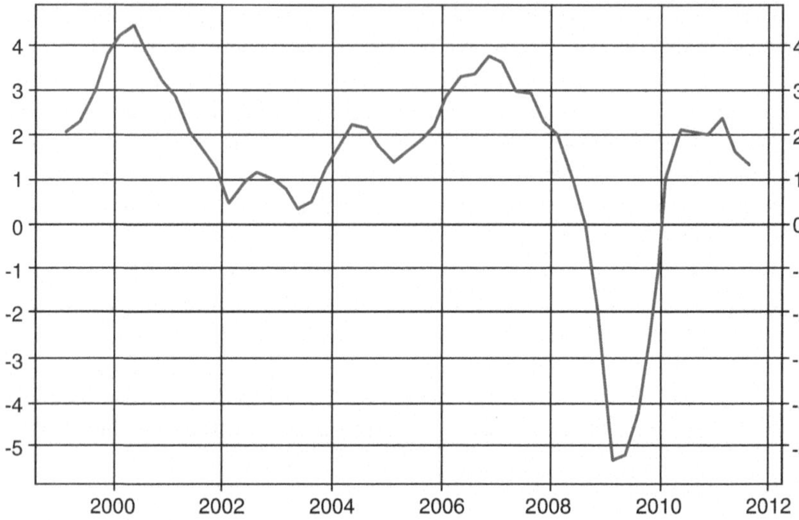

Fig. 4.11 Change in GDP Europe 2000–2012. (Source: Ashgate Publishing Talani (2014a, p165))

If the severity of the crisis in Europe is based on the change in GDP, when the fall of 9% from 3.8% to –5.2% in 2009 is compared with global fall of 6%, which was stated as the largest in history, the very serious nature of its overall impact on the EU is apparent, and Fig. 4.11 shows that the recovery to previously levels has not been accomplished, but that recovery is very fragile (Talani, 2014a).

By the end of 2010, when other economies were recovering, the IMF reported that EU had the weakest GDP growth level globally at 1.7%; the US grew by 3%, Africa 5%, Asia, excluding Japan, 9.5% (Slay, 2011). The IMF (2018) data released in 2018 demonstrated that Europe still had one of the lowest GDP growth rates globally in 2017, with average of 2.4%, whilst Asia Pacific grew at 5.5%, Nepal 5%, Africa 3.8%; within Europe GDP growth ranged from 1.5% to more than 5% with former communist countries experiencing higher growth than mature ones. The World Bank (World Bank, 2019) states that the GDP growth in the Euro area averaged 2.0% in 2018 but that Poland experienced 5.1% growth, Hungary 4.9%, Estonia 3.9% and Czech Republic 2.9%, whilst the economies of Italy, the UK and Greece grew by 0.9%, 1.4% and 1.9% respectively. The EU had been in a precarious position regarding unity for some time, with the UK currently attempting to negotiate its exit but having been offered a Withdrawal Agreement by the EU, which failed to be passed three times by the British Parliament and resulted in the resignation of the Prime Minister Theresa May. The new prime minister is a founding member of the Leave The EU Movement and has assembled a Cabinet of Brexiteers focused on exiting by the delayed deadline of 31 October 2019, and threatening to leave without a deal, a situation that is not beneficial to the EU considering the value of British trade to its economy (Aljazeera, 2019).

Italy has had a populist government for more than a year and is a huge threat to the EU as its third biggest economy; Italy's leaders are in constant conflict with EU regarding continuous austerity budgets that have driven the nation into economic decline. Although a compromise was reached in recent budget negotiations, relationships remain tense (Tondo & Giuffrida, 2018). Several other members have been in conflict with EU immigration policy; populist governments in Austria and former communist states, for instance Hungary, are continuing to refuse to accept EU policies (Behr, 2018).

Securitisation Trends in EU

The asset-backed securities market in Europe had been at its peak prior to the 2008 crisis, but new securities to a value of \$1.2 trillion were sold in EU in 2008; Germany, Italy, Spain, Netherlands and UK were the main issuers, Fig. 4.15. However, by 2013 the level had declined to \$239 billion of ABS products (Fig. 4.12).

The lending criteria, the rating of borrowers and default laws vary in each of the EU countries and in their national banks, therefore, the banking sector loan pool is specific to individual nations. A report by Blommestein et al. (2011) stated that securitised financial instruments had much less effect on the financial crisis, which emerged in Europe in 2007, owing to the generally tighter underwriting criteria existing in Europe. However, investors lost money on these securities because market contagion occurred, the price fell because their reputation elsewhere was associated with toxic investments; most of the price decline was a factor of liquidity risk, inability to sell quickly enough, rather than credit rating risk. Only 0.95% of European securitised instruments defaulted from 2007 to 2010, compared with 7.7% in the US. However, the securitised investment market was severely affected (Blommestein et al., 2011), and was

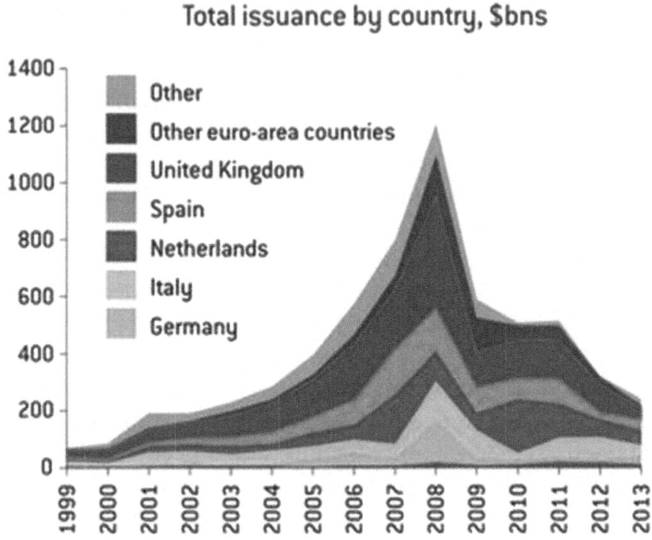

Fig. 4.12 Securitisation levels in EU countries. (Source: SIMFA Altomonte and Busselli (2014. p.4))

further negatively impacted by the freeze in European inter-bank lending. Once the financial crisis began in 2007–2008, the European Central Bank (ECB) changed its rating of these securities, and also the requirements for accepting Asset-Backed Securities (ABS) as repo collateral. Repo collateral refers to the security that the bank has for a loan it provides to a client, with the promise that client will repurchase the security at a later date for a higher price, and the bank therefore earns a fee (Fleming & Garbade, 2003).

The ABS market had been heavily dependent on the financial services sector, particularly insurance funds, so that the tighter regulation that emerged hindered the sale of securities. Ireland, although reliant on financial intermediation to drive its GDP growth, had relatively little exposure to ABS (Altomonte and Bussoli 2014), so that the negative reaction to these securities was not a major cause of the high impact of the financial crisis in Ireland mentioned by Rivera (2012). The EU ABS markets most badly affected were: the UK securities marked declined by 90%, Germany experience a fall of 80%, whilst the markets in Italy, Spain and the

Netherlands fell by 73%. Overall, the volume of ABS issued in the EU fell from $US 766 billion to $US 175 billion. After the crisis only 10% of new ABS were placed on the market by financial institutions, in contrast to the 70% previously available on the market (Altomonte and Bussoli 2014).

In 2017, the ECB agreed to reignite the ABS market simultaneously ensuring that risk was low; all types of asset-backed debt are considered for the development of the ABS, and strict rules have been devised regarding the source of the assets, the capital charges permitted, supervising their trading and mitigating risk. The high levels of caution regarding the reintroduction were the result of mortgage-backed securities being the trigger for the 2008 crisis, according to Buck (2017) so that the new version is described as being Simple, Transparent And Standardised (STS). The original lender must hold at least a 5% interest in the ABS and a database must be kept and available to the European Securities and Markets Authority (ESMA). Whilst the European Parliament accepted this proposal in October 2017, it demanded new laws on securitisation since the Member State in which the instrument is issued will be responsible for the legislation. This insistence on regulation was a consequence of Brexit, because a UK STS will not have the same inferences to an investor as an EU STS, and vice versa.

The new ABS has been applauded by the UK and is forecast to raise up to €150 billion, but the new legislation is likely to take a long time period as new UK law relating to other more important areas such as NHS will take priority. Some financial and economic experts perceive the new ABS as being merely relaxing of regulation and of no benefit to citizens (Glover 2017). The bond is being treated with caution as the debt concerned is a predefined pool of euro government sovereign bonds, but the security will be packaged and sold by the private sector and the risk is not shared by the Eurozone Member States (EC 2018). In fact, this strategy allows European banks and investors to diversify their holdings of sovereign bonds, in order to prevent an accumulation of such securities by banks as occurred prior to 2018. The bonds will comprise those from all 19 Eurozone countries but the risk will not be evenly spread across them, a factor which has raised criticism that investors will not be attracted towards them because they are no different from the bonds they are derived from. Two bonds with different risk levels seem to be planned; low and higher risk (Guarascio 2018). The trends in ABS purchase in Europe have moved from predominantly private debt to public debt in the past five years, in 2017 the proportion was 55% to 45%; the Collateralised Loan Obligation (CLO) has been growing in popularity in both Europe and the US. In Europe the proportion of CLO investment was very low but had grown to €13.1billion by 2016, and the US trend was an increase from $US 72.42 billion in 2016 (SG 2017) to $US 89.7 billion by November 2107. However, Santini (2014) describes this ABS as comprising several high-risk commercial debts, which are combined, but very small parts of different risk levels are sold to investors, the risk varies according to investor's risk appetite. If the original debtor defaults on loan payments the riskier parts of CLO experience the higher losses, whilst low-risk portions provide a consistent return. CLOs are similar to CDOs which were one of the prime instruments causing the 2008 recession, but instead of mortgage debt, they are leveraged loans deriving from firms that have large debt and poor means to repay it.

The first of the new ABS are denominated as Simple Transparent and Standardised (STS) asset-backed securities, because of the new rules applying to their composition and risk; they were issued in the first quarter of 2019 and approval of more similar securities is expected. The first UK version was released in April 2109 and followed the newly created SONIA rate that replaced the discredited LIBOR mechanism. Investors in the EU continue to shun this type of security owing to its past reputation, which is why the regulators devised the STS version with the purpose of stimulating the securities market (Engelen and Glasmacher 2018). The US market has recovered much more strongly with sales amounting to $US 292 billion in the first quarter of 2019 (Jones 2019). Despite STS being inferred as a simple ABS it is extremely complex according to Engelen and Glasmacher (2018), who stress that the prior reputation of ABS seems to have been ignored in favour of the political need to revive the stagnating economy. This is an interesting suggestion, as the EU is also accused of failing to restart the economy by other means such as quantitative easing and austerity measures; STS is consequently the perceived solution.

Initial European Reaction

In the initial stages of the global financial crisis, little attention was drawn to public sector debt in EU countries, but in 2010 the total amount of sovereign debt across the Eurozone was stated as amounting to €7862 billion and during this period Greece announced that its debt was twice that previously stated (Santacana and Siles 2013). The total EU debt level declared to be US$1.4 trillion was even higher than debt levels in the US of US$ 1 trillion, and European banks had a higher proportion of bad loans than US banks (Lucarelli 2014). The emergence of the sovereign debt crisis in the EU in 2010 was described by Rivera (2012) as involving Greece, Ireland and then the remainder of the other so-called PIIGS group, consisting of Portugal, Italy and Spain. This situation initiated the establishment of a Financial Stability Package of €86 billion, with €35 billion allocated for Ireland, which reflected its critical position. However, the market increase on bond yields of all the PIIGS countries invoked a new rescue initiative, referred to as the European Stability Mechanism (ESM), in 2012 (Talani 2014a); this sovereign debt threat, exemplified by the rising security yields, was considered very dangerous for French and German Banks (Lucarelli 2014). By the end of 2010, the EU economy continued to be fragile, predominantly because of the sovereign debt issues in many countries combined with weak banking institutions in some Eurozone nations; the future of the Euro was therefore perceived to be at risk. Consequently, the ECB identified two distinct issues, an appraisal of the financial system for countries in the European Monetary Union (EMU) and another for those outside of it (ECB 2010a, b). The ECB had microeconomic and macroeconomic challenges, related to EU Member States inside and outside the EMU, including the perception that fiscal policies in some Member States were unsustainable (Talani 2014a). The concerns regarding countries outside the EMU incorporated those relating to non-financial companies with serious financial problems of high gearing and weak profitability, particularly in some sectors. The possibility of consumer credit defaults if unemployment remained high was a further concern. A major macroeconomic fear was the risk that the global financial imbalances experienced in the 2008 crisis would reappear (ECB 2010a).

In contrast, uneasiness about those countries in the Eurozone was predominantly focused on financial risk, particularly public sector debt levels in some countries, for instance Greece, and to a lesser extent Portugal. The degree of debt exposure in the banking sector, the volatility in financial markets and little sign of global economic recovery were also disquieting. Increasing unemployment was a challenge, Spain, Slovakia and Ireland had the highest levels, and credit was difficult to obtain. Many banks were reliant on the ECB's Euro financing mechanism for funds, a continuing problem, because banks had to compete for funds with public sector (ECB 2010a; Talani 2014a, 2014b). The public sector financial risks had caused investors to speculate, causing widening of interest rate spreads on sovereign bond debt (Talani 2014a), also described by Panico and Purificato

(2013) (Fig. 4.8). Further consequences of this debt were low economic growth, poor credit availability and fiscal imbalance (Talani 2014a). In addition, there were concerns about further increases in bond spread, which occurred with varying seriousness in 2011 (Fig. 4.10) from Greece with a 1600 point spread from German bonds, to France with just 90 points. These imbalances required rapid remedial action, most critically in countries with growing debt, and by banks that had been bailed out. The banks in difficulty needed to restructure and to reduce their balance sheet values, according to ECB (2010a). In contrast, some large banking groups operating from within the Eurozone were able to regain profitability at the end of 2010, mainly as a consequence of interest earned, but trading risk inferred that this position was potentially unsustainable (ECB 2010a; Talani 2014a). Commercial property prices were severely affected by the crisis in Europe because they were used as loan collateral and negotiating new loans when the current ones reached maturity was considered to be a severe challenge. By 2010 property prices had begun to recover but had not reached the 2006-2007 level, meaning that property investors were vulnerable as were the banks, which had provided the original loans (ECB 2010a).

In late 2010 the European Central Bank commented that, although EU governments had acted to enhance confidence in the EU financial sector in an effort to reduce the level of systemic risk, the continuing presence of high public sector financial debt levels and other financial sector weaknesses were a major source for concern. Governments were therefore urged to create and implement strategies to increase their national competitiveness and by implication that of whole EU area, and banks were asked to improve their capital structures to meet those suggested by Basel III so that they had higher capacity to survive further turbulence in the banking sector (ECB 2010a).

The EU Crisis Timeline

A timeline for the emergence of sovereign debt in the countries is provided by Santacana and Siles (2013), highlighting the major events and outlining interventions, whilst summarising points made in earlier sections. The researchers suggested that the origins of the crisis could be traced back to the signing of the Maastricht Treaty in 1992 when the EC transformed to the EU, and that the fiscal requirements were the key factor that determined the sovereign debt crisis. As early as 2004, Greece revealed that, in order to gain entry to the Eurozone, it had not been transparent about its fiscal convergence criteria and had adjusted them as necessary to gain entry. By 2009 Greece was the first country to announce an unacceptable budget deficit of 12.7% GDP, substantially outside EU criteria, resulting in its global credit rating by Standard and Poor falling from A to BB+. At this point Greece implemented three austerity packages. However, Portugal, Spain and Ireland also had their credit ratings reduced by 2, 1 and 1 points respectively, with Greece's rating being lowered again to Ba1, equivalent to junk status. Loans were provided to all Eurozone nations affected subject to the Member State implementing austerity packages; by the end of 2010 a permanent bail-out process was installed (Santacana and Siles 2013), details of which will be presented and discussed in the next section, which concentrates on research findings regarding the EU reaction to the crisis. In 2011, fiscal rules were tightened across all EU countries and debt yields on bonds rose considerably, owing to investor nervousness regarding the stability of the Eurozone.

In 2012 Greece was subject to bail out, and the EU introduced a new funding package to support countries in difficulty, as well as the central EU body, ECOFIN, tightening the fiscal flexibility of the individual countries, and hence gaining more control over their budgets. Eurozone GDP levels overall reduced to 0.1%, but with some countries experiencing much lower economic growth than others. EU finance ministers agreed to a banking union, with ECB as the banking regulator, banks were to have higher capital ratios, and some banks were forced to close. In 2015 following the election of a left-wing government headed by Tsipras, the latest EU bailout terms were subject to a referendum, and to prevent investors including the general public from causing a bank crisis and capital flight, Tsipras limited cash withdrawals to €60 per day. After the ECB refused to support Greek banks, the Tsipras government conceded to a third bailout of €86 billion in 2018 offered by EU to avert Greece's exit from the Euro, but with further austerity measures demanded; agreement to the new support for Greece took some weeks to implement, as various Eurozone members, particularly Germany, became involved in defining the bailout terms. In early 2017, the IMF refused to support the measure, stating that Greek debt was unsustainable, with the consequence that the ECB made the terms of the bailout less harsh; the country's poverty and weakening economy, however, remaining subject to further tax and pension reforms (CFR 2017). In April 2018, Weltman (2018) warned of the impending prospect of the Italian election in June being won by the 5 Star Alliance and a potential threat to an exit from the Euro by a new Italian government. The Italian economy remained weak and its forecast growth was one-third to one-half the European average, whilst its sovereign debt was the second highest in the Eurozone and bank stability 5.3/10 compared with 7.3 in the Netherlands. The situation was described as the volcano waiting to erupt. In June 2018, the 5 Star Alliance won the election with 32% vote and eventually formed a government with the Lega, a right-wing party led by Matteo Salvini. Their policy regarding Europe is to focus on the needs of the Italian people rather than the dictates directed from the ECB and EU; raise spending, cut taxes and reverse EU-driven reforms approved by previous unelected governments (Bastasin 2018). The situation is totally different from Greece, it is not a question of financial weakness as private wealth is very high compared with the rest of the world, 70% Italian sovereign bonds are held by Italians, as well as other sovereign bonds, and Italy does not require net capital imports. If interest was not paid on the current government debt, there would be a stable primary surplus. These facts mean that the Italian populist government has an alternative to following EU directives (Bastasin 2018); a parallel currency is stated to be in place should Italy decide to exit the Euro rather than conform to austerity measures that EU continues to apply. The mini-bot would be Italy's Treasury bill, a cash equivalent in electronic trading, a government debt instrument with zero interest and no maturity date (Mauldin 2018). The words of the former BIS chairman William White (Mauldin 2018) stated that:

> the trigger for a crisis could be anything if the system as a whole is unstable. Moreover, the size of the trigger event need not bear any relation to the systemic outcome. The lesson is that policymakers should be focused less on identifying potential triggers than on identifying signs of potential instability. (White 2018, p. 368)

At this time Italy is considered a case that could be the instigator (Mauldin 2018) since it continues to threaten reversal to its own currency if the EU continues to impose austerity measures that have impacted negatively on its economy for several years. The Italian economic growth is the lowest in EU, it declined by 0.1% in quarter 4 of 2018 and again in the first quarter of 2019. As a country's debt increases the EU imposes stricter austerity rules that restrict government spending to boost the economy, a vicious circle emerges. In contrast, whilst Greece has a larger debt to GDP ratio than Italy, the Greek economy has begun to grow but that is a response to the number of EU bail-outs it has received and the much more favourable terms on which the debt is to be repaid than those imposed on Italy. Italy is the EU's third biggest economy much higher than that of Greece, but its debt has now reached €2 trillion and as it rises, the threat of a financial crisis is a bigger danger to the EU than Brexit (Edwards 2019). The threat to the Euro from the parallel currency represented by the mini-bot has re-emerged in June 2019 as the government leaders are once more in open conflict with the EU regarding the measures imposed on it to reduce its debt levels (Horowitz 2019).

The Crisis in Different European Countries

The emergence and subsequent development of the global financial crisis in Europe highlighted substantial differences between its regions, revealing huge gaps between north and south, with regard to sovereign debt, economic growth and unemployment levels (Santacana and Siles 2013). It is important to analyse these differences further, rather than merely consider the statistics on debt and GDP, and general comments previously made about the EU as a whole. These differences are likely to impact on understanding of EU actions towards different countries and how the single methodology employed affected each of them. Several regional groupings will be considered, northern Europe, PIIGS and former eastern European nations. The published literature does not reveal an equal focus on each of these groupings, the majority relate to the troubled PIIGS countries.

Northern Europe

One of the objectives of EU membership was to improve the member country competitiveness, which was the trend over the ten years from 1999 onwards; Fig. 4.13 reveals huge variations. The countries in the northern region show growth with Finland and Sweden experiencing high growth, and Germany having a flat economy.

The initial reaction to the crisis in Northern Europe, particularly in France, Germany and the Netherlands, was one of self-righteousness regarding their less liberal financial systems compared with the US and UK, in which the crisis appeared to have been initiated, and hence the expectation was that continental Europe would be less affected. However,

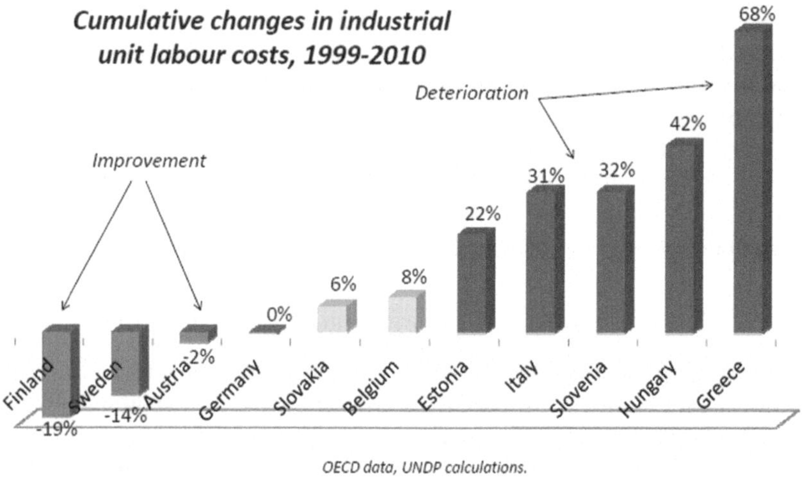

Fig. 4.13 Competitiveness across the EU from 1999 to 2010. (Source: Slay (2011, p. 17 OECD data))

when these countries' governments realised contagion existed, their strategies were developed quickly and without careful consideration of the consequences of their actions, according to Dieter (2009). Germany, for instance, had been a high capital exporter at the time of the crisis, and had substantial exposure to sub-prime lending in the US, because it had exported machines and cars and received Lehman derivatives as payment for the goods (Dieter 2009). At the end of 2008, as the crisis began to affect Europe more severely, national solutions were generally instigated for banks in crisis, rather than an integrated EU solution and, according to Dieter (2009), ING, the Dutch bank, was bailed out by its government, IKN by the German government and RBS by the UK government. However, those banks that with cross-border operations had to be altered to national banks to be eligible for a rescue package, such as Belgian-Dutch Finance, for instance. There was little regard for the principle of market failure, which is based on capacity to create sufficient profitable demand to survive, as applied to other industry sectors, so that even small banks, such as IKB, were rescued. In the case of IKB, €10 billion of state funding was consumed; however, this bank was re-privatised, being bought by an American equity company for an uncertain sum (Dieter 2009); considerably less than the bailout, €2 billion was the purchase price reported by Taylor (2012). Unlike the US reaction to Lehman, Germany set the example for the rest of the EU by stating that all banks would be rescued, even though there had not been a run on the banks prior to this announcement. This statement created panic amongst the population leading to withdrawals being made from Eastern European banks whose governments could not bail them out (Dieter 2009).

The sovereign debt levels represented by the budget deficit or surplus against GDP, from 2005 to 2012, are shown in Table 4.1, and diagrammatically in Fig. 4.14

Table 4.1 Budget surplus (deficit) as percentage of GDP

Year/nation	*2005*	*2006*	*2007*	*2008*	*2009*	*2010*	*2011*	*2012*
Denmark	5.2	5.4	4.9	3.6	-2	-2.5	-2	-3.8
Finland	3.3	4.2	5.3	4.6	-1.9	-2.5	-0.5	-1
France	-2.7	-2.1	-2.3	-2.8	-7	-6.8	-5.1	-4.8
Germany	-2.3	-1.2	-0.3	-0.4	-2.1	-3.1	-0.4	0.1
Netherlands	-0.1	0.5	0.3	0.9	-4.6	-3.9	-3.5	-3.3
Norway	15.1	18.4	17.8	20	11.6	17.2	14.2	14.6
Sweden	1.4	2	3.2	2.2	-0.7	-0.2	0.3	-0.3
UK	-2.9	-2.6	-2.6	-4.5	-10.4	-9.5	-7.2	-5.5

Source: World Bank (2015a)

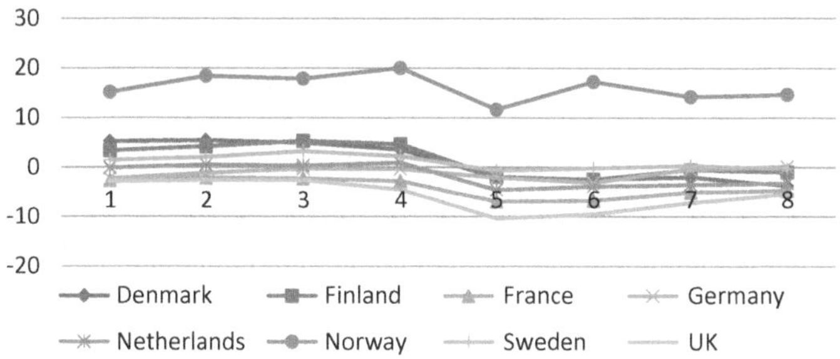

Fig. 4.14 Budget surplus (deficit) as a percentage of GDP. (Source: World Bank (2015a))

Trends in budget deficits in Northern European countries were much less pronounced than elsewhere in Europe, with Norway having a large budget surplus compared to its GDP and, prior to the crisis Finland, Denmark and the Netherlands also had a positive relationship between the two factors. The UK and France both had a budget deficit before 2007 but this was still within the EU 3% limit. However, this changed by 2008 for UK and 2009 for France, both of which remained outside of that limit. The Netherlands also had deficits beyond the limit, whilst both Finland and Sweden were within it, and Sweden was less affected than Finland (World Bank 2015a). In 2003, France already had a budget deficit above the EU imposed 3% limit at 3.9%, but by 2007 had returned within the limit and the deficit stood at -2.5% GDP. However, it then increased steadily to -9% in 2009, falling back to -4% in 2014 (Eurostat 2015).

The trends in GDP in some northern European countries for the years from 2005 to 2010 are shown in Fig. 4.15 (Kowalski 2012).

The trends to 2010 demonstrate Germany's recovering GDP growth but not quite to 2007 levels, whilst the other Northern European economies shown in Fig. 4.15 are all in growth mode; however, the GDP figures remained negative. In comparison with the rest of the world, the GDP of most Northern European countries fell sharply in 2009 to a lower level than the world average decline, and by 2013, no country had reached the world average growth of 2.3%; the UK was closest with 1.7%, Sweden experienced 1.5%, Norway 0.6%, France 0.3%, Germany 0.1% and the Netherlands -0.7% (World Bank 2015b). The effect of the crisis on Sweden and Finland was severe, since their economies relied heavily on exports, which were less in demand once the crisis spread; Finland is a member of the Eurozone whereas Sweden retains its own currency. The crisis caused a drop in the Swedish Krona exchange rate, which then benefitted its export trade and explains its better growth pattern (Gylfason et al. 2010). The only Northern European country to regain export levels as a percentage of GDP by 2010, which it had before 2008, was the Netherlands; in contrast, Finland was exporting approximately 85%, France 92% and Germany 99%, as shown in Fig. 4.15 (Kowalski 2012). Most of these countries had experienced a current account deficit since 2005, whereas Germany had a current account surplus, varying from 4.5% of GDP in 2005 to 6.9% in 2013, and never dipping below 5.8% between those dates. Constant surpluses across this period were also experienced by the Netherlands, Sweden and Norway with higher percentages of GDP than Germany (World Bank 2015c). The current account balance reflects the level of net exports and of

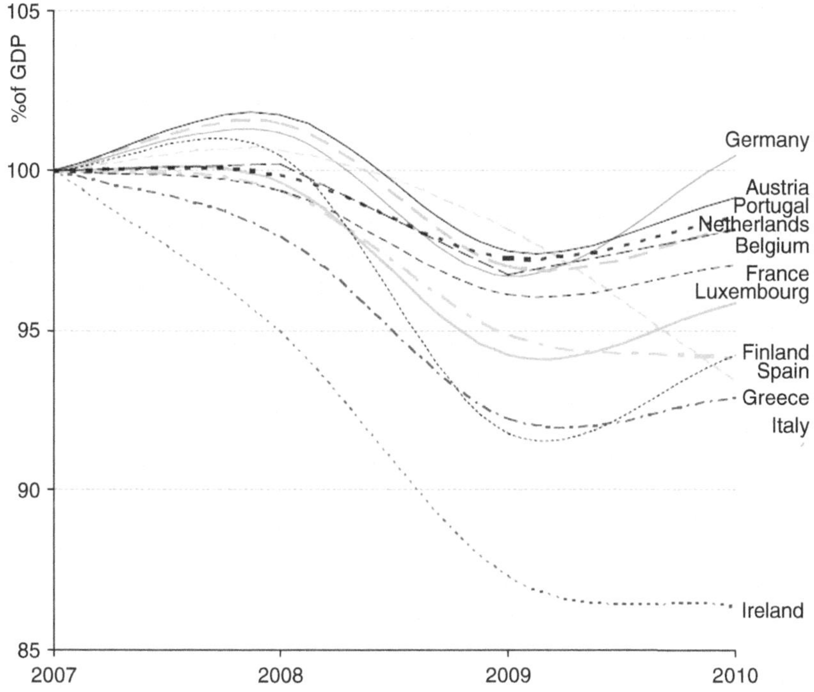

Fig. 4.15 GDP trends for Northern Europe 2005–2010. (Source: Kowalski (2012, p. 24))

net primary and secondary income, highlighting the better economic growth in the northern part of the EU (World Bank 2015c).

Germany's current account surplus from the early years of the twenty-first century was suggested as having fuelled the bubble in other countries and was partly a result of German households' saving levels and low domestic demand while its exports of manufactured goods, such as machinery and cars, were high, for instance exports to Spain and Ireland. Germany lent funds to these governments but also to firms and individuals, enabling loans at low interest rates, which created an economic boom (Dieter 2009; Doukas 2012). In fact, the creation of the Eurozone greatly benefitted the German economy, since its currency moved from the strong Deutschmark to the weaker Euro, which stimulated higher export levels and permitted it to move from a current account deficit to a huge surplus (Doukas 2012).

Germany invested heavily in ABS prior to 2007, and Joeg Asmussen, the individual who encouraged Germany to invest in these securities when he worked as a department head in the German Finance Ministry, suggested that they did not need testing. Asmussen was a board member of the failed IKB bank but was later promoted to Deputy Finance Minister for Germany, to be responsible for bank rescues and promoted liberalisation/deregulation of the German banking system. Asmussen was one in a group of influential people who came from a purely academic background and believed in freer market economics that characterised the US and UK. Hence, his views impacted substantially on Germany's financial services policies and regulations during that period.

Portugal, Ireland, Italy, Greece and Spain (PIIGS)

The public debt situation in the PIIGS countries, as discussed previously, was of much greater seriousness than other EU member countries, whereas Ireland met the EU criteria of less than 60% GDP; even Belgium based in northern Europe had a public debt of 90% GDP, and the average EU public debt just exceeded the limit. By 2010, Ireland had the largest overall percentage rise compared with 2008, as shown in Fig. 4.16 (Slay 2011).

These increases were partly due to governments attempting to support private companies by providing tax incentives and reducing social security payments but, concurrently, tax revenues as a percentage of GDP were

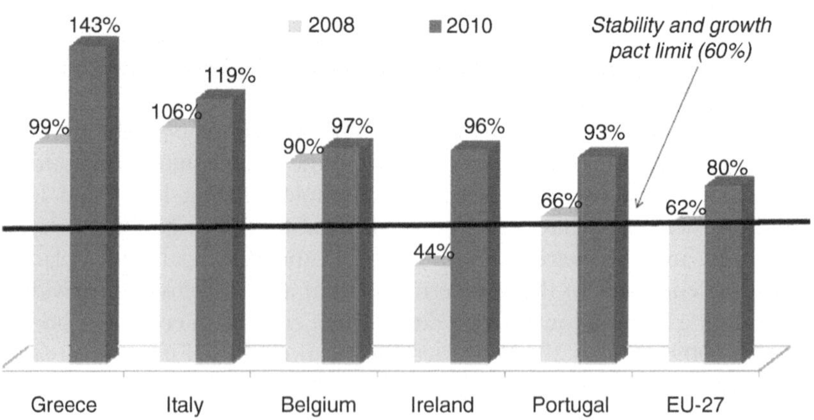

Fig. 4.16 Rise in public debt levels for 2008–2010 in PIIGS. (Source: Slay (2011, p. 16))

declining in all countries except Italy. From 2005 to 2009, for example, they fell in Ireland from 32.3% GDP to 29.6% GDP; in Greece 34.1% GDP to 32.9% GDP; in contrast, in Italy tax revenues grew from 40.7% to 43.4% GDP (Cukurcayir and Tezcan, 2013). However, these percentages were merely an indication of the actual fall in revenues, since the GDP levels in this period also fluctuated, for instance, Ireland's GDP fell dramatically from 2008–2010 and Italy's from 2008–2009, shown in Table 4.2. In addition, international trade levels were also generally declining (Kolwaski 2012) as was competitiveness (Slay 2011). The unemployment generated by the lower trade levels drove increases in social security in all PIIGS countries, particularly from 2008–2010. These increases were partly intended to stimulate economic demand. An additional contribution to the public debt was the support given to banks that would have otherwise gone bankrupt; the PIIGS nations chose to borrow from other countries to save the banks, predominantly from Germany, UK and France, in varying amounts, as shown in Table 4.2.

Public debt levels rose as well as the interest payable on them, a factor which also contributed to the upward trend (Cukurcayir and Tezcan 2013). The gap between expenditures and incomes in the PIIGS group is exemplified by Spain with public revenues of 37.0% and 35.1% GDP for

Table 4.2 PIIGS borrowing levels from other countries

PIIGS country	*Lender*	*Sum $US million*	*Total debt $US million*
Greece	Germany	45	135
	France	75	
	UK	15	
Portugal	Germany	47	116
	France	45	
	UK	24	
Italy	Germany	190	778
	France	511	
	UK	77	
Spain	Germany	238	572
	France	220	
	UK	114	
Ireland	Germany	184	432
	France	60	
	UK	188	

Source: Cukurcayir and Tezcan (2013, p. 5)

2008 and 2009 and public expenditures of 41.5% and 46.3% GDP, respectively. The gap in Greece was higher at an income of 40.7% and 35.0% GDP for 2008 and 2009, however, expenditure levels were 50.6% and 53.8%, respectively (Cukurcayir and Tezcan 2013). In view of this data and the actions of the PIIGS group, researchers comment that EU administration's tardiness to deal with the financial crisis, as it emerged in the US, had a direct impact on the PIIGS and other EU governments, in terms of them attempting to meet the challenges of the crisis using their own strategies. As a consequence, other macroeconomic indicators were affected, such as international trade, competitiveness and GDP levels.

The change in levels of international trade in the period from 2004 to 2009 was part of Kowalski's (2012) study and demonstrated that the openness of the economies of different Eurozone countries and the freedom to trade with them had impacted on their comparative trade levels after 2007 (Fig. 4.17).

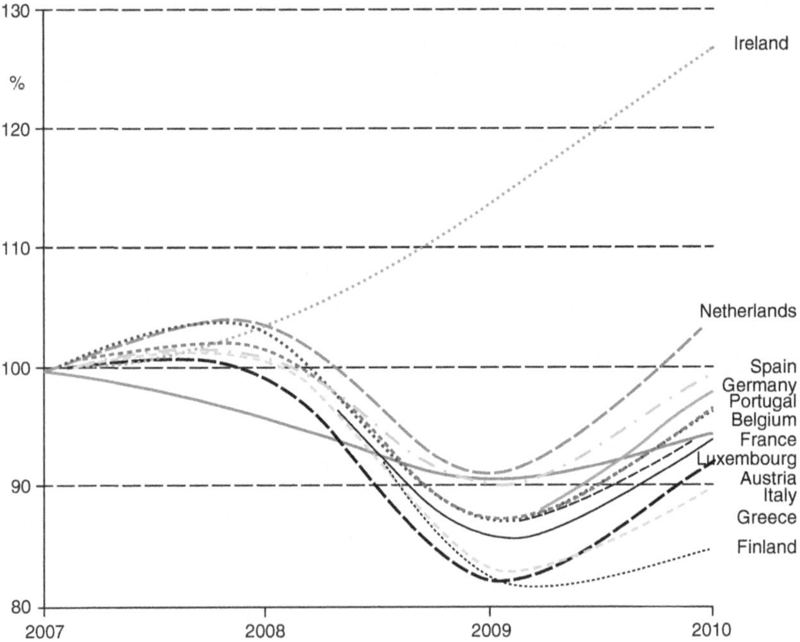

Fig. 4.17 Exports of goods and services and a percentage of GDP (2007–2010) level = 100. (Source: Kowalski (2012, p. 20))

Whereas Ireland had a very open economy and its exports soared as a percentage of GDP, the actual volume declined, but so did internal demand and the related GDP, factors which accounted for the trends. The percentage of exports in relation to GDP in most other EU countries fell dramatically; in 2007, the most open economies were Northern European countries, such as the Netherlands, with Italy, Spain and Greece rating at least five multiples lower on openness. The other countries in the PIIGS group had not regained their previous export to GDP ratio by 2010, with Greece and Italy being most affected, whereas the Netherlands had done so (Kowalski 2012).

The actual changes in GDP levels for countries in the PIIGS group are illustrated in Fig. 4.18.

These figures reinforce Kowalski (2012) regarding the huge fall in Ireland's actual GDP level, which was still relatively negative in 2010, compared to 2007 levels. However, Italy had a low level of -5.1% GDP in 2009, and was also more negatively affected than the average EU decline, but had recovered better than the other PIIGS nations. All PIIGS countries had made some recovery by 2010 except for Greece, in which GDP levels continued to fall. Hence, the comparative crisis severity levels of the PIIGS countries fluctuated in that period, with only Greece continuing on

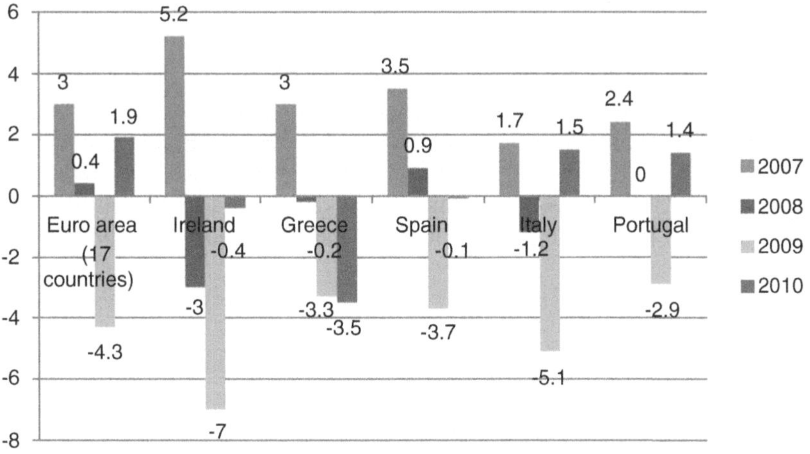

Fig. 4.18 GDP fluctuations in PIIGS group 2007–2010. (Source: Talani (2014b, p. 6) Eurostat Data)

a downward trend. These movements matched the loss in competitiveness of the PIIGS nations from 1999 to 2010, which are a consequence of uncompetitive labour rates (Fig. 4.13, Slay 2011). The huge deterioration of the competitiveness of Greece and of Italy exemplifies and highlights different conditions in the north and south regions of the EU.

The research conducted by Cukurcayir and Tezcan (2013) focused on the PIIGS group and sought to appraise the crisis in the group, its initial effects on the countries concerned and the effectiveness of initial interventions. The findings inferred that attempts to stem the crisis had not resulted in minimising the tensions and that the fundamental issue was the weakness of the Euro system, which required substantial reformulation. The difficulties of individual countries were described as emanating from the fact that they had become part of group that operated as if it were a multinational company, and therefore individual national economic policies were relatively insignificant. At the beginning of the crisis and until 2013, PIIGS countries were promoted by the northern regional group as inefficient and unable to control their spending, which was at the core of their difficulties (Lynn 2014). The findings from Lynn's (2014) study reinforced those of Cukurcayir and Tezcan (2013), regarding the functioning of the Euro system. Portugal, Spain, Ireland and Greece were all showing GDP growth, according to GDP figures for 2013, whilst the northern EU countries such as Germany and Finland were not, in contrast to 2010 (Fig. 4.11). Whereas the northern countries were formerly expected to rescue the PIIGS, stating that PIIGS nations had to reform and run their economies in a manner more similar to that of Germany, the economic problem has moved north, suggesting that there was no rapid end to the economic and financial crisis in Europe (Lynn 2014) and that the problems in the Eurozone cannot be solved by PIIGS reform, as was the theory. Lynn (2014) also commented that Italy's GDP failure commenced from the time it joined the Euro and its economy remained flat.

Eastern Europe

The highly negative and variable effects of the global recession on the eight Eastern European countries that had joined the EU prior to 2007, but had not yet become members of the EMU, were documented and trends discussed in a report by ECB in 2010 (ECB 2010b); the crisis stemmed inward investments by ECB into the region referred to as CEE (Central and Eastern Europe), resulting in GDP decline. In 2009, Poland was the only country in which GDP growth did not fall, but Latvia, Hungary and Romania had experienced such a large GDP decline that they sought economic assistance from the IMF and the EU. Prior to 2008, there were huge differences between the economic development of the eight countries, some had very substantial increases in GDP, which were referred to as unsustainable by ECB (2010b). These increases in GDP were export led and resulted in huge net inflows, which fuelled a credit boom, rising house prices, increased general demand and high inflation. In addition, expansionary government fiscal policies enhanced GDP growth, and governments accumulated significant debt. Private and public sector labour rates also grew as a consequence of this demand, which was particularly noticeable in Bulgaria, Poland and Romania, as well as the Baltic states of Estonia, Latvia and Lithuania. The public sector debt grew as these changes occurred and borrowing from external sources was common, and in foreign currencies, with the Baltic states receiving investments considered as being from risky sources. Bulgaria, Lithuania, Hungary and Poland had much higher proportions of foreign loan capital than those derived internally. Additionally, Hungary Romania, Lithuania and Latvia had fixed exchange rate mechanisms, which greatly affected the import/export trade and made investors wary, owing to high currency risk (ECB, 2010b). Hence, after 2008, the sharp decline in GDP growth was caused by a combination of a lack of domestic demand and demand for exports. Inflation rates quickly dropped, particularly in those countries that had experienced the highest growth rates and had the greatest financial imbalances. These countries also became most deprived of incoming investments, owing to the perceived risk in the private sector, as a consequence of debt levels/foreign currency loan levels. Estonia and Latvia, which were the most exposed, suffered a credit squeeze (Shostya 2014), whilst Czech Republic with very low levels of currency loans was less affected; as a consequence, the Baltic states and Romania experienced massive GDP contraction compared with Poland, for instance. The CEE were part of a larger group of transition economies that were former Soviet bloc members, and the research by Shostya (2014) found that those countries which had a much larger agricultural sector and natural resources were less affected by the global financial crisis. Therefore, the Baltic group of countries, which had depended on the service sector and foreign capital inflows, experienced considerable disadvantage in the time of economic crisis; they were highly sensitive to external shocks compared with other transition economies. The loss of competitiveness owing to labour rates

(Slay 2011), as shown in Fig. 4.13, demonstrates the overheating in the Baltic states mentioned by Shostya (2014). However, the data also reinforces the highly negative impact of the crisis on other countries in the region, for instance Hungary and Slovenia (Slay 2011).

The Eastern European countries were reported as being the most impacted by the Eurozone crisis (Ewing, 2011) by the European Bank for Reconstruction and Development (EBRD). The EBRD is a major source of public and private funding for the former communist countries and with funding underwritten by 61 countries, including EU and the US. EBRD also forecast substantial uncertainty regarding the future prospects of these countries, many of which had experienced a fall in GDP of more than 5%, since the beginning of the crisis. EBRD also stressed that their economies depended greatly on EU for trade, and access to capital funding from the richer EU countries, citing Hungary and Slovakia as being heavily reliant on them. In the Eastern European region, the banking sector was less affected, since most banks in this region were foreign-owned. However, the financial consequences for the countries were difficulty in accessing loans and fear that the Western European banks and other institutions would leave these countries with a severe credit crunch. In addition, many of the current domestic and business loans had been borrowed in Swiss francs or Euros, those in the former currency being susceptible to currency fluctuations, as stated by ECB (2010b) and substantial loan defaults had occurred. The EBRD did not forecast a recession in the region but lowered its economic growth forecast for most of the countries, for instance, Poland from 3.3% to 2.2% in 2012.

The level of public debt in EU member countries and its impact on economic growth in each of them were studied by Szabo (2013), using quantitative methods and data from reliable institutions and categorising the 27 EU countries into three groups: the original members, new members up to 2004 and countries that became members after 2004. Overall, the findings were that higher levels of public debt stifled economic growth in the ratio of a 1% increase in debt, resulting in a 0.027% decline in GDP. However, the effects across member countries were uneven and greater for countries that had been former communist countries in Eastern Europe; the findings also suggested that there was no definite linear relationship between the two factors of GDP and debt level. The specific debt and public expenditure of a country is a result of its historical and current economic policy, which impacts on economic development. In cases in which yields relating to long-term government securities rise, public spending cuts were necessary to service higher interest payments; a decline in GDP also affected education budgets. Hence, the study by Szabo (2013) adds a different perspective to the impact of the crisis on Eastern European countries.

Bibliography

Aljazeera. (2019, July 28). UK Government Working 'on Assumption of No-Deal Brexit'. *Aljazeera*. https://www.aljazeera.com/news/2019/07/uk-government-working-assumption-deal-brexit-190728085027307.html. Accessed 28 July 2019.

Altomonte, C., & Busselli, P. (2014, July 24). *Asset-Backed Securities: The Key to Unlocking Europe's Credit Markets?* Bruegel. http://www.bruegel.org/publications/publication-detail/publication/842-asset-backed-securities-the-key-to-unlocking-europes-credit-markets/. Accessed 10 Apr 2015.

Avgouleas, E. (2009). The Global Financial Crisis, Behavioural Finance and Financial Regulation: In Search of a New Orthodoxy. *Journal of Corporate Law Studies, 9*(1), 23–60.

Baker, J. (2010, June). *Sustainable Dialogue*. Griffith University Asia Pacific Centre for Sustainable Enterprise.

Balcerowicz, L. (2014). *Economic Growth in the European Union*. The Lisbon Council.

Barker, M. M. (2011, April). Manufacturing Employment Hard Hit During the 2007–09 Recession. *Monthly Labour Review*, pp. 28–33.

Bastasin, C. (2018, June 14). *"The People vs. Finance": Europe Needs a New Strategy to Counter Italian Populists*. Brookings Institute. https://www.brookings.edu/blog/order-from-chaos/2018/06/14/the-people-vs-finance-europe-needs-a-new-strategy-to-counter-italian-populists/. Accessed 13 Aug 2018.

BBC. (2019, July 25). Eurozone prepares for interest rate cut as growth slows. *BBC* [online]. https://www.bbc.com/news/business-49113728. Accessed 28 July 2019.

Behr, R. (2018, March 9). Populist Gains in Italy Show the Scale of Europe's Anger Epidemic. *The Guardian*. http://www.bbc.com/news/world-europe-17373216. Accessed 12 Aug 2018.

Blommestein, H. J., Keskinler, A., & Lucas, C. (2011). *Outlook for the Securitisation Market*. OECD.

Borio, C. (2008). *'The Financial Turmoil of 2007–?' A Preliminary Assessment and Some Policy Considerations* (Working Paper 251). Bank of International Settlements.

Borio, C., & Zhu, H. (2008). *Capital Regulation, Risk-Taking and Monetary Policy: A Missing Link in the Transmission Mechanism?* (Working Paper 268). Bank of International Settlements.

Boyd, S. (2007, August 9). BNP Paribas Freezes Funds as Loan Losses Roil Markets. *Bloomberg News*. http://www.bloomberg.com/apps/news?pid=newsarchive&sid=aW1wj5i.vyOg. Accessed 4 Apr 2015.

Bramble, T. (2009). Crisis and Contradiction in the World Economy. *JAPE, 64*, 22–36.

Bris, A. (2010). *The Lehman Brothers Case: A Corporate Governance Failure, Not a Failure of Financial Markets*. IMD.

Buck, G. (2017, May 31). *EU Agrees Measures to Revive Asset-Backed Securities Market*. The Global Treasurer. https://www.theglobaltreasurer.com/2017/05/31/eu-agrees-measures-to-revive-asset-backed-securities-market. Accessed 12 Aug 2018.

Buffett, W. (2003). *Chairman's Letter: Berkshire Hathaway Annual Report 2003*. Berkshire Hathaway Inc..

Caballero, R. J., & Krishnamurthy, A. (2009). Global Imbalances and Financial Fragility. *American Economic Review, 99*(2), 584–588.

CFR. (2017). *Greece's Debt Crisis 1974–2017*. Council on Foreign Relations. https://www.cfr.org/timeline/greeces-debt-crisis-timeline. Accessed 13 Aug 2018.

Coffee, J. C. (2009, June). What Went Wrong? An Initial Inquiry into the Causes of the 2008 Financial Crisis. *Journal of Corporate Law Studies*, 1–23.

Crotty, J. (2008). *Structural Causes of the Global Financial Crisis: A Critical Assessment of the 'New Financial Architecture'* (Working Paper 2008–14). University of Massachusetts, .

Cukurcayir, S., & Tezcan, K. (2013). Investigations on the Euro Area Public Debt Crisis: The Case of PIIGS. *European Scientific Journal, S*(1), 1–94.

Desjardins, J. (2019, January 14). *This Is What Government Debt Looks Like Across the Globe*. World Economic Forum. https://www.weforum.org/agenda/2019/01/visualizing-the-snowball-of-government-debt/. Accessed 28 July 2019.

Dieter, H. (2009). Europe's Crisis Management: Missed Opportunities. *Journal of Australian Political Economy, 64*, 141–157.

Doukas, J. (2012, May 23). *With a Rising Current Account Surplus, Germany Has Benefitted the Most from the Adoption of the Euro. Its Plan for EU Austerity Will Likely Make Things Worse*. LSE. http://blogs.lse.ac.uk/europpblog/2012/05/23/germany-current-account-euro-benefit/. Accessed 28 May 2015.

EC. (2015). *Who Can Join and When?* European Commission [online]. http://ec.europa.eu/economy_finance/euro/adoption/who_can_join/index_en.htm. Accessed 29 April 2015.

EC. (2018, May 24). *Frequently Asked Questions: Enabling Framework for Sovereign Bond-Backed Securities*. EC. http://europa.eu/rapid/press-release_MEMO-18-3726_en.htm. Accessed 12 Aug 2018.

EC. (2021). *EU Countries and the Euro*. EC. https://ec.europa.eu/info/euro-0/eu-countries-and-euro_en. Accessed 17 Jan 2021.

ECB. (2010a, December 9). Financial Stability Review – December 2010 Issue. *ECB*. http://www.ecb.europa.eu/pub/fsr/html/summary201012.en.html. Accessed 28 Apr 2015.

ECB. (2010b, July). The Impact of the Financial Crisis on the Central and Eastern European Countries. *ECB Monthly Bulletin*, 85–96.

Edwards, J. (2019, February 3). *Italy's 'Perma-Recession' Could Trigger a €2 Trillion Financial Crisis that Threatens the Eurozone Itself.* Business Insider. https://www.businessinsider.com/italy-perma-recession-systemic-crisis-threatens-eurozone-2019-4?IR=T. Accessed 28 July 2019.

Ehrbar, A. (2013, February 3). The great bond massacre (Fortune, 1994). *Fortune*. http://fortune.com/2013/02/03/the-great-bond-massacre-fortune-1994/. Accessed 5 Apr 2015.

Elliott, L. (2011, August 7). Global Financial Crisis: Five Key Stages 2007–2011. *The Guardian*. http://www.theguardian.com/business/2011/aug/07/global-financial-crisis-key-stages. Accessed 19 Apr 2015.

Engelen, E., & Glasmacher, A. (2018). The Waiting Game: How Securitization Became the Solution for the Growth Problem of the Eurozone. *Competition & Change, 22*(2), 165–183.

Eurostat. (2015). General Government Deficit (-) and Surplus (+) – Annual Data. *Eurostat* [online]. Available at: http://ec.europa.eu/eurostat/tgm/table.do?tab=table&plugin=1&language=en&pcode=teina200. Accessed 22 May 2015.

Eurostat. (2018). Government Finance Statistics. *Eurostat*. http://ec.europa.eu/eurostat/statistics-explained/index.php?title=Government_finance_statistics#Government_debt. Accessed 12 Aug 2018.

Evans-Pritchard, A. (2007, June 25). BIS Warns of Great Depression Dangers from Credit Spree. *The Telegraph*. http://www.telegraph.co.uk/finance/economics/2811081/BIS-warns-of-Great-Depression-dangers-from-credit-spree.htm. Accessed 18 Apr 2015.

Ewing, J. (2011, October 17). Euro Crisis Weighing On East European Growth. *New York Times* [online]. http://www.nytimes.com/2011/10/18/business/global/euro-crisis-weighing-on-east-european-growth.html?_r=0. Accessed 28 April 2015.

Fabozzi, F. J., & Choudry, M. (2004). *The Handbook of European Structured Financial Products*. Wiley.

Fang, H., Lu, Y., & Su, C. (2013). Impact of the Subprime Crisis on Commercial Banks' Financial Performance. *Panoeconomicus, 5*, 593–614.

Farlow, A. (2009). *The Global Financial Crisis: Causes and Cures*. International Consulting Economists Association; 2009 Feb 10; Institute of Commonwealth Studies.

Farrell, S. (2010, March 10). 'Repo 105' at the Heart of Lehman Report. *The Telegraph.* http://www.telegraph.co.uk/finance/newsbysector/banksandfinance/7431165/Repo-105-at-the-heart-of-Lehman-report.html. Accessed 17 Apr 2015.

Fingleton, J. (2009). *Competition Policy in Troubled Times – Annual Charles River Associates Conference. Competition Policy in Troubled Times. Brussels, 3 December 2008.* Office of Fair Trading.

Fleming, M. J., & Garbade, K. D. (2003). The Repurchase Agreement Refined: GCF Repo. *Current Issues in Economics and Finance, 9*(6), 1–7.

Garber, J. (2018, February 11). *Here's How the US Housing Market Has Been Impacted by the 2008 Crash.* Business Insider. https://www.businessinsider.com/impact-of-2008-crash-on-housing-2016-2?IR=T. Accessed 12 Aug 2018.

Glover, J. (2017, October 27). *Brexit Set to Create Two Securitization Laws Where One Sufficed.* Bloomberg. https://www.bloomberg.com/news/articles/2017-10-26/brexit-set-to-create-two-securitization-laws-where-one-sufficed. Accessed 12 Aug 2018.

Gorton, G. B., & Souleles, N. S. (2005). *Special Purpose Vehicles and Securitization.* Federal Reserve Bank of Philadelphia Working Paper No. 05–21.

GR. (2018). *Central Banks – Summary of Current Interest Rates.* Global Rates. https://www.global-rates.com/interest-rates/central-banks/central-banks.aspx. Accessed 12 Aug 2018.

Guarascio, F. (2018, May 24). EU Proposes New Sovereign Bond-Backed Securities, Faces Criticism. *Reuters.* https://www.reuters.com/article/us-eurozone-sovereign-sbbs/eu-proposes-new-sovereign-bond-backed-securities-faces-criticism-idUSKCN1IP1G2. Accessed 12 Aug 2018.

Gylfason, T., Holmstrom, B., Korkman, S., Soderstrom, H. T., & Vihriala, V. (2010). *Nordics in Global Crisis.* Taloustieto Oy.

HMRC. (2015). *CFM72010 – Other Tax Rules on Corporate Finance: Securitisation: Background.* Her Majesty's Customs and Revenues. http://www.hmrc.gov.uk/manuals/cfmmanual/cfm72010.htm/. Accessed 5 Apr 2015.

Horowitz, J. (2019, June 13). Italy's Toying with a 'Mini-BOT' Worries E.U. and Investors. *New York Times.* https://www.nytimes.com/2019/06/13/world/europe/italy-mini-bot-eu-brussels-debt.html. Accessed 28 July 2019.

Jolly, J. (2019, June 7). German Trade Decline Raises Fears Over Global Economy. *The Guardian.* https://www.theguardian.com/world/2019/jun/07/german-trade-decline-raises-fears-over-global-economy. Accessed 28 July 2019.

Jones, H. (2019, May 9). Glimmers of Light Emerge from Europe's Securitization Slump. *Reuters.* https://www.reuters.com/article/us-europe-abs/glimmers-of-light-emerge-from-europes-securitization-slump-idUSKCN1SF1ZG. Accessed 28 July 2018.

Juhas, G. (2013). Securitization – Great Benefits and Potential Cause of the Global Financial Crisis. *Megatrend Review, 10*(4), 115.

Kenins, A., Hatges, P., & Hassen, D. (2013). *Securitisation Vehicles – Is IFRS the End of the Road*. KPMG. http://www.kpmg.com/ca/en/issuesandinsights/articlespublications/insights-into-canadian-banking/pages/securitization-vehicles-is-ifrs-the-end-of-the-road.aspx. Accessed 12 Feb 2013.

Klimechi, R., & Wilmott, H. (2009). From Demutualisation to Meltdown: A Tale of Two Wannabe Banks. *Critical Perspectives on International Business, 5*, 120–140.

Kodres, L. E. (2013). What Is Shadow Banking? *Finance and Development, 50*(2), 42–43.

Kopechi, D., & Dodge, C. (2009, July 20). *US Rescue May Reach $23.7 Trillion, Barofsky Says*. Bloomberg. http://www.bloomberg.com/apps/news?pid=newsarchive&sid=aY0tX8UysIaM. Accessed 5 Apr 2015.

Kowalski, T. D. (2012). *The Economic and Monetary Union Countries vs. the Global Crisis* (WP/2012/04). Poznan University of Economics.

Krishnamurthy, A., & Muir, T. (2015). *Credit Spreads and the Severity of Financial Crises*. Stanford Graduate School of Business and Yale School of Management.

Liang, Y. (2012). Global Imbalances and Financial Crisis: Financial Globalisation as a Common Cause. *Journal of Economic Issues, XLVI*(2), 353–363.

Llewellyn, D. T. (2009). *The Northern Rock Crisis: A Multi-Dimensional Problem*. Secretariat The European Money and Finance Forum (SUERF).

Lucarelli, B. (2014). German Neomercantilism and the European Sovereign Debt Crisis. *Journal of Post Keynesian Economics, 34*(2), 205–225.

Lynn, M. (2014, August 21). Bond Investors Will Find Out that PIGS Can't Fly. *Marketwatch*. https://www.marketwatch.com/story/bond-investors-will-find-out-that-pigs-cant-fly-2014-01-15. Accessed 28 Apr 2015.

Macchiarelli C. Giacon R, Georgosouli A, Monti M. 2019, March 23. *Why Non-Performing Loans Are Still Putting the European Banking Union at Risk*. London School of Economics. https://blogs.lse.ac.uk/europpblog/2019/03/27/why-non-performing-loans-are-still-putting-the-european-banking-union-at-risk. Accessed 26 July 2019.

Manne, R., & Knight, D. (2010). *Goodbye to All That? On the Failure of Neo-liberalism & the Urgency of Change*. Black Inc. Agenda.

Marshall, W. C., & Concha, E. (2012). Fannie Mae and Freddie Mac: A Bailout for the People? *Journal of Economic Issues, XLVI*(2), 557–565.

Mauldin, J. (2018, June 7). Italy's Proposed Parallel Currency Is The Biggest Threat to the Eurozone. *Forbes*. https://www.forbes.com/sites/johnmauldin/2018/06/07/italys-proposed-parallel-currency-is-the-biggest-threat-to-the-eurozone/#3d97cdbf6cb0. Accessed 13 Aug 2018.

McBride, J. 2016, October 12. *Understanding the Libor Scandal*. Council for Foreign Relations. https://www.cfr.org/backgrounder/understanding-libor-scandal. Accessed 12 Aug 2018.

McConnell, P. (2014). Reckless Endangerment: The Failure of HBOS. *Journal of Risk Management in Financial Institutions, 7*(2), 202–215.
McKibbin, W. J., & Stoeckel, A. (2009). *The Global Financial Crisis: Causes and Consequences* (Working Paper No. 2.09). Lowy Institute for International Policy, .
Merrouche, O., & Nier, E. (2010). *What Caused the Global Financial Crisis? Evidence on the Drivers of Financial Imbalances 1999–2007* (IMF Working Paper WP/10/265).
MGM. (2018, December 27). *US vs EU – A GDP Comparison*. MGM Research. https://mgmresearch.com/us-vs-eu-a-gdp-comparison/. Accessed 26 July 2019.
Mishkin, F. S. (2008). *How Should We Respond to Asset Price Bubbles?* Banque di France Financial Stability Review, No. 12.
Morris, C. (2008). *The Trillion Dollar Meltdown*. Perseus Books.
Nicholas, T., & Chen, D. (2010, February). Lehman Brothers. *Harvard Business Review*, pp. 1–21.
Noeth, B., & Sengupta, R. (2012, April). A Look at Credit Default Swaps and Their Impact on the European Debt Crisis. *The Regional Economist*, pp. 10–11.
OECD. (2009). *Competition in Financial Markets*. OECD.
Panetta, F. (2018). *Italian Banks: Where They Stand and the Challenges Ahead. Bank of America Merrill Lynch Italy Day Conference; 2018 Feb 10*; London.
Panico, C., & Purificato, F. (2013). Policy Coordination, Conflicting National Interests and the European Debt Crisis. *Cambridge Journal of Economics, 37*, 585–608.
Partington, R. (2018, February 16). Home ownership among young adults has 'collapsed', study finds. *The Guardian*. https://www.theguardian.com/money/2018/feb/16/homeownership-among-young-adults-collapsed-institute-fiscal-studies. Accessed 12 August 2018.
Pilbeam, K. (2005). *Finance and Financial Markets* (2nd ed.). Palgrave Macmillan.
Piovacarri, G. (2019, July 23). Italy Banks to Rescue Carige via Depositor Protection Fund. *Reuters*. https://uk.reuters.com/article/uk-eurozone-banks-carige/italy-banks-to-rescue-carige-via-depositor-protection-fund-idUKKCN1UI1BA. Accessed 28 July 2019.
Reinhart, C. M., & Rogoff, K. (2009). *This Time Is Different: Eight Centuries of Financial Folly*. Princeton University Press.
Rivera, P. P. (2012). Crisis and Regional Distribution in the European Union: Considerations of Economic Policy. *Journal of Economic Issues, XLVI*(2), 459–469.
Rudd, K. (2009). The Global Financial Crisis. *The Monthly, 13*(42), 14.
Rumney, E. (2018, October 29). UK Government Plans to Sell Remaining RBS Stake by 2024. *UK Reuters*. https://uk.reuters.com/article/uk-britain-economy-rbs/uk-government-plans-to-sell-remaining-rbs-stake-by-2024-idUKKCN1N32E7. Accessed 28 July 2019.

Sanati, C. (2014, April 10). Collateralized Loan Obligations: Our Next Financial Nightmare. *Fortune*. http://fortune.com/2014/04/10/collateralized-loan-obligations-our-next-financial-nightmare/. Accessed 13 Aug 2018.

Santacana, R., & Siles, J. (2013). Rating Agencies and the European Union Sovereign Debt Crisis: An Ethical Approach. *Journal of International Business Ethics, 6*(1–2), 27–42.

SG. (2017). *Debt Capital Markets 2017 Review*. Societe Generale.

Shostya, A. (2014). The Effect of the Global Financial Crisis on Transition Economies. *Atl Econ J, 42*, 317–332.

Slay, B. (2011). *The Eurozone Crisis: Causes and Implications*. UNDP [PPT Presentation], December 14.

ST. (2019). List of European Countries by GDP Per Capita. *Statistical Times*. http://statisticstimes.com/economy/european-countries-by-gdp-per-capita.php. Accessed 28 July 2019.

Stanford, J. (2009). Understanding the Economic Crisis: The Importance of Training in Critical Economics. *JAPE, 64*, 9–21.

Szabo, Z. (2013). The Effect of Sovereign Debt on Economic Growth and Economic Development. *Journal of Public Finance, 38*(3), 251–270.

Talani, L. (2014a). *European Political Economy: Issues and Theories*. Ashgate Publishing.

Talani, L. (2014b). *The Origins of the Euro-Zone Crisis: The EMU and the Loss of Competitiveness*. EUI. https://www.eui.eu/Projects/PierreWernerChair/Documents/MIKE-ARTIS/MikeArtiscommemorationpaper.pdf. Accessed 11 Jan 2021.

Taylor, E. (2012, September 10). IKB Repays 2 Bln Euros German Bailout Guarantees. *Reuters*. http://uk.reuters.com/article/2012/09/10/ikb-bailout-idUKL5E8KADHK20120910. Accessed 28 July 2019.

TE. (2019a). European Union Unemployment Rate. *Trading Economics*. https://tradingeconomics.com/european-union/unemployment-rate. Accessed 28 July 2019.

TE. (2019b). European Union Home Ownership Rates. *Trading Economics*. https://tradingeconomics.com/european-union/home-ownership-rate. Accessed 28 July 2019.

TE. (2019c). Euro Area Interest Rate. *Trading Economics*. https://tradingeconomics.com/euro-area/interest-rate. Accessed 28 July 2019.

TE. (2019d). Interest Rate. *Trading Economics*. https://tradingeconomics.com/country-list/interest-r. Accessed 28 July 2019.

Telegraph. (2009, January 23). UK Recession: Timeline of How the British Economy Has Been Hit. *The Telegraph*. UK Recession: Timeline of how the British Economy Has Been Hit. Accessed 4 Apr 2015.

Tondo, L., & Giuffrida, A. (2018, December 19). Italy Avoids EU Sanctions After Reaching 2019 Budget Agreement. *The Guardian*. www.theguardian.com/

world/2018/dec/19/italy-avoids-eu-sanctions-after-reaching-2019-budget-agreement. Accessed 28 July 2019.

Vaskova, N., & Vaskova, V. (2010). Breakdown of Trust in Financial Institutions in Light of the Global Financial Crisis. *Journal of Advanced Studies in Finance, 1*(1), 108–205.

Verick, S., & Islam, I. (2010). *The Great Recession of 2008–2009: Causes, Consequences and Policy Responses.* IZA.

Waiglein, H. (2017). *Understanding Bank Recovery and Resolution in the EU: A Guidebook to the BR*. World Bank Group.

Warner, J. (2018, May 12). RBS Turns the Page on the Financial Crisis, but Not So the Bank of England. *The Telegraph.* https://www.telegraph.co.uk/business/2018/05/12/rbs-turns-page-financial-crisis-not-bank-england/. Accessed 12 Aug 2018.

Weltman, J. (2018, April 27). Italy Is the Volcano Waiting to Erupt. *Euromoney.* https://www.euromoney.com/article/b12yz8xr8wj161/country-risk-italy-is-the-volcano-waiting-to-erupt. Accessed 13 Aug 2018.

White, W. (2018). Recognising the Economy as a Complex Adaptive System. In P. Hartmann, H. Huang, & D. Schoenmaker (Eds.), *The Changing Fortunes of Central Banking* (pp. 359–375). Cambridge University Press.

World Bank. (2015a). *Budget Surplus (Deficit) as Percentage of GDP.* http://data.worldbank.org/indicator/GC.BAL.CASH.GD.ZS?page=1. Accessed 16 Jul 2015.

World Bank. (2015b). *GDP Growth (Annual %).* World Bank. http://data.worldbank.org/indicator/NY.GDP.MKTP.KD.ZG/countries/1W-DE-FR-NL-SE-GB-FI?display=default. Accessed 22 May 2015.

World Bank. (2015c). *Current Account Balance (% of GDP).* World Bank. http://data.worldbank.org/indicator/BN.CAB.XOKA.GD.ZS?page=1&display=default. Accessed 22 May 2015.

World Bank. (2018). *GDP Growth (Annual %).* World Bank. https://data.worldbank.org/indicator/NY.GDP.MKTP.KD.ZG?locations=EU. Accessed 12 Aug 2018.

World Bank. (2019). *GDP Growth (Annual %).* World Bank. http://data.worldbank.org/indicator/NY.GDP.MKTP.KD.ZG. Accessed 28 Jul 2018.

CHAPTER 5

Interventions by Governments

Options for Government Intervention

Intervention in Markets

Free markets are often considered as failing to operate in a perfect manner so that if there was no intervention, the market economy would not operate in a socially or economically practicable way. From an economic perspective, the term social efficiency relies on the balance between two concepts, Marginal Social Benefit (MSB) and Marginal Social Cost (MSC). MSB is the additional benefit to society that results from production or consumption of a good or service, whereas MSC is the cost of doing so, which can be financial or non-financial. Social efficiency occurs when Marginal Social Cost is equal to Marginal Social Benefit and, therefore, in economic terms, there is an assumption that a perfect market exists only when perfect knowledge regarding costs and benefits that impact on society also exists (Sloman et al., 2018). Firms are considered to be ill informed about the microeconomic and macroeconomic factors that impact on their businesses, and hence make forecasts and plans based on uncertainty and ignorance regarding future conditions, competitors and market opportunities. Consumers also lack knowledge about the goods or services that they consume, which is often exacerbated by the marketing claims of the manufacturer or the service provider. Hence, the rationale behind governments intervening in markets is to make sure that they are

S. Weißschnur, *The Proportionality of State Intervention*,
https://doi.org/10.1007/978-3-030-75676-5_5

socially efficient, since they consider that firms would not do so if left to make such a decision (Sloman et al., 2018; Lipsey & Chrystal, 2015; Tirole & Rendell, 2017).

Intervention by governments is described as a discretionary act by Boettke and Coyne (2011), and there are opposing views on whether or not government intervention in markets is preferable. Groups that propose intervention in markets support the view that the role of governments is to reduce the negative effects of market activities, either by regulation or fiscal policy without reducing the benefits of an economy based on competition. In other words, the role of the state is to define the rules and the regulations therefore the associated responsibilities of firms that take priority over their self-interest (Tirole & Rendell, 2017). The opposing parties suggest that the forces of demand and supply are sufficient to rectify imbalances caused by events such as recession and that overall, leaving the market to rebalance naturally will make the economy stronger (Aikins, 2009). The latter is referred to as laissez-faire economics, which literally infers that government should not interfere in markets but leave them to self-regulate, allow free information flow and consumption behaviour based on consumers' revealed preferences. However, the consequence is that the consumer will be excluded from possessing the preferred good/service unless s/he can pay for it. Therefore, the opposite economic approach, which justifies intervention, is that if companies are able to stifle competition or fix prices, then consumers will not have sufficient information to choose the most appropriate option. Existing firms may also prevent new companies from entering the market, which can result in huge social inequalities, relating to income and wealth. Economists holding this viewpoint believe that governments must take action to prevent this inequality, one method being to enact legislation to prevent it (Aikins, 2009). Interventionism has actually grown exponentially from the beginning of the twentieth century, in terms of the scope and expenditure to effect market interventions, and more so after globalisation exposed the inequalities in different parts of the world. However, Boettke and Coyne (2011) state that this level of public expenditure on intervention is unsustainable and cite the fourfold growth from 1914 to 2009 as the underlying reason. Market failure has also been employed by governments as the rationale for intervention, so that four major contexts are evident: controlled monopoly power, externalities, public goods and macroeconomic instability (Tirole & Rendell, 2017). These opposing views are important to this study because, after the 2008 economic crisis markets fell and indicated the risks from laissez-faire economics, such that many governments were compelled to intervene.

Market Failure

Governments regulate industry for economic and social reasons using a range of interventions. The economic regulation of firms has the purpose of reducing monopoly power, in cases of lack of competition as exists in the utilities sector exemplified by the electricity and water industries. Social regulation is concerned with monitoring externalities, which are the cost or benefit that an independent third party experiences as a consequence of the economic activity of a firm (Tirole & Rendell, 2017). A positive externality might be planting new trees, which benefit the community, for instance, for visual impact, as well as enabling the exchange of carbon dioxide and oxygen in the air and for wildlife to prosper. In contrast to this, an example of a negative externality is factories dumping waste into rivers, an action that needs rectification and incurs public expenditures (Sloman et al., 2018; Zerbe & Mc Curdy, 1999). The government may also intervene in markets to ensure access to public goods; those products or services that are not practical or profitable for private firms to offer; government may provide public goods directly or by paying private firms to supply them (Zerbe & Mc Curdy, 1999). Two types of public goods exist, merit and demerit goods; merit goods or services are beneficial to society, whilst demerit products or services are considered harmful. Merit goods, for example education and libraries, may not be provided in sufficient quantities by private firms and/or not consumed frequently enough if consumption decisions were made by consumers (Poterba, 1994). Therefore, governments tend to either provide merit goods/services free of charge to the public or subsidise them. Demerit goods are products such as tobacco and alcohol, which are associated with ill health or negative social behaviour, so that the government intervenes in an attempt to suppress their consumption, often by taxing them highly (Sloman et al., 2018).

Government intervention in commercial activities, by means of legislation and regulation, is directed at protecting consumer interests, those of workers and the environment; for instance legislation on health and safety standards in the workplace, fair terms and conditions of employment, restricting environmental damage by imposing of emission limits (Tirole & Rendell, 2017). Legislation is also enacted to prevent the advertising of certain goods or services to certain age groups, making false claims about them associated with product safety and to prevent firms from colluding in ways which are not in the best interest of consumers (Sloman et al., 2018; Wolf, 1993; Winston, 2006).

Instruments Employed for Government Intervention

Taxation may be used to lower consumption of demerit goods, whereas subsidies are incentives for the production of certain goods and services in cases in which the market is likely to produce too little. However, if these subsidised goods are stockpiled, market price can be inflated, causing consumer dissatisfaction (van Doren, 2000). Intervention by regulation and legislation is frequently used to restrict certain commercial and social practices; it either prevents or regulates certain behaviours in productive operations, including providing misleading information and producing products that are harmful to individuals and/or to society (Wolf, 1993). In commercial activities, regulation is primarily used to restrict the activities of monopolies or oligopolies, so that they do not use their market power to exploit their position to negatively impact on the interests of consumers (Zerbe & Mc Curdy, 1999; van Doren, 2000). Single producer or service supplier, which possesses market monopoly, is considered likely to generate prices that are excessively high, whilst keeping costs to a minimum, and subsequently creating unjustified profit unless regulated. A monopolistic producer or supplier would not be threatened by new entrants and would be able to maintain market power at this level, for instance utility providers in many countries have historically had monopoly power. The action taken to eliminate this monopoly was denationalisation of vital industries such as rail, telephone, gas, water and electricity; industries subsequently operated by several competing firms. In the case of utilities, governments continue to regulate them because they remain quasi monopolistic industries, and there is a perceived need to restrain prices and the generation of excessive profits, so that the market is relatively efficient. However, these principles imply that the regulator has perfect information, and there is no cost in instigating and maintaining the regulation (Joskow & Rose, 1989; Winston, 2006). In general, legislation is employed to discourage firms from adopting anti-competitive practices, particularly regarding price. In the UK, for instance, there was a general regulatory body, the Office of Fair Trading (OFT) until 2014, which was dedicated to ensuring that the markets operated competitively:

> markets work well when businesses are in open, fair and vigorous competition with each other for the consumer's custom. (OFT, 2014, p. 1)

This advisory and regulatory body offered information and advice to the public about product safety and consumer debt agreements, but also appraised impending mergers and acquisitions. Its responsibilities have been passed to two new bodies, the Competition and Markets Authority (CMA) and the Financial Conduct Authority (FCA) (OFT, 2014).

Command and control regulation are often employed by governments to control environmentally related issues, permissions, prohibition and setting and enforcing standards resulting in fines for failure to comply. The main disadvantage of this type of regulation is the cost of enforcing it, despite providing government revenues. In contrast, financial incentivisation is associated with rewards from governments (OECD, 2001), exemplified by providing green credits for organisations that control emissions to remain below the stated limits (Galinato & Yoder, 2010); this approach has the negative effect of disincentivising organisations to reduce levels below the maximum permitted (Galinato & Yoder, 2010; Winston, 2006). Consumer protection laws are interventions to protect consumers from unfair practices, for instance, unacceptable product quality and safety, and unfair trading methods including distance trading that has become more important with the growth of e-commerce. Standards are set regarding information required by law, for example, delivery arrangements, returns and cancellation rights and the legislation comprises laws relating to goods and services from consumable products, such as food, to non-consumables, such as electrical goods and property. Other examples of legislation are the regulation of loans to customers who wish to purchase goods and services on credit, and anti-competition legislation against business cartels, a form of monopoly (Wolf, 1993: Sloman et al., 2018). Employment rights and conditions comprise legislation and regulation relating to employment contracts, working conditions for instance working time, workplace discrimination, equal pay, dismissal, redundancy and health and safety (Joskow & Rose, 1989). Legislation that relates to social issues and affects individuals and society includes any type of discrimination, direct or indirect, and human rights (Winston, 2006: Sloman et al., 2018).

Fiscal Policy Intervention

Fiscal policies are the instruments used by governments to influence the direction of the economy, for instance, government spending and taxation. Traditionally, these policies were attributed to John Maynard Keynes, who published the book entitled the *General Theory of Employment, Interest, and Money* in 1936, at the time of the Great Depression. The underlying principle of this theory was that the major factor driving a nation's economy was the aggregate demand created by households, businesses and the government, rather than the dynamics of free markets. Keynes considered that free markets did not have a self-balancing mechanisms to lead to full employment, so that Keynesian economics justified government intervention in the economy, which had the purpose of ensuring full employment and price stability. Aggregate demand was stimulated by following four principles: in an economic downturn, governments should instigate employment opportunities for the unemployed population; increased government spending should occur when the economy needed stimulation; interest rates should be lowered as a means of stemming rising prices, or rates should be raised during deflationary periods; since consumer spending is necessary for economic growth, governments should maintain full employment by spending as required (Musgrave, 1987/88; Sloman et al., 2018; Wolff & Resick, 2012).

Therefore, fiscal policy relies on the adjustment of tax rates and government spending to control unemployment, growth and inflation (Aikins, 2009). In a recession, deflationary fiscal policy, often referred to as expansionary policy, would be employed; governments would increase government expenditures and/or cut taxes. The impact of this policy was to stimulate demand and GDP growth, while concurrently reducing unemployment. In practical terms, this expansionary policy is often effected by government investment in new projects to create jobs. However, if the economy is expanding too quickly and inflation is rising too fast, the government should raise taxes and/or reduce its level of spending, referred to as contractionary fiscal policy. Hence, the uncertainties of the economic cycle, namely the highs and lows, could be reduced by this combination of approaches (Bullard, 2012).

A deflationary fiscal policy may result in a budget deficit, if government spending exceeds its income generated by taxation, and the national debt will increase. However, Keynes suggested that this was a necessary short-term measure to stimulate the economy and the amount invested had a multiplier effect on growth; for each unit of expenditure, a higher multiple of economic growth would result. A budget surplus will occur only if the level of taxation collected is greater than government expenditures. Discretionary fiscal policy is the term given to deliberate government intervention in markets and is accomplished by altering government expenditures or taxation policies (Wolff & Resick, 2012; Sloman et al., 2018).

However, fiscal policy has the limitation that it cannot completely prevent unemployment. Tax cuts also have less impact on GDP than increasing expenditure, since the latter ensures that the sum injected into the economy is totally spent, whereas consumers cannot be guaranteed to spend the extra disposable income that tax cuts provide. The actual effect of fiscal policy on GDP, unemployment and inflation is not easy to forecast for a number of reasons discussed in this appraisal of fiscal policy, such as crowding out, tax and savings links, and the unpredictable nature of the multiplier (Sloman et al., 2018; Wolff & Resick, 2012). Therefore, a rise in government expenditure may not result in an equal amount being injected into the economy, since other types of financial injection into the economy could decrease, for instance, business investment. Government budget deficit rises when its expenditure increases and is facilitated by either boosting the money supply or borrowing money from individuals and firms. If the option selected is to borrow money, the government will compete with the private sector for financing, which increases interest rates and subsequently results in reducing borrowing levels by businesses and diminishing their investment into the economy. This phenomenon is referred to as crowding out businesses from borrowing, as well as deterring consumers from using credit facilities to purchase products/services. Therefore, the increase in government expenditures could be counteracted by lack of consumption and declining business investment (Wolff & Resick, 2012). Tax reduction has no certain link with changes in savings or consumption, because individuals may perceive that a tax cut is temporary, and/or they lack confidence about future prospects, and may fail to consume the additional disposable income.

The time lag between the injection of extra government spending and business investments into the economy is uncertain and hence the multiplier effect cannot be predicted; in a recession, the lack of business owner confidence may also prevent the multiplying effects from showing in the economy until it begins to recover and moves towards a boom (Sloman et al., 2018). According to Bullard (2012), modern political processes are not able to handle macroeconomic shocks in the timely manner that Keynesian policies demand and, rather than being a short-term measure, these policies were likely to be more effective as a medium- or long-term intervention. For several decades prior to the global crisis many governments, particularly in developed countries such as the US and UK, considered that intervention to stabilise the market using fiscal policy was an ineffective measure. However, as nominal interest rates decline to a very low level, in some cases to almost zero, fiscal policy seemed to be appropriate (Bullard, 2012); fiscal policy was employed by the US for three years from 2008, and in many OECD countries. Governments did not employ traditional methods such as taxation to enable increased government spending during the aftermath of the 2008 global crisis, instead it was debt financed. The potential consequence of this strategy is to remove the longer term positive effect that fiscal policy was intended to deliver; excessive national debt has not been studied in regard to fiscal stabilisation policies (Bullard, 2012).

Monetary Policies Intervention

Monetary policy intervention refers to managing the national money supply by manipulating interest rates and other monetary tools, to influence consumer spending levels and aggregate demand in the economy. The government may also set targets for the inflation rate so that the national central bank adjusts interest rates to keep inflation within the target level or it may monitor additional macroeconomic variables, for instance, growth and unemployment (Scaberd & van Wijnbergen, 2014; Abdymomunov & Kang, 2015). In the UK, monetary policy is set by the Bank of England's Monetary Policy Committee (MPC), independently of the government, but if the Committee fails to meet the target inflation rate, it must confer with the Chancellor of the Exchequer, who represents the government. The Bank of England monitors a variety of inflationary trends involving economic variables, for instance, unemployment, consumer confidence, house prices, GDP growth and exchange rates (HM Treasury, 2013). The government may lower interest rates as a tactic to increase the demand for money, for example to stimulate economic growth in a recession; governments or central banks increase the money supply to encourage investment and consumption (Scaberd & van Wijnbergen, 2014). Quantitative easing, or simply printing more money, usually electronically, is one method of increasing the amount of money in the economy and is particularly important to this study, since when bank interest rates are already very low, interest manipulation is not feasible. The new money generated is used to buy bonds from banks, pension funds or other investors, therefore, the amount of liquidity in the financial system increases, allowing financial institutions increased capacity to lend to businesses and individuals, which can either consume more goods or services or expand their businesses to stimulate economic growth. However, quantitative easing increases the market value of government bonds, reducing the income paid to investors, with a negative impact on them. Pension funds, for instance, which were invested in bonds prior to the recession, have experienced a fall in their investment income, whilst continuing to pay the pensions in force. Consequently, deficits on pensions have increased substantially since 2007, generating a concern regarding future pay outs. To reduce inflation, interest rates can be raised or the money supply decreased, or the government may choose to sell government bonds, which are bought by investors. These actions reduce bank reserves and hence the supply of money in circulation (Fawley & Neely, 2013). Monetary policy is referred to as being accommodative, neutral or tight, according to whether interventions are made to increase, stabilise or reduce the money supply, respectively (Sloman et al., 2018). However, monetary policies also have limitations, for instance, managing aggregate demand by means of interest rates may not reduce consumption until rates are high, and speculation regarding interest rates, inflation and exchange rates tends to cause money fluctuation. On a global level, monetary policy was the accepted way of controlling inflation globally, usually by interest rate manipulation, until the latest economic crisis (Sloman et al., 2018).

In response to the 2007 economic crisis, central banks reduced interest rates to almost zero in many countries, as shown in Fig. 5.1.

During the current crisis, monetary policy has been effective in stabilising the economy, according to Bullard (2012), despite interest rates of almost zero in many countries; in the UK and US, for example, this has been achieved by means of several tranches of quantitative easing. In the UK, quantitative easing began in 2009 with two asset purchase programmes and a private asset purchase up to a £50 billion limit, as the means to alleviate specific credit conditions as well as established purchases related to quantitative easing, which amounted to £250 billion that year. During the economic crisis, the US Federal Reserve took similar measures to ensure that both central banks acted as the market maker of last resort, to enable the market to function again (Bullard, 2012). Quantitative

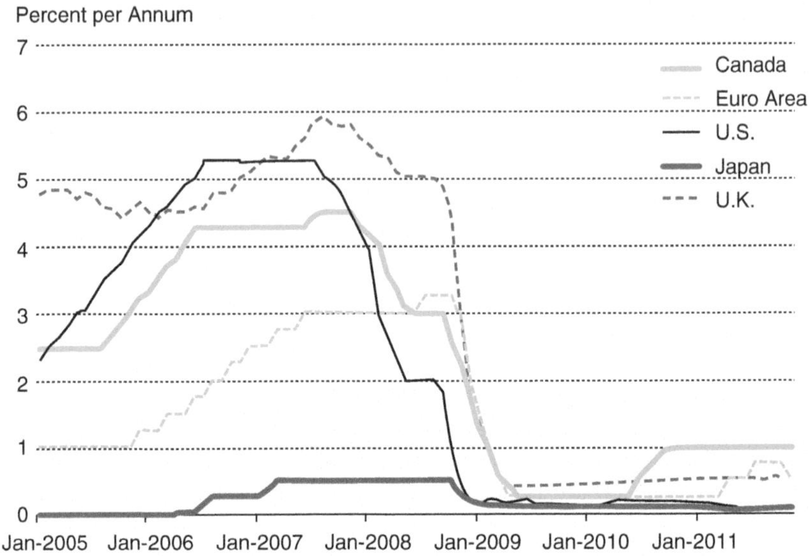

Fig. 5.1 Interest rate trends for G7 countries 2005–2011. (Source: Federal Reserve Bank of St Louis—Bullard (2012, p. 87))

easing was used extensively by the ECB to stimulate economic growth, which has continuously failed to meet expectations and, whilst the German economy, which is regarded as the indicator for the whole EU group, increased significantly, other EU countries either had stable growth or continued to make little progress from 2014 to 2017. The US Federal Reserve stopped using QE in 2015 and adopted a normalisation monetary policy; interest rates were raised from 0.25% to 0.5% and gradually increased to the 1.5% set in December 2017 (Federal Reserve System, 2017); US interest rates in 2019 are 2.5% (MGM, 2018).

The ECB also announced that QE would end in December 2018 so that interest rates would be normalised from that date. The ECB was also forecast to retain low interest rates until mid-2019 at the latest. QE was introduced whilst inflation was below 2% so that it was assumed that once it reached 2%, normalisation would actually occur and interest rates would start to rise. The factors impacting on normalisation in the EU are changing, and an ageing population and shift from manufacturing to services would be expected to lower inflation. Therefore, the EU was expected to monitor the effects of the US normalisation strategy before deciding on how its interest policy was shaped (Mariathasan, 2018). Quantitative easing ceased as planned by the EU, but in July 2019, the ECB announced new plans for monetary stimulus to address the stagnant economy, which might comprise lower interest rates and renewed asset purchases (Look, 2019).

The perceived negative effect of QE was emphasised by Mariathasan (2018) who regarded it as an experimental measure that had generally distorted the global economy by enabling inflation in the price of assets. A quantitative study by Hohberger et al. (2018) tended to confirm this perspective because it found that QE had stimulated inflation by 0.3% in 2015 and 0.6% in 2015, and GDP by 0.3% to 0.5% in 2015 compared with 0.3% to 0.7% in 2016. However, the study does not provide any indication of how these averages represented the positions of inflation and GDP in individual Eurozone countries. The research by Hausken and Ncube (2013) suggested that QE had been far more effective in US and UK because it focused on bond purchases to diminish interest rates rather than on lending to private financial institutions, the ECB strategy. QE generally had little effect on economic growth but had stimulated manufacturing in UK and US and reduced unemployment in US. There was little evidence that QE had stimulated consumer confidence or house prices so that other measures such as structural reform were required as complementary stimulants. The evidence on the impact of QE in the Eurozone conflicted suggested that it had supported a fall in unemployment from an average of 12.1% to 9.3% and growth of 5.1% in total since December 2015. However, the uneven impact across the EU was highlighted by Giles and Jones (2017) who highlighted 0.4% growth for the third largest EU economy, Italy, in 2017, whilst even Portugal had registered 1.0%. The latest analyses demonstrate that the ECB has been forced to rethink its exit from extraordinary economic stimulus because it did not accomplish its inflation target of 2% and there had been a downturn in its manufacturing sector. The decline in market confidence in EU economic policy is evident from the decline in the Euro to US dollar exchange rate by 0.3% and the German 10-year bond rate reaching its lowest yield to date at -0.42% (Look, 2019). Therefore, the EU is in a weak position to meet the additional challenges of the forecast slowdown in global growth (Look, 2019).

Intervention in Banks

The importance of the financial services sector to every national economy was highlighted by OECD (2009), which added that if one financial services organisation failed to deliver acceptable service as a consequence of poor practice, it led to contagion and lack of confidence that impacted on the whole financial sector and had extreme and negative impacts on economic outcomes. This statement explains why governments intervene in the banking and financial services sector by means of regulation, which rapidly changed if failure occurred in the sector (Cariboni et al., 2010). Prior to 2007, the financial services sector had become increasingly deregulated in developed countries, so that credit became more accessible to the population (Rudd, 2009). Governments take a neoliberalist approach to failing companies because they consider that their success and failure should be left to market forces (Phelan & Dawes, 2018), in contrast to the rationale taken in the case of banks, which is interventionist. A bank failure affects a large number of companies and individuals who may have no control over an event and, if all bank clients failed, the economy would be badly affected. Hence, bank failure has been generally considered unfavourable, and banks had the image of being too big to fail (Lipsey & Chrystal, 2015).

The agreement to the introduction of the new European ABS is another new intervention in the market, an attempt to direct risk away from the banks holding sovereign debt by selectively pooling government bonds from the 19 Eurozone countries and offering them to private sector financial institutions. Whilst this policy may have positive externalities for the banks because they hold less debt and can therefore meet their asset reserve targets more readily, investors purchasing the riskier elements of these securities are the potential recipients of huge losses in an economic turndown (Buck, 2017). This perspective was reinforced by Engelen and Glasmacher (2018), who also suggested that the ECB had developed a complex version of the ABS, called STS, which was subject to stricter rules but nevertheless neglected the toxic nature of the original ABS. In fact, Engelen and Glasmacher (2018) proposed that the main reason for this intervention in the banks was not to reduce their risk but to stimulate the economy by increasing monetary flow: rational choice (Blakely, 2019).

EU Government Intervention

EU Subsidiarity and Proportionality

The EU comprises several governance levels, the EU, the Member States and those related to individuals and its policies (Sauter, 2013). The Principle of Subsidiarity, which is contained in Article 3b of the Maastricht Treaty, is stated to be a fundamental principle of EC operations (Poto, 2009), which enables it to take action at lower government levels, to ensure the enhancement of competency levels within the group. According to Stoain (2013), this Principle infers that the EU would provide support to others, individuals or groups, which may lack specific skills or knowledge to accomplish an agreed goal, to make decisions or to solve a problem. Therefore, Stoain (2013) suggests that the EC interpret this principle as supporting Member States to meet any aspect of treaty objectives, if it considers that they do not have the appropriate competencies, and that it could achieve the objective more effectively (Stoain, 2013). The implication is that the principles are adopted as a method of dividing power between the EU bodies and its Member States, such that decisions should be taken at the appropriate level on a continuum between the EU with supranational power and the Member State with sovereign power (Golbu, 1996). This interpretation of the term reflects the original meaning of this Principle, which was to protect the independence of smaller entities from larger ones, according to Syrpis (2004). However, the EU definition of the Principle of Subsidiarity infers that it will determine the degree of intervention required, the position along that continuum, relevant to the competencies shared between the EU and the Member State(s). Consequently, the level of EU control will be made based on its perceived capacity to be more effective than the state concerned but with no justification for which competencies the EU possesses that the Member States do not, and Pelkmans (2006) proposes that subsidiarity is used as a political tool. The stages in the test for subsidiarity are shown in Table 5.1.

Therefore, tensions are likely to arise between the Member State(s) and the EU when it considers that the EU is less effective, and/or its interventions are perceived to conflict with national sovereign rights. In contrast, if the test suggests that the issue should be centralised, the Principle of Proportionality is applied (Pelkmans, 2012). Proportionality forms the basis of all EU decision making related to Member State rights that can be limited by governmental interventions in the public interest, to what

Table 5.1 The subsidiarity test

	Stage	*Detail*
1	Verify whether the issue is relevant to shared or exclusive powers, in this case the EU	If exclusive, the treaty rule cannot be undone by the test If shared, the test can be applied
2	The need to act together occurs if regulation at the national level is either ineffective or too expensive because of scale of externalities	If one criterion (or both) applies (apply); there is a 'need to act' in common
3	Evaluate whether shared action could avoid centralisation at the exclusive power for instance by cooperative action among some or all Member States coordination, joint acceptance of constraints on national regulation	Non-centralised common action retains some national powers, hence it is preferred, provided it is • feasible • adequate • durable If not, non-centralisation is not credible to market players and will not solve the issue, while inducing costs (e.g. uncertainty)
4	Centralisation at the EU level is justified, if previous stage is not credible	

Source: Springer Pelkmans (2012, p. 11)

extent they should be limited and in which cases there is no justification for government intervention (Sauter, 2013). However, Harbo (2010) states that it is the mechanism by which judicial decisions are legitimised, whereas Portuese (2013) proposes that it is a principle employed to maximise efficiency, because it focuses on overcoming market failures. The Principle accomplishes this objective by considering the public expenditure involved in projects and has the purpose of determining the balance between intervention in the public interest and restricting the freedom of individuals and groups. Since market failures, such as those associated with public goods or with monopolistic and oligopolistic power, can have high cost, these costs must be appraised with regard to the cost of managing or regulating them (Portuese, 2013).

The Proportionality Principle applies to the EU, to each Member State and to matters including competition law, so that Sauter (2013) perceives attempting to define the scope of the Principle, and of what it comprises, is extremely difficult especially as it must consider competing principles; it is considered ideal for resolving disputes by some groups, whilst others suggest that it has no meaning. In legal terms, Proportionality refers to balancing that enables the diverse rights and principles of a number of groups to be considered, and constitutional judgements to be made, which will only have validity if balance is demonstrated; balancing contravenes liberty so that a justified reason is crucial (Alexy, 2002). Proportionality has its origins in French and German laws, and in EU law is based on three precepts (Portuese, 2013), the cost or value of intervening in the interest of individuals, taking full account of public interest, and public interest concerns as sufficient to reduce the rights of the individual (Sauter, 2013). In relation to EU Member States, Proportionality emerged as they assumed responsibility for the rule of law and were responsible for balancing individual freedom with the public interest. However, this changed when the EEC treaty was originally signed; it legally limited the sovereign rights of the Member States and their citizens, which have gradually been eroded by subsequent developments, including the requirement to enforce EU law in national courts and to establish its principles with regard to individual rights and proportionality. The EEC treaty committed Member States to invoke free competition between them and the Maastricht Treaty in 1993 initiated the principle of free movement of people and EU citizenship. The Charter of Fundamental Rights was implemented later and states what is meant by the term individual rights, including the definitions of third-generation rights, for instance, data protection and bioethics (EU, 2010). The Principle of Proportionality is the most important innovation as the basis of governance since the EU became legally integrated, according to Sauter (2013), because it enables the EU to define EU law, its scope and limitations and how diverse rights and principles can be balanced but it fails to question the competence within the EU to conduct balancing.

Proportionality is explained by Pelkmans (2012) as applied in two distinct ways to actions relating to the EU and to those of Member States; the consistency of the actions with regard to EU law is appraised in each case. However, the test is considered to be substantially different in each case. The appraisal of consistency of action is determined by the degree to which policies are centralised at the EU level, as sometimes member nations will have negotiated national public policy exceptions (Pelkmans, 2006). Similarly, the strictness of the test to which EU measures are subjected depends in part on whether common policies are involved. However, tests also exist regarding individual rights, in which a Member State may be overruled by EU law regarding individual preference, for instance, crossing borders for the purpose of healthcare treatment (Sauter, 2013).

The EU Level Proportionality test has four parts that also determine necessity: the measure taken is appropriate; its purpose is legitimate; the measure taken is the least restrictive effective means; the cost versus benefit is not overtly disproportionate. When the relevant power is with the EU, it uses its discretion but not all of these steps are applied in practice, and often either the last or third forms part of the test. There is no requirement for the proportionality test to consider public interest when applied to Member States, but it must be focused on what is essential, and not go beyond what is absolutely required, such that it could be replaced by another less restrictive intervention. However, if the proposed intervention by an individual Member State has a highly negative effect on trade between community states, when taken in the context of its purpose, it would have to be eliminated (Pelkmans, 2006; Harbo, 2010). On examination of EU rulings, Sauter (2013) suggested that the use of the least restrictive means test was rarely applied at the EU level, and similarly the excessively disproportionate test was used infrequently. The case in which an intervention was considered regarding manufacturers providing details to consumers of the exact composition of animal feedstuffs, to ensure there was no chance of contaminating the food cycle, is an example cited by Sauter (2013); this was overthrown by the concern that manufacturers would be required to disclose secret composition, which would have a higher economic impact on them. In relation to legal judgements made by the European Court of Justice, Harbo (2010) found there was a huge variation in how the Proportionality Principle was applied, and that often there appeared to be no logical approach. In practical terms, the EC employs the Proportionality Principle for reviewing EU legislation and for defining EU policy, in terms of degree of intervention in areas such as consumer protection regulation, international anti-terrorism policy, health, advertising including that relating to demerit goods such as tobacco, as well as agricultural, environmental and social policies (Portuese, 2013).

EU Government Intervention in the Market

Monetary and Fiscal Policies

The Euro is the common currency of 17 EU countries or of the 331 million people within the countries that are members of the Eurozone. This characteristic makes the Euro one of the most important global currencies and is a key achievement of the EU, according to EC (2015b). In the Eurozone, the EMU initially controlled monetary policy, whilst the Member States had sovereignty over their fiscal policies. This division of responsibility implied that Member States could shape their fiscal policies in a way that negatively affected people living in other member countries. Therefore, EU intervention to coordinate national fiscal policies with EU-directed monetary policy was considered necessary; three types of coordination policy were devised, referred to as the soft, hard and unified regimes. The soft coordinated regime had the purpose of encouraging appropriate Member State behaviour and was applied to social policies by employing interventions, such as discussion, monitoring, peer reviews and cautionary advice. In contrast, the hard coordinated regime related to the national fiscal policies, which employed similar interventions to those of soft coordination, but also added measures, for example appropriate budget planning and budget deficit limits, which form the basis of the Stability and Growth Pact (SGP) (Panico & Purificato, 2013; Buti et al., 2003). The unified regime concerns the organisation of monetary policy by the ECB and the central banks of the 27 nation states, which in combination form the European System of Central Banks (ESCB), and the Eurosystem, comprising EU and the 17 countries belonging to the EMU (Panico & Purificato, 2013). The Eurosystem actually takes the decisions on monetary policy and implements them according to the relevant treaties and European |law; the treaties include the Consolidated Treaties of the European Union, and law associated with ECB and ESCB (EU, 2011). This framework has the purpose of eliminating uncertainty for Member States in the Eurosystem about such decisions and their implementation, according to Panico and Purificato (2013).

Although the SGP is regarded as one of the pillars of the EMU and has been described as extremely innovative in terms of policy coordination, it has proved to be unpopular with academics and with other groups having influence on public opinion from inception. The SGP is compared with the Bretton Woods system (Buti et al., 2003) devised in 1944, a framework for economic cooperation and development from which the IMF and the World Bank (WB) emerged. The rigidity of the procyclical SGP rules, for instance, raising interest rates in boom times and lowering them in economic downturns could not allow for the variations in the needs of different member country economies with diverse growth potentials (Kaminsky et al., 2004). In addition, Buti et al. (2003) stressed that this rigidity caused some member countries to operate outside the required budget deficit limit in 2001, and this resulted in EU sanctions being applied but never actually being enforced (Jonung & Larch, 2006). Hence, at that time it was suggested that the ESCB needed to be revised to allow individual nations some capacity for country-specific conditions, which might result in the Member States being more compliant with the SGP, owing to the higher flexibility permitted (Buti et al., 2003).

Setting Monetary Policy

The ESCB governing council comprising members of the ECB and governors of national central banks of Eurozone countries defines monetary policy and its objectives, and does so by making formal decisions and rules for implementing them, for instance, managing interest rates and the supply of reserves. The executive board of the ECB is responsible for implementing these monetary interventions, and national central banks must carry them out or be subject to sanctions by the ECB (EU, 2011).

The role of the ECB is to stabilise prices and maintain inflation below 2% in the medium term, where inflation is defined as a Harmonised Index relating to Consumer Prices (HICP) across EU Member States. The inflation rate is the method of assessing price stability used by the governing council and trends in inflation since 2000 demonstrate the effectiveness of the policy. Prior to the 2007/2008 financial crisis, the EU inflation rate was generally higher than 2% and rose steeply between 2007 and mid-2009 (Fig. 5.2, ECB, 2015a). According to ECB (2008), price stability was the most vital purpose of its monetary policy, as this was the route to economic growth and social stability. Price stability was promoted as generating positive improvements in labour markets through job creation and would lead to higher overall levels of affluence in the group. However, this was a medium-term objective and, therefore, inflation must be managed over a longer term, not merely in the short term. The inflation review in the same report (ECB, 2008 suggests that inflation policy had been very successful, since it had been much lower than the average annual rates of

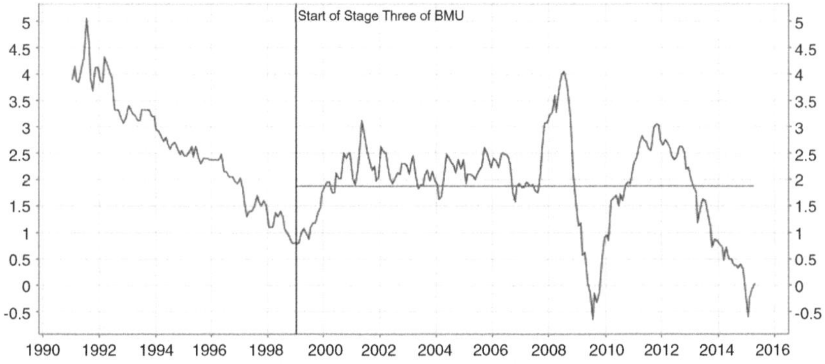

Fig. 5.2 Inflation rate trends EU 1990–2015. (Source: ECB (2015a))

individual Eurozone member countries before they joined the Euro (Fig. 5.2).

When national banks required liquidity support, it was available by means of their national central bank and according to monetary policy procedures, but also through an emergency liquidity procedure, which is not regarded as part of the single monetary policy operations. Emergency Liquidity Assistance (ELA) funds are those provided by the national central bank of the Eurozone member, to one or a group of solvent financial institutions with temporary liquidity issues, and/or other assistance that it could give that could lead to an increase in central bank money supply (ECB, 2015b); any risks arising from such assistance are stated to be the concern of the national bank providing the funds. The national central bank must inform the ECB of any ELA granted within two days of it being completed, accompanied by a long list of information regarding the loan, for instance, the collateral for the loan, its value, maturity date and the interest rate agreed, as well as the reasons for granting the loan. However, ELA is only permitted by ESCB if it is regarded as not hindering the objectives of the Eurosystem, and in cases where ELA would be considered to conflict with Eurosystem objectives, the specific ELA would be subject to a vote of at least two-thirds of the governing council in favour of granting it. There are other specific conditions relating to limits exceeding €500 million and also at the €2 billion level (ECB 2015b). Therefore, the ECB does not act as the lender of last choice, as happens in other countries, for instance the US and the UK, where the central banks,

Federal Reserve and Bank of England, respectively, have the ability to create money, as they are not subject to profit making. This banker of last resort is an EU principle that is invoked as required (Herr, 2014).

Fiscal Policy Intervention

Fiscal policy coordination is initiated by the EC, and its Economic and Financial Committee (ECOFIN) is responsible for environmental analysis. However, ECOFIN, composed of economic and finance ministers from the 27 Member States plus EC and ECB representatives, makes formal decisions as to how Member State fiscal policies are coordinated. In reality, the Member States could choose to disregard ECOFIN's supranational formal decisions on fiscal policies, since no real sanctions were taken in the original agreements, unlike monetary policy in which Member States can be forced to comply (Panico & Purificato, 2013). However, the Lisbon Treaty in 2007, which was due to come into force in 2009, modified the Excessive Debt Procedure (EDP) so that decisions regarding non-compliance by members of the Eurozone were taken only by those countries, and without the non-compliant Member State being involved in the decision making (ECB, 2008).

The review of fiscal policy by ECB (2008) found that its success varied, with some countries yet to achieve targeted outcomes, and to create policies that reduced their level of government debt, the consolidation of public finances in periods of economic boom had not taken place in these countries and remained a concern. Since fiscal and monetary policies were linked, lax fiscal policies that affected the ECB's capacity to manage the inflationary target were considered undesirable. The ECB demanded that monetary policy must take precedence over an individual member country's budgetary deficit and that in the extreme situation, the fiscal authority was forced to default on outstanding debt, monetary policy must be protected through a no bailout clause (ECB, 2008). If one Member State increased its public debt and did not redress the situation by increasing its taxes, all EU members were affected by the threat to price stability. Therefore, fiscal policy should be based on long-term fiscal sustainability, instead of being short term focused and influenced by events such as Member State elections. The ECB stressed that many Eurozone countries still had unacceptable public expenditure and taxation that must be managed, in order to align with the price stability goals of monetary policy (ECB, 2008). Several Member States were identified as failing to meet even the minimum requirements set by the EU and if a moderate economic crisis were to occur they were likely to return to excessive deficit levels. The deficits and the underlying reasons for them were the subject of a study by Jonung and Larch (2006), who concluded that several factors operating in Euro Member States were responsible, for example, over optimistic economic growth forecasts, which led to avoidance of economic reform by either taking no action or delaying it, the influence of elections, the structure of budgetary institutions and impending elections.

Intervention in Banks

The EU intervention in banking and financial services was driven by the need to ensure economic growth, which bank failure would threaten (Cariboni et al., 2010). An example of EU intervention in the financial services sector was the EU Directive 94/19/EC intended to protect the deposits of bank clients up to the sum of €20,000, and was applicable to all EU members; however, there was discretion on how the Directive was implemented so that huge variations existed. From 2005–2006, this Directive was reviewed, and recommendations were made by the EC about self-regulatory arrangements, accompanied by a review of the different ways in which the original Directive had been implemented. The purpose of the review was to monitor whether some procedures impeded fast action for clients when financial institutions failed (Cariboni et al., 2010). The second banking coordination Directive in 1992 allowed banks within the EU Member States to open branches in other states, using the procedures and processes adopted in the home country, and based on licences provided by the home country. Identical financial services, investment services and investment funds could be offered to those available in the home country. But it was mandatory that subsidiaries be supervised by the home country. The supervision of the subsidiary by the home country was limited in terms of staff and incentives, so that generally it was weak and the host country showed little capacity for their supervision. The huge issues that had occurred in financial service in Iceland were cited to be consequence of similar lack of supervision. Branches of EU Member State banks had expanded but compliance with the EU legislation to protect bank deposits was ignored, so that the host countries were implicated when the bank failed.

In so far as official regulation was concerned, the Committee of European Banking Supervisors (CEBS), the Committee of European

Insurance and Occupational Pensions Supervisors (CEIOPS) and Committee of European Securities Regulators (CESR), level 3 Committees, had been created by the EC to assist with legislative initiatives on regulation, in order to drive cross-national information exchange and to strengthen enforcement of legal compliance. Banks were subject to the Basel II agreement and the associated Capital Requirements Directive (CRD), the implementation mechanism (Konoe, 2010). An independent report by Stichele (2008) commented on the fragmented regulation and supervision of financial services within the EU, and noted the risky financial instruments being sold. The core purpose of the legislation to encourage cross-border financial services was to increase the global competitiveness of the financial services sector and to reduce costs. The legislation was influenced by observing some sectors of the US financial services industry that contributed substantially to the economy, such as investment banking; an opportunity for economic growth (Stichele, 2008). In reference to the three committees, which all contributed to development of the EU directives on financial services and markets and had overlapping responsibilities, Stichele (2008) proposed that the regulation for the decision-making process to coordinate and harmonise financial regulation and supervision was complex. ECOFIN and the Economic and Monetary Affairs Committee were also involved in the decision-making process of these Directives. However, the financial services industry had an extensive, strong formal and informal lobbying presence and academic and financial experts, who were cautious about the looser regulation, had their warnings dismissed; consumers also had minor influence in any decisions on the sector regulation and supervision. Since the implementation of the financial services sector supervision was the responsibility of the Member States, and no EU wide supervisory framework had been imposed, the agreements in place were voluntary rather than mandatory. Regulatory costs and supervision were considered risky to the competitiveness of the financial services industry in member countries. The ECB did not participate in the regulation or supervision of the financial services industry, and Stichele (2008) states that its role was primarily financial stability.

Intervention by Means of Taxation, Subsidies and Regulation

A study by Gaul and Jodar (2006) reported that state aid to industry by means of taxation and subsidies was a major EU initiative to drive efficiency and hence economic growth. However, the nature of this support, which was contained in EU Industrial Policy, was more restricted on an internal EU basis than in a sovereign state. Industrial policy focused on the causes of market failure, such as market power, externalities and public goods, and regarded Research and Development (R&D) as a positive externality in which it could intervene to achieve overall EU goals. The intervention was implemented by providing incentives to small- and medium-sized firms across all countries to innovate and considered necessary because banks were deterred from lending to such firms for R&D purposes, owing to asymmetric information regarding them. Consequently, EU Member States were able to focus their policies on nationally important industrial sectors. An additional intervention was to encourage firms to form industrial clusters for enhancing levels of innovation because information gaps in individual countries might prevent firms from considering this solution and/or knowing how to organise and fund it. The EU had previously intervened to set national standards for mobile phones, by making GSM technology mandatory throughout Europe, and this intervention was considered to account for greater speed of adoption of mobile phones than in other parts of the world. The major objective of the EU state aid policy was regulatory so that it was able to monitor the actions of member countries to ensure that national industrial policies did not negatively impact on market competition and trade within the EU or cause a war over subsidies; providing support to industry was the means to accomplishing this objective. The associated categories of state aid were specified in Articles 87 and 89 of the Treaty of Amsterdam (Gaul & Jodar, 2006); this Treaty also incorporated discretionary exceptions, for example in Article 87(3) cases of very high unemployment, culture and heritage conservation and serious economic change. Certain sectors were considered sensitive, for example fisheries and agriculture, coal and steel, and those that recently experienced high competition, as exemplified by financial services; the importance of manufacturing and R&D to the EU was also stressed by Allen et al. (2006). Therefore, these interventions were core EC industrial policy; technology development, standard setting and purchase of public goods driven by the EU, in cases in which market failure conditions would have an economic impact (Gaul & Jodar, 2006). However, Pelkmans (2012) states that regulation is the core feature of EU intervention and Principles of Subsidiarity and Proportionality employed in its implementation. EU regulation necessarily involves Member States making some adaptations to national regulations. The EU framework for regulation and intervention is a five-stage process (Table 5.2).

Table 5.2 EU regulation framework

Box 1: Proper economic framework for EU regulation. Why intervene?
- Identify market failures and the benefits of their removal
- If beneficial effects are non-trivial and
- If market-based incentives or cooperative solutions are impossible

At what level?
- Subsidiarity test
- Explicitly consider cooperative (but credible) solution among member states
- Consider two-levels solutions, if appropriate

What instruments are available?
- Constraints at EU level
- National or EU subsidies sometimes; or taxes at national level
- Usually regulation, including economic instruments

Least-cost regulation
- Minimize costs of centralization
- Minimize degree of binding, where possible
- Consider different types of regulatory solutions

Maximize net benefits
- Assess options as to effectiveness
- Use appropriate analytical tool (e.g. models, cost-benefit analysis, etc…)

Source: Springer; Pelkmans (2012, p. 5)

The application of this procedure enabled the internal market to be appraised for regulation, creating common approaches across Member States, and assessing what that regulation should be, if it was deemed a requirement. However, liberalisation that creates freer markets between Member States is also an intervention within the range available in the EU environment. Member States had to prove their capacity to deal with specific market failures, in order to avoid EU internal market intervention.

EU regulations focus on risks regarding health, transport and industrial equipment safety, consumer protection, the environment, food, chemicals and pharmaceuticals and financial markets. However, Pelkmans (2012) states that the biggest challenge for the EU is to avoid overregulation that is too rigid, too wide and too costly to enforce, which is the reason for regulation being focused on technical standards. In contrast, high-risk products and services attract a command and control approach, for instance food risk and certain types of environmental damage. In the case of emissions, incentivisation was the approach as demonstrated by the EU Emissions Trading Policy. The EU intervention strategy has been to maximise outputs while minimising costs, which the five-stage process accomplishes (Pelkmans, 2012).

EU competition law is employed extensively with the purpose of reducing monopoly and oligopoly power and accomplished by means of several interventions, to support consumer interests relating to fair prices and sufficient choice. The EC monitors businesses to ensure that collusion between firms to form cartels is detected, and so that mergers and acquisition do not give organisations a dominant market position by lowering competition. However, the EU also proactively promotes competition by liberalising services, for example traditional nationalised industries, such as telecoms and postal services, and collaborates with national competition agencies in member countries to ensure that EU competition law is applied homogeneously (EC, 2015c).

Intervention in Labour Markets

The implementation of a single monetary policy across Eurozone members is cited by Bean (1998) as inferring that the EU should intervene in labour markets, and reform them to create greater flexibility, because Eurozone Member States no longer have the option of devaluing their currencies when macroeconomic shocks affect their economies. The extent of these shocks was considered likely to be low in economic unions characterised by: high integration relating to trade and services; similar production structures and business cycles; nominal wage policies implemented; high labour force mobility and/or high price flexibility. At the time the EMU was formed, none of these characteristics was common but monetary integration was expected to lower the diversity in business cycles through lower foreign transaction costs owing to common currency, and compulsory competitive tendering, for instance (Bean, 1998). The types of reform required are exemplified by considering the high unemployment rates within EU member countries: lowering unemployment benefits to reduce government spending; reducing the cost of redundancies that allowed firms with excessive employees to restructure; encourage Member States to reduce labour rates and business taxes to provide firms with incentives to locate there and/or start new ventures. The EC introduced a labour reform strategy in 2006, referred to as flexicurity, to effect such change and it had the purpose of benefitting employers and employees in terms of flexibility of labour practices for employers, whilst providing income security for employees. The principles and formula for flexicurity were devised by the EC, and member countries were responsible for adapting the details to their specific labour market features. The EC commission specified four methodologies for policy design and implementation: contracts that embraced flexible but secure policies; active labour market policies that made transition to the flexicurity policies effective, in other words security regarding changing jobs; implementing life-long learning approaches that were systematic and correlated with workplace career needs; social security policies that matched modern labour conditions and that drove labour mobility in the employment market, including supporting the unemployed to get back into work (Bekker & Wilthagen, 2008). The EU continues to use this strategy with a long-term goal of 75% employed by 2020 and states that the main measures to accomplish this are to strengthen the four principles on which it is based, by ensuring that people of working age have the skills that match future job opportunities, ensuring working conditions improve and encouraging states to devise strategies to create more jobs. There was also focus on young people acquiring the requisite qualifications, skills and experience, and adopting mobility as a prerequisite for gaining employment; all underpinned by better publicly funded employment services for finding jobs and supporting career development. The EC monitors progress in the success of flexicurity policies by visiting the parties involved in delivering within individual Member States and discussing progress with them (EC, 2015c).

Bibliography

Abdymomunov, A., & Kang, K. H. (2015). The Effects of Monetary Policy Regime Shifts on the Term Structure of Interest Rates. *Studies in Nonlinear Dynamics & Econometrics, 19*(2), 183–207.

Aikins, S. K. (2009). Political Economy of Government Intervention in the Free Market System. *Administrative Theory and Praxis, 31*(3), 403–408.

Alexy, R. (2002). *A Theory of Constitutional Rights.* Oxford University Press.

Allen, C., Herbert, D., & Koopman, G. (2006). The European Commission's New Industrial Policy. *BIG Papers, 11*(2), 135–143.

Bean, C. (1998). The Interaction of Aggregate-Demand Policies and Labour Market Reform. *Swedish Economic Policy Review, 5*(2), 353–382.

Bekker, S., & Wilthagen, T. (2008, March/April). Flexicurity – a European Approach to Labour Market Policy. *Intereconomics*, pp. 68–111.

Blakely, J. (2019). How Economics Becomes Ideology: The Uses and Abuses of Rational Choice Theory. In P. Rona & L. Zsolnai (Eds.), *Agency and Causal Explanation in Economics* (pp. 37–52). Springer.

Boettke, P. J., & Coyne, C. J. (2011). The Debt–Inflation Cycle and the Global Financial Crisis. *Global Policy, 2*(2), 184–189.

Buck, G. (2017, May 31). *EU Agrees Measures to Revive Asset-Backed Securities Market.* The Global Treasurer. https://www.theglobaltreasurer.com/2017/05/31/eu-agrees-measures-to-revive-asset-backed-securities-market. Accessed 12 Aug 2018.

Bullard, J. (2012, March/April). Death of a Theory. *Federal Reserve Bank of St. Louis Review*, pp. 83–104.

Buti, M., Eijffinger, S. C. W., & Franco, D. (2003). *Revisiting the Stability and Growth Pact: Grand Design or Internal Adjustment?* (CEPR Discussion Paper No. 3692).

Cariboni, J., Joossens, E., & Uboldi, A. (2010). The Promptness of European Deposit Protection Schemes to Face Banking Failures. *Journal of Banking Regulation, 11*, 191–209.

De Grauwe, P. (2015, January 21). The Sad Consequences of the Fear of QE. *The Economist.*

EC. (2015a). *Flexicurity.* European Commission. http://ec.europa.eu/social/main.jsp?catId=102. Accessed 24 May 2015.

EC. (2015b). *The Euro.* European Commission. http://ec.europa.eu/euro/index_en.html. Accessed 25 May 2015.

EC. (2015c). *What Is Competition Policy?* European Commission. http://ec.europa.eu/competition/consumers/what_en.html. Accessed 26 May 2015.

ECB. (2008, July). One Monetary Policy and Many Fiscal Policies: Ensuring a Smooth Functioning of EMU. *ECB Monthly Bulletin*, pp. 65–78.

ECB. (2015a). Monetary Policy. *ECB.* https://www.ecb.europa.eu/mopo/html/index.en.html. Accessed 24 May 2015.

ECB. (2015b). Emergency Liquidity Assistance (ELA) and Monetary Policy. *ECB.* https://www.ecb.europa.eu/mopo/ela/html/index.en.html

Engelen, E., & Glasmacher, A. (2018). The Waiting Game: How Securitization Became the Solution for the Growth Problem of the Eurozone. *Competition & Change, 22*(2), 165–183.

EU. (2010). *EU Charter of Fundamental Rights.* Brussels.

EU. (2011). *Institutional Provisions.* Brussels.

Fawley, R. W., & Neely, C. J. (2013, January/February). Four Stories of Quantitative Easing. *Federal Reserve Bank of St. Louis Review.*

Federal Reserve System. (2017). *Open Market Operations.* Federal Reserve System. https://www.Federalre-serve.gov/monetarypolicy/openmarket.htm. Accessed 15 Aug 2018.

Galinato, G. I., & Yoder, J. K. (2010). An Integrated Tax-Subsidy Policy for Carbon Emission Reduction. *Resource and Energy Economics, 32*(3), 310–326.

Gaul, J., & Jodar, S. (2006). Vertical Industrial Policy in the EU: An Empirical Analysis of Effectiveness of State Aid. *EIB Papers, 11*(2), 81–105.

Giles, C., & Jones, C. (2017, June 5). Eurozone Recovery Becomes Surprise Economic Story of 2017. *Financial Times*. https://www.ft.com/content/8db37b0a-46be-11e7-8519-9f94ee97d996. Accessed 13 Aug 2018.
Golbu, J. (1996). Sovereignty and Subsidiarity in EU Environmental Policy. *Political Studies, XLIV*, 686–703.
Harbo, T. (2010). The Function of the Proportionality Principle in EU Law. *European Law Journal, 16*(2), 158–185.
Hausken, K., & Ncube, M. (2013). *Quantitative Easing and Its Impact in the US, Japan, the UK and Europe*. Springer.
Herr, H. (2014). The European Central Bank and the US Federal Reserve as Lender of Last Resort. *Panoeconomicus, 1*(S), 59–78.
HM Treasury. (2013). *Review of the Monetary Policy Framework*. H.M. Treasury.
Hohberger, S., Priftis, R., & Vogel, L. (2018). *The Macroeconomic Effects of Quantitative Easing in the Euro Area: Evidence from an Estimated DSGE Model*. Bank of Canada.
Jonung, L., & Larch, M. (2006, July). Improving Fiscal Policy in the EU: The Case for Independent Forecasts. *Economic Policy*, pp. 491–534.
Joskow, P. L., & Rose, N. L. (1989). The Effects of Economic Regulation. In R. Schamalensee & R. D. Willig (Eds.), *Handbook of Industrial Organization* (Vol. 11, pp. 1449–1506). North Holland.
Kaminsky, G., Reinhart, C., & Vegh, C. (2004). *When It Rains, It Pours: Procyclical Capital Flows and Macroeconomic Policies* (NBER Working Paper No. 10780).
Konoe, S. (2010). *International Finance and Policy Cooperation: Before and After the 2007–2010 Financial Crisis* (EUI Working Paper MWP 2010/24).
Lipsey, R., & Chrystal, A. (2015). *Economics* (13th ed.). Oxford University Press.
Look, C. (2019, July 25). *ECB Signals Rate Cut, QE as Global Stimulus Push Picks Up*. Bloomberg. https://www.bloomberg.com/news/articles/2019-07-25/ecb-signals-rate-cut-qe-ahead-as-global-stimulus-push-picks-up. Accessed 28 July 2019.
Mariathasan, J. (2018). *Euro-Zone: What Comes After QE?* IPE International Publishers Ltd. https://www.ipe.com/investment/asset-class-reports/government-bonds/euro-zone-what-comes-after-qe/10025514.article. Accessed 13 Aug 2018.
MGM. (2018, December 27). *US vs EU – A GDP Comparison*. MGM Research. https://mgmresearch.com/us-vs-eu-a-gdp-comparison/. Accessed 26 July 2019.
Musgrave, R. A. (1987/88). US Fiscal Policy, Keynes and Keynesian Economics. *Journal of Post Keynesian Economics, X*(2), 171–183.
OECD. (2001). *Command-and-Control Policy*. OECD. Available at: https://stats.oecd.org/glossary/detail.asp?ID=383. Accessed 24 May 2015.
OECD. (2009). *Competition in Financial Markets*. OECD.

OFT. (2014). *Office of Fair Trading*. GOVUK. https://www.gov.uk/government/organisations/office-of-fair-trading. Accessed 24 May 2015.

Panico, C., & Purificato, F. (2013). Policy Coordination, Conflicting National Interests and the European Debt Crisis. *Cambridge Journal of Economics, 37*, 585–608.

Pelkmans, J. (2006, October). An EU Subsidiarity Test Is Indispensable. *Intereconomics*, pp. 249–254.

Pelkmans, J. (2012). The Economics of Single Market Regulation. *Bruges European Economic Policy Briefings, 25*(12), 1–39.

Phelan, S., & Dawes, S. (2018). Liberalism and Neoliberalism. In *Oxford Research Encyclopedia, Communication*. Oxford University Press. https://oxfordre.com/communication/view/10.1093/acrefore/9780190228613.001.0001/acrefore-9780190228613-e-176?print=pdf. Accessed 24 Jan 2020.

Portuese, A. (2013). Principle of Proportionality as Principle of Economic Efficiency. *European Law Journal, 19*(5), 612–635.

Poterba, J. M. (1994). *Government Intervention in the Markets for Education and Health Care: How and Why?* (NFER Working Paper No. 4916).

Poto, M. (2009). Principle of Proportionality in Comparative Perspective. *German Law Journal, 8*, 835–870.

Rudd, K. (2009). The Global Financial Crisis. *The Monthly, 13*(42), 14.

Sauter, W. (2013). Proportionality in EU Law: A Balancing Act? In C. Barnard, A. Albors-Llorenc, M. W. Gehring, & R. Schütze (Eds.), *Cambridge Yearbook of European Legal Studies 2012–2013* (pp. 439–466). Hart Publishing.

Scaberd, A., & van Wijnbergen, S. J. G. (2014). Sovereign Default and the Stability of Inflation-Targeting Regimes. *IMF Economic Review, 62*(2), 1–28.

Sloman, J., Garrett, D., & Guest, J. (2018). *Economics* (10th ed.). Pearson.

Stichele, M. V. (2008). *Financial Regulation in the European Union*. World Economics, Environment & Development Association.

Stoain, A. (2013). Influences of the Principle of Subsidiarity in the Activity of the Public Administration. *Social-Behavioural Sciences, 4*(72), 383–482.

Syrpis, P. (2004). In Defence of Subsidiarity. *Oxford Journal of Legal Studies, 24*(2), 332–334.

Tirole, J., & Rendell, S. (2017). *Economics for the Common Good*. Princeton University Press.

van Doren, P. (2000, May 1). Strangulation by Regulation. *National Review*, pp. 43–47.

Wearden, G. (2015, June 29). Greek Crisis: Banks Shut for a Week as Capital Controls Imposed – As It Happened. *The Guardian*. http://www.theguardian.com/business/live/2015/jun/28/greek-crisis-ecb-emergency-liquidity-referendum-bailout-live. Accessed 16 July 2015.

Winston, C. (2006). *Government Failure v Market Failure*. AEI-Brookings Joint Center for Regulatory Studies.

Wolf, C. (1993). *Markets or Governments: Choosing Between Imperfect Alternatives* (2nd ed.). Rand Books.
Wolf, M. (2012, March 6). The Pain in Spain Will Test the Euro. *Financial Times.* http://www.ft.com/intl/cms/s/0/f54332d2-66dc-11e1-9e53-00144feabdc0.html#axzz3dEXYMemL. Accessed 17 June 2015.
Wolff, R. D., & Resick, S. A. (2012). *Contending Economic Theories: Neoclassical, Keynesian, and Marxian*. MIT Press.
Zerbe, R. O., & Mc Curdy, H. E. (1999). The Failure of Market Failure. *Journal of Policy Analysis and Management, 18*(2), 558–578.

CHAPTER 6

Overview of EU Responses to the Global Economic Crisis

Introduction

This chapter appraises, in outline, the measures that the EU took to ensure financial stability, growth and employment after the global financial crisis emerged in 2007–2008. It also considers the interventions regarding corporate governance to enhance protection again risk that a similar crisis would occur in the future. The emphasis of this chapter relates to the context of the legal framework and ESFS; further chapters then evaluate the measures taken for financial stability, economic growth and employment, in greater detail. The EU actions towards the crisis in Greece, which occurred in 2015, are included in this chapter as a case study example of the EU's more recent actions. These EU responses have significant relevance to the research question and to the implementation of EU measures. The responses also expose conditions under which support is granted or not, and their implications regarding proportionality, which this study appraises.

Overview of EU Response to the 2007–2008 Crisis

A major reason for the global crisis resulting in financial losses was that nations failed to understand the interconnectedness of their financial systems in a global context. They also failed to realise that the impact of the crisis was not equal across different world regions, in terms of the severity

S. Weißschnur, *The Proportionality of State Intervention*,
https://doi.org/10.1007/978-3-030-75676-5_6

of decline in demand and the length of the recession, according to Konoe (2010). Europe was more affected by financial loss than any other world region except for the US; the annual average bank write-downs across the EU amounted to 4.6%, and were generally higher for non-Eurozone members at an average of 5.1%, than for Eurozone members which experienced an average of 3.6% (Konoe, 2010; IMF, 2009). The study by Barnard (2012) found that the EC's response to the crisis could be categorised into four main strategies: financial reform to monitor the banking sector and changes to legislation, including the amount of capital funding retained and the level of deposit guarantees; establishing a financial stabilisation programme, which would support granting funds to Member States, based on the issuance of debt instruments in capital markets; enhancing economic governance by overseeing Member State budgets, focused particularly on EMU Member States; measures to generate economic growth, which impacted on employment. The fourth strategy regarding economic growth was the least developed of the four, according to Barnard (2012). This four-part perception of the EC reaction to the crisis sets a framework for this chapter, although the interrelationship of the measures often makes it difficult to effectively categorise them in the way Barnard (2012) suggests; this researcher has attempted to appraise the diverse interventions as logically as possible.

Financial Reform

The financial reforms were based on creating a new European banking authority and a programme for recapitalising the banks, as well as redefining the amount of capital that must be retained by the banks, securitisation and risk, commission and reward guidelines to reduce risk/fraud by employees, in addition to raising deposit guarantees up to €100,000 (Barnard, 2012). In December 2008, the EU stated that it had devised a European Economic Recovery Plan, and intervened in the banking sector, in an attempt to stabilise it, so as to restore to its previous levels and to devise bank reform (EC, 2009). However, Dieter (2009) suggested that the initial EU reaction to the crisis had been one of complacency, led by the stronger Member States, such as Germany and France, and later followed by implementation of measures that had been decided and implemented in a fragmentary and hasty manner and lacked a coherent strategy. Consequently, the challenges of managing the crisis were not attempted in an effective manner for more than two years after it had occurred; one of these quickly enforced measures was the initial deposit guarantee scheme. In 2008, national provisions were the only type of bank deposit guarantee levels in force, with wide variations in the speed of pay out and processes to enable banks to continue trading. Consequently, deposit flow from countries with poor guarantees to those with robust ones was possible, and intra-country deposit flows from banks with headquarters in other countries that offered poor guarantees to those with better terms. The potential financial instability driven by Ireland guaranteeing 100% of all bank deposits after the crisis, setting a precedent that other countries could either not match, or wish to match, forced the EU to quickly react to stem negative consequences for other Member States: ECOFIN reacted to suggest a new higher guarantee scheme across the EU within three working days of Ireland's announcement (Pisani-Ferry & Sapir, 2009). This intervention demonstrates that the stronger Member States initially collaborated in an attempt to resolve the situation without supranational EU involvement as an intergovernmentalist type of stance to protect their national interests (Hoffmann, 2000). The EU eventually applied the Principle of Subsidiarity in the context of its better capacity to resolve the crisis than leaving the matter to individual Member States (Buxbaum et al., 2011). In fact, prior to the crisis doubts had been raised regarding the EU's capacity to manage liquidity and solvency in the region, according to Pisani-Ferry and Sapir (2009). There were no robust guidelines for bank liquidity levels or plans to install a banker of last resort in cases in which the national banks throughout the EU faced difficulties. This was an omission in the Maastricht Treaty; it had failed to make provision for the ECB to take over the role of lender of last resort. Therefore, the ECB did not have the authority to supervise national banks or force them to provide confidential information and no provision for solvency issues existed, for instance to create processes for cross-border banking crises that might occur; in this case emphasis was placed on mechanisms for shared fiscal burden. In addition, no Treasury function had been implemented in the EU or Eurozone areas, which had the consequence that there was no resource pool available for potential lack of solvency, so that national treasuries were responsible for banks within their borders. However, banks operating across borders, namely pan-European banks, had no crisis resolution pathway available (Pisani-Ferry & Sapir, 2009). The former president of the Bank of International Settlements was quoted as referring to the EU arrangements at the time as being less than ideal (Pisani-Ferry & Sapir, 2009); the inference is that the EU considered that nation states had sufficient competence to manage their financial services appropriately.

After the 2007–2008 financial crisis, the EU acknowledged that there were substantial, very serious structural and practical weaknesses in existing monitoring mechanisms throughout the EU financial system, including those for Member State national financial institutions. This was exacerbated by the degree to which many of them operated on an international basis (NCA, 2015) and the IMF (2015a) report also cited cross-border lending as more sensitive to global economic shocks than local lending. The IMF emphasised that cross-border lending heightened the effect of the difficulties in obtaining credit from domestic sources; cross-border banks had expanded rapidly, and when they were threatened with insolvency, financial stability was endangered (Eisenbeis & Kaufman, 2007). The European Parliament amended the Capital Requirements Directive (CRD) in 2009, to ensure that banks held more capital, which reduced their exposure to risk, and instructed the EU to present its proposals regarding this matter by the end of 2009; these proposals were to include measures for cross-country integrated financial supervision throughout the EU. Therefore, the interconnectedness of European banks and financial markets, mentioned by Konoe (2010), was acknowledged by the European Commission after the crisis. In 2009 a supranational body, the European System of Financial Supervision (ESFS), was proposed to rectify the situation and the new institutional supervisory framework came into force in January 2011 (NCA, 2015). The IMF report in 2008 also recommended the creation of a new body to accomplish this integration, which is referred to as the European Systemic Risk Council (ESRC); it was later renamed the European Systemic Risk Board (ESRB) and supervised by the ECB. The ESRB came into force in December 2010, as an integral part of the ESFS.

The EU commissioned Jacques de Larosière to chair a high-level committee charged with the task of devising ESRB legislation; de Larosière was responsible for creating the IMF document which had recommended a systemic risk body. The legislation was based on consideration of how to strengthen European supervisory arrangements for rebuilding trust in the EU's financial system and focused on the supervision of individual firms and the stability of the entire financial system (ESRB, 2015). The purpose of the ESRB legislation was to provide macroprudential supervision of the whole financial system; it confirmed that the previous arrangements were regarded as too weak and fragmented to accomplish this. The legislation ensured that risks would be identified and warnings issued with recommendations for actions that should be taken to mitigate them and to create consistency between micro and macroprudential supervision (ESRB, 2010; Perrut, 2012). However, Buiter (2009) suggested that the ESRB was formed too quickly and that the general Board and committees, which made the decisions, were overly dominated by the ECB. The general ESRB Board consisted of 61 members, which Buiter (2009) proposed was too high to be effective and the voting rights structure meant that ECB members would always have the power to ensure their agenda was accepted. This situation was a consequence of the 12-person Steering Committee set up to support ESRB decision making having seven ECB members, the Board and Steering Committee having the same individual as chairperson, and the identity of this individual likely to be the ECB President. In addition, most of the Member State representatives were employees of their central bank, which inferred that the advisory technical committee was also dominated by ECB influence. The role of the central banks on this Board was highly tenuous because they lacked the technical knowledge, the tools and instruments, and the legitimacy to dominate a macroprudential financial stability framework of this nature according to Buiter (2009). Therefore, ESRB was stated to be dominated by individuals with no record of competence in the matters for which the Board was devised, since they had contributed to bank failure in their Member States but were being given responsibility for future macroprudential matters. Consequently Buiter (2009) suggested that empire building was the core reason for these individuals seeking membership of ESRB. The proposed structure did not include any central fiscal dimension related to financial stability, whereas fiscal bodies needed to have equal voting rights. The Board membership also lacked a mechanism for new expertise to be included and there was no industry and commerce representation. The membership structure of ESRB inferred that none of the accountability cited in the legislation was likely to be practised because ECB members would be unwilling to reprimand or dismiss other ECB members. In addition, no sanctions for incompetence or poor performance were included in the legislation (Buiter, 2009). However, Kaldor and Vizard (2011) suggested that the ESRB's role was merely advisory, to issue warnings and recommendations as the ESRB (2010) stated but no legal pathway existed for these warnings and recommendations to be made compulsory. This situation inferred that the Member States were not forced to implement the warnings and recommendations, but if they did not implement them, they were obliged to explain the reasons for non-compliance with the ESRB (Perrut, 2012). The two main instruments employed to minimise systemic risk under this new Board were capital and liquidity ratios, the percentage of a bank's capital as a proportion of its risk-weighted assets and the value of liquid assets; its liabilities were also taken into account. This liquidity coverage ratio reduces that capacity of Member State banks to provide short-term loans (EU, 2013). The ESRB was described as an independent body within the ESFS, and part of its supervisory function was to support the effective functioning of the EU market and to generate growth in the financial sector, which was a significant contributor to economic growth (Arestis & Sawyer, 2013). The ESRB's incapacity to assist Member States in a fiscal capacity, if they should experience an emergency situation, or to bail out banks was also highlighted by Arestis and Sawyer (2013).

The ESFS comprises six bodies including the ESRB, the remaining five being three European sector supervisory authorities, which were intended for microprudential supervision and known as ESAs, and the Joint Committee of the European Supervisory Authorities (JCESA) for microprudential supervision, and the national Member State supervisors. The three ESAs were the European Banking Authority (EBA), the European Insurance and Occupational Pensions Authority (EIOPA), the European Securities and Markets Authority (ESMA). These bodies are the competent or supervisory authorities for the banking, insurance and occupational pension sectors in the Member States and have the purpose of microprudential supervision of securities institutions and markets, as specified in the legislation when they were created (NCA, 2015). Although these three bodies were intended to be independent, they reported to political leaders and rarely used their power to enforce policies on financial institutions, possibly because the associated procedures were complex (Perrut, 2012). The new ESFS legislation, which was implemented as the ECB lowered interest rates, had the purpose of: reducing money market term rates, in order to encourage banks to increase lending to customers; improving market liquidity, particularly to key parts of the private debt funding sector; generating easier funding for banks and businesses. Quantitative Easing (QE) was simultaneously employed to enable these objectives to be met (Arestis & Sawyer, 2013); it is further appraised later in this chapter. Hence, the ESFS integrated EU and Member State level supervisory bodies, with the purpose of overseeing national bodies by monitoring their national financial institutions on a daily basis to instil a common supervisory culture (Perrut, 2012). In reality, the EU had increased its control on national competent authorities (NCA, 2015) in alignment with its interpretation of the Subsidiary Principle. These bodies had a second purpose, which was to resolve conflicts between organisations operating across Member State borders (Perrut, 2012). The increase of EU control in the financial services sector was also highlighted by Schmieding (2012), who proposed that the crisis had provided the EU with the opportunity to develop a more integrated Europe in a stepwise manner, and that the ECB had shown reluctance to manage the tensions this had created, as Member States were subjected to turmoil in their national markets.

The banking sector underwent further reform as a result of the Single Supervisory Mechanism (SSM) regulation, which came into force in November 2013. This resulted from the EC Development Plan for a banking union, which it had presented in 2012, with the purpose of EU-level supervision of all banks, a European deposit guarantee scheme and common regulations across all Member States, regarding the financial services industry. This further strengthened the EU's position as a supranational body which can be interpreted as increasing technocratic decision making in a neofunctionalist context (Niemann & Schmitter, 2009, p. 45). The ECB instigated its new supervisory responsibilities in 2014, which were to identify the risks that might threaten the viability of banks operating in the banking union with a balance sheet asset value of €30 billion or greater. These banks were obliged to conform with the ECB rules, which applied to the entire internal market, whilst the EBA retained its existing powers for developing and consistently applying the common legislation for financial services across all Member States, and reinforcing their supervisory practices (NCA, 2015).

The SSM also included the Bank Recovery and Resolution Directive (BRRD), introduced with the purpose of ensuring that banks and national authorities had made sufficient preparation for another crisis. This objective was accomplished by means of national authorities installing the tools to intervene rapidly in any bank being perceived as potentially failing at an early stage. It also provided for Member States to cooperate in the case of cross-border bank failure and for banks to make contributions to assist with bank restructuring costs. This Directive comprised four main elements: banks and national authorities devise recovery and resolution plans for financial stress or impending bank failure; banks implement changes to their legal and corporate structures to enable any potential failure to be resolved quickly, without use of taxpayer funding; official ECB bank supervisors have the power to intervene if the bank is likely to breach capital regulatory requirements, including dismissing bank management, installing own administration and devising debt restructuring plan with creditors; resolution of bank financial issues at minimal costs to the state and taxpayers, which can include the power to sell the institution, force a merger or implement a temporary bridging bank, for instance, to categorise bank assets and write down the debt of failing banks, referred to as bank bail-in. The concept of bank bail-in avoided the requirement for bail-out funding (EC, 2014).

The IMF suggested that SSM had improved the strength of banks, but had failed to manage asset quality, since more than €900 billion non-performing loans still existed in EU, and they needed to be written off because they would never be repaid. In addition, current legal frameworks for corporate and individual bankruptcies were inadequate. These factors impeded bank lending capacity and subsequently GDP growth. The ECB had direct supervisory control of the 120 most important banks, which held 85% of all Eurozone bank assets, but it also controlled 3500 smaller banks because their national competent authorities were subject to implementing compulsory controls (IMF, 2015a). The ECB could control these banks directly if a situation arose which had a systemic effect on the Euro. The IMF considered this centralisation of bank supervision effective in reducing the fragmentary nature of the Eurozone banking system, in ultimately transforming it to single market status, but that it lacked a fully effective fiscal backstop so that the links between banks and their sovereign governments could be reinstated, according to IMF (2015a).

The European Banking Union was described as strengthening the banking system by eliminating the potential for Member States to consider their national banking interests as more important than Eurozone combined interests, a tendency that was characteristic of economic crises (Schoenmaker, 2014), and highlighted by IMF (2015a). Therefore, the Banking Union eliminates the link between banks and national governments and perceived as better prepared to absorb externally generated shocks; the global crisis demonstrated that if the national bank was weak, the national fiscal system was negatively affected, for instance, in Spain and Ireland (Schoenmaker, 2014). This perception justified the EU's intervention in the banking sector.

Many of the financial regulations have been amended since 2011 to make sure that EFSF remains effective, for instance those relating to banks, insurance companies, financial markets and consumers as well as credit rating agencies, which are supervised by ESMA and strive to create higher levels of consumer and investor protection (NCA, 2015). These changes in EC regulation demonstrate how the EC has gradually gained significant control over the EU banking sector and reduced the sovereign power of Member States.

Financial Stabilisation

The initial fiscal stimulus injected into the economy had the purpose of supporting demand so that business and labour markets might revive (EC, 2009). However, the EC's Director General of Economic and Financial Affairs suggested that Member States would need to take measures to reduce their public debt, and to gradually withdraw the support given to financial institutions, in order to create growth (EC, 2009). The stimulus package was expected to generate the demand and growth in 2009 and 2010, and the EU allowed Member States, which complied with the request to fund the stimulus package to increase their budget deficits beyond the required 3% GDP (Tait, 2008). However, there was uncertainty about the wisdom of the stimulus package because of the expectation that the 27 Member States would provide the majority of the funding by means of national tax and infrastructure planning; opposition to the plan was received from Germany and Italy (Tait, 2008);

The EC instigated the European Financial Stability Facility (EFSF), which it described as a temporary measure, in June 2010, and intended to provide financial support to Ireland, Portugal and Greece; this support was financed by issuing a range of debt instruments on capital markets. This formal financial stabilisation, which followed the initial stimulus packages, relied on two main measures, the European Financial Stabilisation Mechanism (EFSM) and the European Stability Mechanism (ESM) (Barnard, 2012), which were a part of the EFSF. The EFSM was based on the *Treaty on the Functioning of the European Union* (TFEU), Article 122(2), to provide financial support for Member States that experienced exceptional difficulties considered beyond their control. The ESM was described as an intergovernmental organisation under public international law, so that the ESM Treaty provided for the private sector to participate in financial assistance programmes that could be granted to Member States (Olivares-Caminel, 2011). The study by de Witte (2011) provides some background on how the ESM was instigated and tends to support the argument put forward by Schmieding (2012) and NCA (2015), of increasing EC control over Member States, and is therefore, important to this research. The ESM was enabled by Treaty amendment to replace the EFSM, which was specifically instigated to deal with the sovereign debt crisis, and was devised using international, EU and private law. The amendment was based on Article 122(2) TFEU and was subject to legal interpretation challenges, according to de Witte (2011). The EFSM resulted from Eurozone countries agreeing loans to Greece, whilst the EU was only informally involved, but de Witte (2011) emphasises that the EC was asked to coordinate the lending operation. Article 122(5), derived from the Maastricht Treaty, specifically permits the EU to provide financial support to Member States experiencing severe difficulties as a result of exceptional events, outside of their control, for instance, national disasters. However, Germany argued that the governments of Greece and Ireland were not facing circumstances beyond their control, as they had responsibility for creating their sovereign crises, and therefore assisting them financially was contrary to Article 122(2). In 2010, ministers from Member States committed support for the new, separate intergovernmental credit mechanism the EFSF, for which a Special Purpose Vehicle (SPV) was created via a company based in Luxembourg but controlled jointly by the EMU Member States; EFSF had no limited period of existence but a six-month rolling review period. This idea was derived from German Chancellor Merkel gaining support from France to generate a limited amendment to the Treaty (De Witte, 2011), an intervention that reflects the earlier influence of these two countries in shaping the response to the initial stage of the crisis, as it affected Europe in their own interests and reflected intergovernmentalism. The support mechanism adopted in 2010 was considered to have two constitutional problems, the uncertainty that the measures implemented by the Eurozone Member States were in compliance with Article 125 of TFEU, which prevents Member States from supporting each other financially, and that giving that support on the basis of severe conditions, which must be complied with by the recipient, had no precedence in the contents of Article 125. Hence, the Treaty amendment put forward by Merkel was able to resolve these doubts, since it gave the Euro Member States the authority to support each other when there were budget or financial difficulties, by means of an internal mechanism, which did not widen EU powers and without changes to Article 125. Consequently, an amendment to Article 48(6), which related to internal policies, was instigated instead, and the draft amendment presented to the European Parliament made some suggestions so that the EU institutions could have a complementary role, for instance setting the conditions for the financial assistance. An additional paragraph to Article 136 was used as the implementation vehicle (De Witte, 2011). Article 136 states:

> The Member States whose currency is the Euro may establish a stability mechanism to be activated, if it is indispensable to safeguard the stability of the Euro area as a whole. The granting of any required financial assistance under the mechanism will be made subject to strict conditionality. (EUI, 2015, p.1)

The constitutional importance of this change was not revealed, the change was referred to as merely a simple revision of the relevant treaty so that approval could be effected, whilst de Witte (2011) states that it may have needed ratification by means of Member State referendum and this was avoided by the wording 'revision', in other words this was a highly controversial and potentially illegal intervention.

Once the ESM was in place, the EFSM programme was closed to all other Eurozone members except Greece, which continued to receive funding from EFSM until June 2015 (EFSF, 2015). The EFSM continued to receive interest payments from Eurozone members, which had been granted loans, and to make payments to the purchasers of the financial debt instruments created by the EC. In addition, it made arrangements for loan rollovers issued to Eurozone Member States, because the debt instruments that had been used had a shorter maturity than the loans issued to Ireland, Portugal and Greece.

The ESM was referred to by EFSF (2015, p. 1) as a "permanent rescue mechanism" and initiated in October 2012 and became the sole funding mechanism in operation for Eurozone members from July 2013 (ESM, 2015). ESM was used to grant loans requested by Spain, stated to be for bank recapitalisation, and to Cyprus for macroeconomic adjustment, described as restoring the viability of its banks and implementing reforms to generate sustainable economic growth.

The ESM governance structure has two boards, the Board of Governors and the Board of Directors, the former set policies and operating guidelines, whilst the latter implemented them and managed the daily operations. Unlike ECB institutions, each ESM Board member has a single vote and the Managing Director is its legal representative. The process is that the Eurozone Member State must formally ask for financial assistance from the Chair of the Board of Governors, who liaises with EC and ECB to assess the risk of the Member State situation to Eurozone stability, and liaises with the IMF to appraise the debt sustainability, as well as to evaluate financing needs and any private sector involvement. Once this process has been completed, the Board of Governors make the decision whether to grant the loan and, if the result is positive, the EC, ECB and IMF are involved in devising the Memorandum of Understanding (MoU) with the Member State. The draft MoU must be approved by the Board of Governors before being forwarded to the EU for signatures, on behalf of ESM. The ESM implements a warning system to remind the borrower to make the relevant payments on time, and the EC and possibly the IMF monitor Member State compliance with the terms of the MoU (Olivares-Caminel, 2011).

The MoU contains the conditions on which the loan is based, referred to as the adjustment programme; the conditions vary according to the Member State's perceived weaknesses. The MoU focuses on the reductions that must be made to public expenditure, and exactly how these will be implemented, for instance the original MoU for Greece in 2010 included compulsory reforms of the healthcare system and labour market, whereas Portugal was forced to reduce pension expenditure, reform healthcare, tighten eligibility rules on other social benefits and reduce the amount paid to recipients (Touri & Touri, 2014). Since debt instruments were employed to raise the ESM funding, the EC could state that no taxpayer money was used to support the Eurozone Member States. The capital available for lending was €500 billion, of which loans amounting to €47 billion had been granted at that time. The interest rate on loans varied, since recipient Member States were responsible for paying the costs incurred in setting up the arrangement but each bundle of loans issued also had a different rate. The type of debt instrument employed also affected the rate. ESM stated that the interest rates paid by the Member States were lower than those they would be subject to if they accessed funding from financial markets. However, the ESM loan was granted only when the specified policy conditions in the MoU were accepted; these conditions were devised by the EC, ECB and Member States concerned, as sometimes the IMF was involved. A major condition was that loans must be repaid in full at the maturity date. The Eurozone Member States were also committed to providing €700 billion in collateral for the fund, to ensure that investors had confidence in purchasing the debt instruments. However, the €500 billion fund was considered to be of much too low a value to support ongoing funding requests (Schoenbaum, 2012).

The debt instruments used by the EFSF are deemed to be very similar to SPVs, the collateralised debt instruments (CDOs) first created in the US, which were the underlying cause of the 2007–2008 global financial crisis, and, according to Olivares-Caminel (2011), the CEO of the EFSF denied that this was the case. However, academics and industry experts suggest that they are identical to SPVs and the method of awarding credit ratings to the EFSF debt instrument is the same as was employed for CDOs. The use of primary and secondary markets by EFSF indicates that any difference is increasingly minor. Whilst EFSF appears to have been employed to rectify long-term structural failure, these instruments represent a relatively short-term measure, and Olivares-Caminel (2011) commented that these debt instruments, which had already been issued, had a shorter expiry date than previous loans made to the Member States concerned, for instance, Ireland (ESFS 2015). The inference is that a further facility could be required on maturity. If the Member State fails to make loan payments, further instalments of the loan amount are withheld (Olivares-Caminel, 2011).

A study of EU policies to create financial stabilisation undertaken by Cayla (2013) also found that the EU tended to take a short-term approach to sovereign debt issues, by means of the funding mechanisms described above, because the Member States could not gain access to funding from financial markets. The EU policies attempted to control the debt levels in the short term by instigating legislation, whilst in the medium to long term the EU strategy was to solve the imbalance issues by attempting to enforce the countries in the Southern EU region to improve their trade balances, by implementing EU devised processes for added competitiveness. The underpinning EU rationale and assumption was that current economic challenges were a result of public debt, and that the reason that Southern EU countries were unable to solve their debt problem was a structural matter related to their uncompetitive products and services. However, Cayla (2013) argues that the assumption was a fallacy.

Austerity is considered as the most effective means to force Member States to reduce their deficit by reducing public sector spending, as this would then be offset by more spending by the private sector. However, politicians formulated the austerity policies to apply to countries requesting loans on rather dubious empirical theories put forward by Barro (1989) and Alesina et al. (2012), according to Keen (2014). The result of austerity is that growth has declined and created significant levels of unemployment, as exemplified by Greece and Spain. The IMF Chief Economist is cited by Keen (2014) as providing the logical explanation for the failure of the austerity measures to generate GDP growth. The measures failed in Europe because the change in government deficit to GDP and a change in GDP were much greater than one; a 1% decline in government deficit generated more than a 1% fall in GDP. The ESM regulations imposed greater austerity, which Krugman (2015) proposed has historically led to higher levels of economic depression and resulted in investors being more convinced that some Member States would not have the capacity to repay the debt, so that there was a lack of confidence to invest in their bonds. Deflation, which was a consequence of the EU austerity package, reduced wage and price levels so that an inflationary environment, which would reduce the public debt in real terms, was not possible (Cayla, 2013). Another option to austerity policies as a means of reducing public debt is to completely restructure the debt by means of QE; public debt could be used by the financial sector as risk-free assets, which help them to borrow from the central bank, and lend to private sector investors at higher interest rates (Cayla, 2013).

The ESM currently represents the Eurozone's fiscal backstop, according to Schoenmaker (2014), since the loans it provides to Member States may be used for bank restructuring, however, that is the extent of its jurisdiction. A fiscal backstop is the support of last resort, normally relating to a national government by means of its central bank or deposit insurance, so that a bank is judged on the strength of its fiscal backstop; in the case of countries such as Iceland and Ireland, the backstop was perceived as weak. In order for ESM to directly recapitalise banks and act as the fiscal backstop, it would need to have the power to exert appropriate supervision by Single Supervisory Mechanism (SSM) and resolution by Single Resolution Mechanism (SRM), in a similar but suitable manner to the way those processes are applied by ECB. This type of arrangement would strengthen EC power over Member States and was a concept at the development stage at the time of ESM (Schoenmaker, 2014).

Enhancing Economic Governance

The purpose of the EU strategy to improve economic governance was to communicate to financial markets that the EU had restored market stability and that a recurrence of crisis could not occur, according to Barnard (2012). In 2005, the two aspects of the Stability and Growth Pact (SGP) were amended, the preventative and corrective parts. The preventative aspect focused on accomplishing medium-term budgetary targets (MTOs), related to stability and convergence with annual reporting, and on early warning procedures. It focused on managing excessive debt and devising a timetable for its correction, with a potential sanction being described. However, after 2007/8, these reforms to the SGP were regarded as insufficient to encourage member countries to accumulate funds in an economic growth period, in order to prevent recurrence of the huge economic impact on Member States, which occurred in 2007/8. SGP was also criticised for lack of emphasis on the dynamics of debt, on the levels of debt in individual member countries, on imposing any debt limits, and enforcing existing procedures, according to Arroyo (2011). In addition, the Member States were accused of providing inaccurate budget statistics, which led to inaccurate fiscal monitoring, whilst in the macroeconomic sense, monitoring fiscal policy was the main concern, which resulted in limited knowledge of the wider implications (Arroyo, 2011). Hence, the SGP was initially extended by widening macroeconomic monitoring, inside and outside the EU, particularly relating to relative competitiveness and structural reform. Recommendations were also made to strengthen corrective measures, especially relating to imbalances. The statistical inaccuracy was rectified by greater use of EUROSTAT, which could produce higher-quality fiscal data and enforcement of corrective measures, and by imposing sanctions quickly, since automatic triggers exposed lack of compliance (Arroyo, 2011).

These changes were the basis of the instrument referred to as the Six Pack, a set of measures to ensure macroeconomic and fiscal survival (Barnard, 2012), to accomplish or maintain a strong fiscal position in the medium term (MTO). The Six Pack refers to a bundle of five measures and one directive, intended to reinforce the Stability and Growth Pact; the Six Pack came into force in December 2011. The EC stated that it contained secondary law and some specified rules relating to financial sanctions, which applied to all 27 members. Overall, it concerned fiscal and macroeconomic monitoring, plus a macroeconomic imbalance programme (EC, 2012). Each country would have a budgetary balance, which aligned with its specific medium-term objective of limiting government deficit to 3% of GDP limit, and sovereign debt to no more than 60% GDP, as required by the EU guidelines. Hence, the Six Pack provided a more precise quantitative statement regarding deviation from these targets, and methods for their correction, in order that Member States returned to the specified limits or lower (EC, 2012). These regulations were also imposed on those Member States without excessive deficit and/or debt, according to Barnard (2012). This legislation also changed the voting rules regarding EC recommendations or proposals, from votes registered to the introduction of Reverse Qualified Majority Voting (RQMV) regarding sanctions. This change meant that the Commission would regard a motion as adopted in the Council, unless a qualified majority of Member States voted against it (EC, 2012; Barnard, 2012). The Treaty on Stability, Coordination and Governance (TSCG) was to run parallel to the Six Pack once it was ratified, and integrated several of the objectives set out in the Six Pack; the part of the TSCG relating to fiscal matters was referred to as the Fiscal Compact (EC, 2012). The Treaty on Stability, Co-ordination and Governance in the EMU was devised in 2012 and agreed by 25 states, with UK and the Czech Republic not included (Schoenbaum 2012). It required ratification by 12 states to become law (Schoenbaum 2012), and came into force in June 2013 (Cramme & Hobolt, 2014). The TSCG Treaty was intended to ensure permanent fiscal union between EU Member States and particularly Eurozone members. Article 3 of this Treaty described as the 'balanced budget rule 1'is highlighted by Schoenbaum (2012, p. 42) as being unrealistic, since the terms demand the incorporation of the Article's terms into national laws. This committed the Member States to an annual budget deficit of less than or equal to 0.5% nominal GDP, and an annual reduction in their present public sovereign debt levels of 5%, in cases in which the sovereign debt exceeds 60% GDP (EC, 2012; Shoenbaum 2012); the latter being referred to as a debt brake mechanism (Cramme & Hobolt, 2014). These terms can be enforced by national and EU law and any non-complying Member State can be subject to legal action by the EU in the European Court of Justice (ECJ), with possible sanctions of monetary value up to 0.1% of its GDP. Any Member State, which refused to sign the Treaty, would be unable to access ESM funding, and Barnard (2012) stated that this new regulation effectively enforced the EMU Member States to implement macroeconomic monitoring. If the Member State failed to comply with corrective action recommended by EC, an interest-bearing deposit could be demanded, and that if lack of compliance was repeated, a fine of up to 0.1% GDP would be imposed. An EC alert system comprising ten indicators for macroeconomic imbalances was employed by the EC, which Barnard (2012) referred to as a scorecard. Hence, the EU initiated a rigorous study to investigate whether suspected imbalances in a Member State's budget would ultimately result in crisis.

The Treaty was regarded as severe austerity by Schoenbaum (2012), since it would impose spending cuts and generate further recession; it was referred to as an orgy of austerity. This Treaty contained much more limiting but credible rules than the Six Pack or the original Stability and Growth Pact, according to Cramme and Hobolt (2014). However, Schoenbaum (2012) doubted that full integration of fiscal policies would occur, or that one Member State would implement legal action against another at the European Court of Justice. In addition, Wolf (2012) commented that the Treaty had significant legal, economic and political implications, referring to the EC as unelected bureaucrats threatening court action on elected governments. In addition, Wolf (2012, p. 1) made the following statement:

> Would elected governments accept the guesstimates of unaccountable technocrats? How, moreover, are judges to reach a decision? Are they to evaluate the merits of alternative econometric models? Since huge changes in estimates of structural deficits are likely, how is a government to adapt? Putting an unmeasurable concept into the law seems mad.

In economic terms, structural deficits are impossible to calculate, as demonstrated by the substantial errors made by the IMF in 2007 (Wolf, 2012).

An annual timetable was also set for collective scrutiny of Member State budgets and economic structural policies, and then for their coordination; this timetable was referred to as the European Semester by Cramme and Hobolt (2014). The provision was a part of the TSCG for economic governance in the Eurozone, EC (2012) refers to a minimum of two of these Euro summits annually, with the purpose of strengthening economic cooperation. The European Semester had broad implications, for instance, Azzopardi-Muscat and Brand (2014) stated that it was an instrument to scrutinise economic policy coordination across certain sectors, which were expected to generate substantial employment prospects and economic growth, healthcare for example. However, analysis of the country-specific recommendations for the years 2011–2013 revealed that all but 3 of the 25 recommendations focused on sustainability. They were linked to sustainability of public finances and governance, a trend that concerned public health experts, because considerations of equity and quality of healthcare were being relatively ignored, and public health and investment in it were generally receiving much less attention. Whilst balanced country-specific recommendations could support enhancement of health systems, there was a danger that the prescribed recommendations would not be appropriate to some countries and could be enforced, if those countries were participants in the EMS programme, although this was not transparent at the time (Azzopardi-Muscat & Brand, 2014).

Funding the Measures

The EU predominantly employs monetary policies that focus on managing prices, meaning that inflationary stability is the prime purpose (Sloman et al., 2018). In order to do so, QE may be employed; the Bank of England (2015) refers to QE as unconventional monetary policy intervention in which the Central Bank creates new money electronically to buy financial assets, for instance, government bonds. The QE process then encourages the private sector to invest in the economy to return the inflation rate to the targeted level. The EU was very reluctant to use QE after the 2007–2008 crisis, whereas the US and UK were adopting typical Milton Friedman monetary policy interventions to raise inflation, by increasing the money stock. In other words, EU's policies were initially based on deliberately not increasing the money supply by means of an open market purchase of government bonds. By the end of 2014, inflation in the EU had become negative; which meant that deflationary pressures were being experienced (De Grauwe, 2015). However, Fawley and Neely (2013) proposed that the ECB had initially adopted a style of QE policy in 2008 to 2009, which primarily relied on lending to banks, whereas the US and UK had implemented the traditional monetary method based on bond purchases. The difference in emphasis was a result of banks having a more important role in Europe, where they were the means to liquidity and to supporting the respective financial systems, depending on the economic structure of the nation/region, according to Fawley and Neely (2013). Immediately after the Lehman Brothers' collapse, the ECB began a one month special term refinancing operation, which was intended to improve liquidity throughout the EMU banking system. However, within two weeks the ECB used QE for the first time by means of bidding, a methodology that was contrary to its previous rules of offering a defined sum for which rates were fixed, owing to the worsening liquidity of the Euro. On this occasion, banks were informed that they could borrow limitless funds at a fixed interest rate, providing that they had the collateral, referred to as Fixed Rate Tender Full Allotment, and the EU extended the acceptable items representing collateral. The standard ECB lending for refinancing involved two levels of interest rate lending arrangement, usually three months, relative to a two-week Main Refinancing Operation or a Longer Term Refinancing Operation. In October 2008, the fixed interest rate was 4.25% but fell to 1% in May 2009 invoking a huge increase in lending (Fig. 6.1).

Although these Fixed Rate Tender Full Allotments were in good supply and at low rates, there were fears of default risk. Therefore in the first half of 2009, the ECB adopted the same strategy as the US and UK with the introduction of asset purchase programmes as its core refinancing strategy, even though it had no experience with this financial instrument. A 12-month long-term financial operation was offered at 1% interest and a Covered Bond Purchase Programme, in the Securities Held for Monetary Policy Purposes category. Therefore, from 2009, significant long-term financial operational growth occurred, and Covered Bond Purchase Programme growth from 2010 to 2012. Covered Bond Purchase Programmes are described by Fawley and Neely (2013) as differing from asset-backed securities because the issuer and the underlying collateral were the means for payment if the bond defaulted, and banks could not

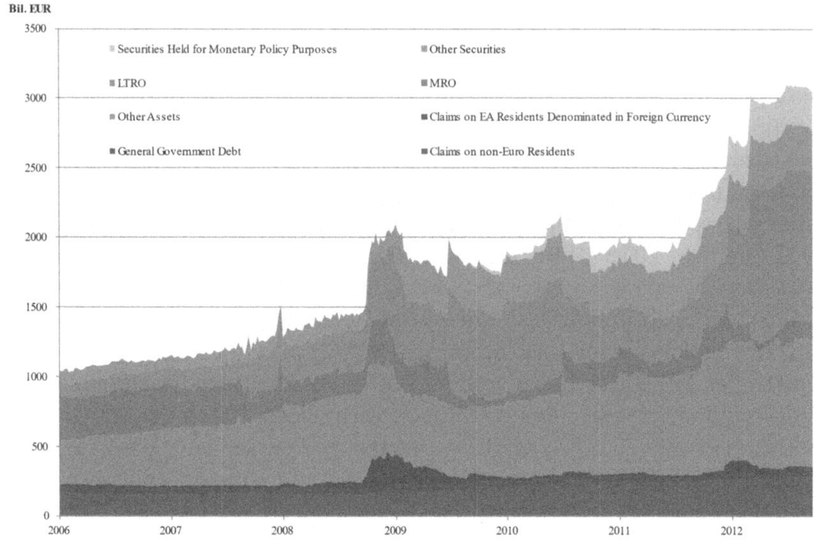

Fig. 6.1 Lending trends ECB 2006–2012. (Source: Federal Reserve Bank of St. Louis Fawley and Neely (2013, p.69))

take them off balance sheet. This strategy reduced bank preference for securitising poor quality loan packages and were a major reason for Covered Bond Purchase Programme growth. The ECB publicly planned to purchase Covered Bond Purchase Programmes to the value of €60 billion in May 2009, and the ECB President denied that they represented a QE measure that would expand the ECB balance sheet (De Grauwe, 2015). However, this action would relieve the tight credit conditions and revive the EU market, including improving its liquidity. Whilst €60 billion provided stimulation of €130 billion, much of the increase resulted from swaps from uncovered bonds, which generally had little impact on credit risk.

In 2010, the Member State sovereign debt crisis was worsening so that the ECB introduced the Securities Market Programme to enable its purchase of government debts in the secondary market. This strategy was necessary because Article 123.1 of the Treaty on the Functioning of the European Union prohibited the ECB from providing extended credit to Eurozone Member State governments or directly purchasing their sovereign debt in primary markets (Marta, 2015). Therefore, this programme was not acknowledged as one that supported Member States, but as a general strategy to improve liquidity in certain market segments, such as the securities market, and to regularise monetary policy. On this occasion, there were limits to the nature of the interventions, as support was given as considered necessary and not publicly announced. Therefore, the extent of support implemented could not be determined until the release of the next balance sheet; asset purchases were sanitised so that EMU monetary policy was not affected. The ECB suggested that quantitative easing had not occurred because the monetary base increase had not been detected (De Grauwe, 2015), but Securities Market Programme purchases were observed by some experts who suggested that they depressed rates on Italian and Spanish debt in August 2011. The ECB held €208.5 billion in sovereign debt from the Securities Market Programme initiative in December 2012 and it was argued that the central bank operated credit rationing, rather than monetary policy, with selected Member States benefitting (Fawley & Neely, 2013), a factor that aligns with ESM (2015). The EU financial crisis, sovereign debt crisis and banking policy were all linked in Europe, according to Fawley and Neely (2013). The financial crisis created a recession, which reduced Member State tax revenues and growth, whilst it concurrently increased social spending and consequently, public debt. Therefore, private banks that held higher risk sovereign debt were most likely to fail and because governments guaranteed bank deposits, the associated Member State sovereign debt increased when they did.

The EU sovereign debt crisis disrupted the global financial markets and in late 2011, the ECB issued more Covered Bond Purchase Programmes and one year long-term refinancing operations to fund the banks, followed by three year long-term refinancing operations issued in December. The introduction of the three year financing operation was intended for purchasing sovereign debt at low cost, rather than for increasing liquidity, according to Buiter and Rabhari (2012). This option enabled the ECB to publicly comply with its Charter but various forms of financial repression had generated this strategy.

The Outright Money Transactions programme replaced the Securities Market Programme in September 2012 and allowed the ECB to purchase sovereign debt in the secondary markets, if the Member State complied with its rules. This strategy which was impossible under the previous programme had no effect on its monetary targets and enabled the ECB to enforce its rules on Member States (Buiter & Rabhari, 2012). There was also no limit to the debt that could be purchased, and Touri and Touri (2014) state that the ECB effectively became a stakeholder in the sovereign nation's finances, since banks purchase national bonds with ECB loans, and banking and fiscal issues became integrated. Consequently, the ECB undertook a political stance during the political crisis in these Member States and became one of their creditors (Touri & Touri, 2014), a perception strengthened by the fiscal and economic policies, which the states were forced to accept. The increasing direct and indirect role of the ECB in lending to Member States was equivalent to spending taxpayer's money and led to substantial conflict with Germany resulting in two German ECB officials resigning (Touri & Touri, 2014, p. 266).

The initial ECB reluctance to use traditional QE was a consequence of German resistance to the measure, since it believed that if the ECB bought the bonds from Greece, Italy or Portugal and those governments defaulted, the ECB would have to record losses on its balance sheet, and the German taxpayer would be the ultimate source to remedy the losses. Therefore, the ECB did not employ QE until 2014 (De Grauwe, 2015) but German taxpayer fear of being subjected to paying ECB losses was not an accounting reality, according to De Grauwe (2015), since the accounting conventions relating to such a loss had no implications for taxpayers. A proposed ECB compromise was that each national central bank within the Eurozone acted independently to buy its government's bonds. This proposed policy is contrary to the risk sharing and unified action on which the EU monetary was based, and threatened the Eurozone as a future monetary union (De Grauwe, 2015). When the ECB altered its QE methodology to buying government bonds to increase liquidity, the central banks of those countries, which had received bailout funding, were made responsible for the majority of any losses that occurred. The time taken to adopt this policy for driving economic growth inferred that it would be less effective than in other countries, which had acted more quickly (Economist, 2015). The action taken by Germany is another instance of its influence on ECB strategies and on its self-interest being more important than the EU Principle of Justice and Fairness for all Member States.

In terms of the comparative measures taken by the US and Europe to manage the global crisis, QE has proven to be more effective than austerity, according to Keen (2014). However, neither measure accomplished what was expected by the politicians implementing them. The underlying reason suggested by Keen (2014) was that both sets of politicians had ignored why the global financial crisis had occurred and subsequently generated a huge decline in economic growth. The fact that private sector spending based on credit had substantially reduced since the crisis resulted in rapid fall in aggregate demand because of lack of availability of private sector credit. However, the EU considered the cause of the crisis to be rising public debt and implemented austerity; this was a fallacy, and it was caused by the decline in private sector borrowing. QE had partly succeeded in generating growth but only because it had encouraged the private sector to borrow again, meaning that private debt levels remain the highest in history and that the underlying cause of economic crisis has not been removed. This fact is also emphasised by IMF (2015a), which states that gross corporate debt levels in France, Italy, Portugal and Spain would remain at approximately 70% of GDP until 2020, and that action was needed for economic growth to be restored.

Generating Economic Growth

A fiscal stimulus of the equivalent of 2% EU GDP was injected into the economy (EC, 2009), amounting to 200 billion euro (Tait, 2008), with the purpose of increasing domestic demand, since purchasing power would be increased and therefore business and labour markets stimulated. The Euro Plus Pact (EPP) or Competitiveness Pact was a plan generated by the French and German governments, in which some EU states agreed to political reforms that intended to make their economies more competitive by increasing their fiscal strength; it was a more rigorous form of the SGP. The EPP, although another governance reform, actually considerably impacted on labour law and could be imposed on states who had signed the MoU, as part of the EFSM and ESM. The comment made by Barnard (2012) was that the EU had devised a notion that individual country deregulation was the most effective formula for escaping from the crisis. The argument presented by Barnard (2012) was that EC policy relied on a monetarist approach to the economy; but if this was combined with highly restrictive and severe austerity measures, economic growth was not likely to occur and employment prospects would worsen, including potential job losses. Whilst the EC refers to its 2020 growth strategy, Member States would need to make significant investments to accomplish the inclusive, sustainable growth targets; however, sovereign debt and deficit rules prevented this. The option of generating growth by currency devaluation was not an option for EMU members (Barnard, 2012). This strategy reflects the strong political influence of the most pro-European Member States, France and Germany, which favoured monetarist policies rather than the Keynesian-based policies, which were representative of the Southern European Member States, particularly Italy (Bibow, 2013).

The Major Eurozone Crises 2015 to 2018: Case Studies Greece, Italy and UK

A report by Evans-Pritchard (2014) in December 2014 suggested the potential for a new relationship between Greece and the EU, since a left-wing candidate for Greek Prime Minister, Alexis Tsipras, was expected to win the election and be prepared to cease adhering to what was referred to as the EU-IMF Troika regime; in other words, to refuse to comply with MoU that had been agreed upon by previous governments. Tsipras was convinced that the EU, and especially Germany, would not enforce the MoU or debt repayment because the perception would be that the Eurozone had failed to manage the financial crisis appropriately. In the previous seven years, Greece had experienced a 29.5% decline in GDP, whilst its debt to the EU and IMF had reached €245 billion. Investment in Greece had also declined by 63.5%, 43.9% of young people were unemployed and almost a quarter of all jobs had disappeared (McKinsey, 2012; Evans-Pritchard, 2014). The Greek government sought to stay in the

Euro, but not if the price of doing so was too high. It planned to ask for an increase in EU subsidies, raise the minimum wage and pension levels, increase social benefits for the poorest, write off much private debt and ask for 62% of its debt to EU to be written off, in a similar way to how Germany had been given relief at the end of World War Two. The EU management of the Greek crisis had been disastrous, according to Evans-Pritchard (2014) but the logical forecast was that Greece would be ejected from the Euro within a short period. The events that followed the election of Tsipras in January 2015 and the EU's responses to the situation are a contemporary manifestation of the increasing changes to the legislation. They expose the various motivations for changing it for the national or institutional personal interest and provide further rich data for answering this research question regarding the proportionality of intervention made by the EU.

A brief review of the events that primarily involve Greece from 2007 to 2015 is first undertaken to provide background to the ongoing processes that subsequently occurred, including the different objectives and motivations of the various actors. In the case of Italy, developments during 2018 are the focus, combined with recent history, and for the UK an overview of the behaviours exhibited by the EU since the UK electorate decided that Britain should leave the group.

Greece

Greece in the Eurozone 2007–2014

The financial crisis that engulfed Greece from 2009 was suggested by Crysoloras (2013) as a mirror image of that which firms had recently experienced, high growth and increasing prosperity followed by catastrophe and seemingly irreversible instability. However, the difference was that a country was the entity involved in the financial crisis and, although EU and OECD had previously remarked on the high levels of Greek debt and deficit, no public statement was made regarding a possible collapse. In reality from the time of joining the Euro, the Greek economy appeared to be reasonably robust, owing to lower interest rates on bonds and bank loans, and increases in tourism and shipping, wage increases also generating demand. However, between 2001 and 2009, Greek GDP had declined from surplus of 4.1% GDP to a deficit of 16.9% GDP, whilst wages had risen, productivity had declined; competitiveness decreased by over 20% in

2009. Corruption and tax evasion were also high, underpinned by weak administration to rectify them (Crysoloras, 2013; McKinsey, 2012).

Despite the rhetoric that Greece had high levels of debt in 2009, the proportion was lower than that of Germany and half that of the UK (McKinsey, 2012). In 2010, Greece was given financial support by the group of emergency lenders referred to as the Troika, EU, ECB and IMF, but the austerity measures imposed as a condition of funding drove the country into deeper recession, and public perception of the EU considerably worsened. While some of the imposed reforms were instigated such as social benefits, these were regarded as too minor by the EU; it considered that too little had been done to sell off public assets to the private sector and other measures were equally slow to emerge. The reasons for this situation were that the EU demands in the MoU were unrealistic, the Greek administration was weak and could not coordinate the reforms, and there was a lack of commitment to the reforms from the main political parties (Crysoloras, 2013). Public deficit declined from 16.0% to 6.6% GDP between 2010 and 2012, and primary deficit from 10.5% to 1.4%, much greater than other Southern European Member States (Crysoloras, 2013); the achievement by Greece was also recognised by Stiglitz (2015). However, this improvement in deficit was accomplished by: unemployment rising to high levels with little prospect of new jobs being created; the country having the highest proportion of long-term unemployment in the EU; homelessness, suicide and crime increases (Crysoloras, 2013; Stiglitz, 2015). The economic position prior to the 2012 elections in Greece was that GDP was forecast to decline by 28.5% by 2013 compared with its position in 2018, so that the EU was approached to provide financial support. The population was disillusioned in the period leading up to the 2012 elections, since it had believed that the 2010 bailout and MoU reforms would be a unique event, and that within three years they would be able to borrow from the financial markets once more; but these expectations were not achieved. After the election of the existing government, which preferred to stay in the Euro, Greece renegotiated the terms of the original loan but the MoU conditions were also altered to enforce greater austerity. The new conditions included a two year extension for meeting the fiscal targets and lower interest on the original loan. During the Greek financial crisis in 2012, the German Chancellor was quoted as being extremely close to demanding the removal of Greece from the Eurozone (Evans-Pritchard, 2014).

The Greek economic structure was based on non-tradable goods, high self-employment, a large public sector and few large firms, meaning that economies of scale could not be used to leverage productivity and that imports levels were high (Crysoloras, 2013; McKinsey, 2012). The economic structure, which was contrary to the EU Stability and Growth and Pact, had been ignored by the EU, according to Crysoloras (2013) and reinforced by Wolff (2015), who stated that measures to increase competitiveness should have been included as part of the conditions of the first loan. The high bureaucratic levels and complex tax systems characteristic of the Greek public sector deterred business expansion. Therefore, austerity to rectify fiscal imbalance without a robust, sustainable growth strategy inferred that little improvement was possible (McKinsey, 2012).

Greek Crisis 2015

Shortly after Tsipras was elected Greek leader in January 2015, the Greek government negotiated an extension to their 2012 loan agreement, in exchange for not implementing the intended measures that would conflict with the terms of the existing MoU, and pledging to carry out its agreed terms (BBC, 2015). The agreement that was implemented from February to June temporarily removed the possibility of Greece leaving the Eurozone and stemmed further withdrawals from Greek banks by nervous investors. However, this negotiation was the precursor to very challenging negotiations regarding Greece's financial future, and its relationship with other EU governments was stated as weakened, especially with Germany (Steinhauser & Dalton, 2015). As the end of the four month period approached, little progress had been made between EU bodies and Greece, and the Greek government threatened to default on payments. The Greek government had held discussions with the Russian leader Putin during this period, which raised EU fears of a Greek pact with Russia to raise funds. The discussions also caused highly negative reactions from EU and US governments; several leaders predicted that Greece would leave the Eurozone (Evans-Pritchard, 2015).

In June, the ECB ended the emergency funding it had granted to Greece so that banks were forced to close, and capital controls were introduced (BBC, 2015). The new austerity demands from the EU were subject to a referendum by the Greek people, which took place on 5 July, and the population rejected the terms for a new bailout (BBC, 2015). The actual terms offered to Greece were difficult to determine because different information had been leaked by parties to the negotiations to the press. However, Zartman (2019) suggests that Greece had been offered a further five-month extension on the current bailout loan programme but with specific reforms to implement. The offer was considered extraordinarily generous by Germany whilst Tsipras considered it as unworkable because there would be an immediate negative impact on the labour market and huge tax increases for working population. The Greek government proposed a reduction of public sector debt of €8 billion by means of value-added tax increases, a wealth tax and defence spending cuts. However, these proposals were rejected by IMF as insufficient and it insisted on public sector salary and pension reductions. As a consequence of the impasse, capital controls were imposed by the Greek government that restricted Greek citizens to being able to withdraw a maximum of €60 per day from banks. Bank holidays were also introduced from the time the talks broke down until the end of the referendum, in order to reduce capacity for bank withdrawals (Wearden, 2015).

The EU demands were severely condemned by Stiglitz (2015), who stated that the Troika directed dire conditions in Greece relating to unemployment levels and declining GDP on a weak government, rather than considering that austerity measures detailed in the MoU were incorrect, such as the forecast budget surplus of 3.5% GDP by 2018, even when global economists had commented that it was unrealistic. These unrealistic conditions were also emphasised by Wolff (2015), and Stiglitz (2015) predicted that Greece would not emerge from the economic depression, if the results of the referendum had been to accept the Troika terms. The highly charged conflict between European leaders demonstrated that the continuing debt dispute was more concerned with power and democracy than with money and economics, according to Stiglitz (2015).

In its country report on Greece at the end of June, IMF (2015b) concluded that there were signs that Greek debt was sustainable a year earlier and that no further debt relief would be required other than that provided in 2012 if the MoU was adhered to. However, recent policy changes in Greece had led weak reform, which negatively affected the impact of growth and privatisation measures, and inferred that new loans were needed. When new funding was combined with existing increased debt levels, the situation was considered to be unsustainable and the conclusion was made that any further weakening of the agreed reforms would require debt write-downs. Greece failed to make the second payment that was due to IMF shortly by the end of June 2015 such that it owed €2 billion (BBC, 2015).

The Greek referendum had resulted in a majority vote to reject the proposed measures required by the EU/IMF, therefore created considerable instability and renewed fears that Greece would be ejected from the Eurozone; this was reinforced by the German proposal that Greece be awarded a five-year temporary exit. After the US government intervention to avoid a Greek exit from the Euro, Troika demands increased (Khan & Wright, 2015). Negotiations continued and the Greek Prime Minister was reported having agreed to the new EU demands on 13 July 2015, in exchange for more than €86 billion in new loans from ESM; the loan comprised approximately $35 billion to support economic growth and to reduce unemployment (EC, 2015 g). This unratified agreement imposed much harsher terms on Greece than had been suggested by the EU/IMF before the Greek referendum (Khan, 2015a) and need to be agreed by the European Parliaments. In effect Greece was still be unable to make the missed payment whilst this situation existed (Holehouse, 2015; EC, 2015) but committed to making a €12 billion interest payment to IMF and ECB on its current loans by the end of August (Strupczewski, 2015). However, making the payment would have resulted in collapse of the Greek banking system and €4.2 billion of this sum was due to ECB almost immediately. As a consequence, EC President suggested reviving the EFSM solely to support Greece (EC, 2015 g), since this mechanism could be used to borrow short-term funds from financial markets; the EFSM had been replaced by ESM in 2012 and had no such options. The €8.6 billion short-term bridging finance obtained to support Greece was reported by Holehouse (2015) as having collateral based on the EU budget, but this had significant implications for the UK government, since the UK was not a Eurozone member but would be required to make a contribution of £1 billion to the bailout. This proposed action was in breach of a written agreement made in 2010 between the EU and countries outside the EMU that the EFSM would not be used again, meaning that they would not contribute to Eurozone bailouts from 2013. This agreement had been made by the EU in exchange for the agreement of non-Eurozone members to the legislation that created the ESM.

The published terms of the agreement were that Greece must increase tax revenues collected by means of changes to value-added taxation base; comprehensive reform of the pension system must occur; there must be full implementation of the EC Treaty on EMU stability, coordination and governance, particularly the banking system and ensuring fiscal council was operational; spending cuts were automatically made to rectify deviations from previous target before any MoU could be finalised. However, reorganisation of the civil justice system to reduce cost and bureaucracy created delays. The agreement also required compliance with the Bank Recovery and Resolution Directive, and the new MoU included defined timetables to implement the necessary legislation and policies to meet the structural benchmarks detailed in the agreement. Market reforms were those proposed by OECD including enabling Sunday trading; eliminating trade union closed shops in macroeconomic critical trades, such as in ferry transport; privatising national companies for instance electricity; modernising labour markets including employment law and practices to align with relevant EU directives and best practice, so as to drive growth; improve bank governance; exclude state influence on management appointments. The Greek government was also obliged to agree to the transfer of valuable Greek assets valued at €50 billion to an independent fund. This fund was managed by the Greek government but under supervision from EU institutions, which would sell them to ensure that loans granted were repaid; 25% of the sum raised would be used to recapitalise the banks, 25% to decrease debt to GDP ratio; 50% for investment. Sales pricing was also required to comply with OECD guidelines. Apart from the humanitarian crisis bill, the legislation installed by the Tsipras-led government from February 2015 was to be reviewed, so that it met the terms of previous MoU. These extensive demands were the minimum requirements of the issuance of the third bailout fund, and needed to be agreed rapidly, owing to pending interest payment. The Greek government was also made responsible for ensuring that negotiations were finalised so that the banks could reopen. Bank capitalisation requirements represented between €10 and €25 billion of the total ESM funding and a private account was set up for this purpose (Rankin & Smith, 2015: CFR, 2021).

The IMF issued a press release after the terms of the agreement had been decided, stating that Greek debt was unsustainable and would reach 200% of GDP by 2018 (IMF, 2015c). IMF emphasised that Greek debt would become sustainable only if the EU provided debt relief of a much higher amount than the sum announced. The statement also indicated that because most Greek debt was outstanding to EU creditors, on lower than market terms, the framework of the 2012 loan could be altered to extend repayment terms, especially as Greece would be unable to raise money from financial markets until its debt levels were much lower. The

Governor of the Bank of England reinforced the IMF stance that Greek debt was unsustainable and commented that the bailouts in 2010 and 2012 had made it very difficult for the Greek government to repay its debts (Evans-Pritchard, 2015). The EU demand that the Greek government privatise the nation's assets to pay off its loans was also condemned as a negative strategy and a third loan agreement to be almost impossible to contemplate (Khan, 2015b, p. 1). Senior economists in Germany also expressed doubts that the bailout would solve the economic and political issues in Greece, owing to its huge underlying structural problems, and that EU politicians continued to act in a dishonest manner insisting on the same austerity strategy. A five-year exit plan would have served Greece better, according to a former German Finance Minister. Greece was granted a bridging loan of €7.16 billion by the EFSM, with a three-month maturity so that arrears to the IMF and ECB could be paid (Spence & Bradshaw, 2015). A sum of €89 billion in emergency liquidity assistance was granted to Greek banks so that they could reopen; this action was perceived as a blatant political strategy by the ECB President to appear reasonable towards Greece (Spence & Wright, 2015). Greece could not receive quantitative easing since it did not meet the criteria, 33% of its debt was already owed to ECB, the maximum debt any Member State could have. Once repayment of the interest on ECB loan was made on 20 July 2015 Greek debt would fall below the maximum, but the ECB could not purchase Greek debt because its credit rating was too low (Spence & Bradshaw, 2015). Political turmoil was expected to return in Greece, despite the funding because 38 members of Tsipras' political party voted against acceptance of the bailout terms (Evans-Pritchard, 2015). Shortly afterwards, Tsipras called an election (Palaiologos, 2015). At this time the IMF had still not agreed to become involved in the bailout and Germany preferred to have IMF agreement to the bailout terms because this was considered to add greater economic rigour (Carrel, 2015).

Greece 2018–2019

The OECD (2018) forecast an increase in GDP of 2.3% for the Greek economy in 2019, generated predominantly by exports. Domestic demand was expected to increase as consumption demand rose to a level that had been recorded for a brief period in 2009, and investment confidence was stated as returning but businesses continued to experience difficulty in accessing loans. In addition, private consumption was limited by the type of employment that had been created, predominantly temporary or part-time work with minimum wage pay levels; continuing high public debt levels restricted price and wage rises as well as overcapacity reducing price pressure. The country would require additional funds from the ECB to enable the required reforms to take place, a major goal being to reduce child poverty by more effective social protection targets and distribution of funds. However, a study by Mavradis (2017) suggested that many of the published economic improvements had been gained at huge social cost, including a declining birth rate, increased homelessness and continuing loss of young, educated people. The potential of the UK leaving the EU without any agreement regarding trade and other matters has been expressed in Greek government report as a threat to its recovery, owing to the loss of the UK's contribution to the EU budget. This event would mean lower funding for Member States, adding pressure on the EU to come to an agreement with UK or to experience further budgetary issues concerned with other EU members (Rothwell, 2018).

The recent Greek election results, in which the Tsipras government was not re-elected, suggested that further tensions between the EU and Greece could be expected even though the EU bailout conditions had officially ended in August 2018. The perception of the electorate was that Tsipras had betrayed the country by finally agreeing to the EU demands for further austerity. The new prime minister's policies include lowering taxes, privatising some government services and attempting to stimulate economic growth especially as youth unemployment remains at an unacceptable level and its general unemployment level is more than double the EU average (BBC, 2019).

Italy

The Threat to the EU and the Eurozone from Italy

Although the high level of Italian public debt, the riskiness of its bond yield and the instability of banks owing to the level of non-performing loans have been alluded to in previous sections, the political changes that have occurred since 2016 represent several new threats to the EU and to the Euro (Rachman, 2016). In 2016, the pro-EU Italian Prime Minister Matteo Renzi resigned after losing a referendum on constitutional reform, a situation which Rachman (2016) considered a greater threat to EU than Brexit, particularly as Italy is one of the six original members. The Italian population's perception of EU membership changed from enthusiasm to delusion as a consequence of flat economic growth, the Euro, excessive forced immigration, the loss of 25% industrial capacity since 2008 and 40% youth unemployment. The rising popularity of populist parties, for instance the Five Star Movement, which suggested a referendum on leaving the Euro, posed a second threat to the EU. The Italian banking crisis implied potential for an EU bailout of banks, which would be far more difficult than the Greek situation, owing to the size of the Italian economy, ten times that of Greece (Jones & Bindi, 2018).

In June 2018, the left-wing Five Star Movement and the far right Northern League created a populist government; their election was the predicted consequence of the stagnant economy and concern about the growing, uncontrolled immigration that was not shared by other EU members (Jones & Bindi, 2018). The result of the election and the increasing public debt levels led to investors moving money out of the country raising fears of a financial crisis similar to that of Greece in 2015, according to Jones and Bindi (2018). In addition, the impending crisis has unsettled the European and international markets and could impact negatively on economic growth in Europe.

The lack of a coherent, forceful EU immigration policy is stressed by Mickonyte (2018), who states that the EU attempted to reduce the immigration burden on Greece and Italy, which faced unprecedented arrivals of asylum seekers during the 2015–2016 crisis. It had tried to impose mandatory immigration targets per member state, but some countries such as Hungary and other former communist states refused to acknowledge them and the Austrian government had opposition to immigration at the centre of its policies. The most challenging issue of the EU policy for Italy was that EU rules required that the country where the immigrants landed should complete the asylum process (Mickonyte, 2018), which meant that Italy had responsibility for them. An earlier OECD report by Hall (2000) had identified that immigration to Italy created huge issues concerning how to overcome the challenges of the large numbers of illegal entries into the country and to halt the people trafficking on a huge scale. Italy was targeted by immigrants who perceived it as a route to the wealthier North European countries of UK, German and Switzerland, rather than a country to begin a new life; accessing Italy was relatively easy owing to its long coastline and access by means of its islands.

The position taken by Matteo Salvini, Italy's Interior Minister, regarding the unequal financial burden that the immigration crisis had placed on

Italian budgets, whilst the EU and other European countries refused to allow immigrants across their borders from Italy, for instance France and Austria, was treated with horror. Salvini closed Italian ports to migrant ships, referring to Sicily as the refugee camp of Europe because 690,000 refugees had entered Italy since 2013 and 500,000 of these still resided in the country. The cost of immigration to Italy in 2017 alone was €4.2 billion and associated with sea rescues, caring for the immigrants and medical assistance; asylum seekers are not allowed to work according to EU rules (Robinson, 2018). The Interior Minister accused non-governmental organisations (NGOs) of trafficking immigrants and forced the EU Summit to provide a solution to balance the burden, but no satisfactory solution has been developed. Several Central European countries had already rejected an EU scheme to relocate 160,000 refugees remaining in camps in Italy and Greece, and longer term EU members were considered likely to reject suggested policy changes to set up centres across Europe to receive immigrants (BBC, 2018; Robinson, 2018).

In September 2018, the new Italian government devised its budget, which stated it would raise public spending significantly, and possibly beyond the levels the EU austerity programme permitted, tax cuts and income support were also intended, such that EU would need to make special adaptations to support reigniting the Italian economy (Costeloe, 2018; Jones & Bindi, 2018). Since Italy is the third largest economy in Europe its threat of instigating a parallel currency to the Euro to enable the budget measures to be accomplished needed to be taken seriously. The demands potentially inferred a change of EU policy regarding Member States in which the current measures imposed have not produced the forecast economic growth. This dilemma is ongoing, particularly as the public support for the Interior Minister and Deputy Prime Minister Matteo Salvini had increased to a level in which his potential to win an election was extremely high. Salvini had become the Italian politician representing the major threat to the EU, and tensions between the two groups remained potentially explosive in July 2019 (Economist, 2019).

The UK: Brexit

The UK held a referendum on 23 June 2016, which required those eligible to vote to state whether the UK should continue to be a member of the European Union (EU) or not, a no vote allowing the nation to return to its pre-EU Sovereign State, in other words its status before 1973 (Kerr,

2016). The leave vote renewing sovereignty is interpreted as meaning that the country will become an independent territory, people and a government, which devises its own laws and policies (Fowler & Bunck, 1996). In 2016, the largest proportion of extra-EU trade was by Germany, 28.7% of exports and 18.8% imports, whereas the UK accounted for 11.1% exports, and second to Germany, but had the highest level of EU imports at 16.6% of the total; the UK had the second largest trade deficit in the group at €89.7 billion (EC, 2017). The level of UK exports of goods and services to the EU has declined from 55% in 2002 to 43% in 2016, and UK imports also fell from 58% in 2002 to 51% by 2011 (Ward, 2019). In 2018, UK imports from EU amounted to £353 billion and exports £88.9 billion, whereas direct trade with the rest of the world was worth £345.1 billion in exports and £312.1 billion in imports, a trade surplus (Ward, 2019). Despite the declining trend in exports and imports between the UK and EU, the loss of UK trade would be damaging to EU as further demonstrated by £2.6 billion increase in UK payments to the EU in the year ending 31 March 2019, owing to the increase in the UK's gross national income; the UK contribution to EU budget is 13% of total (Rayner, 2019). Whilst some groups argue that UK trade will be negatively impacted by Brexit, others oppose such a view, hence the subject of Brexit and trade is controversial. However, UK House of Commons data show that the deficit between UK imports from, and exports to, the UK has gradually widened from 1999 and doubled from £41billion in to £82 billion between 2012 and 2016, the reason cited by a leading economist is that the EU Single Market and customs union are not advantageous to the UK, in fact Germany gains the most benefit (Elliott, 2018).

The process of withdrawing from the EU, Article 50 of the Treaty, comprises four steps, according to Renwick (2017); decision to leave, notifying the UK of that decision, negotiation of a deal, agreement to its terms, but Brexit is the first time it has been invoked. This process generates five possible outcomes (Renwick, 2017) and whilst UK wishes to operationalise Brexit without transitional arrangements, the EU prefers Brexit with transitional arrangements in order to have time to decide any future relationship. No deal and UK exit within two years is another option (Renwick, 2017), which originally appeared probable, as an agreement was expected to be reached by October 2018, for exit in March 2019. However, negotiations aroused particularly bitter reaction and a stubborn approach from senior EU officials that would prefer UK to remain in EU. The UK was also forced to agree to continue to pay into the EU budget as a part of the Brexit negotiations, a condition demanded by the EU before it would grant any talks on ongoing trade between the two parties (Hunt & Wheeler, 2018). According to David Davis, the former UK Brexit Secretary, the unwillingness to attempt to find a compromise exit strategy that was mutually advantageous was contrary to Article 8 of the Lisbon Treaty in which it is stated that EU

> develop a special relationship with neighbouring countries, aiming to establish an area of prosperity and good neighbourliness, founded on the values of the Union and characterised by close and peaceful relations based on cooperation. (Rayner, 2018. p.1)

Hence, the conclusion of the UK politicians was that EU is contravening its duties under Article 8 (Rayner, 2018).

After considerable political and legal challenges by politicians and their supporters opposing Brexit, the UK and EU agreed the UK Withdrawal Agreement, on 25 November 2018, with a date of 29 March 2019 for the official UK exit. However, this agreement was rejected by the UK Parliament on three occasions, owing to the alleged problems regarding the need for arrangements to stop a hard customs border between Northern Ireland, which is part of the UK, and Southern Ireland which would remain an EU Member State. The EU negotiators were aware that the backstop would create severe problems for the UK, since it possibly contravened the terms of a previous politically sensitive peace agreement between the UK and Southern Ireland (Walker, 2019; Timothy, 2019). The imposition of the backstop was widely perceived as a ruse by the EU to force the UK to accept a Customs Union solution to its withdrawal from the EU, which effectively forced the country to remain subject to EU regulations and payments, without any voting power (Timothy, 2019). Although the UK Prime Minister attempted to renegotiate the Withdrawal Agreement to allow its terms to be altered and therefore acceptable to Parliament, the EU refused but it agreed to an extension of the exit deadline until 31 October 2019. After the UK Prime Minister Theresa May resigned in June 2019 as a result of her failure to deliver Brexit, the subsequent election was won by the founder of the Brexit, or Leave movement, Boris Johnson as Conservative Party Leader. Johnson has pledged to leave the EU with no deal if the EU is not willing to reopen negotiations including removing the backstop. However, the UK Conservative Party had a majority of two seats in Parliament when he took office on 24 July, which is considered insufficient to ensure that either a new agreement will be passed by Parliament or that it will agree to leave the UK with no deal, even though the default position is no deal if no agreement with EU has been reached by that deadline (New Statesman, 2019). Therefore, uncertainty remains as to the exact nature of the ongoing relationships between the EU and the UK.

Bibliography

Alesina, A., Favero, C., & Giavazzi, F. (2012). *The Output Effect of Fiscal Consolidations* (National Bureau of Economic Research Inc. NBER Working Papers: 18336).

Arestis, P., & Sawyer, M. (2013). *Economic and Monetary Union Macroeconomic Policies: Current Practices and Alternatives*. Palgrave Macmillan.

Arroyo, H. T. (2011). *The EU's Fiscal Crisis and Policy Response: Reforming Economic Governance in the EU*. European Commission.

Azzopardi-Muscat, N., & Brand, H. (2014). The 'European Semester' – A Growing Force Shaping Health Systems Policy and Reform in the European Union. *European Journal of Public Health, 24*(2). http://eurpub.oxfordjournals.org/content/24/suppl_2/cku164.089. Accessed 17 June 2015.

Bank of England. (2015). *What Is Quantitative Easing?* Bank of England. http://www.bankofengland.co.uk/monetarypolicy/pages/qe/default.aspx. Accessed 24 June 2015.

Barnard, C. (2012). The Financial Crisis and the Euro Plus Pact: A Labour Lawyer's Perspective. *Industrial Law Journal, 41*(1), 98–114.

Barro, R. J. (1989). The Ricardian Approach to Budget Deficits. *Journal of Economic Perspectives, 3*(2), 37–54.

BBC. (2015, July 14). Greece Profile – Timeline. *BBC News*. http://www.bbc.com/news/world-europe-17373216. Accessed 6 July 2015.

BBC. (2018, June 30). Migrant Crisis: Italy Minister Salvini Closes Ports to NGO Boats. *BBC* [online]. Available at: https://www.bbc.com/news/wo. Accessed 18 Aug 2018.

BBC. (2019, July 8). Greece Elections: Centre-Right Regains Power Under Kyriakos Mitsotakis. *BBC*. https://www.bbc.com/news/world-48902766. Accessed 28 July 2019.

Bibow, J. (2013). *On the Franco-German Euro Contradiction and Ultimate Euro Battleground*. Bard College Levy Economics Institute.

Buiter, W. (2009, October 28). The Proposed European Systemic Risk Board Is Overweight Central Bankers. *Financial Times*. http://blogs.ft.com/maverecon/2009/10/the-proposed-european-systemic-risk-board-is-overweight-central-bankers/#axzz3dDt1LAgs. Accessed 16 June 2015.

Buiter, W., & Rabhari, R. (2012). *The ECB as Lender of Last Resort for Sovereigns in the Euro Area* (CEPR, Discussion Paper No. 8974).

Buxbaum, R., Hertig, G., Hirsch, A., & Hopt, K. (2011). *European Economic and Business Law: Legal and Economic Analyses on Integration and Harmonization*. De Gruyter.

Carrel, P. (2015, March 11). Germany Wants IMF Involved in Greek Bailout for Reform Rigour: Sources. *Reuters*. https://www.reuters.com/article/instant-article/idUSKCN0QP1HJ20150820. Accessed 18 Jan 2021.

Cayla, D. (2013). European Debt Crisis: How a Public Debt Restructuring Can Solve a Private Debt Issue. *Journal of Economic Issues, XLVII*(2), 427–437.

CFR. (2021). *Greece's Debt 1974–2018*. Council of Foreign Relations. https://www.cfr.org/timeline/greeces-debt-crisis-timeline. Accessed 18 Jan 2021.

Costeloe, K. (2018, July 23). *Italy's Populist Spending Plans Start to Strain Coalition*. Bloomberg. https://www.bloomberg.com/news/articles/2018-07-23/italy-s-league-pushes-for-challenge-to-eu-budget-restrictions. Accessed 18 Aug 2018.

Cramme, O., & Hobolt, S. B. (2014). *Democratic Politics in a European Union Under Stress*. Oxford University Press.

Crysoloras, N. (2013). *Rebuilding Eurozone's Ground Zero: A Review of the Greek Economic Crisis*. London School of Economics.

De Grauwe, P. (2015, January 21). The Sad Consequences of the Fear of QE. *The Economist*. https://www.economist.com/free-exchange/2015/01/21/the-sad-consequences-of-the-fear-of-qe. Accessed 18 Jan 2021.

De Witte, B. (2011). The European Treaty Amendment for the Creation of a Financial Stability Mechanism. *European Policy Analysis, 6*, 1–8.

Dieter, H. (2009). Europe's Crisis Management: Missed Opportunities. *Journal of Australian Political Economy, 64*, 141–157.

EC. (2009). *Economic Crisis in Europe: Causes, Consequences and Responses: European Economy 7/2009*. European Commission.

EC. (2012). *Implementation of the Compact for Growth and Jobs*. European Commission.

EC. (2014). *EU Bank Recovery and Resolution Directive (BRRD): Frequently Asked Questions*. European Commission.

EC. (2015, July 13). *Agreement on Greece; President Juncker Satisfied: "There Will Not Be a Grexit"*. European Commission. http://ec.europa.eu/news/2015/07/20150713_en.htm. Accessed 15 July 2015.

EC. (2017). *International Trade in Goods*. European Commission. http://ec.europa.eu/eurostat/statistics-explained/index.php/International_trade_in_goods. Accessed 12 June 2017.

Economist. (2015, January 24). Quantitative Easing in the Euro Zone: Better Late Than Never. *The Economist*. https://www.economist.com/finance-and-economics/2015/01/22/better-late-than-never. Accessed 18 Jan 2021.

Economist. (2019, July 11). The Most Dangerous Man in Europe: How to Defuse the Threat That Matteo Salvini Poses to the Euro. *The Economist*. https://www.economist.com/leaders/2019/07/11/how-to-defuse-the-threat-that-matteo-salvini-poses-to-the-euro. Accessed 28 July 2019.

EFSF. (2015). About EFSF. *European Financial Stability Facility Commission* [online]. http://www.efsf.europa.eu/about/index.htm. Accessed 17 June 2015.

Eisenbeis, R. A., & Kaufman, G. G. (2007). *Cross-Border Banking: Challenges for Deposit Insurance and Financial Stability in the European Union* (Federal Reserve Bank of Atlanta Working Paper 2006–15a).

Elliott, L. (2018, April 8). Why the UK Trade Deficit with the EU Is Woeful and Widening. *The Guardian*. https://www.theguardian.com/business/2018/apr/08/why-the-uk-trade-deficit-with-the-eu-is-woeful-and-widening. Accessed 18 Aug 2018.

ESM. (2015). *ESM Factsheet*. European Stability Mechanism.

ESRB. (2010). Regulation (EU) No 1092/2010 of the European Parliament and of the Council. *Brussels: Official Journal of the European Union, 331*(1).

ESRB. (2015). *Establishment of the ESRB*. ESRB [online]. http://www.theguardian.com/business/2011/aug/07/global-financial-crisis-key-stages. Accessed 16 June 2015.

EU. (2013). Recommendation of The European Systemic Risk Board of 4 April 2013 on Intermediate Objectives and Instruments of Macro-Prudential Policy. *Brussels: Official Journal of the European Union, 170*(2), 1–19.

EUI. (2015). *Constitutional Change Through Euro Crisis Law*. EUI. http://eurocrisislaw.eui.eu/topic/tfeu/. Accessed 14 July 2015.

Evans-Pritchard, A. (2014). Greek Candidate Willing to Call European Leaders' Bluff. *The Telegraph*. http://www.telegraph.co.uk/finance/comment/ambroseevans_pritchard/11286477/Greek-candidate-willing-to-call-European-leaders-bluff.html. Accessed 15 July 2015.

Evans-Pritchard, A. (2015, January 26). Greek Coalition Braces for Debt Showdown as Germany Rattles Sabre. *The Telegraph*. http://www.telegraph.co.uk/finance/economics/11370960/Greek-coalition-braces-for-debt-showdown-as-Germany-rattles-sabre.html. Accessed 15 July 2015.

Fawley, R. W., & Neely, C. J. (2013, January/February). Four Stories of Quantitative Easing. *Federal Reserve Bank of St. Louis Review*.

Fowler, M. R., & Bunck, J. M. (1996). What Constitutes the Sovereign State? *Review of International Studies, 22*(4), 381–404.

Hall, B. (2000). Immigration in the European Union: Problem or Solution? *OECD Observer*. http://oecdobserver.org/news/archivestory.php/aid/337/Immigration_in_the_European_Union:_problem_or_solution_.html. Accessed 18 Aug 2018.

Hoffmann, S. (2000). Towards a Common European Foreign and Security Policy? *Journal of Common Market Studies, 38*(2), 189–198.

Holehouse, M. (2015, July 13). EU Demands Britain Joins Greek Rescue Fund. *The Telegraph*. http://www.telegraph.co.uk/finance/economics/11737286/EU-demands-Britain-joins-Greek-rescue-fund.html. Accessed 2 Nov 2020.

Hunt, A., & Wheeler, B. (2018, July 31). Brexit: All You Need to Know About the UK Leaving the EU. *BBC News*. https://www.bbc.com/news/uk-politics-32810887. Accessed 18 Aug 2018.

IMF. (2009). *Global Financial Security Report: Navigating the Financial Challenges Ahead*. International Monetary Fund.

IMF. (2015a). *Global Financial Stability Report April 2015*. IMF.

IMF. (2015b). *Greece Preliminary Draft Debt Sustainability Analysis* (IMF Country Report No. 15/186).

IMF. (2015c). *Greece: An Update of IMF Staff's Preliminary Public Debt Sustainability Analysis* (IMF Country Report No. 15/186).

Jones, E., & Bindi, F. (2018, July 31). *Will Italy's Divided Politics Cripple Europe's Economy – or Worse?* University of Philadelphia Wharton School Knowledge Wharton. https://knowledge.wharton.upenn.edu/article/instability-italy-crisis-will-impact-europe/. Accessed 18 Jan 2010.

Kaldor, M., & Vizard, P. (2011). *Arguing About the World: The Work and Legacy of Meghnad Desai*. Bloomsbury Publishing.

Keen, S. (2014). Austerity or Quantitative Easing? *Ecodate, 28*(1), 5–7.

Kerr, F. (2016). Comment: Post Brexit. *New Blackfriars, 97*(1072), 659–660.

Khan, M. (2015a, April 1). Greece Threatens Default as Fresh Reform Bid Falters. *The Telegraph*. http://www.telegraph.co.uk/finance/economics/11509302/Greece-threatens-international-default-without-fresh-bailout-cash.html. Accessed 2 Apr 2015.

Khan, M. (2015b, July 14). Greece News Live: Osborne Fights Brussels Plans for Greek Bailout as Athens Reels from 'Humiliating' Deal. *The Telegraph*. http://www.telegraph.co.uk/finance/economics/11738150/Osborne-fights-Brussels-plans-for-Greek-bailout-after-Greeks-reel-from-humiliating-deal.html. Accessed 14 July 2015.

Khan, M., & Wright, B. (2015, July 13). Crucified Tsipras Capitulates to Draconian Measures After 17 Hours of Late Night Talks: As It Happened. *The Telegraph*. http://www.telegraph.co.uk/finance/economics/11735609/Greece-news-live-Crucified-Tsipras-capitulates-to-draconian-measures-after-17-hours-of-late-night-talks.html. Accessed 16 July 2015.

Konoe, S. (2010). *International Finance and Policy Cooperation: Before and After the 2007–2010 Financial Crisis* (EUI Working Paper MWP 2010/24).

Krugman, P. (2015, April 29). The Case for Cuts Was a Lie. Why Does Britain Still Believe It? The Austerity Delusion. *The Guardian*. http://www.theguardian.

com/business/ng-interactive/2015/apr/29/the-austerity-delusion. Accessed 10 Aug 2015.

Marta, R. S. J. (2015). *The Financial Obligation in International Law*. Oxford University Press.

Mavradis, S. (2017). Greece's Economic and Social Transformation 2008–2017. *MDPI Social Science, 7*(9), 1–14.

McKinsey. (2012). *Greece 10 Years Ahead*. McKinsey & Co.

Mickonyte, A. (2018). *Divisions in Europe Expose the Need for an Ambitious Reform of the European Union* (OGFE Policy Brief 11).

NCA. (2015). *The European System of Financial Supervision*. Netherlands Court of Audit. http://www.courtofaudit.nl/english/Publications/Topics/EU_governance_to_combat_the_economic_and_financial_crisis/The_European_system_of_financial_supervision. Accessed 24 June 2015.

New Statesman. (2019, July 22). What Is the Government's Working Majority in Parliament? *New Statesman*. https://www.newstatesman.com/politics/uk/2019/07/what-governments-working-majority-parliament. Accessed 29 July 2019.

Niemann, A., & Schmitter, P. (2009). Neo-functionalism. In A. Wiener & T. Diez (Eds.), *Theories of European Integration* (2nd ed., pp. 45–66). Oxford University Press.

OECD. (2018). Greece. *OECD Economic Outlook, 1*, 150–152.

Olivares-Caminel, R. (2011). The EU Architecture to Avert a Sovereign Debt Crisis. *OECD Journal, 2011*(2), 1–32.

Palaiologos, Y. (2015, August 31). Some Questions for Alexis Tsipras. *Wall Street Journal*. http://www.wsj.com/articles/some-questions-for-alexis-tsipras-1441048578. Accessed 3 Sep 2015.

Perrut, D. (2012). Financial Regulation After the "Subprime" Crisis: What Has Been Learned and What Reforms Made? *Foundation Robert Schuman/European Issues, 246*, 1–13.

Pisani-Ferry, J., & Sapir, A. (2009). *Banking Crisis Management in the EU: An Interim Assessment* (Bruegel Working Paper, 2009/07).

Rachman, G. (2016, December 5). Italy's Threat to Europe's Future. *Financial Times*. https://www.ft.com/content/cedfc28c-b884-11e6-ba85-95d1533d9a62. Accessed 17 Aug 2018.

Rankin, J., & Smith, H. (2015). The Great Greece Fire Sale. *The Guardian*. https://www.theguardian.com/business/2015/jul/24/greek-debt-crisis-great-greece-fire-sale. Accessed 18 Jan 2021.

Rayner, G. (2018, August 5). No-deal Brexit will break the EU's own laws, ministers warn Brussels. *The Telegraph* [online]. https://www.telegraph.co.uk/politics/2018/08/05/brussels-will-break-laws-refuses-compromise-brexit/. Accessed 18 August 2018.

Rayner, G. (2019, July 19). Britain's EU Contribution Rises by 20 Per cent in Year, as Uk's Booming Economy Props Up Brussels' Budget. *The Telegraph*.

https://www.telegraph.co.uk/politics/2019/07/19/britains-contribution-eu-rises-20-per-cent-year-uks-booming/. Accessed 29 July 2019.

Renwick, A. (2017). *The Process of Brexit: What Comes Next?* (UCL European Institute Working Paper).

Robinson, T. (2018). *Italy Has Closed Its Ports to Migrant Ships and Refugees*. Borgen Project. https://borgenproject.org/italy-has-closed-its-ports/ https://borgenproject.org/italy-has-closed-its-ports/. Accessed 18 Aug 2018.

Rothwell, J. (2018, August 17). Greece Warns 'No-Deal' Brexit Would Plunge Country into 'Financial And Political Instability'. *The Telegraph*. https://www.telegraph.co.uk/politics/2018/08/17/greece-warns-no-deal-brexit-would-plunge-country-financial-political/. Accessed 17 Aug 2018.

Schmieding, H. (2012). Tough Love: The True Nature of the Eurozone Crisis. *Business Economics, 47*(3), 177–189.

Schoenbaum, T. J. (2012). *The Age of Austerity: The Global Financial Crisis and the Return to Economic Growth*. Cheltenham: Edward Elgar Publishing.

Schoenmaker, D. (2014). *On the Need for a Fiscal Backstop to the Banking System* (VU University DSF Policy Paper, No. 44.SG, 2017).

Sloman, J., Garrett, D., & Guest, J. (2018). *Economics* (10th ed.). Pearson.

Spence, P., & Bradshaw, J. (2015, July 17). Greece News: Europe Gives Go Ahead for Third Greek Bailout Talks – As It Happened 17 July 2015. *The Telegraph*. http://www.telegraph.co.uk/finance/11745779/Greece-live-Germany-and-Austria-prepare-to-vote-on-bailout-talks.html. Accessed 18 July 2015.

Spence, P., & Wright, B. (2015, July 16). Greece News: Brussels Prepares to Release Emergency Loan to Get Greece Through July – As It Happened 17 July 2015. *The Telegraph*. http://www.telegraph.co.uk/finance/economics/11743163/Greece-news-live-Brussels-prepares-to-release-emergency-loan-to-get-Greece-through-July.html. Accessed 18 July 2015.

Steinhauser, G., & Dalton, M. (2015, February 20). Eurozone Agrees on Four-Month Extension of Greece Bailout. *Reuters*. http://www.wsj.com/articles/eurozone-approves-greece-bailout-extension-1424435121. Acessed 16 July 2015.

Stiglitz, J. E. (2015). Europe's Attack on Greek Democracy. *Project Syndicate* [online], June 29. Available at: http://www.project-syndicate.org/commentary/greece-referendum-troika-eurozone-by-joseph-e%2D%2Dstiglitz-2015-06#wh1z1FhUvZgLI3VQ.99. Accessed 16 July 2015.

Strupczewski, J. (2015, July 14). EU Exec to Recommend Use of EFSM for Greek Bridge Financing – Officials. *Reuters*. http://www.reuters.com/article/2015/07/14/eu-greece-financing-efsm-idUSL5N0ZU36E20150714. Accessed 16 July 2015.

Tait, N. (2008, November 26). EU's stimulus plan met with doubts. *Financial Times* [online]. http://www.ft.com/cms/s/0/0b216d84-bba6-11dd-ae97-0000779fd18c.html#ixzz3dEYyxmuW. Accessed 16 June 2015.

Timothy, N. (2019, July 28). Varadkar Can Blame Britain All He Likes – but He Is the Real Threat to Peace. *The Telegraph*. https://www.telegraph.co.uk/politics/2019/07/28/varadkar-can-blame-britain-likes-real-threat-peace/. Accessed 29 July 2019.

Touri, K., & Touri, K. (2014). *The Eurozone Crisis: A Constitutional Analysis.* Cambridge University Press.

Walker, N. (2019, May 23). *Brexit Timeline: Events Leading to the UK's Exit from the European Union* (House of Commons Briefing Paper Number 7960).

Ward, M. (2019, July 24). *Statistics on UK-EU Trade* (House of Commons Briefing Paper Number 7851).

Wearden, G. (2015, June 29). Greek Crisis: Banks Shut for a Week as Capital Controls Imposed – As It Happened. *The Guardian*. http://www.theguardian.com/business/live/2015/jun/28/greek-crisis-ecb-emergency-liquidity-referendum-bailout-live. Accessed 16 July 2015.

Wolf, M. (2012, March 6). The pain in Spain will test the euro. *Financial Times* [online]. http://www.ft.com/intl/cms/s/0/f54332d2-66dc-11e1-9e53-00144feabdc0.html#axzz3dEXYMemL. Accessed 17 June 2015.

Wolff, G. B. (2015, July 14). *Olivier Blanchard fails to recognise two major IMF mistakes in Greece - the IMF needs to draw the right conclusions.* Breugel [online]. http://data.worldbank.org/indicator/GC.BAL.CASH.GD.ZS?page=1. Accessed 16 July 2015.

Zartman, I. W. (2019). *How Negotiations End.* Cambridge University Press.

CHAPTER 7

EU Initiatives

The Economic Recovery Plan

Plan Details

The consequence of the 2008 crisis was to influence substantial labour reform as quickly as possible and was effected by temporary income support for the unemployed, accompanied by short-term working initiatives that were integrated into the EC Economic Recovery Package. The communication from the EC to the European Council regarding the first Economic Recovery Plan (ERP) in November 2008 contained the following statement in its introduction:

> The current economic crisis gives another opportunity to show that Europe serves its citizens best when it makes concrete action the touchstone. Europe can make the difference.

In difficult times, the temptation is to feel powerless but Europe is not powerless according to EC (2008): the levers of government, and the instruments of the European Union, the influence of intelligent coordination combine to produce a potent force to arrest the trend towards a deeper recession. The plan states that the particular contribution of the European Union is its ability to help partners work together, and its harnessing of Member States and community action represents a powerful

S. Weißschnur, *The Proportionality of State Intervention*,
https://doi.org/10.1007/978-3-030-75676-5_7

lever for change to exist (2008, p. 2). The document stated that national governments had already started to devise plans to resolve the effects of the crisis and these were underpinned by the common principles agreed for the single market (EC, 2008, p. 2). Member States were urged to exploit the EU's strengths to support growth: effective coordination, credible frameworks, such as the Stability and Growth Pact and the Lisbon Strategy; the enormous scale that the Euro and the largest global single market offered. The proposed recovery plan, which the EU/EC and Member States were asked to approve, was intended to enable joint action to limit the extent of the economic downturn, to stimulate demand, to inspire confidence, to allow business continuation and to preserve jobs until the economy moved back into the growth phase. The principle on which the plan was based was one of 'solidarity and social justice' (EC, 2008, p. 4), to support those Member States with the greatest need, and supported by the European Globalisation Adjustment Fund and an accelerated European Social Fund.

The plan comprised two major interventions: a €200 billion financial injection, €170 billion expansion of Member State budgets and €30 billion from EU, amounting to 1.5% GDP. This would create more demand and represented an action within the confines of the Stability and Growth Pact, a programme to increase European competitiveness in the short term, referred to as smart investment. Smart investment was described as investing in the most important skills for future productivity and growth, becoming a knowledge economy. It also meant concentrating specifically on energy efficiency, clean technologies based on low carbon emissions, which would be drivers of growth and would create new jobs, for example, in the automobile and construction sectors. This strategy would reduce Europe's reliance on imported energy and reduce domestic and business energy costs. In addition, infrastructure investment and improved connectedness were vital, reference being made to enhancing internet skills and use of internet, to increase innovation and productivity. Monetary policy was to be employed to support this by lowering interest rates, but also renewing the financial system, specifically the banking sector, which needed to lend to businesses and apply the lower interest rates (EC, 2008). The European Investment Bank (EIB), which focuses on lending for investment products, raising finance from other sources and advising Member States on how to raise finance for projects and managing them, has the purpose of supporting EU growth and employment, promoting innovation and skills, and financial support for smaller businesses, and creating strategic infrastructure and climate-related projects (EIB, 2015). Hence, the EIB played a significant role in delivering the plan, increased its annual investment budget by €7.5 billion for the coming two years and aimed to attract additional funding from external sources; EC (2008) urged Member States to use EIB resources. The European Bank for Reconstruction and Development (EBRD) was originally established to manage the reunification of Germany, currently offers project finance and business advice globally, mainly to emerging economies (EBRD, 2015), and was expected to increase its funding for new EU members by €500 million per year (EC, 2008).

The plan also emphasised the different financial and economic positions of each Member State, and the need for them to monitor and rectify their imbalances when devising their individual plans based on the EU Recovery Plan. Member States were encouraged to boost employment and economic growth by using discretionary spending rather than reducing taxes, to create domestic demand, for instance, financial support for projects related to climate change or improving infrastructure for SMEs. Concurrently, Member States were urged to minimise the social benefits provided to citizens, in order to focus on the poorest households, and to temporarily lengthen the term of unemployment benefits. They were also encouraged to provide bridging loans for companies in temporary financial difficulties, and incentives to initiate projects related to energy efficiency or green technologies. The lowering of employee taxes and social contributions should take place to boost disposable income and to create demand, and was to be accompanied by a temporary reduction in the rate of value-added tax. All measures taken by Member States were required to align with the SGP, in other words, common targets should apply across all EU countries. The plan envisaged that the 3% GDP deficit could be breached, and the ERP stated that this additional deficit could be rectified as recovery occurred. Member States were expected to provide updated stability or convergence programmes for the medium term, and to include the measures that would be taken to reverse any breach of the deficit, and hence to restore sustainability in the medium term, by means of budgetary policy that focused on better procedures and frameworks. Structural reform would be needed, such as market functioning to reduce prices, wages linked to productivity, more flexible working time, enhanced employment services support and reduction in state bureaucracy/regulation to increase productivity (EC, 2008).

Therefore, a fiscal stimulus should align with the Lisbon strategy priorities of people, business, infrastructure and energy, research and innovation, and ESF funding would support these initiatives, which intended to protect jobs and to promote entrepreneurship. Specific proposals regarding people were a major employment initiative, and the objectives were to upgrade the skills of the low skilled by means of personal counselling, intensive training, apprenticeship schemes and employment subsidies, and to provide financial support for new self-employed start-up businesses. Employability of the low skilled was to be improved by better management of job vacancies and lower social charges on low-income jobs; these measures would enable more individuals to enter the labour market and this objective would be further improved by subsidised child care, and the creation of temporary jobs for vulnerable groups. In addition to reducing bureaucracy for businesses, for which the Small Business Act had been introduced, start-ups should receive the requisite authorisation within three days, without any cost being incurred. When start-ups wished to employ their first employee, a simple, single process should be possible and the costs of start-up patent applications and trademarks were to be reduced by 75% and 50% respectively. Micro enterprises were also allowed to cease producing mandatory annual accounts and would be able to set up a company for a one Euro fee. Member States could access the increased EIB financial resource, but grants were limited to projects in the specified key industries and on training. Grant authorisation would be particularly available for research into products, which had environmental standards beyond the present EU minimum. Member States should also adopt European Private Company law to allow SMEs to operate under single market rules. Public sector invoices should be paid to all their creditors within 30 days, as a means to support business cashflow, and e-invoicing adopted for speed and cost-saving purposes (EC, 2008).

The ERP devised for 2010 to 2013 appeared to be a continuation of the 2008 ERP, but with the development of three related partnership initiatives. The Commission and industrial partners were described as committed to intensive collaboration to develop the implementation plans for the three partnership: Factories of the Future, referred to as being focused on the manufacturing sector and attracting R&D funding of €1.2 billion; Energy Efficient Buildings, an initiative directed at the construction sector, with €1 billion of R&D; the automobile sector initiative entitled Green Cars, with €5 billion funding, which included €1 billion for R&D (EC, 2009). The Commission proposed to provide a contribution of 50%

to the total R&D budget from the 7th Framework Programme budget, with matching investment coming from the private sector.

EU 2020 Growth Strategy

The 2020 Growth Strategy, devised in 2010, referred to long-term employment and growth, an integral part of the ERP, in which five interconnected targets could be delivered: minimum employment levels of 75% for EU citizens aged between 20 and 64 years; 3% GDP invested in innovative R&D; reduction in school drop-out rate to less than 10%, whilst increasing participation to 40% of the population in tertiary education, degree or diploma; reduction in poverty and social inclusion levels by 20 million; reduction in carbon emissions by 20%, whilst enhancing renewable energy usage by 20% and energy efficiency by 20%. Individual Member States were encouraged to convert these priorities into national targets, which would reflect the different initial positions regarding them; the targets were politically binding, and two were legally binding on Member States, reducing carbon emissions and renewable energy use (EC, 2014b).

The EU Compact for Growth and Jobs and Youth Initiatives

In June 2012, the European Council agreed on further measures in an attempt to ensure that the 2020 targets could be achieved. A €120 billion increase in funding available from EIB was recommended, and pilot project bonds were to be introduced. The EC suggested this new initiative would act as a catalyst for growth and attract private funding. The project bonds were intended to drive major investments in infrastructure, transport, broadband and energy, and Member States were allowed to reallocate other funds with EC approval. In addition, measures should be implemented for unemployment reduction, whilst supporting improvement in business growth, initiating tax reforms and creating the EU Single Energy Market (EC, 2012a).

A Youth Employment Package was introduced in December 2012, specifically to support Member States to assist the under 25s to obtain jobs, and was to take place by means of a Youth Guarantee Scheme, which ranged from finding jobs, to creating apprenticeships, and education and training for those who had completed their education or who had become unemployed up to four months previously. In order to implement the scheme, Member States were advised to form partnerships with organisations that could support the initiative, individual Member State progress was monitored and advice was given in the European Semester meetings. In addition, traineeships were launched to provide work experience for school children, and the quality and number of apprenticeship schemes to be enhanced by formation of the European Alliance for Apprenticeships, sharing best practice, and helping Member States to remove mobility barriers for young people seeking employment (EC, 2012b).

The Youth Employment Initiative, an intervention suggested in February 2013, required a budget of €6 billion and was targeted to be in operation from 2014 to 2020. It would be focused on Member States with youth unemployment exceeding 25% in 2012, and its intention was to increase the speed of implementation of the Youth Employment Package. A dedicated budget of €3 billion would be directed from Youth Employment budget, and a minimum of an extra €3 billion would be granted from the ESF; however, this part of the funding required an additional contribution from the Member State concerned (EC, 2013a).

Monitoring the ERP and 2020 Strategy

The EC used the LABREF database to monitor labour market policies in relation to the EU economic policy; the data suggests two well-defined phases. Immediately after 2008, reforms were directed at labour taxation, social welfare and unemployment benefits, to reduce the impact of the recession and to stabilise redundancy levels, by means of Member States initiating or extending short time work initiatives. The purpose was to encourage better management of Member State labour costs after the recession whilst concurrently containing job losses. The second phase after 2010 was characterised by tax wedge reductions and unemployment benefit reform; reforms that concentrated on job protection, wage level management and working hours. The implementation of this phase was most evident in Southern European Member States. Unemployment benefit reform related to reducing the degree of passive labour market policies because the lower availability of benefits appeared to be most effective in reducing unemployment (Turrini et al., 2014). Tax wedge is a term that relates to labour market taxes and includes employer taxes, employee taxes, social security contributions and employee personal income tax. The variation in tax wedge rates across the Member States in 2012 was substantial, for instance, 20% in Malta and over 50% in Belgium; Italy had the highest level of the South European group at approximately 44%, almost equivalent to Germany (EC, 2013b). In addition, active labour market policies were most evident in Belgium, Luxembourg and Denmark where long-term unemployment was low, but very weak in Italy, which had one of the worst instances of long-term unemployment. Passive labour markets are characterised by paying unemployment benefits, which are considered by some to reduce incentives to apply for low-paid jobs, and their existence was particularly high, for example, in Ireland and Estonia (EC, 2013c).

Review of 2020 Targets

The EC review undertaken in 2014 found that progress across Member States was mixed in relation to formal education, an overall decline of 3% to 12.7% was recorded for the years from 2005 to 2012 and it was acknowledged that this could be partly a consequence of lower employment prospects (EC, 2014c). However, the review stated that structural changes were evident and had contributed to over 50% of Member States reaching their targets but no statement was made about whether national and EU targets were in alignment. In terms of tertiary education completions over the same period, an increase from 27.9% to 35.7% was recorded, and considered to be a result of structural change. Employment levels declined by 0.1% from 2010 to 2012, measured as 68.4% compared with 70.3% in 2008; the forecast was 72% in 2020. However, the variation in Member States was substantial, for instance Sweden and Germany had high employment levels (Fig. 7.1).

Some Southern and Eastern European countries had failed to meet their targets by significant amounts and failure was suggested as being due to a huge decline in employment in these Member States since 2000, and limited mobility across borders. In addition, older workers and immigrants had lower skills, which did not match the labour market need for knowledge workers, and therefore Member States needed to drive lifetime learning programmes to be able to meet employment goals (EC, 2014c). The innovation goal of 3% of GDP was forecast as unlikely to be met, since the level was just 2.06% by 2012 and envisaged to reach only 2.2% by 2020.

The achievement of green issue targets was forecast since EU had already accomplished 18% of greenhouse gas reduction by 2012, renewable use was at 14.4%, almost double that in 2000, and primary energy consumption fell by 8% in the six years to 2012. However, poverty and

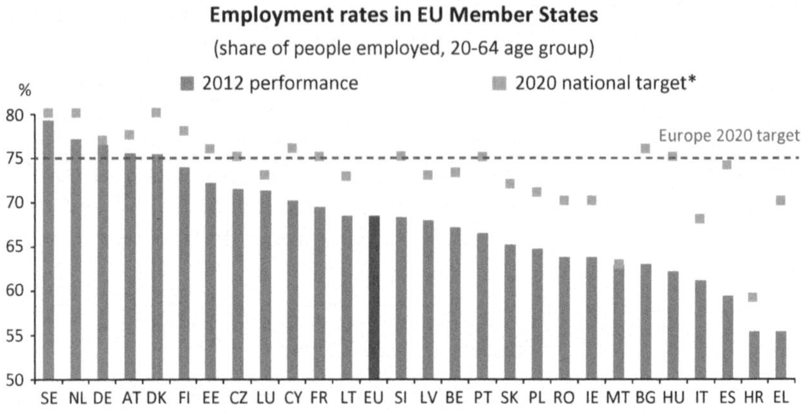

Fig. 7.1 2012 Employment level versus 2020 target in EU Member States. (Source: EC (2014c, p. 5))

social exclusion targets, which included jobless households, rose by 10 million from 2009 to 2012 when the total was 124 million, with 100 million at risk of poverty. The comment made on this situation by EC (2014c) was that the level of poverty was related to conditions in specific Member States, which had many jobless households and many were also severely deprived in material terms.

External Assessment of ERP

An appraisal of the 2008 ERP by Cameron (2010) suggested that it was unsuccessful in meeting its targets for two reasons: a solely fiscal stimulus was implemented; the EU was not characterised by fiscal and monetary union. The consequence of these factors was that Member States had discretion in how they implemented their responses in terms of national fiscal policies, and the outcome of the initiative varied considerably across Member States. The diversity in application of the intervention was largely a consequence of the EU taking no further active participation in the implementation other than preparing the plan. Some states quickly regulated their financial sector, whilst others took a laissez-faire approach, and the creation of part-time or flexible working to reduce unemployment in some countries contrasted with inaction in others, in which no interventions were made. Therefore, a few states had experienced some economic recovery by 2010 but others were still in deep recession, and Cameron (2010) proposed that the EU had massively underestimated the severity of the problem. The data available provided evidence that a severe worsening of the impact of the crisis had occurred before the plan was implemented and, despite advice from the OECD and US Administration to increase the fiscal stimulus from 1.5% GDP to at least 4% GDP, the EC president and colleagues chose to continue as planned. However, Cameron (2010) acknowledged that changes in policy would have also been difficult as 27 countries were involved, and proposed that the EC had little understanding of Keynesian measures to stimulate the economy. In addition, EC had insufficient budget, approximately 1% GDP, whereas the combined nation states had over 50% GDP, and EC could not issue debt. The ERP acknowledged the deficit status of some Member States and that these would be further beyond the required EU's 3% GDP limit when they implemented the plan, and suggested they do so, but should also devise additional plans to redress the issue as their economies grew. This was poor advice by Cameron (2010) and hypocrisy by Rommerskirchen (2012), noting that it was the first time EMU had encouraged rather than condemned deficits. Hence, the policymakers devising the ERP had facilitated the path for nation states to use Keynesian style spending as a means to end the recession, accompanied by vague advice on how to do so. However the ERP inferred that it was advisable to record the accomplishment of the relevant activities in a systematic manner during the period in formal language; the recommendations were communicated as if the policymakers were consultants to the Member States (Rommerskirchen, 2012).

The assessment of the ERP by Cameron (2010) was that some Member States had budget surpluses at the time, which enabled then to implement it but those with deficits would have difficulty in doing so, and could and did choose to ignore the EC proposals, especially as growth contraction had been greater than in the 1930s' depression. Since fiscal policy was a national responsibility but monetary policy was controlled by EC, there could be no coordination of the two, as was needed (Cameron, 2010.). Similar conclusions were drawn in other studies regarding lack of coordination of fiscal policy and the increase in Member State deficits that occurred during this period, possibly as a result of following ERP guidelines. Consequently, the forecast economic growth did not emerge (Coenen et al., 2012). An appraisal of the EC interventions to stem unemployment during the crisis also focused on the lack of coordination, because the 27 EU states all had different labour laws and labour market policies. Each country had employed a range of policies, so that attempting to identify which ones had been used most frequently and to compare their effectiveness was not possible (Davulis & Petrylaitė, 2012).

The OECD (OECD, 2009) commented on the lack of progress regarding the EU innovation targets set in 2000 and again with ERP (2008), stating that Europe lagged behind the US and Japan. The report proposed that relying on measuring innovation inputs, rather than the outputs they produced, was a flaw in the plan, since measuring output provided the knowledge to amend the innovation policy effectively; EU measurement methodology was also suggested as weak. In regard to energy policies, OECD also commented that these should be strengthened, several shortcomings were identified and the measurement process considered less than optimum (OECD, 2009). Suggested amendments to the policy included ensuring that the renewable energy policy was accomplished in the most effective way, for instance, by making sure that the public procurement policies favoured renewables, and that joint projects on renewables between Member States were encouraged, as well as taking measures to ensure the benefits of policies for reducing renewable energy exceeded their costs.

The EU Single Market

The EU Single Market: Drivers for Growth

The ERP (2008) suggested that the fundamental drivers for growth as a single market were the creation of a knowledge economy, energy efficiency relying on increased usage of green technologies and greater connectedness based on optimising internet usage by businesses and citizens. These themes are developed further in later publications, for instance, the amendments to the Single Market Act in 2011 and 2012 defined the four major drivers of growth. The revision of the legislation was stated as vital owing to the changes in the external environment since the 2008 financial crisis. The fundamental means of achieving the EU vision of a highly competitive social market economy, a single market visibly representing Europe's competitiveness in global terms, was that it would foster growth through consistent and complementary policies (EC, 2012c). The major growth drivers were stated as development of fully integrated energy and transport networks across all Member States within the single market; enabling movement of people and businesses across borders; driving the digital economy within the Member States to enhance productivity and creativity; intensifying social entrepreneurship, consistency and consumer confidence by making opportunities available to all individuals and businesses on the basis of fair, robust and equitable rules (EC, 2012c).

The concept of the digital single market as a driver for economic growth had emphasised on three principles: access, economy and society and environment. Access referred to business and citizens employing the internet to purchase and sell goods and services, whilst economy and society stressed the importance of digital skills, on which 90% of all future jobs were forecast to rely 47% of EU population currently lacked those skills. In terms of the environment, innovative digital services were fundamental to EU economy so that EC intended to facilitate conditions for an advanced Information Communication Technology (ICT) infrastructure. It suggested that cloud technology and Big Data be employed for integrating regulatory conditions for investment in digital networks, so that all Member States were able to be equally competitive in the market (EC, 2015b). Investment was therefore required to create the ICT infrastructure so that EU society was more inclusive, would receive enhanced public services and ensure digital skills training for EU citizens (EC, 2015b).

Investment for Growth

The new EC Investment Plan, announced by the EC President in 2014, had three strands: investment, structural reform and fiscal responsibility. Finance would be raised from the EU budget, the SGP would provide the flexibility Member States required for strategic investments, and the existing European structural and investment funds would be more effectively allocated. Finance would therefore be targeted at strategic projects, which would be subject to a selection process, technical assistance would be given with preparation for selection, and outreach activities should provide real work experience. The investment environment was forecast to improve owing to new quality regulation, new sources of long-term finance, removal of barriers in key sectors and improvement in the quality of the taxation and public administration in Member States, so that funding could be allocated appropriately. The associated funding of €315 billion would be provided by various European funds, with €75 billion focused on SMEs and the remainder on long-term projects (EC, 2014a).

At the end of 2014, European growth was described as dire and as impacting negatively on the world economy, with GDP average growth of less than 1%, unemployment more than 11% and inflation at 0.4%, which bordered on deflation (Economist, 2014). The EC's three-year investment plan was not scheduled to begin until mid of 2015 and suggested as likely to have little effect by Economist (2014); the allocated sums were far too low, and the plan also relied on raising extra funding from private sources and Member States. In fact, no new funds were available and the allocation a mere 1% GDP, which had been redirected from other parts of the EU budget, which was limited and 40% of that budget was allocated to farm subsidies. Whilst supporting the idea of attracting private funding, Economist (2014) commented that finding the appropriate projects and passing the required legislation would be time consuming. Hence, the EC President's proposal that this plan would reverse the stagnating EU economy was not honest and could lead to Member States reducing the level of existing national measures. Economist (2014) suggested that highly targeted action was needed to include looser monetary policy, quicker structural reform by Member State governments, which in general were not convinced these were effective, and a fiscal policy that was more supportive of growth.

Investment for Growth in Greece

The measures proposed in the third Greek bailout for growth and job creation were that the EC should liaise with the Greek government to invest up to €35 billion to promote economic activity according to a range of EU initiatives, implied as already in place; investment in SMEs was part of this policy. In addition, the EC would increase pre-financing by €1 billion immediately to boost investment once the MoU was signed but EU control was demonstrated by a legislation for co-control; an investment plan for Europe was to be the means to fund opportunities for Greece (EC, 2015b). These recent proposals align with the policies appraised in Chap. 6.

Bibliography

Cameron, D. R. (2010). *Fiscal Responses to the Economic Contraction of 2008–09*. Yale University.

Coenen, G., Straub, R., & Trabandt, M. (2012). *Gauging the Effects of Fiscal Stimulus Packages in the Euro Area*. US Federal Reserve International Discussion Paper 1061.

Davulis, T., & Petrylaitė, D. (2012). Labour Regulation in the 21st Century. In *Search of Flexibility and Security*. Cambridge Scholars.

EBRD. (2015). *What We Do*. European Bank for Reconstruction and Development. http://www.ebrd.com/what-we-do.html. Accessed 2015 Jul 17.

EC. (2008). *Communication from the Commission to the European Council: A European Economic Recovery Plan*. European Commission.

EC. (2009). *Joint Statement & Press Package: European Economic Recovery Plan 2010–2013 Public Private Partnerships in Research Activities*. European Commission. http://ec.europa.eu/research/index.cfm?pg=newsalert&year=2009&na=ppp-310309. Accessed 2015 Jul 17.

EC. (2012a). *Implementation of the Compact for Growth and Jobs*. European Commission.

EC. (2012b). *Youth Employment: Commission Proposes Package of Measures*. European Commission.

EC. (2012c). *Single Market Act II: Together for new growth*. European Commission.

EC. (2013a). *Commission Proposes Rules to Make Youth Employment Initiative a Reality*. European Commission. http://ec.europa.eu/social/main.jsp?langId=en&catId=89&newsId=1829. Accessed 2015 Jul 2015.

EC. (2013b). *Tax Burden on Labour*. European Commission.

EC. (2013c). *Active Labour Market Policies*. European Commission.

EC. (2014a). *An Investment Plan for Europe*. European Commission.

EC. (2014b). *Q&A: Taking Stock of the Europe 2020 Strategy for Smart, Sustainable and Inclusive Growth*. European Commission. http://europa.eu/rapid/press-release_MEMO-14-149_en.htm. Accessed 2015 Jul 17.

EC. (2014c). *Taking Stock of the Europe 2020 Strategy for Smart, Sustainable and Inclusive Growth*. European Commission., 130 final/2.

EC. (2015a). *The EU at a Glance*. European Commission. http://ec.europa.eu/cyprus/eu_glance/index_en.htm. Accessed 2015 Apr 2.

EC. (2015b). *The Digital Single Market: Driving the Economic Growth*. European Commission. http://ec.europa.eu/digital-agenda/en/news/digital-single-market-driving-economic-growth. Accessed 2015 Jul 18.

Economist. (2014). *The European Commission's Investment Plan: Fiddling While Europe Burns*. The Economist. https://www.economist.com/leaders/2014/11/27/fiddling-while-europe-burns. Accessed 2021 Jan 18.

EIB. (2015). *EIB at a Glance*. European Investment Bank. http://www.eib.org/about/index.htm. Accessed 2015 Jul 17.

ERP. (2008). *A European Economic Recovery Plan*. Brussels: European Commission.

OECD. (2009). *OECD Economic Surveys: European Union 2009*. OECD.

Rommerskirchen, C. (2012). *The Difficulties of Fiscal Policy Coordination in Times of Economic and Financial Crisis*. Scotland Debates EU Economic Governance; 2012 Jun 1: University of Edinburgh.

Turrini, A., Koltay, G., Pierini, F., Goffard, C., & Kiss, A. (2014). *A Decade of Labour Market Reforms in the EU: Insights from the LABREF Database*. European Commission Economic Papers 522.

CHAPTER 8

Effects of Government Intervention

Overview of the Effects of State Intervention on Employment and Growth

Unemployment and Economic Growth Trends

The employment rates in the EU have been severely affected by the slowdown in aggregate demand, but this has been significantly worsened by the austerity policies imposed to reduce budget deficits, since such policies invoked job losses and wage reductions. The EU imposed countercyclical economic policies in an attempt to reverse the recession in 2009–2010, when an economic upturn appeared to be occurring, but then imposed procyclic economic policies, which were intended to accelerate the recovery but these had the opposite effect, leading to a double dip recession (ILO, 2013). The ILO (2013) report suggests that the EC adopted disjointed monetary and fiscal policies and did not approach difficulties in the financial sector including sovereign debt issues logically across members, which led to uncertainty in Member States and outside the region. Therefore, continued uncertainty led to lack of investment and job creation by employers, which hoarded cash or paid higher dividends instead. The consequence of this environment was that recessionary conditions continued and weakened job creation rates, and in relation to employment inflow, the number of unemployed continually increased whilst employment outflow representing individuals getting jobs decreased, so that the

S. Weißschnur, *The Proportionality of State Intervention*,
https://doi.org/10.1007/978-3-030-75676-5_8

overall trend was job destruction. The consequences were evident from the severity of the job crisis in the EU, in which a 1% contraction was experienced and expected to get worse, since being unemployed for long periods in which there is weak demand for goods and services deterred individuals from remaining in the employment market.

Youth unemployment in EU was 23.8% at the end of March 2013 (Eurostat, 2015), compared with a global figure of 12.7% (ILO, 2013), and had declined slightly to 21.4% at the end of 2014 (Eurostat, 2015). Long-term youth employment figures in EU, which relate to individuals out of work for more than six months, were amongst the highest globally at 35%, a rise of 6.5% since 2007 (ILO, 2013). The International Labour Organisation (ILO) report (ILO, 2013) also highlighted the fact that young unemployed people were not engaged in education or training, and that a 2% growth in youth unemployment had been experienced since 2008. The additional issues for the long-term unemployed were the loss of professional and social skills, combined with lack of recent job experience, which damaged their long-term prospects. Even when the long-term unemployed returned to work, their productivity was lower, reducing the speed of economic recovery. When job creation and economic growth were compared with GDP growth from the end of 2008 to the end of the Q3 2012, the stark differences in the north and south of the Eurozone Member States were evident. Whereas Germany experienced some GDP growth from 2009 to early 2012, which then flattened to almost zero, Greece had experienced negative GDP growth since the end of 2008 and Italy had a period of very low growth in 2010 and 2011, with negative growth at other times; the employment trends were similar. Employment levels contracted in Germany only once in Q3 2009, whilst Greece registered 9% losses in Q4 2012, although ILO forecasts that the losses would decline (2013). Hence, the indication seems to be that GDP growth is required for unemployment levels to fall and jobs to be created; however, other more current sources suggest this is not the case. Currently, most Eurozone countries are showing year-on-year economic growth, the average was 0.3%, but its uneven nature is illustrated by Germany registering 0.7% and Spain 2% and by Italy continuing to have declining GDP growth, whilst economic growth in France was marginally positive (Economist, 2015). The Economist (2015) highlights these growth figures as a concern because France and Italy are the two largest economies after Germany, inferring stagnation in the region. In contrast, most of the northern Eurozone countries had positive growth, for instance, Luxembourg, and the Netherlands had GDP growth varying from 3.8% to 1% and Portugal in Southern Europe had 0.4% growth in 2014; non-Eurozone members had higher year-on-year GDP growth than Euro Member States, for example, Hungary and Poland had GDP growth of more than 3%. When economic growth is compared with the levels of unemployment, there is no clear alignment, for instance, Spain had GDP growth, but its unemployment rate remained high at 24%, and Portugal at 14%, whereas Germany had less than 5% unemployed. In most other northern Eurozone states, unemployment was 8% or lower, but for many non-Euro members some alignment was shown between the two factors, as was the case in Italy with unemployment of 12.5% and Greece 26%, both of which had negative GDP growth levels (Economist, 2015). Youth unemployment in Greece and Spain remained at over 50%, Italy 42% and Portugal 34%; the serious nature of youth unemployment in Europe was also emphasised by the United Nations (UN, 2014), which stated that little progress would be made to rectify unemployment without GDP growth in the countries affected. Whilst public debt levels in most north Eurozone countries were below 100% GDP, the debt levels in Belgium, Spain, Portugal, Italy, Cyprus, Malta, Greece and Ireland remained at over 100%, despite some of these countries, including Greece, having budget balances of less than -3% GDP. The indication was that even though some change in economic growth was demonstrated, its effect on job creation was not occurring in the same direction and continued to be an issue; austerity strategy did not appear to affect the ECB/IMF forecast when the terms of the bailout loans were devised. However, the ECB, the IMF and many northern Eurozone countries continued to insist that standard solutions would resolve the issues with these non-growth economies, despite evidence to the contrary.

Portugal an Exemplar for Success of Austerity Strategy

A major example of the success of the austerity programmes was stated to be Portugal, which received a €78 billion EU bailout loan in 2011, and austerity measures were imposed as a condition of it being granted. Portugal recently paid off the debt and the country was considered the exemplar of the effectiveness of the EC/IMF austerity strategy and programme (Khan, 2015a). Whilst the country has experienced approximately 0.7% year-on-year GDP growth, many issues remain with job creation. The loan repayment masked severe internal problems, for instance, the country's deficit was rising again, with public and private debt of €360 billion, the highest in the Eurozone, which IMF stated was the consequence of the austerity package. Whilst IMF predicted 1.6% GDP growth for 2015, which it suggested would be a result of a weak Euro and low commodity prices, productivity gains were not mentioned; PWC (2015) states that Portugal has shown weak improvement in competitiveness. The current level of Portugal's debt is forecast to reduce demand (Khan, 2015a), and job creation in Portugal is declining; a gradual overall decline in the labour force had been experienced since 2010, although the jobless total was currently 12.9%, as compared with 13.7% at the end of March 2015; no details were given of the composition of jobs, for instance, the proportions of part time and full time work. Structural reforms were reported to have slowed, since the loan had been paid off and there was considerable political risk of ECB/IMF forecasts for growth and reduction of debt not being met, if anti-austerity political parties won an impending election, according to the IMF (Khan, 2015a). The high levels of debt in Portugal were mainly owned by foreigners, and Lynn (2015) suggests that Portugal may default on them, as its debt levels are beyond the 130% GDP considered sustainable. An associated factor was that GDP growth was generated by internal demand, not exports, which continued to fall. In addition, GDP needed to grow at a minimum of 3% per annum to sustain the debt at current level (Lynn, 2015). Despite seven years having passed since the global crisis, Portugal's banking sector had not solved the legacy of bad loans, the value of which was reported to have grown by 12.3% in the first quarter of 2015.

The Beveridge Curve as an Employment Indicator

The Beveridge Curve, which compares job vacancy rates in the market with unemployment figures, is an additional employment key indicator. In an ideal situation, there would be a perfect match between job vacancies and the number of unemployed job seekers. However, the trend was for the curve to move outwards when the skills of those seeking employment did not match the needs of the jobs available. Therefore, ILO (2013) proposed that the extent of match was reliant on the quality of labour market intervention and labour supply conditions; consequently policy makers must understand the determinants of labour market creation and destruction in recessions. In other words, policymakers must select the labour market policies that will be effective in creating jobs, based on their forecast demand, but the accuracy of the policies implemented also relied on the expected future profit streams by the employer. The Beveridge Curve as related to Greece and Spain had already moved away from the ideal match situation prior to 2008, suggesting that labour market matching was poor, and this indicates one of two possibilities: either the job vacancies existed but the skills to fill them were not available in the country, or the countries were not reacting to a stronger growth trend. According to ILO (2013) these Beveridge Curve trends should have been noticed by ECB/IMF, and they should have been aware that a continuing trend of inappropriate/inactive labour market intervention made it more difficult to rectify and had reduced the impact of the policy interventions that were intended to stimulate the economy. This comment suggests that these factors were not fully considered, and nor was the self-sustaining relationship between low activity and weak employment that led to slow economic growth.

Impact of Uncertainty on Unemployment

The ILO (2013) report stated that the governments of developed countries, such as EU Member States, needed to reduce the uncertainty in the labour market that resulted from the vagueness of their policies. The EU should have created plans that had predictable outcomes, rather than general statements, and should have subsequently made the financial investment to stabilise the banks, so that they could provide the loans to expand the small and medium enterprise (SME) sector, the driver of the economic growth. The EU should also have devised exit strategies for the countries most affected by the debt crisis. This ILO proposal highlights the plight of EU countries and particularly Greece in this period when youth unemployment exceeded 50% (ILO, 2013); most was long-term unemployment, and uncertainty regarding investment had been risen throughout 2015. The increasing uncertainty was driven by the lack of solidarity of other EU countries and infighting between agencies such as ECB and IMF (Holehouse, 2015a; Khan, 2015b), and was completely contrary to the rhetoric of the European Economic Recovery Plan (EC, 2008). It also conflicted with the Principle of Proportionality, which Portuese (2013) suggests as a means to shape human behaviour, so that individuals react in a reasonable manner and ensure that social justice prevails.

The ILO (2013) report comments on the lack of coordination of EU policy, which had failed to enhance competitiveness across Member States, especially in cases in which it was combined with the austerity measures it had imposed. The EU was stated to be far from meeting the objectives of its policies and risked a deflationary spiral typified by low demand and low wages, but it had tried to rectify the EU Single Market problems by worsening the issues in many of its Member States. In other words, the EU adopted 'beggar thy neighbour' economic policies, underpinned by encouraging countries to change social protection policies so that the unemployed received fewer benefits and by depressing wage levels. Whilst the general principles of an active labour market and pro-employment macroeconomic policies are included in the ERP, it was the lack of appropriate application that appeared to be the reason for the failure to redress the situation. The ILO (2013) stated three principles for success: encourage youth entrepreneurship; improve youth employability, for instance, through apprenticeships, job search support and youth employment guarantee schemes; promote the labour standards and employment rights of young people, such as equal treatment and bargaining rights. The ERP (EC, 2008), whilst emphasising the first two of these principles, appears to have put little emphasis on promoting the employment rights of young people, in terms of equal treatment and bargaining rights, even in the later announcement (EC, 2012a).

Intervention Austerity Measures, Problems and Effects

Economic Cycles, Policies and Effect on Economic Growth

Cyclisation of economic policy concerns how the government varies its key policies during the economic cycle. A procyclical economic policy has the purpose of accelerating recovery, it is expansionary, whilst countercyclical or contractionary economic policy is used to slow economic growth to prevent a boom, and to slow down a recession. A government employing countercyclical fiscal policy could increase taxation or reduce its public spending to slow the economy, since this intervention reduces disposable income or slows demand, subsequently impeding economic growth. If the government employs a monetary rather than a fiscal policy, it will use interest rates or money supply, increase interest rates or allow less money in circulation, for instance, through issuing debt bonds, with the purpose of slowing economic growth, and lower interest rates or place more money in circulation to generate a recovery (Abbot & Jones, 2011). During a recession, therefore, the government has two alternative policy options: either increase spending, adopting a countercyclical economic policy or decrease spending, a procyclical economic policy. The latter is usually the case, according to Riera-Crichton et al. (2014). Each cycle is characterised by two main phases: a recessionary phase, represented by decline in economic activity, followed by an expansionary phase in which activity increases. However, the macroeconomic conditions in a particular cycle influence its characteristics. In most economic cycles, recessions are usually shorter and less frequent with a decline of approximately 2.75% GDP, while an expansionary phase could be up to 20% GDP. However, financially related recessions tend to last longer and are combined with the steeper decline in GDP, so that when recovery occurs, it is slower because consumer demand is weak and credit is often hard to obtain. This was certainly the case in the Eurozone, and very evident in those countries, which had been the recipients of bailout funding. The procyclical economic policy was not effective when there was a large budget deficit, according to OECD (2010), and although countercyclical monetary policy can be effectively employed to shorten the length of recessions, it is not the solution if the recession is linked to financial crisis, according to Kannan et al. (2009); expansionary fiscal policies appear to be a better solution in such cases. When monetary policy was employed in past recessions, it was effective in ending them and driving recovery but if the cause of the recession was financially based, monetary policy was weak. Hence, fiscal stimulus is associated with strong recoveries in these macroeconomic conditions, but recovery is limited in economies with larger levels of public debt. In cases where government spending is decreasing during a recession, fiscal stimulus takes longer to make an impact and the multiplier is smaller, according to Riera-Crichton et al. (2014). Therefore, the size of the multiplier depends on whether the government spends its way out of recession or reduces spending.

In the Eurozone countries, some Member States had high budget deficits and, when forced to undertake a procyclical economic policy, it was evidently much less effective in creating fiscal stimulus than those stated to have small budget deficits or budget surpluses (OECD, 2010). The difference is exemplified by the fast German recovery from contraction of 5.1% in 2009 to 4% growth in 2010 (Oxfam, 2013c), whilst Greece with a huge budget deficit had experienced contraction since the beginning of the crisis (ILO, 2013). A study by Truger (2013) also observed that Eurozone countries remaining in recession were those that had the worst budget deficits and, when this factor was combined with the 2008 recession, it ensured that all other Eurozone countries had poor economic growth. Hence, OECD (2010) proposed that the EU was mistaken in forcing member countries with high deficits to adopt a procyclical economic policy and needed to allow them much wider fiscal margins, since monetary policy might not align with the stabilisation needs of those countries; it categorically stated that fiscal rules such as balanced budgets were totally inappropriate and destabilising.

These examples demonstrate that EU approach to the Principle of Subsidiarity in which its stance was that it was more equipped to resolve the growth and employment issues of individual Eurozone Member States was flawed; authority was removed from them despite the different preferences that Member States had for these issues based on their unique contexts. It could also be implied that such actions prevented EU citizens in many countries from accessing the human right to decent work contrary to the Principle of Proportionality.

State Intervention and the Consequent Problems

The details of interventions and their consequences in specific Member State markets are discussed now, including how the austerity packages affected those nations; intended and actual effects of austerity are appraised in this section. The evaluation is extended beyond Member States' granted bailouts to others that were pressured into adopting the ECB/IMF strategy because their public debt levels did not meet the 3% maximum imposed by the EC. The German context is also assessed because Germany has had the greatest influence on the shape of interventions, and hence the outcomes. The analysis enables an overall conclusion to be drawn about the nature of the interventions and their impact on the nations involved. It also highlights the emerging backlash against the standard austerity solution, which serves to drive those nations worst hit by recession and unemployment into further recession, not recovery; the political left in Greece, Portugal, Spain and Italy, for instance, have increasingly gained public support.

Portugal

Portugal's Memorandum of Understanding (MoU) for the 2011 bailout was based on structural adjustment policies intended to reduce the government deficit and debt, and to balance the current account by internal devaluation, which meant wage cuts. The various versions of the MoU contained 222 actions and more resembled a plan devised by central planners in a planned economy than that appropriate to a market economy, according to Cabral (2013). However, the prior austerity measures initiated in March 2010 were already increasing recession and raising unemployment rates, which reached 15.6% by early 2012; the main Portuguese trade union suggested the real figure was much higher (Oxfam, 2013a). In the six months to March 2012, wages declined by 3.9% and the deficit continued to rise, indicating that austerity measures were not working, according to Caldas (2012), since the debt continued to rise. However, no alterative action was offered by the EU or the IMF, even though reform fatigue had commenced and caused the population to be highly alienated towards the EU; Cabral (2013) observed that every Troika review demonstrated that debt levels were rising. Political infighting occurred between the various political parties regarding austerity policies, for instance the Socialist Party that agreed to them, but lost the election to a centre right government, which implemented the austerity programme. After their election defeat, the Socialist Party opposed the implementation of the MoU.

The measures implemented for increasing government revenues were to reduce tax allowances and to increase tax rates, employee pension contributions and VAT rates (Caldas, 2012); these measures would substantially affect disposable income, and therefore demand. Social protection was also reduced with the consequence that citizens were forced to make co-payments for the National Health Service, and public transport costs increased. Government expenditures were concurrently reduced by cutting public sector workers' wages and pensions, reducing health and education budgets, and renegotiating the terms of private-public sector partnerships. Oxfam (2013a) reported a 23% cut in educational funding in two years, and subsequently teachers being the group whose use of job centres increased the most. The fees for health emergency appointments were set at €20.60 and a further €50 for examinations, so that many citizens were unable to afford healthcare. However, part of the increased revenues was used to save a failing small bank, and an unknown amount of the loan awarded by EC had to be used to save other banks. According to Cabral (2013) €12 billion of the €78 billion borrowed by |Portugal was allocated to the banks by the terms of the MoU, bank recapitalisation chosen by the ECB on political grounds rather than best practice, which would have involved creating a special resolution for banks, as recommended by IMF and considered best international practice. If Portuguese banks had failed, the ECB as the largest creditor would have been most affected by taking the loss; as ECB was both creditor and designer of the MoU plan, a double role and a conflict of interest, enabled the action selected. The existing bank shareholders continued to choose the management staff, so that bank practices were unlikely to change, and measures taken regarding the banks also reduced domestic credit by 12% (Cabral, 2013), a factor that would reduce demand in the economy.

The effect of the ERP (EC, 2012a) is evident from Caldas' (2012) study, which stated that unemployment benefits were cut from 3 years to 18 months (Oxfam, 2013a): labour law changed to make dismissal and flexible working easier to implement, holiday entitlement and other paid holidays were reduced, the power of the unions weakened by decentralising collective bargaining. In addition, apart from unemployment benefits, further social protection cuts included every individual being means-tested before receiving social security payments, and some recipients being forced to do unpaid work in return (Caldas, 2012). In the period from 2010 to 2013, the number receiving social insertion benefits, the most in need, had dropped to less than 274,000 from 571,000, and the monthly payment in 2013 was just €81.90 (Oxfam, 2013a). State assets in the form of public sector bodies were also sold with privatisation of energy companies, naval and defence construction, transport and media. Processes for setting up companies and operating them were also made simpler (Caldas, 2012). Both trends also aligned with the EC (2012b) strategies for growth.

Overall, the results of the austerity measures had been minimal until 2012, according to Caldas (2012), who compared the Portuguese economic stability before and after joining the EU. The budget deficit in 1995 was 3.5% but had reached 12.5% GDP by 2008; private debt in 1996 was 88% GDP but 249.1% GDP in 2011, whereas public debt was 50.4% GDP in 2000, it was 68.3% in 2007 and 107.8% by 2011; the 68.4% employment rate in 2000 had declined to 64.2% by 2011. Caldas (2012) considered that Portugal had become more sensitive to external shocks and had reached the state of economic stagnation and high debt, arising from the combined effect of joining the Euro, the expansion of the

EU, relaxation in credit rules so that credit was easily obtained and cheap imports from non-EU sources. However, Cabral (2013) suggests the theory that entry to the Euro had worsened Portugal's trade deficit and competitiveness was questionable, as the country had a trade deficit before entering the Euro. However, Cabral (2013) agreed that the deficit value was much lower and had lower impact in the pre-Euro period because the country was free to devalue its currency. The fact that Portugal has higher external debt levels, rather than sovereign debt, meant that the deficit was larger and high public borrowing was required. However, Cabral (2013) concluded that after 13 years in the Euro, Portugal had lost more than it had gained by joining.

In terms of consequences on citizens, austerity affected the unemployed more than any other group, and young educated people were emigrating to get jobs (Caldas, 2012); the official emigration figure was 43,998 in 2011 but the real figure was probably higher (Oxfam, 2013a). Hence, the country's current and future human capital, the major driver of growth in a knowledge economy, was being depleted, according to the ERP (EC, 2012a); a report by Oxfam (2013a) also emphasised this factor. Inequality was increasing: Portugal had the seventh highest inequality level in Europe, with a Gini coefficient of 0.34; the top 20% of the population had income of 5.7 times that of the lowest 20%. The number of business bankruptcies in 2012 was 6600, with construction companies and restaurants being the most common failures and, in the latter case, the raising of VAT rates had impacted substantially on the whole tourism sector, which was a key industry (Oxfam, 2013a).

Politically, the public has become disenchanted with the democratic form of government and therefore political unrest was expected to grow. The rhetoric used by the government and media influencers was that the measures were painful but were needed to meet the challenges of demographic trends and declining resources. However, Caldas (2012) remarks that the labour and social policies that had been agreed in the MoU could not be stated as government policy and put to the vote; in other words, citizen's democratic rights had effectively been breached.

Spain

The aftermath of the housing market bubble was the key factor in Spain's economic collapse after 2008 because it had collected substantial revenues from taxes related to the housing boom and its economy was generally reliant on labour-intensive sectors, such as construction. These factors had a significant influence on why Spain remained in recession in 2012 with high debt levels and one of the highest unemployment rates in the EU at 26% of active labour market (Conde-Ruiz & Marín, 2013; Witte, 2012). The increasing debt levels were generated by a huge imbalance between increases in government expenditure, which remained lower than the EC average in 2011, whilst its tax revenues were severely reduced, partly as a consequence of the existence of a large informal economy. However, the expenditure forecasts had been based on previous housing-related tax revenues, so that when these were no longer generated just after the crisis, maintaining the planned expenditure became challenging. Consequently, there was a negative change in government revenues from 2007 to 2011, the worst in the Eurozone. The Spanish government followed the advice of the EC and IMF by adopting an expansionist fiscal policy in the first two years after the crisis, and then a policy to reduce government deficit, which was fiscal consolidation. However, Conde-Ruiz and Marín (2013) are critical of the strategy imposed by the EC/IMF, since fiscal consolidation was unlikely to be effective until there was sustained economic growth, which had not yet been experienced; this point is also emphasised by Krugman (2015). In addition, the original stimulus package had encouraged Eurozone state members to increase their deficits, to fund the expansion (Tait, 2008). Spain applied a stimulus package of 4% GDP using fiscal policy measures, employing various tax cuts and stimulating demand with, for instance, a child benefit lump sum for new babies and investment projects focusing on reviving business sectors, such as construction. In the period 2008 to 2009, Spain moved from a +2% GDP budget surplus to a deficit of 11% but no structural reforms of pensions or labour markets had occurred, as were recommended by the stimulus programme.

As with many other Eurozone countries, the fiscal expansion that caused the increasing deficit engendered a new phase of economic crisis, which is referred to as the sovereign debt crisis. This second phase was a consequence of the difficulty of selling public debt in the form of bonds, and the spreads on them, which varied as confidence in EU fluctuated, particularly owing to worsening debt in some countries. In order to comply with sudden new EC guidance, Spain increased taxes from 2010 to 2012, for instance, VAT rose from 16% to 21%, excise tax also increased, tax credits were withdrawn and expenditure reduced, for example by minimising drug costs in the health sector. Spain also reduced public sector salaries by 5% and froze any public sector increases (CESR, 2012), whilst simultaneously extending the working week from 35 to 37.5 hours (Witte, 2012). The increased revenues were forecast as equivalent to 3.9% GDP whilst the expenditure as 3.5% GDP. However, no measure of structural reform, such as pensions or a tax system, was implemented again. The higher VAT rate applied to only 42% of Spanish goods/services, much lower than other EU countries, so the proportion of potential increased revenue was minimised. Spain failed to meet the EU consolidation objectives, so that expected changes did not occur, and Conde-Ruiz and Marín (2013) suggest that the existence of the autonomous regions in the country is a key underlying reason for this failure. These regions represent 35% of all Spain's expenditure but receive only 19% of revenues and, therefore, their sense of responsibility regarding spending was weakened. The revenues these regions received were estimated at the beginning of the tax year, which also led to discrepancies between forecast and annual tax and differences were not rectified for two years, such that the lagging factor was responsible for the large increase in deficit for 2010 and 2011. In other words, the autonomous regions' deficit was related to an earlier period and approximately 40% to 55% of the total (Conde-Ruiz & Marín, 2013). These anomalies were a major reason why fiscal adjustment did not work in Spain, because the whole region had started implementing the austerity measures later than anticipated, and Spain's international reputation suffered as a consequence. Conde-Ruiz and Marín (2013) suggested that the EU should have enabled Spain to set different objectives over a longer period, in order for the economy to recover but UN (2014) reports that the EU has given Spain until 2016 to rectify its deficit. In the labour market, generally, some structural reforms had occurred, with union power being weakened, and dismissing employees and wage setting was made easier (Witte, 2012).

The social costs of the austerity measures are highlighted by the Centre for Economic and Social Rights, CESR (CESR, 2012), which found that in excess of 40% of the unemployed were long-term unemployed. The number had quadrupled since 2008 and income inequality had widened, with a Gini coefficient of 0.34 and a rapidly expanded income gap of seven times between the lowest and highest 20% of the population, the third highest in the EU; from 2006 to 2008, the Gini index was 0.31 (Witte, 2012). High youth unemployment in Spain continued (UN, 2014) and is explained by Conde-Ruiz and Marín (2013) as initially being a consequence of the way in which young people were employed in Spain prior to the crisis. At that time young people had temporary contracts, which were not renewed and many of them had left education without completing it, in order to work in construction during the pre-crisis boom; therefore they had two barriers to permanent employment. Employees on minimum wage received a sum that was one-third of the average income, lower than 40% to 60% recommended by ILO (2013), with 31% of workers earning minimum wage or less. In addition, the growth in the informal economy was valued at 24.3% of GDP. The austerity measures have failed to reform the labour market in accordance with the International Convention on the Protection of the Rights of All Migrant Workers and Members of their Families, with immigrant males earning 50%, females 40% and Spanish females 74% of that being paid to national males (CESR, 2012). The expenditure cuts had resulted in only 2% of housing stock being available for social housing, in contrast with an 11.7% average in the EU top 15, and with low-cost rental accommodation for less than half the EU average number. Low-cost housing was available to one-third of poor households, whilst concurrently Spain had more vacant properties than any other EU country. In addition, Spain had the third lowest expenditure on health, education and social protection in 2009, at €6087 per citizen but was the fifth largest EU economy (CESR, 2012). The lack of focus on education within the Spanish system is also evident from the very high rate of those not completing secondary school, which was 24.8% in 2010, and from the wide variation in education spending amongst the autonomous regions. Education improvement was stated to be a driving force that was vital to accomplishing the ERP objectives, including reducing early school leavers to 10% by 2020 (EC, 2012a), however, measures to meet the challenges did not receive government attention. Budget cuts in 2012 were the highest ever imposed in Spain, with education spending declining by 28.2%, and job promotion reduced by 25.6%, whereas both were considered vital in the ERP. Access to housing declined by 45.3% whereas pension expenditure rose by 7%, an expenditure that EC/IMF sought to decrease (CESR, 2012). CESR suggested that the Spanish government had substantial alternatives to austerity, which created these social costs, for instance, reducing/eliminating the informal economy would increase government revenues (CESR, 2012). GESTHA, the Technical Union of the Spanish Ministry of Finance, estimated that 10% reduction in the black economy alone would raise €38 billion, which was more than the value of the budget cuts imposed in 2012. The tax revenues could also have been generated by alterations to the tax system to reflect social and economic equality, by increasing the relatively low levels of taxation on the wealthiest, in contrast to the austerity strategy of cutting public expenditure, which had most affected the poorest sections of the community.

In contrast to the political situation in Portugal, the Spanish government was stable with no pending elections in 2012, and the new government at that time had mentioned implementing austerity measures as part of its policies. However, Witte (2012) observed that tax increases were not mentioned, reflecting the government's limited democratic approach to voters' wishes expressed in election; the public were informed that austerity was the only solution to the deficit issue. Most regions have adopted austerity except Andalusia, which devised its own alternatives and the Basque province, which did not experience the issues in other parts of Spain.

A recent report by European Commission suggested that the 0.8% GDP growth in Spain at the beginning of 2015 showed that austerity had worked. The lower energy prices, market confidence and job creation advances had been the underlying factors, although the unemployment rate remained at 23.7% for the first quarter and debt levels remained high (Matsangou, 2015). However, the local elections in May 2015 reflect the population's displeasure at the outcomes of austerity, since left-wing parties obtained local government seats and the national election.

Italy

In Italy, there was no banking crisis, since Italian banks had few business transactions with international markets, but the global crisis invoked a lack of trust between Italian banking institutions, as well as the capacity of Italian small- and medium-sized businesses to overcome the challenges in the market. Hence, banks stopped providing loans and credit to businesses, which resulted in recession (Oxfam, 2013a). After the crisis, the government planned to introduce reforms to enhance growth, as had previously been recommended by OECD and other institutions (Goretti & Landi, 2013). The initial focus was on simplifying bureaucratic administration and reforming apprenticeships, despite resistance by unions. However, by 2011, the changes elsewhere in Europe evoked fear of contagion so that Italy experienced significant threat to its financial stability, as a consequence of bond market turbulence. The resignation of the government at this time resulted in the appointment of Mario Monti to deal with the impending crisis, and measures were introduced including new legislation to reduce the growing budget deficit and to improve competitiveness. The reduction in public sector expenditure was a part of the action to attain a balanced budget by 2013; from 2011 to 2012, the deficit declined from -3.6% to -0.9% GDP, and the economy was expected to grow by 2.4%. However, unemployment and poverty levels both rose. From 2007 to 2012, public sector employee numbers declined by 4.3%, sector pay by 2.3% and some functions were merged; the number of local governments reduced from 86 to 51 by 2014 and state assets were sold to reduce debt. The emergency measures had worked, according to Goretti and Landi (2013), but the social situation was serious. The reduction in deficit was attributed to revenues from taxes and expenditure cuts of 43.9%; extra tax revenue was generated by increases in VAT, higher taxes on some business sectors and reducing tax evasion. However, expenditure cuts were focused on education and healthcare and complemented by some pension reforms and action on public sector procurement. The approach taken is very pro-government and fails to capture public opinion or the weak action of government in dealing with the overinflated public sector or promoting job creation and business growth. The debt level of 135% GDP in 2014 demonstrated the continuing issues, this level was suggested as unsustainable, and some groups considered that Italy should have negotiated to restructure its debt (Goretti & Landi, 2013); Mazzolini and Mody (2014) proposed that more modest austerity with active stimulus packages would have resulted in better outcomes for countries such as Italy.

The social and political outcomes of the austerity measures given in detail by Oxfam (2013b) contrast with the positive report by Goretti and Landi (2013). Partly as a result of the lack of credit, company bankruptcies were huge, with 104,000 businesses closing in 2012, and 45,000 companies in loan default from 2009 to 2013. Monti's government was referred to as being responsible for increased taxes on households to 44.7% income by Oxfam (2013b), and this included a new property tax on houses, which many citizens did not have the income to pay. The reform to pensions, which immediately raised the retirement age, left 140,000 people due to retire with no job or pension. Over the previous 10 years, net family wealth had reduced by 40.5% from €26,000 to €15,600 per family, and the gap between the top 20% and the bottom 20% of income earners increased from 5.1 times to 5.6 times from 2008 to 2011. Poverty levels rose, families bought the cheapest goods, stopped travelling and growing their own vegetables and child poverty rating rose to 32nd out of the 35 OECD countries. The income situation would have been worse if most Italians had not been savers, although savings levels have dropped since 2008. Whilst unemployment levels, particularly youth unemployment, rose dramatically, there was no social system to provide income for most of the jobless, since they were not on the long-term contracts, referred to as the Busta Paga, which assured substantial benefits. Oxfam (2013b) concluded that austerity has failed to significantly reduce debt or to initiate growth in Italy.

Germany

There is very sparse published data on the effect of the 2008 crisis or austerity on Germany. However, a report by Oxfam (2013c) emphasises that the impact that the global economic crisis had on the German economy was quite different from that of other EC countries. In the initial stages, the German banking sector was rescued from failure by the government, the cost estimated by IMF was €70 billion, government debt levels rose from 65.4% to 82.5% in the three years to 2010 but were expected to return to the lower level by 2018 and the country's economy was also negatively affected. Economic growth fluctuated over the period from 2008 to 2013, recording a 5.1% GDP contraction in 2009, but returning to 4% growth in 2010, as a result of stimulus measures, and low but positive growth followed. Owing to investor confidence, German debt instruments did not experience large spreads as occurred in Spain and Greece, and therefore in these economic conditions, Germany was able to pay the interest on its debt. Little change in the labour market occurred initially, and over the period from 2008 to 2012, unemployment declined from 7.8% to 5.5%, but it rose to 6.8% in 2013 (Oxfam, 2013c). The high employment rate was partly a result of the flexible labour law that already existed at the time of the initial downturn and government wage subsidies for those working on short-term temporary contracts, according to Oxfam (2013c). In addition, Germany was more technologically advanced than many other Member States and had a highly skilled labour force, with manufacturing competence enabling high global competitiveness.

The contrast between the impact of the crisis on Germany and Southern European countries was a consequence of very different economic conditions, because Germany has a large export market. Exports increased from 30.5% GDP in 2002 to 41.5% in 2012, enabling a current account surplus from 2008 onwards, the second largest globally at a time when most developed countries had a deficit (Oxfam, 2013c). However, German success was considered to have impacted very negatively on many other EU members, since it underpinned the imbalances in other Member States, hindering their recovery; the US government had requested Germany to reduce its export drive for this reason, as well as the effect the policy was having on global growth (WP, 2013). Whilst there was a lack of domestic demand and encouragement to save in Germany, and EC insisted that the remainder of Europe curb imports to dampen internal demand, Germany also supressed own demand by its self-imposed austerity (WP, 2013).

The German population experienced some social hardship, which had begun in 2002 when the labour market and welfare benefits system changed and many national companies were privatised to increase the nation's competitiveness, for instance, utilities. Concurrently VAT rates were increased to balance the loss of revenue from tax cuts for businesses, and labour market reforms were made possible by weakening union power and reducing social benefits, such as unemployment benefits, pensions and lengthening retirement age. In effect, these measures reduced the value of real wages, making labour and therefore production prices lower and more competitive. The labour reforms did not include legislation to provide equal pay for female workers, who were paid at a rate of 19.4% lower than men up to 2010. In general, these reforms resulted in a substantial quantity of low-paid work, with little employment security and few employment rights; from 2001 to 2010, low-paid employment increased from 4.3 million to 7.8 million, with almost three times as many women as men employed in this sector (Oxfam, 2013c). Consequently, income inequality also increased; the Gini index rose to 0.47 in 2010 as compared with 0.41 in 1991 but by readjusting taxes and transfers, it was reduced to 0.29 in 2013. However, the wealthiest 10% owned 60% of the country's assets, whilst the poorest 50% had virtually no assets. In general, both the working poor and poverty have increased, with 16.8% of women classified as poor, and poverty remaining higher in East Germany (Oxfam, 2013c); Germany had the third highest number of millionaires, 1,015,000 individuals, after the US and Japan (Fuchs, 2013). The very rich live in cities, typified by the Ruhr, which have decaying infrastructure since municipal governments have been forced to return a balanced budget; in 2011 approximately 40% local governments were required to devise and submit a plan to achieve a balanced budget within ten years. In these local government areas, voluntary services were described as meagre or non-existent; day care centres for the elderly, children's language training and disabled transport services are examples (Fuchs, 2013). The social protection cuts in Germany affected women more than men: 5% more women receive unemployment benefits; the amount is €200 less than for men; proposals for double parental leave benefits were suspended (Fuchs, 2013; Oxfam, 2013c). Germany also planned further reductions to its aid budget administered via the Official Development Assistance (ODA) (Oxfam, 2013c). The ODA helped developing countries and provided humanitarian aid (WH, 2015), but the 2014 amount was €245 million lower and a further reduction of €150 million was planned for 2015 (Oxfam, 2013c).

Greece

An outline of the consequences of austerity in a social and political context is summarised, as the main interventions and processes were appraised in Chap. 7. The lack of structural reform in Greece for many years prior to 2008 crisis was described as enabling large informal economies to exist, social services were poorly managed, and tax evasion and benefit fraud were common, to the extent that 110,000 individuals, who were not registered by the census received stated pensions. IMF commented that the fiscal system was in disarray and successive political parties had no will to impose change. The public sector, which had continued to grow, paid its staff 130% salary compared with private sector employees, and 14 payments a year plus providing excessive pension benefits; many of the issues in Greece were hidden by the apparent boom prior to 2008 (Oxfam, 2013d; Monastiriotis, 2013). In the period up to 2012, Greece had received two bailouts by the EC, and some progress had been made in reducing the deficit (Crysoloras, 2013), as described in Chap. 7, however, the manner in which loans were granted meant that Greece was directly responsible for repayment, which was added to public debt levels. Consequently, additional loans from EU were made directly to banks, to stem the level of official public debt but Greece was forced to request an extension to the second bailout as a result of negative GDP growth. The very long process involved in negotiating the extension created lower investor confidence in Greece, but was eventually agreed in August 2015, although finalising the detail added to uncertainty. However, economists suggested that the loan would be granted subject to achieving impossible targets; primary deficit of no more than 0.25% GDP in 2015, and surpluses of 0.5% GDP in 2015 rising to 3.5% by 2018 (Chan, 2015).

The primary reforms were to be related to pensions, increasing the retirement age, higher taxes for shipping firms and privatising the ports and energy sectors and reorganising pharmaceuticals (Chan, 2015). However, 57 prior actions were needed before agreement was finalised, and Germany had taken a long period of time to agree to the bailout, extending uncertainty, according to Holehouse (2015b). When the consequences of austerity so far are appraised, the effect of this planned and very much harsher MoU is likely to exacerbate social and political issues. Youth unemployment levels in Greece are the highest in the EU, and the fact that half of all young people have never worked was a counterproductive effect of the austerity package, according to Zen (2015), who cites Adam Smith as stating that the young were the drivers of economic growth and human progress. Austerity measures imposed on Greece, which severely reduced the size of its economy, have made the opportunities to implement the needed institutional reforms much more challenging (Zen, 2015). Since 2009, the gap between average income in Greece and other OECD member countries has considerably widened; consequently, poverty levels were rising, with 327,000 at risk in 2011 and a third of the population formally categorised as below the poverty line in 2012. Since Greece was the only Eurozone member without any last resort social safety net, the situation was worsening; 17.5% of all households were jobless and there were 20,000 homeless people, a rise of 25% since 2009. The sense of hopelessness had resulted in a 26.5% rise in suicides between 2010 and 2011; access to health services was not available to a substantial proportion of the population, and crime rates had risen (Oxfam, 2013d). The population had become very disenchanted with the EU, as a direct result of the effects of the parts of the austerity packages that had been implemented.

France

France is the second largest economy in the Eurozone and subject to implementing austerity programmes, since its debt is above the prescribed 3% GDP, and mainly generated as a result of poor practice in the banking sector. In fact, France's debt grew at a much faster rate than that of any of the other major economies. Whilst public expenditure in Greece and Ireland had been reasonably flat/decreasing, France increased spending by 8% from 2008 to 2012 because the President initially refused to bow to EC policymakers' pressure to impose austerity on the population. The increased expenditure was partly funded by raising more tax revenues from individuals and companies, whilst VAT remained unchanged. Economic growth had declined since 2009 and in 2013 was expected to be zero (Oxfam, 2013e). In this period, unemployment was rising and young people were emigrating to find work; there were 600,000 job losses from 2007 to 2013, by which time almost five million people were unemployed, with under-25 and older age groups most affected. In 2012, 16,000 companies went into liquidation (Oxfam, 2013e).

The French Prime Minister was closely involved with Germany until 2012, but the French election resulted in a new socialist government that had opposed austerity, indicating public resistance to it (Stratfor, 2013). However, in 2014, with the largest government spend in developed countries of 57% GDP, the French Prime Minister implemented austerity measures, lowering employment taxes and balancing the loss in government tax revenue by cutting its expenditures; the rationale was to stimulate economic growth (Dorfman, 2014). However, this change caused public protests, since changes to healthcare provision, deregulation of professions and other employment law legislation were planned (Euronews, 2014). Even before this change, Oxfam (2013e) had assessed how five rounds of austerity measures employed by the previous prime ministers had affected the social fabric in France.

The austerity measures initially employed were described by Fofana (2011) as very minor changes to pension rules, no other structural reforms, and with no significant cuts in government expenditure. However, Oxfam (2013e) stated that the 2011 measures involved higher taxing of households and cuts in public spending, and in 2014, although tax on the wealthiest was proposed, VAT increases would most affect the poorest. Poverty levels had risen from 2008 onwards, with an additional 600,000 categorised as poor within five years, making a total of 8.6 million by 2010, including 2.7 million children. Income inequality had increased, with the top 20% receiving wage increases of 0.9% in 2009–2010, whereas the lowest 20% had a decrease of 1.3%, at the same time prices of essential items were rising. However, from 2000 to 2010, the richest 10% had experienced more than three times the income increases of the lowest 10%, a rise of 18.9%. France had also reduced ODA to other countries, as well as focusing aid on those countries likely to repay. Healthcare costs were also rising with the population choosing to neglect dental and eye care and having to pay a greater contribution for general healthcare, although France still had a free service for the poorest groups; funding of healthcare in the future was a serious public concern (Oxfam, 2013e).

In 2013, the French Minister of Industrial Renewal accused the ECB of failing to deal with growth and supporting the unemployed, as well as stating that it was not caring for European citizens generally, which was its duty. As a founding member of the EU, and relatively less affected by the global crisis than some other members, the effects were still impacting on the economy and affecting its political position (Strafor, 2013).

Conclusions

The Euro crisis was caused by poor EU governance, according to Cabral (2013), who states that the third phase of the EMU had a flawed structure, which was a consequence of the nature of the group of approximately 100 individuals selected to devise it. These individuals were mainly bank staff and ministers appointed to key EU positions from the most important Member States and had been responsible for devising most EU treaties, SGP and ECB legislation. However, scrutiny of their proposals was weak and/or occurred too late in the process for changes to be made (Cabral, 2013). In strategic management terms, this group of individuals shares an embedded culture, which does not look outside its own institutions for different perspectives, either because it does not have the capacity or it does not wish to do so, and therefore no real learning took place, as is demonstrated by the inability to offer different alternatives to suit different member experiences and environments (Schein, 1991; Argyris, 1976) or to divert from the course of action once made, an approach if adopted in a company would cause it to fail (Mintzberg, 1987; Miller, 1992).

The myopic approach to resolving EU/EC officials' problems is also cited for the same reasons by Zen (2015), who states that if the key EU policymakers had enabled public discussion instead of making autonomous decisions, their policy errors could have been avoided, since the proposed interventions would have been scrutinised by means of a set of standard procedures, and weaknesses would have been highlighted; a study by Truger (2013) reinforces these same points. The lack of institutional democracy, or government by discussion, is severely criticised by Zen (2015) who suggested that EC policymakers failed to validate their knowledge by referring to how recovery had taken place in the past, or to consult the public. The errors of leaders of the EU Member States were demonstrated by the number who lost elections as a result of the austerity measures to which they agreed (Zen, 2015), without the consent of voters (Witte, 2012).

The political motive behind austerity is to cut public spending permanently according to Krugman (2015), and this factor at least partially accounts for the unwillingness to adopt Keynesian type policies, to expand the economy in times of recession, and is further underpinned by the unpopularity of such measures by big businesses. However, the results of austerity from the past five years have shown that the countries that were subject to the harshest austerity measures have experienced the least economic growth, substantially less that the Eurozone nations, which were not subject to austerity. In the period 2009–2013, Germany averaged approximately 2% GDP growth whilst Spain and Portugal had 1–1.5% GDP contraction, and Greece 6% contraction, the latter generating the opposite outcome to that proposed by pro-austerity economists. Harsh austerity damages rather than improves economies, according to Krugman (2015) and Mazzolini and Mody (2014), and the social costs are evident in the outcomes for EU citizens in Spain (Oxfam, 2013b), for example. The insistence on the 'golden rule' of balanced budgets that represent austerity is also stressed as erroneous by Ladi and Tsarouhas (2014, p. 173). The unwillingness of EC policymakers to use Keynesian measures to restore economic growth is also highlighted by Zen (2015), who observes that only recently the ECB employed quantitative easing of €1 trillion in recognition that expansionary measures were required, rather than the consolidation strategies introduced in 2012, which failed to generate growth.

The Troika tried to impose badly needed institutional reform in many Member States by insisting on undifferentiated austerity measures across them, which had little effect in changing the national systems but resulted in severe pain for the population (Zen, 2015); this is evident from the review of changes under austerity for all countries appraised in section 7.2 in which labour market reforms have been weak. Required institutional reforms, such as removing rigid employment laws and informal economies, should have been treated as a separate agenda, since there was no rational reason for the combination of reform and austerity. The consequences of integrating reform into austerity measures merely resulted in various sets of interventions, with focus on cutting public expenditure, whilst increasing revenues where possible as required by MoUs, and meant that reform strategies were neglected. As a world respected economist, Zen (2015) stated that he had approached EC, BIS, IMF, World Bank an

OECD regularly from 2009 onwards in an attempt to generate their willingness to consider an alternative approach. In Zen's (2015) view, reform was needed in these nations, but austerity was not.

In this study, there have been several instances in which the EC actions have not been specified in the original EC treaty, such as the amendment to Article 48(6), to avoid changes to Article 125 and enable greater power for EC to intervene in Member State markets (De Witte, 2011), as related in section 5.2.2. Ladi and Tsarouhas (2014) observe that the creation of the EU Summit, in which heads of state and government of Eurozone members discussed matters such as a Eurozone budget, as well as creation of three new bodies, EFSF, ESM and EFSM, which enabled EC to initiate, implement, devise and impose macroeconomic adjustment and monitor them, were other examples for which the EC treaties did not provide. The EU Summit was the body that promoted the golden rule of austerity, and again the prime influence was Germany. The German influence on the reform packages devised for Member States with budget deficits above 3% GDP, whether leading to bailout loans and MoUs or not, has been increasingly evident and resented across much of Europe; Germany's political and economic stability and its self-interest, served by preserving the EU and the Eurozone, were given as the underlying reason. Whilst other Member States, for instance France, had urged the German Chancellor to consider the needs of other nations, this had little effect, owing to preserving the position of Germany, according to Strafor (2013).

Austerity was not only imposed on those with huge budget deficits, but also to others without balanced budgets, for instance, Italy and the UK, although the terms were not so harsh. The study by Ladi and Tsarouhas (2014) reinforces comments made regarding individual Member States that austerity policies imposed by Troika resulted in Member States having to implement these radical changes rapidly, and therefore having no opportunity to pursue alternative options for alleviating the issues. This emphasises the new relationship of the EU with IMF, which served to support the creation of the conditions and to use coercive strategies for their implementation; the EU had previously never involved international institutions in its affairs in this manner. The second radical change, as observed by other studies in this chapter, is the decline in the national public sector and the welfare provisions that they represented for citizens, to the extent of a social and political crisis emerging as a consequence of the financial crisis.

The Treaty on Stability, Co-ordination and Governance, which became EC law in 2013, and was appraised in Chap. 6, included a strategy that became known as the debt brake, proposed by the German Chancellor and French President in 2011 (Economist, 2011). The model was forecast to be based on the German framework implemented in 2009 to reduce Germany's structural deficit, in other words, the deficit remaining after recovery or recessionary influences of the business cycle influences are deducted (BB, 2011). This balanced budget strategy would ensure that Member States could never repeat the deficit levels of the past. However, two weaknesses of the debt brake have been highlighted by economists; it prevents governments from borrowing to invest in projects that have long-term positive outcomes, for instance with education, and this approach is likely to hinder recovery; it is not an easy mechanism to enforce and most importantly had not been proven in the German context before implemented by the EC policymakers (Economist, 2011). The strategy had been used in Switzerland and, while Geier's (2011) research suggested the approach was effective, the quality of the budget that was associated with it could not be guaranteed. This budget quality represented a limitation to its use according to Geier (2011) because the elements of the expenditure were not fixed and could result in the required structural reforms failing to be implemented, spending not being allocated or lower amounts being allocated to priority items such as demographic change. This has been the case with the EC approach, as demonstrated by the variation between Eurozone members committed to austerity.

The broad advice given by EC in terms of the recovery plans and youth employment initiative, for instance EC (2012a)), appended no detailed guidance on how to implement them within individual nations (Hemerijck and Vandenbroucke, 2012). The evidence included in this chapter is that, whilst individual Member States were devising measures to cut expenditure and increase tax revenues, sparse attention was given to the structural reforms, such as school completion rates, labour reforms and youth training/employment initiatives, resulting in little change taking place; social policies were the responsibility of the national governments, whilst supranational macroeconomic policies that of EC. The consequence of imposition of the letter, driving social inequalities to higher levels than before 2008, including educational attainment and poverty. It reflected the initial EC architectural flaw of separating monetary policy as a supranational EC responsibility and fiscal policy as a Member State responsibility.

When the interventions prescribed for stimulus and for consolidation are examined, the accompanying austerity packages demonstrate a very close resemblance to the German measures taken from 2002 onwards that led to its strong and sustained growth throughout the period from 2007, as described by Oxfam (2013c); the model for austerity appears to be based on reducing social protection to drive competitiveness and growth, and a move in power from labour to capital (Oxfam, 2013c). However, the speed at which the MoUs expect the austerity policies to be effective is quite unrealistic, if compared with the time period that reforms were effected in Germany. Whilst the key objective of the EC was to increase economic growth, it was concurrently expected to increase the standard of living for its citizens, but for many it has had the opposite effect, and EC has become a much more divided society of haves and have nots than it was before 2007. The social effects of austerity experienced by Member States were also experienced by Germany, as a result of its reforms from 2002 onwards, suggesting that the most powerful voice in the Troika could have had little doubt of these consequences while driving other Member States to accept MoUs to receive financial support.

The impact of the 2008 global economic crisis in the European Union was originally considered by the EC to be a consequence of its failure to regulate the financial services sector appropriately, so that a banking crisis ensued. However, there has been a challenge to generate economic growth since then, and the measures taken by the European policymakers and their advisers, such as IMF, have resulted in confidence in Europe as a single market project reaching the lowest point since its formation. The political crisis that has emerged has expanded considerably, with Euroscepticism being common and likely to threaten its future (Ladi & Tsarouhas, 2014). This situation has not changed significantly, and the examples considered in exemplifying the growing discontent within particular member countries, particularly the Eastern European and Southern European Member States and the UK. The current situation in Italy is considered a bigger threat to the EU than Brexit since Italy is also a member of the Eurozone and a founding member of the single market, so that a continuing damaging rift between Brussels and Rome generates unease in global markets and internal discontent. The hard stance taken by the EU in the negotiations regarding UK withdrawal from the EU is a consequence of the impact it will have on the EU budget, whilst there are currently 28 Member States, the UK contribution is 13% which is substantial and its economic position is considerably more positive than the average EU Member State.

Principle of Proportionality

This study began by defining the Principle of Proportionality, a principle that is interpreted in a number of ways. Hence, as a concluding section, each concept will be appraised against the evidence accumulated as the research developed.

If proportionality is based on the concept of justice and of protecting the rights of human beings against political actions, which could reduce or eliminate those rights, then the EC/Troika interventions in the countries appraised have not provided protection for social justice or human rights against political actions, since the laws passed and MoUs imposed on those nations in most difficulty have encouraged Member States to take political action. This has reduced the social protection of their citizens and has regularly alienated to them to the extent of political conflict and, in some cases, violence. In addition, the rights of minority groups such as women and immigrants have declined, and income inequality and poverty have increased. An ILO study (Vaughan-Whitehead, 2016) critically analysed the decline in social protection, which occurred in individual Member States from 2008 to 2014. It commented on the speed of actions taken towards social issues post crisis in comparison to the lengthy period the EU had taken to develop the European Social Model (ESM), which comprised welfare policies intended to create stability and peace. In 2013 the EU President stated that "social models are not an expense or a cost but the most profitable investment for the future. With growing individualisation in our societies, Europe needs collective rules" (Vaughan-Whitehead, 2016, p. 1). However, no definition was ever developed for ESM so that quantifying the changes that occurred from 2008 onwards is somewhat challenging, but various presidential pronouncements from 2000 onwards emphasise, for instance: investing in people; a dynamic welfare state reducing the number of people at risk of poverty and unemployment, with employment being the best way of preventing social exclusion; increasing growth, job creation and competitiveness; social cohesion. Article 117 of the Treaty establishing the EC also stresses the need to harmonise social protection systems and Article 118 demanded that EC ensured close cooperation between Member States on social security matters (Vaughan-Whitehead, 2016). ESM is also based on solidarity that "people share their wealth with those in need and they put back their individual interests in favour of collective interests or for the benefit of the wider public" (Hermann, 2013, p. 18). The quantitative data available from Oxfam

(2013a, 2013b, 2013c, 2013d, 2013e) exemplifies the reduction in social protection in many Member States and the rising gap between rich and poor in many EU states. The analysis of EU trends by Tsarou (2016) and Vaughan-Whitehead (2016) reinforces data previously included in this research. Exemplary data includes employment rates in Eurozone in 2012 being lower than in 2004 for all Member States except Germany, with EU youth unemployment averaging 23% compared with 15% in 2004. However changes in wage setting in Germany skew comparative data and enabled Germany to lower real wage levels to remain globally competitive (Dustmann et al., 2014). Those citizens classed as the economically inactive population rose to 137 million by the end of 2013, when all unemployment had increase by 3.8% since 2008, and long-term unemployment 2.5% of active population (Frazer et al., 2014). Income gaps, even in the most affected EU and Eurozone members, had widened, for instance the media income of the 20% richest in Bulgaria, Romania, Greece and Portugal was six times higher than that of the poorest 20% (Frazer et al., 2014). Pension reforms increased retirement ages in Italy, Spain, Ireland, UK, Romania and Hungary for instance, with other pension changes occurring in some of these, such as extension of contribution periods in Italy, Spain and Romania and reduction of payments in Portugal and Hungary (Hermann, 2013). Although the EU unemployment rate had almost returned to pre-2008 levels by the end of 2018, the most affected Southern European countries still experienced higher levels; youth unemployment for 15- to 25-year-olds had also returned on average to 15.6% as in the second quarter of 2008. In Greece it remained at 43.8%, in Spain 35.5% and in Italy 32.5%, whereas only 6.3% of this age group were without employment in Germany.

According to Harbo (2010), proportionality embraced a liberal rights-based constitutional rationality with a strong commitment to a welfare state; the commitment to dismantling the welfare state has been a strong characteristic of the austerity plans, and further actions mentioned earlier, as well as legislation to weaken the power of unions and to implement minimum wage. This objective is evident in the data trends and emphasised by Vaughan-Whitehead (2016), who demonstrated that although countries such as Portugal and Spain had a minimum wage, growth in the sum was frozen in 2012 so that it failed to keep pace with price increases, and in Greece it was reduced by 22% for the unskilled and 32% for under 25 year olds as part of the austerity measures imposed by EU. Collective bargaining was also weakened so that annual adjustments of real wages declined.

The Principle of Proportionality in the EU stated that its power was restricted to taking the specific actions necessary to accomplish Treaty objectives, which were combined into the Treaty of Lisbon and based on values including respect for human rights and dignities, democracy, equality and freedom (EC, 2015). The EU has used its power to change laws, which it considered no longer appropriate; however it used indirect means, so that it did not have to alter specific articles in the Treaty, which would have meant consulting other parties. Hence, the principle of democracy was violated (Kerikmae et al., 2013) and, in doing so and in creating new legislation related to providing financial support to countries in financial difficulties, it forced them to change their national laws to enable receipt of funding. This action was against the spirit of the original intention of this Principle; the inference being that EU policymakers were more competent than those in each of the Member States concerned, so that its intervention appeared to align with the Principle of Proportionality. The disproportionate influence of Germany on these changes of legislation, and the design of austerity measures so that its own economic and political agenda were achieved, has been suggested by several sources (Zen, 2015; Krugman, 2015), inferring that democratic processes have not been utilised. Other EU policymakers have been highly criticised for their increased lack of consultation with other experts and Member State communities on other occasions, throughout the period since 2008. Two of EU's major policy defects are exposed: setting up the ECB as a separate rather than a European Central Bank: adopting Alesina's flawed theory on austerity and retaining it after it had been discredited, even by the IMF, a member of the Troika that implemented it initially (Blyth, 2013; Kuttner, 2013). The other major consequence of EU policies during the recession, and evidenced in this research, has been to flout the values on which it was formed whilst espousing a policy of "respect for human dignity and human rights, freedom, democracy, equality and the rule of law" (European Parliament, 2015, p. 1), a point reinforced by Douglas-Scott (2012).

More recent events reinforce the EU's lack of adherence to the Principle of Proportionality, for instance it has failed to become sufficiently involved in resolving the immigration crisis, which has disproportionately and deeply affected the social environment of EU citizens in Greece and Italy owing to the high numbers unable to move to other EU countries, which refuse or fail to offer to equalise the burden. It has also condemned Italy and other countries that have refused to continue to receive immigrants, despite being aware that their particular geographical location makes them particularly attractive as a migrant destination. The disproportionate and unreasonably high social and economic cost to those EU Member States receiving most immigrants has been virtually ignored by EU. This lack of concern is contrary to the EU's founding principles (Harbo, 2010). The EU is also failing to the objectives of its Treaties with regard to its stance on Brexit, owing to fear of contagion to other countries, in other words encouraging other Member States to exit the EU. This fear is compounded by continuing austerity measures that are not meeting their objectives, for instance in Italy (Panico & Purificato, 2013), which continues to experience low or no growth. The continuing involvement in bond markets and creation of ABS that diverts debt risk for banks to citizens are not an EU function envisaged in the original Treaties (Panico & Purificato, 2013). In fact, the EU motives for creating the STS are perceived as being a political means of stimulating the economy and ignoring the risk to its citizens that these securities have previously been proven to represent (Engelen & Glasmacher, 2018). It is evident that EU citizens in some countries are becoming more disillusioned with being a part of the EU, not only those mentioned in detail in Chap. 6, because they do not perceive that the EU is using its powers appropriately, as set out in the original Treaties (Braniff, 2011).

Hence, the question which was the basis of this study has been answered, with evidence to the effect that the strategies taken by the EU, as a consequence of the global financial and external public debt crisis, did not align with the Principle of the Proportionality of State Intervention in the Market Economies of European Countries, but were generated to accomplish other political and economic goals related to specific member countries and to force political and economic integration with a EU wide social system that was contrary to the Lisbon Treaty.

Spillover Effects of EU Policies

This research has indicated significant spillover effects of EU policies, which have extended beyond the direct financial and political interventions to aspects such as declining standards of living, higher unemployment and poverty levels, particularly in the southern Eurozone Member States (Oxfam, 2013a, 2013b, 2013c, 2013d, 2013e). However, an outline of spillover effects in this conclusion focuses on financial and economic EU policies adopted from 2008 to 2020.

The fundamental cause of the sovereign debt crisis which emerged in its first stages in 2010 was caused by foreign central banks increasing their investment in French bonds, which were considered a safe haven, and subsequently German investors divesting their Italian and Spanish bonds, debt instruments in favour of French bonds. Hence French investors were forced to buy debt issued by sovereign banks, in other countries, such as those in Italy and Spain. After the crisis Italian and Spanish investors sold their French bonds (D'Auria et al., in t'Veld & Zeugner, 2014). This sudden change in activity generated high uncertainty in the Eurozone financial markets. The spillover consequences of sudden changes in activity in the sovereign credit markets of Eurozone members and their associated banks are illustrated in an ECB report (Alter & Beyer, 2013), which analysed daily changes in Credit Default Swaps (CDS) using quantitative data. The spillovers were evaluated and reported as a Contagion Index, derived by measuring the systemic effects of unexpected shocks to the creditworthiness of one Eurozone Member State's bank index on those of other banks' CDS in the period October 2009 to July 2012. Contagion is relevant because it refers to extensive financial volatility and uncertainty which generate crisis throughout a financial system so that competent authorities must take action to contain it (Constâncio, 2012). CDS are debt instruments, bonds or other securities and are similar to insurance protection in that an investor can protect itself against default on a loan and other risks; the purchaser of a CDS makes regular payments to the CDS seller, until the CDS maturity date, whilst the CDS seller guarantees that if the original debt issuer defaults it will pay the purchaser the total amount of premiums and interest that it would have received up to the CDS maturity date (CFI 2020); fundamentally CDS is a type of contract in which an investor can swap its credit risk with the credit risk of another investor. The main findings were that shock change in creditworthiness of Spanish CDS had a high impact on Euro area sovereign debt and banks in the first half of 2012, and later in 2012 to non-Eurozone Member States. The analysis also revealed increasing interdependence between banks and sovereign debt that was likely to generate systemic risk and a decreasing trend in the creditworthiness of all Eurozone members. However, the EBS suggests that the EU's monetary policy interventions, EFSF and long-term refinancing operations implemented in December 2011 somewhat mitigated the effect overall, and implementation of joint IMF/EU interventions reduced the systemic impact of creditworthiness shocks in Greece, Portugal and Ireland (Alter & Beyer, 2013).

The spillover effects on non-Eurozone countries are given sparse attention in the ECB report despite their impact on other EU Members States, and found to be substantial in the study conducted by Potjagailo (2016). This research embraced effects on 13 non-Eurozone countries, 10 Central and Eastern European (CEE) states and 3 Western European nations, and effects on production, prices and financial market variables. Although not Eurozone members, expansionary monetary policy or a reversal of it affected national policies of other EU members, owing to the degree of integration associated with trade and technical markets. These strong ties had encouraged some CEE states to peg their currencies to the Euro and were vulnerable to contagion from the systemic creditworthiness shocks; others with high foreign currency lending had limited exchange rate fluctuation against the Euro. Sweden, Denmark and UK had retained their own currencies but their involvement with the Euro also exposed them to spillover effects from both the contagion and the EU/ECB policies to contain it (Potjagailo, 2016). On average the spillover effect on production was similar to that of Eurozone countries, but was higher in the small open economies of CEE countries with fixed exchange rates, in which production was a response to increased foreign demand; production in non-Eurozone countries with flexible exchange rates was also affected but to a lower degree. Therefore the implication was that spillover effects of EU monetary policy were highest for countries with fixed rates, whereas those with flexible exchange were able to take actions to compensate for EU policy changes, although these are somewhat limited in the context of highly developed, integrated global financial markets. Price increases were experienced in production and consumer markets in the three Western European EU Member States, whilst the effects varied considerably in CEE countries. These Member States tended to use the increases in domestic currency exchange rates to mitigate their foreign currency debt levels whilst simultaneously enhancing risk (Potjagailo, 2016).

The economic policies implemented by the EU and its response to the sovereign debt crisis have induced significant political spillover effects in several EU Members States, the most important being UK's decision to leave the single market in 2016. However, other strong political anti-EU and/or anti-Euro campaigns have been experienced in Italy, France and the Netherlands (Belke et al., 2016). The ongoing uncertainty regarding the final terms agreed by the EU regarding Brexit has already damaged its reputation as a sustainable supranational body, especially as it failed to understand the challenges that Brexit inferred for EU and has continued to fail to address them objectively (Welfens, 2020). The initial effects of Brexit generated negative spillover effect on share prices, CDSs and 10 year interest rates in Eurozone countries, and on Sterling and the Euro. It is also likely to have a negative effect on both EU and UK economies, with the Ireland and the southern Eurozone states Italy, Portugal, Spain and Greece being most negatively impacted. At the end of 2016 business confidence had already declined by 4% and consumer confidence by 12% (Belke et al., 2016). The UK represents one fifth of the EUs national income, so that the potential economic spillover is extremely high; Germany, the Netherlands, Belgium and Ireland are particularly economically vulnerable owing to their reliance on exports to the UK (Welfens, 2020). If the EU continues to maintain a hard stance on Brexit, the UK could easily become its competitor in Asian markets, lower its corporate tax rates and further deregulate banks, all of which represent negative spillovers from the stance it has taken to date (Welfens, 2020). Given the continuing uncertainty in Southern European countries towards their stance on EU, political, financial and economic spillovers are likely to increase in the foreseeable future.

Bibliography

Abbot, A., & Jones, P. (2011). Procyclical Government Spending: A Public Choice Analysis. *Public Choice, 154*, 243–258.

Alter, A., & Beyer, A. (2013, June). *The Dynamics of Spillover Effects During the European Sovereign Debt Turmoil* (ECB Working Paper Series No. 1558).

Argyris, C. (1976). Single-Loop and Double-Loop Models in Research on Decision Making. *Administrative Science Quarterly, 21*(3), 363–375.

BB. (2011, October). *The Debt Brake in Germany – Key Aspects and Implementation.* Deutsche Bundesbank.

Belke, A., Dubova, I., & Osowski, T. (2016, November). *Policy Uncertainty and International Financial Markets: The Case of Brexit* (CEPS, Working Document NO. 427).

Blyth, M. (2013). *Austerity: The History of a Dangerous Idea.* Oxford University Press.

Braniff, C. (2011). *Integrating the Balkans: Conflict Resolution and the Impact of EU Expansion.* I.B. Taurus.

Cabral, R. (2013). The Euro Crisis and Portugal's Dilemma. *Intereconomics, 48*(1), 4–32.

Caldas, J. C. (2012). *The Consequences of Austerity Policies in Portugal.* Friedrich-Ebert-Stiftung.

CESR. (2012). *SPAIN Factsheet 12*. Centre for Economic and Social Rights.
Chan, S. P. (2015, August 11). Greece Reaches New Debt Deal but Critics Brand Targets 'Utterly Unachievable'. *The Telegraph*. elegraph.co.uk/finance/economics/11796970/Greece-reaches-new-debt-deal-but-critics-brand-targets-utterly-unachievable.html. Accessed 12 Aug 2015.
Conde-Ruiz, J. I., & Marín, C. (2013). The Fiscal Crisis in Spain. *Intereconomics, 48*(1), 21–26.
Constâncio, V. (2012). Contagion and the European Debt Crisis. *Banque de France, Financial Stability Review, 16*, 109–121.
Crysoloras, N. (2013). *Rebuilding Eurozone's Ground Zero: A Review of the Greek Economic Crisis*. London School of Economics.
Dorfman, J. (2014, January 18). Hollande Converts, Proposes Austerity and Lower Taxes to Boost Growth in France. *Forbes*. http://www.forbes.com/sites/jeffreydorfman/2014/01/18/hollande-converts-proposes-austerity-and-lower-taxes-to-boost-growth-in-france/. Accessed 13 Aug 2015.
Douglas-Scott, S. (2012). Justice and Pluralism in the EU. *Current Legal Problems, 65*, 83–118.
Dustmann, C., Fitzenberger, B., Schönberg, U., & Spitz-Oener, A. (2014). From Sick Man of Europe to Economic Superstar: Germany's Resurgent Economy. *Journal of Economic Perspectives, 28*(1), 167–188.
EC. (2012a, December 5). *Youth Employment: Commission Proposes Package of Measures*. European Commission.
EC. (2012b). *Single Market Act II: Together for New Growth*. European Commission.
EC. (2008). *Communication from the Commission to the European Council: A European Economic Recovery Plan*. European Commission.
EC. (2015). The EU at a glance. *European Commission* [online]. http://ec.europa.eu/cyprus/eu_glance/index_en.htm. Accessed 2 April 2015.
Economist. (2011, December 10). Is Germany's fiscal straitjacket an example for others? *The Economist*.
Economist. (2015, May 1). Taking Europe's Pulse. *The Economist*. https://www.economist.com/graphic-detail/2016/02/18/european-economic-guide. Accessed 22 May 2015.
Engelen, E., & Glasmacher, A. (2018). The Waiting Game: How Securitization Became the Solution for the Growth Problem of the Eurozone. *Competition & Change, 22*(2), 165–183.
Euronews. (2014). Anti-austerity, anti-Macron Law: Thousands Protest on Streets of France. *Euronews*. http://www.euronews.com/2015/04/09/anti-austerity-anti-macron-law-thousands-protest-on-streets-of-france/. Accessed 13 Aug 2015.
European Parliament. (2015). *Values*. European Parliament. Accessed 12 Aug 2015. http://europarlamentti.info/en/values-and-objectives/values

Eurostat. (2015). Unemployment Statistics. *Eurostat*. http://ec.europa.eu/eurostat/statistics-explained/index.php/Unemployment_statistics#Youth_unemployment_trends. Accessed 8 Aug 2015.

Fofana, I. (2011). More than Words: Austerity in France. *Harvard International Review*, Winter, pp. 9–11.

Frazer, H., Guio, A., Marlier, E., Vanhercke, B., & Ward, T. (2014, October). Putting the Fight Against Poverty and Social Exclusion at the Heart of the EU Agenda (OSE Research Paper No. 15).

Fuchs, S. (2013, September 21). *Poverty Grows in Germany's Large Cities*. WSWS. https://www.wsws.org/en/articles/2013/09/21/pove-s21.html. Accessed 11 Aug 2015.

Geier, A. (2011). *The Debt Brake – The Swiss Fiscal Rule at the Federal Level*. Berne: FFA.

Goretti, C., & Landi, L. (2013). Walking on the Edge: How Italy Rescued Italy in 2012. *Intereconomics, 1*, 15–21.

Harbo, T. (2010). The Function of the Proportionality Principle in EU Law. *European Law Journal, 16*(2), 158–185.

Hemerijck. A.C., & Vandenbroucke, F. (2012). Social Investment and the Euro Crisis: The Necessity of a Unifying Social Policy Concept. *Intereconomics, 4*, 200–206.

Hermann, C. (2013). *Crisis, Structural Reform and the Dismantling of the European Social Model(s)* (Hochschule für Wirtschaft und Recht Working Paper, No. 26/2013).

Holehouse, M. (2015a, July 13). EU Demands Britain Joins Greek Rescue Fund. *The Telegraph*. http://www.telegraph.co.uk/finance/economics/11737286/EU-demands-Britain-joins-Greek-rescue-fund.html. Accessed 5 July 2015.

Holehouse, M. (2015b, August 12). Greece Agrees Draft Deal with Creditors – But Waits for Germany to Say Yes. *The Telegraph*. http://www.telegraph.co.uk/finance/economics/11799008/Cyprus-has-provided-Greece-with-an-object-and-abject-bailout-lesson.html. Accessed 12 Aug 2015.

ILO. (2013). *Global Employment Trends*. International Labour Organisation.

Kannan, P., Scott, A., & Terrones, F. E. (2009). *From Recession to Recovery: How Soon and How Strong*. International Monetary Fund.

Kerikmae, T., Nyman-Metcal, K., & Papageorgiou, I. (2013). "Is This Really What I Voted For?" – On the Legitimacy of European Integration. *Baltic Journal of Law & Politics, 6*(1), 45–62.

Khan, M. (2015a, August 7). Indebted Portugal Is Still the Problem Child of the Eurozone. *The Telegraph*. http://www.telegraph.co.uk/finance/economics/11786694/Indebted-Portugal-is-still-the-problem-child-of-the-eurozone.html. Accessed 7 Aug 2015.

Khan, M. (2015b, July 15). Greece News Live: PM Alexis Tsipras Says Banks Could Stay Closed for a Month. *The Telegraph*. http://www.telegraph.co.uk/

finance/economics/11738150/Greece-news-live-Germans-back-Osbornes-fight-against-Juncker-plan-to-bailout-Greece-as-IMF-calls-for-more-debt-relief.html. Accessed 13 Aug 2015.

Krugman, P. (2015, April 29). The Case for Cuts Was a Lie. Why Does Britain Still Believe It? The Austerity Delusion. *The Guardian*. http://www.theguardian.com/business/ng-interactive/2015/apr/29/the-austerity-delusion. Accessed 10 Aug 2015.

Kuttner, R. (2013). *Debtors' Prison: The Politics of Austerity Versus Possibility*. Penguin Random House LLC.

Ladi, S., & Tsarouhas, D. (2014). The Politics of Austerity and Public Policy Reform in the EU. *Political Studies Review, 12*(2), 171–180.

Lynn, M. (2015, June 24). Forget Greece, Portugal Is the Eurozone's Next Crisis. *Marketwatch*. http://www.marketwatch.com/story/forget-greece-portugal-is-the-eurozones-next-crisis-2015-06-24?page=2. Accessed 9 Aug 2015.

Matsangou, E. (2015, April 30). *It Worked! Spain's GDP Up Thanks to Austerity Measures*. World Finance. http://www.worldfinance.com/home/it-worked-spains-gdp-up-thanks-to-austerity-measures. Accessed 10 Aug 2015.

Mazzolini, G., & Mody, A. (2014, October 3). *Austerity Tales: the Netherlands and Italy*. Bruegel. http://nbn-resolving.de/urn:nbn:de:0168-ssoar-395173. Accessed 10 Aug 2015.

Miller, D. (1992, January–February). The Icarus Paradox: How Exceptional Companies Bring About Their Own Downfall. *Business Horizons*, 24–35.

Mintzberg, H. (1987). The Strategy Concept 1: Five Ps for Strategy. *California Management Review, 30*(1), 11–24.

Monastiriotis, V. (2013). A Very Greek Crisis. *Intereconomics, 1*, 4–9.

OECD. (2010, May). *Counter-Cyclical Economic Policy* (OECD Economics Department Policy Notes, 1).

Oxfam. (2013a). *The True Cost of Austerity and Inequality; Portugal Case Study*. Oxfam.

Oxfam. (2013b). *The True Cost of Austerity and Inequality: Italy Case Study*. Oxfam.

Oxfam. (2013c). *The True Cost of Austerity and Inequality; Germany Case Study*. Oxfam.

Oxfam. (2013d). *The True Cost of Austerity and Inequality; Greece Case Study*. Oxfam.

Oxfam. (2013e). *The True Cost of Austerity and Inequality; France Case Study*. Oxfam.

Panico, C., & Purificato, F. (2013). Policy Coordination, Conflicting National Interests and the European Debt Crisis. *Cambridge Journal of Economics, 37*, 585–608.

Portuese, A. (2013). Principle of Proportionality as Principle of Economic Efficiency. *European Law Journal, 19*(5), 612–635.

Potjagailo, G. (2016). *Spillover Effects from Euro Area Monetary Policy Across the EU: A Factor-Augmented VAR approach* (Kiel Institute for the World Economy, Working Paper, No. 2033).

PWC. (2015). *Five Years of Eurozone Bailouts – But Where Does Each Economy Stand Now?* Price Waterhouse Coopers. http://www.pwc.com/gx/en/issues/economy/global-economy-watch/five-years-eurozone-bailouts.jhtml. Accessed 9 Aug 2015.

Riera-Crichton, D., Vegh, C., & Vuletin, G. (2014). *Procyclical and Countercyclical Fiscal Multipliers: Evidence from OECD Countries* (NBER, WP No. 20533).

Schein, E. H. (1991). *Organizational Culture and Leadership*. Jossey Bass.

Strafor. (2013, March 5). *Worries on Austerity in France and the Netherlands*. Strafor. https://www.stratfor.com/analysis/worries-austerity-france-and-netherlands. Accessed 13 Aug 2015.

t'Veld, J., & Zeugner, S. (2014). Cross-Border Spillovers in the Euro Area. *Quarterly Report on the Euro Area, 13*(4), 7–22.

Truger, A. (2013). *The Sad State of Economic Policy in Germany and the EU* (Institute for International Political Economy Working Paper 22/2013).

Tsarou, D. (2016). Rethinking the European Social Model. In E. Stetter, K. Duffek, & A. Skrzypek (Eds.), *Delivering Empowered Welfare Societies* (pp. 145–164). Brussels.

UN. (2014). *World Economic Situation and Prospects 2014 Update as of Mid-2014*. United Nations.

Vaughan-Whitehead, D. (2016). *The European Social Model In Crisis. Is Europe Losing Its Soul?* ILO/Edward Elgar Publishing.

Welfens, P. (2020). Trump's Trade Policy, BREXIT, Corona Dynamics, EU Crisis and Declining Multilaterism. *International Economics and Economic Policy, 15*, 563–634.

WH. (2015, August 11). *What Is Official Development Assistance (ODA)?* World Hunger. http://www.worldhunger.org/articles/05/us/oda.htm. Accessed 11 Aug 2015.

Witte, L. (2012). *Austerity Policy in Europe: Spain*. Friedrich-Ebert-Stiftung.

WP. (2013, November 1). Germany's Austerity Program Is Hurting Germany, Too. *Washington Post*. https://www.washingtonpost.com/opinions/germanys-austerity-program-is-hurting-germany-too/2013/11/01/34d64fe0-424d-11e3-a62b4-41d661b0bb78_story.html. Accessed 11 Aug 2015.

Zen, A. (2015, June 4). Amartya Sen: The Economic Consequences of Austerity. *New Statesman*. http://www.newstatesman.com/politics/2015/06/amartya-sen-economic-consequences-austerity. Accessed 11 Aug 2015.

CHAPTER 9

EU in 2020

Introduction

This purpose of this additional chapter is to provide a comparison of the economic, social and political development in three of the original EEC Member States from the period of their initial membership until mid-2020. Three case studies and the results of surveys conducted in each of those countries are presented and followed by an epilogue that outlines the present situation. The Member States can be considered representative as they were all established members almost three decades before formation of the EU, so that they were all signatories of the original Treaties and Regulations (UK Parliament, 2020). All three have been subject to the same conditions of membership throughout the past 47 years and are major EU economies, so that the benefits and limitations that they have experienced from membership might be assumed to be similar. However, history has revealed that these same membership conditions have had widely different impact on them. Possibly the decision of the UK to remain outside the Euro could explain the economic differences, and yet Germany and Italy chose to join the Euro yet the outcomes of their decision have proved diverse. Prior to the Maastricht Treaty in 1992, Italy had gradually strengthened its economic performance, and its GDP per capita was 97% that of France, for instance. Despite implementing EU rules relating to fiscal austerity and structural reforms associated with the Maastricht Treaty more closely than most Member States, its economic performance declined

S. Weißschnur, *The Proportionality of State Intervention*,
https://doi.org/10.1007/978-3-030-75676-5_9

faster than major EU economies in income per person, labour productivity, export market share and investment (Storm, 2019a, 2019b). In contrast Germany's economy remains the strongest in the EU. Therefore, these case studies provide an opportunity to explore the underlying reasons for potentially the most diverse outcomes from membership of the same institution; to discover how interpretation of the same rules could have shaped their different relationships with EU by 2020, when one member is exiting, another is in regular conflict and the third is the most powerful in the group.

Case Study 1: United Kingdom

Background

At the end of World War Two, the United Kingdom (UK) was still a major global power and more focused on developing the Commonwealth than participating in a European group (Young, 1989). However, it sent a representative to the Messina Conference in 1955 (NA, 2020) but no further attempt was made to join the six founding nations that signed the Schumann Plan. The Plan was devised by the French in 1950 with the objective of developing a supranational body, which would regulate the production and sale of coal and steel, and later become the European Economic Community (EEC) (Young, 1989; NA, 2020; Bulmer & Quaglia, 2018). The Treaty of Rome was signed by France, West Germany, Italy, Belgium, Luxembourg and the Netherlands in 1957 to establish the European Atomic Energy Community (EURATOM), and the EEC was created in 1958 (NA, 2020). Non-EEC-member countries including the UK had formed the European Free Trade Association (EFTA) in 1959 but it could not compete with EEC as a stand-alone free trade area. The UK attempted to join EEC in 1960s, since the Prime Minister was concerned about the rapid economic growth occurring in France and Germany, but the French President Charles De Gaulle vetoed the application in 1963 and again in 1967, the reason being the UK's close links to US and Commonwealth countries, as well as its domestic agricultural policies. In 1973, the UK application was finally accepted but the change from a Conservative to a Labour Government in 1974 was followed by a referendum on membership. The electorate voted to remain in EU, despite the Prime Minister's disapproval of the retention of its membership (NA, 2020; Bulmer & Quaglia, 2018).

The signing of the Maastricht Treaty in 1992 is regarded by some politicians and economists as the point at which the British Conservative Party began to become divided over the advantages of remaining in the EEC; a major reason cited by Liddle (2019) was the removal of the word economic as the EU was created. The European Research Group (ERG) was formed by Sir Michael Spicer, a group of Eurosceptics that would significantly influence political opinion on remaining in the EU during the twenty-first century (Mudge, 2018).

The UK decided not to join the European Monetary Union (EMU), which was indicated by Margaret Thatcher's rejection of the concept in 1988 (Bulmer & Quaglia, 2018). Subsequently the UK did not sign the Maastricht Treaty, and Kassim et al. (2017) suggest that this is an important example of the UK's general unwillingness to participate fully in major EU policy initiatives and its preference for liberal intergovernmentalism. However, the role of institutions and governmental actions were also evident in this and other UK policy decisions (Kassim et al., 2017). The UK's participation in the EU had been relatively successful before 2008, despite the conflicting perspectives, because it had been able to profit from aspects of the single market, for instance freedom of movement, without being forced to join the Euro, according to Thompson (2017).

UK Relationship with EU from 2008

The UK's reaction to the Eurozone crisis was formulated with respect to protecting City of London interests and domestic issues of concern to the electorate and Parliament, insofar as long-term economic outcomes were concerned. A relatively small group of actors were involved in the decision-making process, often merely Prime Minister and Chancellor, with little discussion taking place in the related EU forum (Kassim et al., 2017). This is somewhat reinforced by the fact that after the financial crisis, whilst the EU adopted a variety of methods to recapitalise banks, for instance the consolidation of Spanish savings banks, the UK government acted alone as single financial regulator and nationalised some of its banks (Eubanks, 2010), most notably Royal Bank of Scotland (RBS) and Northern Rock Building Society. The UK experienced its worst recession since World War Two from 2008, as a result of the banking crisis (Pylas, 2020), and it initially introduced austerity comprising 89% fiscal consolidation; most spending cuts were generated by reducing centralised funds to local governments by 36.3% from 2009 to 2015 (Innes & Tetlow, 2015).

After 2008, successive UK governments continued to oppose joining the EMU (Kassim et al., 2017; Pylas, 2020) so that when the ESFS was proposed in 2011 as the means to prevent a future crisis by tighter regulation of all EU banks and financial firms, substantial opposition was evident from the UK, a non-Eurozone member. The plan was to instigate common supervisory guidelines for all financial firms that aligned with EU laws and regulations. The UK's antagonism occurred because its national financial market was extremely well developed and regulated by the Financial Services Authority, and it did not wish the EU to have the power to control its national regulatory authority. The additional proposition that EU could expect national governments to use taxpayer's money to rescue banks in another EU country was also firmly rejected by the UK (Eubanks, 2010).

The UK Conservative government expressed dissatisfaction with the EU's strategies to resolve the Eurozone crisis, for instance their caution in implementing the actions considered necessary, but also the ways in which it acted towards some countries, for example Greece. The ongoing Euro crisis was considered a potential danger to UK economic recovery and the EU's attempts to strengthen the link between Eurozone and wider EU policies, single market legislation, were also received with suspicion. These developments and the EU's poor economic performance since 2008 served to increase Euroscepticism within the party and the UK electorate (Kassim et al., 2017; Leetim, 2016). The economic problems in Greece were evident to UK government in 2008–2009, and it considered that EU authorities lacked the competence to resolve a sovereign debt crisis of this magnitude. In 2010, the IMF became involved and insisted that the EU participate in the resolution of the problem, but the solution proposed was associated with the EU budget and not provided for by the existing EU Treaties. The UK opposed the idea of a proposed €500 billion stabilisation fund, which would be sourced from the EU budget to which it was a contributor, but it was not a Eurozone member and stated that it should not be forced to bail out the affected Eurozone countries. It also stressed that Article 122(2) did not have any provision for such action because the relevant Member States had not experienced natural disasters or other impacts beyond their control and proposed to veto any attempt to implement the stabilisation fund. However, the UK later reluctantly agreed to a temporary three-year stabilisation fund to alleviate the difficulties encountered by Greece, Spain and other Eurozone members, owing to pressure from US and other G7 countries. All three major UK political parties agreed to this action, since the intervening UK election in 2010 had left a hung Parliament (Kassim et al., 2017), but the UK expressed concern that the borrowers would not be able to repay the loans. The UK's resistance to the pressure to agree to the EFSM allowed the new Prime Minister David Cameron to be able to ensure that the replacement vehicle to the EFSM, the ESM, did not allow bailouts to Eurozone countries, as the change to Article 122 had permitted (BBC, 2019a). The EFSM measure failed to resolve the Euro crisis, and subsequently Article 122(2) was no longer relevant to securing financial stability, but introduction of ESM required alteration to Article 136 of the Treaty, a change promoted by Germany in 2011, in order to implement the Fiscal Compact (De Witte, 2011). This change caused further anxiety regarding backlash on UK economy. The UK responded by asking for a Treaty change that would alter its relationship with EU in terms of no longer being bound by EU financial regulations but was unable to gain agreement and vetoed the Treaty change. This action caused criticism from other Member States as their efforts to appropriately manage the crisis were blocked.

By 2011, the UK Prime Minister and Chancellor were becoming more frustrated with the lack of EU action on recapitalising banks and other measures related to the design of the single currency, the Euro, instead the EU focus continued to be on national problems, which were worsening (Kassim et al., 2017). In regard to bank reform, the EU had to decide on the formation of a banking union that would ensure all banks were strong enough to withstand another crisis. The decision was based on a choice between the European Banking Authority (EBA), the regulatory body associated with the EU, or a European Central Bank (ECB). The UK preferred the ECB because it did not generate powerful EU financial agencies and would be based in Frankfurt, which would threaten The City of London, and possibly because the UK would have less influence on decisions as a non-Eurozone member. The concept of a banking union was complex because, in contrast to the situation before the 2008 crisis when banking issues such as monetary and exchange rate policies had been separated from single market matters, they were likely to become much more intertwined by development of EBA. However, a European Central Bank would be based in the Euro area and allow UK to remain beyond its regulatory controls in the same way as other non-Euro countries. As in 1992, the UK perspective on the Euro was that it was unsound, and this opinion was driven in this period by the increasing Eurozone member integration and fiscal union, and the potential for failure in the Eurozone to spillover into the UK. As a non-Eurozone member, but a continuing EU member, the UK became increasingly marginalised and subject to being unwillingly and excessively influenced by the Eurozone bloc of countries (PCK, 2011; Kassim et al., 2017). In 2011, President Barosso had confirmed this type of ostracisation by stating that belonging to the Euro areas should involve participating in the Eurozone and failing to do so was contrary to EU principles on integration (PCK, 2011). An additional reason that the UK remained Eurosceptical was that it perceived that the EC had a growing capacity to be unable to deliver on the extensive strategies it was proposing (Kassim et al., 2017). The increase in interest rates by EU in 2011, a contractionary measure, met with UK disapproval since its view was that expansion was needed for economic growth in Eurozone countries; the contractionary policy increased UK scepticism about EU competence (Leetim, 2016). In response, the UK sought to assist Ireland, which was experiencing economic difficulties, by providing it with a bilateral loan, in recognition of the long-term relationship between the two countries but did not participate in other loans to the stricken Eurozone states of Italy, Spain and Portugal. The deteriorating situation in Eurozone had induced votes in Parliament by Labour MPs against funding for IMF, because it had also been instrumental in shaping the harsh austerity measures on Greece. In contrast the UK government was able to promote anti-austerity policies at that time because it was not bound by the fiscal rules imposed by the Eurozone and could support government borrowing that did not generate inflationary outcomes (Thompson, 2017; Leetim, 2016).

The difference in economic performance between the Eurozone countries and the non-Eurozone members of the single market, including UK, tends to strengthen the UK's case that the design of the Euro was flawed and was the underlying reason for economic stagnation after 2008 (Fig. 9.1).

The Conservative Party had formed a coalition government with the Liberal Democrat Party in 2011, to resolve the hung Parliament situation by granting it the option of a Referendum on whether the UK should remain or leave the EU (Kassim et al., 2017). According to BBC (2019a), this option was to apply only to a circumstance when the EU attempted to increase its powers over the UK. However, this was not the first time a Conservative Party had suggested a referendum on EU membership; it had also suggested a referendum in 2005 and 2010. In 2015, the

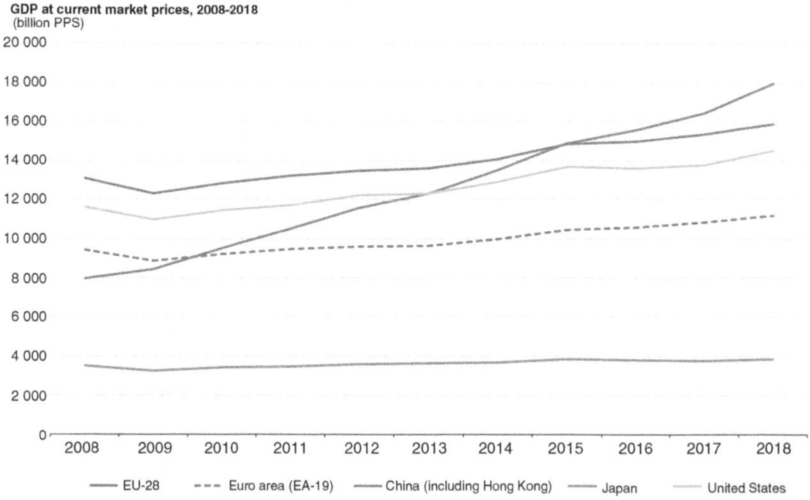

Fig. 9.1 Comparison of Eurozone, non-Eurozone, China, Japan and US GDP 2008–2018. (Source: Eurostat (2020))

referendum option was integrated into the Conservative Election Manifesto (BBC, 2019b; Pylas, 2020).

The referendum held in the UK on 23 January 2016 resulted in 51.9% of the electorate who voted choosing to leave the EU and 48.1% to stay (BBC, 2019b; Raitio & Raulus, 2017). Two social and political aspects are also often cited as furthering Euro scepticism and leading the 2016 referendum result; liberal internal immigration, which grew rapidly when the EU expanded from the early 2000s onwards, and excessive regulation. Although the UK refused to stop border checks required by the Schengen Agreement in 1999, it continues to be forced to allow any immigrants with a Schengen Visa that can be granted to visitors even from beyond the EU countries (Peers, 2015; Leetim, 2016). The increasing quantities of undemocratic economic regulation devised by unelected, unaccountable EU bureaucrats based in Brussels, which limits national freedom of decision making on simple matters, such as the maximum power allowed for a vacuum cleaner, are also cited as a major reason to leave (Leetim, 2016).

In March 2017, the UK Prime Minister Theresa May invoked Article 50, the official notification to the EU that the country would leave the single market (Bulmer & Quaglia, 2018). Whilst the Lisbon Treaty Article

50 states that a Member State is free to leave the EU to meet its own constitutional preference (Pylas, 2020), the UK has met significant resistance and challenges to accomplish the wishes of the electorate; this is contrary to Article 8 of the Lisbon Treaty, which promotes strong relationship building with neighbouring countries (Rayner, 2019). The UK wished to accomplish a comprehensive agreement comprising the terms of Brexit and to shape the UK's future relationship with the EU within two years, whereas the EU has been determined that the UK's transition to leave should last a much longer term (Renwick, 2017). The EU accused the UK government of 'cherry picking', in other words aiming to select strategies that were advantageous to it and avoiding those EU policies that were perceived as disadvantageous (Raitio & Raulus, 2017). The EU stated that a phased approach to exit was required, and the first stage was to agree the terms of exit and must be completed before future relations between the parties could take place, in other words future trade agreement. The EU representatives also stated that UK could not have the same rights as a Member State since it does not commit to the four single market freedoms of the acceptance of the authority of the EU and the ECJ, making appropriate budgetary contributions decided by the EU, and compliance with EU common trade policies (Bulmer & Quaglia, 2018). Under this phased exit, the UK was forced to continue to contribute to the EU budget before it would agree to discuss future trade arrangements (Hunt & Wheeler, 2018). The UK Withdrawal Agreement was originally agreed on 25 November 2018, so that the UK would leave the EU on 29 March 2019. The UK Parliament rejected the agreement presented by Prime Minister Theresa May three times, stating the proposed customs border between Southern Ireland and Northern Ireland required by the EU was unacceptable; this requirement was regarded by the UK as a strategy to force EU preferred terms on UK or to effectively prevent UK from returning to sovereign rule (Walker, 2019; Timothy, 2019). Theresa May resigned as Prime Minister in June 2019 replaced by Boris Johnson, founder of the Brexit also known as Leave.

After three years, and with a change of Prime Minister, the UK officially left the EU on 31 January 2020. The current Conservative government led by Boris Johnson with the largest majority in Parliament this century now faces the challenging task of agreeing a future trade deal with a hostile EU (Pylas, 2020). Whilst the transition period to agree the terms for trade between EU and UK was scheduled to begin on 1 February and to expire on 31 December 2020, the EU appears determined to extend the term by obstructing a quick exit (Sandford, 2020a, 2020b).

The relationship between the UK and the EU reinforces the theory that the UK perceived single market membership with an intergovernmentalist philosophy but there are also substantial instances that reflect postfunctionalism, as the various tensions between the EU and UK demonstrate over the period since the 1960s. In contrast the EEC was founded on neoliberalism principles and there have been several indications of postfunctionalism as an EU integration theory, in regard to its potential for generating conflict situations. These are exemplified by the EU's inability to change its mental model on the single austerity solution for the Eurozone, and resistance to negotiating UK withdrawal terms other than those that comply with its current economic model. In Effect, disintegration has been the consequence with UK and may generate further countries exciting the EU in future (Hooghe & Marks, 2019). The EU's stance on Brexit negotiations and future trade relations appears to be contrary to the Principle of Proportionality in terms of representing the least restrictive solution and not exceeding the objective concerned (Engle, 2012a, 2012b); under the Lisbon Treaty countries are allowed to exit the EU to follow their own constitutional preferences (Pylas, 2020) and strong relationships should be developed with neighbouring countries (Rayner, 2019). The Principle of Subsidiarity has been upheld to the extent that the EU negotiators have continuously stated that the 27 remaining Member States will vote on the outcomes of negotiations. However, the application of the Principle in this case may be more idealistic than realistic indicating its weakness and impacting on future strong relationships (Rayner, 2019).

Primary Research on UK Case Study

A quantitative survey was conducted to gather the opinions of professionals on the UK's performance as a non-Eurozone member of the EU, including its relative capacity to recover from the 2008 recession. It also seeks to establish whether EU policies impacting on the UK aligned with the Principles of Proportionality and Subsidiarity.

The following hypotheses are tested:

H1: UK citizens were increasingly more dissatisfied with the perceived disadvantages of EU membership, examples EU power and influence, so that its advantages such as freedom of movement were less likely to be valued.

H2: The EU had stronger reasons to dissuade the UK from withdrawing from the single market, for instance budget contribution and weakening the EU's position with the remaining 27 states, than its fear that UK trade focus would move to its former commonwealth countries and US.

United Kingdom Survey Analysis and Discussion

The participants of this survey were 1638 professionals with an age range from 19 to more than 60 years, the largest group 47% being in the 30–44 age group: 63% males and 37% females. The highest level of qualification and range of specialisms are indicated in Fig. 9.2.

Whilst the responses to the length of UK membership of the single market vary considerably, 48% of participants stated that it commenced in 1973 and 17.7% in 1992, indicating reasonably accurate knowledge of the relationship span (NA, 2020; Bulmer & Quaglia, 2018).

The responses to all the questions in the survey can be accessed in the Case Study Appendix; in this section the hypothesis testing is overviewed and some major points from the survey.

Hypothesis Testing

The main hypotheses tested in this case, H1 and H2, were related particularly to questions 10 and 12 respectively:

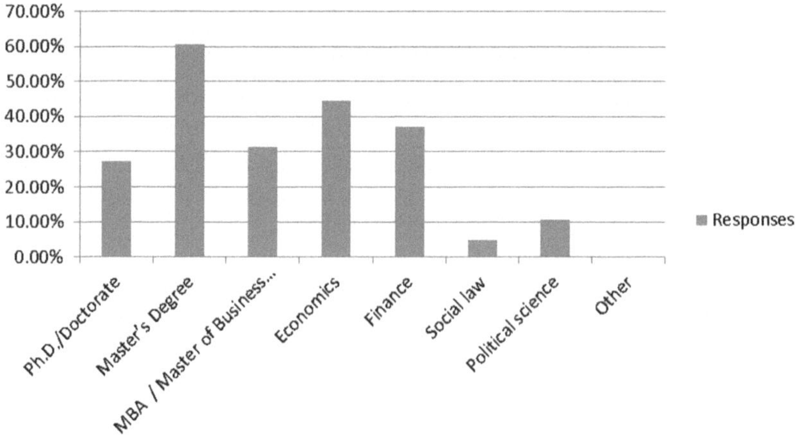

Fig. 9.2 Participant professional profile

H1: UK citizens were increasingly more dissatisfied with the perceived disadvantages of EU membership examples EU power and influence, so that its advantages such as freedom of movement were less likely to be valued.

The spss output from the survey demonstrates that HI must be refuted because it is not proven (Table 9.1).

There is a negative, significant correlation between 10b and both 10c and 10d, meaning that as the first element increases the second will move in the opposite direction. These two pairs basically have the same inference, for instance increase in excessive free movement was not a major reason corresponding with legislation/regulation decreasing. The negative correlation being higher for pair 3, implying more dissatisfaction with perceived inappropriateness of EU legislators than EU regulation. The mean score for 10b was also more than 3 indicating that more voters tended to wish to leave owing to immigration than did not. When paired samples were subjected to a t-test to compare difference in the means and to measure the spread of scores, all three pairs had a high t value, particularly 10b and 10c with a t value of 14.99 and p=0.000.

Table 9.1 Question 10c, d, e versus 10b, f

Paired samples correlations				
Pair 1 Significant!	10b. Excessive free movement, internal immigration was not a major reason for the decision to leave. 10c. Increasing EU regulation in every aspect of trade and life was considered unacceptable to UK population.	1183	-0.060	0.038
Pair 2 Not significant!	10b. Excessive free movement, internal immigration was not a major reason for the decision to leave. 10d. The continuous enlargement of the EU was regarded as indicating its preference for increasing its power rather than the economic growth and prosperity principles of the original EEC.	1176	-0.008	0.784
Pair 3 Significant!	10b. Excessive free movement, internal immigration was not a major reason for the decision to leave. 10e. British voters were tired of being subject to inappropriate legislation passed by EU bureaucrats that had not been elected by them.	1190	-0.177	0.000

The relative scores on the ratings grids in Survey Monkey dataset reinforce these statistics; they show strong agreement that increasing regulation, perceived power seeking and EU enlargement and legislation as reasons for Brexit leave vote with aggregated strongly agree and agree of 58.7%, 60.6% and 61.85% respectively. In contrast only 41.3% agreed with free movement not being a decision to leave, meaning that more people tended to agree that free movement internal immigration was a major issue, and 58.5% agreeing that UK voters did not want to leave owing to loss of free movement. These outcomes particularly on immigration, regulation and legislation tend to be in agreement with studies conducted by Peers (2015) and Leetim (2016).

H2: The EU had stronger reasons to dissuade the UK from withdrawing from the single market, for example budget contribution and weakening the EU's position with the remaining 27 states, than its fear that UK trade focus would move to its former commonwealth countries and US.

The responses to questions 12b and 2c were independently compared with that to 12e, findings in Table 9.2:

There are also statistically significant differences between the two sets of statements, when subjected to t tests, t values of -5.2 and -12.48 respectively.

Hence the significant pair suggests that the undervaluing of EU exports to UK is weakly negatively correlated to lack of fear that UK will trade

Table 9.2 EU Single Market and UK withdrawal

Paired samples correlations

		N	*Correlation*	*Sig.*
Pair 1 **Significant**	12b. The value of UK import trade to other EU members is not being considered seriously enough in the obstinate stance the EU has to the talks. 12e. The EU does not fear UK's ability to sign substantial trade agreements with US and former UK commonwealth countries.	1162	-0.082	0.005
Pair 2 **Not Significant**	12c. The EU has no mechanism for a country to withdraw from the group and fears UK exit will provoke further requests to leave and weaken its power. 12f. The UK will leave the EU without a trade deals and become subject to World Trade Organisation rules.	1176	-0.006	-0.844

more with other countries, suggesting that as a perception that the value of UK exports is not considered important increases, EU's lack of fear that UK might preferentially choose other trade partners declines. Therefore, H2 must be refuted since the correlation is weak and further proof is required.

However, the non-statistical analysis demonstrated that more UK participants agreed or strongly agreed, 64.12%, with the statement that the EU had no mechanism for withdrawal and feared that Brexit would weaken its power with other Member States (Hooghe & Marks, 2019), than those that did not know or disagreed and 55.3% agreed that EU did not value its export trade to UK seriously enough.

The major reasons given for UK leaving the EU were dominated by immigration but to a lesser degree by returning to an independent or sovereign state and many diverse comments about EU legislation, a few alluded to being ruled by unelected bureaucrats. These aspects reinforce studies for instance by Walker (2019) and Timothy (2019). The majority of respondents felt that the mode of exit of UK from the EU followed the Principle of Proportionality, 40% disagreed. These viewpoints are contrary to those expressed by Engle (2012a, 2012b) and Rayner (2019).

When asked for opinions about the Brexit negotiations, three statements were of greatest concern: 55.75% considered that the UK would leave without an agreement on trade and other matters as indicated by Pylas (2020); 55% felt that the EU had not given sufficient thought to the value of EU exports to UK in its negotiations; 47.4% stated that EU was making it difficult for UK to leave in order to retain its budget payments for as long as possible (Hunt and Wheeler, 2018). The percentage of those with no definite opinion for these questions was over 25% despite their professional status. The limitation of this study is also the lack of representation of the entire population, these participants being qualified in economics, politics and finance and predominantly males, for instance, and the lack of capacity to gather qualitative data to expand underlying reasons for responses.

Case Study 2: Germany

Background

The Federal Republic of Germany (FRG) formed after World War Two was referred to as West Germany, whilst the eastern part of the country was under Communist rule until 1989 and known as the German

Democratic Republic (GDR); Germany was created by the unification in 1989 and it became the largest member of the European Union (Bulmer, 2019). FRG was one of the founding members of the European Coal and Steel Community (ECSC) in 1952, became the European Economic Community (EEC) and then the European Union (EU) in 1992. The German Chancellor Helmut Kohl was instrumental in forging European integration, since it provided a vehicle for regaining the trust of Western European nations after the war, especially with France. Kohl also influenced the creation of the European Monetary Union (EMU) in 1992 (Bulmer, 2019), and Werbowski (2013) states that substituting the Euro for the Deutschmark after reunification was an emotional act. In order to restrain German influence after reunification, Kohl also made an informal pact with the French President Mitterrand. However, transfer to the Euro did not have the desired effect of demonstrating lower German power, because it provided Germany with financial and economic dominance when the 2008 crisis occurred. The German policy on Europe has been extremely consistent since unification, reinforcing the original intention of peaceful trading interaction by encouraging further integration, enlargement of the membership, developing the nature of the market and exerting non-military power to secure its goals (Bulmer, 2019). Germany is the world's fifth largest economy, approximately one third greater than the UK economy, and is increasingly export led (Fig. 9.3) relying on automotive vehicles, machinery and chemicals (Haran, 2014).

Prior to the financial crisis in 2008, the average rate of increase in GDP from 2000 onwards was 1.54% but it was relatively volatile, peaking at 3.7 in 2006 and falling to 1.8% in 2008 and dipping to -0.71% in 2003 (Macrotrends, 2020). Germany's unemployment rates rose from 9.2% in 1998 to 11.1%, or 5 million, in 2005, but had fallen to 3 million by 2008 as a consequence of labour market intervention (Dustmann et al., 2014).

German Economic Trends and Relations with the EU from 2008

Economic Trends

After the 2008 crisis, Germany's GDP initially declined, for example by 6.8% at the start of 2009 (Dustmann et al., 2014) and by 2.9% for that year (Anderson, 2009). The German export and internal market were affected by the crisis, domestic consumer and business confidence declined (Fig. 9.4; Anderson, 2009).

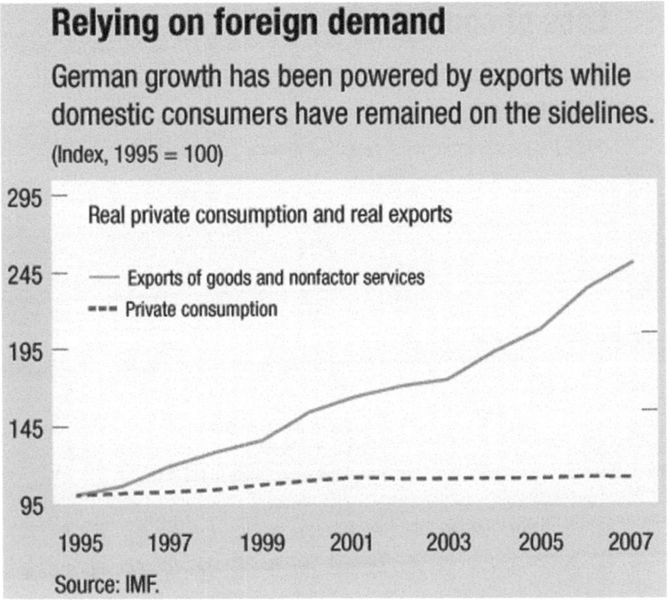

Fig. 9.3 Increasing export-led GDP growth. (Source: IMF Data Anderson (2009))

The GDP decline in Germany was caused by the dramatic fall in global trade flows (Haran, 2014) unlike the situation in the UK and US that was generated by a credit bubble, which was not backed by physical equity assets but by highly toxic debt instruments (Rudd, 2009). In contrast to the US and most EU countries, which experienced rising unemployment, German unemployment fell after 2008 and had declined to 7.7% by 2010. The relative economic impact of the 2008 crisis and recovery from it in the first five years are evident from Fig. 9.5.

Germany recovered from the crisis very quickly regaining its previous GDP growth by quarter 1, 2011 and, whilst the entire Eurozone showed a quicker recovery than the UK, both had a deeper and longer recessions than Germany, and had not returned to positive GDP growth by 2013 (Haran, 2014). The return to growth in Germany is likely to have been supported by the fiscal stimulus of approximately €50 billion applied by the German government in late 2008 over a period of two years, a much larger sum than injected in other global trading nations (Anderson, 2009).

Fig. 9.4 Pre- and post-2008 economic climate Germany. (Source: IMF, Anderson (2009))

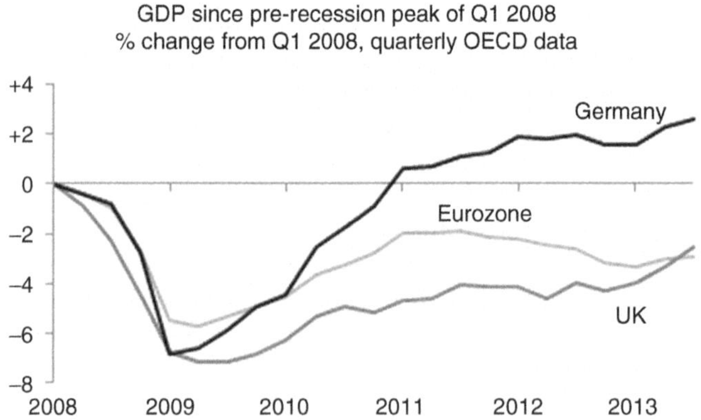

Fig. 9.5 Economic growth trends, Germany, Eurozone and UK 2008–2013. (Source: Haran (2014))

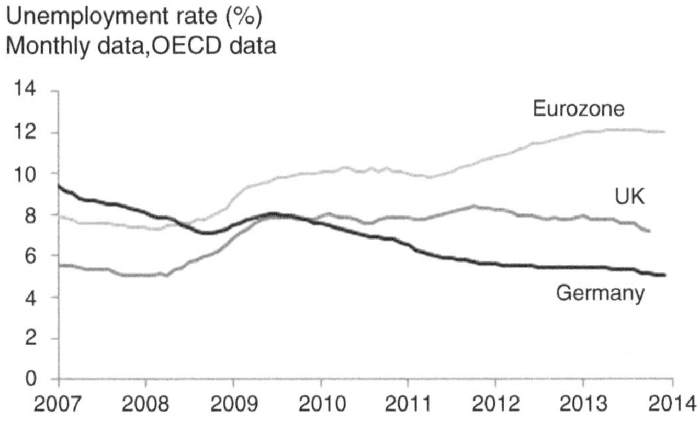

Fig. 9.6 Unemployment trends. (Source: Haran (2014))

The German current account surplus fell by a quarter in 2009 but remained at 5% GDP (Deutsche Bank, 2010). The unemployment trends in the three zones also failed to align (Fig. 9.6), whereas UK employment continued to rise until 2012, Eurozone unemployment was still increasing in 2017, whilst German unemployment dipped slightly in 2008 to 2009 and then continuously declined (Fig. 9.4). In 2014 the average was 5% with youth unemployment at 7% compared with average youth unemployment at 23% in Eurozone and 20% in UK (Haran, 2014).

German export growth from 2012 was negatively impacted by the global and European debt crisis and the large scale of recession in both the Eurozone and neighbouring countries so that economic growth had declined to 0.4% in 2013. In 2012, 40% of German exports were associated with automotive vehicles, machinery and chemicals and total GDP comprised 51% exports, mainly to US, France and UK. Domestic growth was slower over this period, Germany's trade surplus in 2012 amounted to 7% GDP and gross debt was approximately 80% GDP (Haran, 2014). The relatively lower labour costs in Germany, owing to higher productivity per person and decrease in real wage levels, were also cited as a reason for Germany's capacity to recover competitiveness in contrast to Italy and Spain. The UK was a non-Eurozone member, which allowed it to rely on currency depreciation to moderate its relative labour costs and increase its competitiveness; this was no longer an option for EU countries belonging to the Euro (Dustmann et al., 2014). Germany's labour relations structure enabled a high degree of wage setting decentralisation so that reducing wages, especially lower wage levels, had been possible because fewer workers belonged to trade unions, and work councils within individual firms were able to determine the stipend paid (Dustmann et al., 2014). These labour market strategies had severe social consequences, since social inequality increased, and Dustmann et al. (2014) suggested that a minimum wage was likely to be introduced to mitigate the issue. An action of this kind would lower German capacity to increase or maintain competitiveness by means of lower real wages. Eurozone countries such as France, Spain and Italy were unable to regain competitiveness in a similar way by altering relative labour costs through productivity increases because their labour market institutions were controlled centrally and by law, for instance employment market protection was high, whilst active labour market policies and centralised collective bargaining were relatively weak. Hence, political intervention in southern Eurozone countries was characterised by two-tier reforms that only impacted on some employee groups rather than entire labour markets, as had occurred in Germany (Boeri, 2011),

The economic trends since 2013 are summarised in Table 9.3, demonstrating lower GDP increases than prior to 2008, but nevertheless continued growth in contrast to most Eurozone countries.

In 2017, Germany recorded its fourth consecutive surplus of €38.4 billion, 1.2% GDP and highest employment rate since unification (Destatis, 2018). The black zero balanced budget policy is considered to have enabled Germany to generate surpluses since 2014 without any borrowing. In 2018, for instance, it had high employment, its debt servicing costs were low, and its growth was 1.9% GDP (Economist, 2019). However, despite German annual GDP growth for the past ten years up to the first quarter of 2019, Angela Merkel was being urged to remove the black zero budget imposition in Germany to stimulate the economy (Nienaber, 2019; Economist, 2019; DW, 2020) owing to the -0.2% growth in the second quarter and 0.1% expansion in the third quarter; impending recession was the government fear. The stimulus was warranted, according to

Table 9.3 German economic trends since 2013

Year	2013	2014	2015	2016	2017	2018	2019
GDP growth	*0.6*	*1.9*	*1.5*	*1.9*	*2.2*	*1.9*	*0.6*

Sources: Destatis (2018); Economist (2019); Walker (2020)

observers, after a €13.5 billion surplus has been recorded (DW, 2020). The relatively weak GDP growth in 2018 and 2019 was also reflected in Eurozone with overall 0.1% growth in 2019 quarter 4, demonstrating the impact of low German growth and contraction in the Italian and French economies (Walker, 2020). The German growth in 2019 was mainly a consequence of household spending, with export growth considerably slower than previously and business investment weaker; officially recession was avoided because contraction did not occur in two consecutive quarters (Walker, 2020). Brexit and trade conflicts between US and China, which affected its export levels to China, and transition on the car industry from fossil fuel to electric vehicles, were blamed for low growth in Germany in 2019. An increase in company insolvencies is expected in 2020, weaker growth and the end of Germany's golden decade are forecast (DW, 2020). In 2019, the World Economic Forum (WEF) downgraded Germany by four places to seventh position in the global competitiveness ranking owing to its poor adoption of the internet and mobile networks, the weakest aspect of its competitiveness; Germany scored lower on 53 of the 103 categories (DW, 2019). This rating on technology, the comment that Germany's performance in information technology application was lower than all Baltic and Nordic countries, some Gulf countries, as China and Russia, and that fibre optic broadband internet access was used by the privileged few (DW, 2019), contrasts with expectations of the EU Economic Recovery Plan (EC, 2008).

Germany and EU

The surpluses continuously recorded by Germany are considered to be a risk to the EMU (Priewe, 2017; Bernanks, 2015). Germany has the highest surpluses of a bloc of EMU surplus countries, whilst many other EMU members have current account deficits, and a third bloc of countries have relatively balanced current accounts. In the case of Germany, the surpluses are a consequence of its technology-driven industrialised production structure, wage-restraint measures, export-led economy, advantage from the weak Euro and fiscal policies that suppress domestic spending including on imports (Priewe, 2017; Bernanks, 2015). In contrast, other Eurozone countries have become deindustrialised, many are in recession and have experienced the associated high unemployment, whilst having no mechanism to raise spending or reduce taxes to stimulate domestic demand (Priewe, 2017; Bernanks, 2015). Therefore, the Eurozone economies are highly dissimilar in terms of the import and export balances. However, the EMU was designed without a mechanism to control balance of payments issues, so that attempts to correct the imbalance between the German situation and that of other Eurozone members have not been successful. The EU push for low inflation leads to the risk of deflation in periods of recession in those Eurozone countries characterised by huge deficits, which are then forced to devaluate internally. As the dissimilarities between the blocs increase, the differences in GDP per capita also widen, and attempts to use monetary policy become less effective as a means to employ a single solution for all EU members. Unless the rate of growth of German exports as the major surplus generator is substantially reduced in relation to imports, imbalances will continue and represent a risk to EMU (Priewe, 2017) and to global trade since Germany is saving the income earned from its exports, and not using measures to create internal aggregate demand; regarded as trade protectionism (Ellyatt, 2018). This means that the German economy relies on demand from other EU and EMU countries, reducing employment and domestic demand, as is the case in other global economies, but Germany does not contribute to global demand (Bernanks, 2015).

However, the German Council of Economic Experts (GCEE) is not concerned about the surplus but emphasises that the deficits in other Eurozone countries are the consequence of failing to apply Eurozone guidelines on reducing deficits. It also considers the Macroeconomic Imbalance Procedure (MIP) is not required because the Fiscal Compact and banking union are adequate. The EC tends to align with Germany's stance and has failed to take measures to encourage Germany to reduce its surplus, despite knowing the negative spillovers experienced by other EMU members (Priewe, 2017) and that fixed exchange rates systems such as the Euro have historically had negative impact on countries with deficits (Bernanks, 2015). It has chosen not to invoke the Principle of Proportionality, although its objective is to generate trade and mutual benefit between nations and promote justice (Engle, 2012a, 2012b) or the Principle of Subsidiarity in which it could act as the body with exceptional competence (Wolf, 2001).

The IMF identifies Germany as having the largest global surplus and also stresses that it endangers the global economy, because countries with high deficits are unable to rebalance their economies; hence IMF recommended that Germany reduced its surpluses by means of applying MIP (Priewe, 2017). Three major interventions for reducing the German surplus recommended by Bernanks (2015) were for Germany to spend on its transportation infrastructure, which was declining, to create domestic demand for instance using tax incentives for investment, and to raise wage levels. The German government's recent announcement of investing in rail infrastructure indicates that it may be changing its stance on surpluses.

Almost 25 years after German reunification Berlin was described by Werbowski (2013) as the uncontested political and economic centre of Europe and the major force in the EU. Its power over the fate of weaker Member States such as Greece was considered to be a concern to close allies, for example France and the UK. According to Werbowski (2013), as some Eurozone members were considerably more economically weakened by the crisis than Germany, it used the crisis to improve its own position and was the major force that gradually destroyed their sovereignty by means of using the Euro crisis to impose austerity in the weakest nations in the south of Europe, where unemployment was high and growth very low. Werbowski (2013) also emphasises that these countries were simultaneously the importers of German products, which enabled Germany to create huge surpluses, whilst controlling their economies to ensure they had balanced government budgets and were not capable of generating new borrowing (Werbowski, 2013; Ivanovitch, 2019a, 2019b). The effect of German dominance also enabled it to shape labour policies in Eurozone countries that aligned with its preferences, which has similarly resulted in increased levels of poverty and a much reduced social support system (Oxfam, 2013a, 2013b, 2013c). These actions are contrary to the EU Principle of Proportionality and Germany could be interpreted as considering it has exceptional competence in these economic matters, substituting for EU in relation to the Principle of Subsidiarity.

Since 2015, Germany has also been dominant in shaping EU foreign and security policy (Janning & Moller, 2016; Aggestam & Hyde-Price, 2020), an approach that is not usually included in either neofunctionalism (Bergmann & Niemann, 2015; Aggestam & Hyde-Price, 2020) or intergovernmentalist European integration policies. However, in states that do not have strong domestic policies in these matters, intergovernmentalists strive integration in them (Moravcsik, 1993) as appears to be Germany's strategy, especially as it was awarded top marks on the European Council on Foreign Relations' Annual Scorecard in 2015 and 2016. In 2015, Germany led in the Greek Euro crisis, consulting other Northern European countries and the EC, in regard to the European refugee crisis with Italy and the EC, and on conflict in the Ukraine, it involved other Balkan countries. The push for integration on these matters has taken precedence over development of national foreign and security policies according to Janning and Moller (2016). However, in relation to the refugee crisis in 2016, Angela Merkel demonstrated that German domestic needs to stem the flow of refugees being allowed into the country was more vital, and almost unilaterally negotiated an agreement with Turkey to exchange one Syrian refugee from every Turkish refugee camp if Turkey agreed to accept a Syrian from Greek refugee camps. The German need to solve the refugee problem causing domestic unrest became the EU policy directly for the first time, according to Janning and Moller (2016). In addition intergovernmentalist policy had taken precedence with single nations Germany and Turkey negotiating policies that were an advantage to them, but not necessarily to the EU membership of which Germany is a part; EU consensus replaced by German dominance on decisions with intergovernmental coalitions (Janning & Moller, 2016). The survey of Europeans by Janning and Moller (2016) found that other EU members had failed to offer to take refugees in response to earlier pleas from Germany owing to its dominance in the Euro crisis, and the fact that Germany had unilaterally halted the Dublin agreement, which directs refugees to seek asylum in the first EU country they enter, without consulting them. Therefore, failing to support Germany's request was an opportunity for them to mitigate the previous unbalanced power. Brexit and weaker relations between Germany and other EU members such as Poland are a concern to Germany, as is EC leadership that it considers weak, so that Germany may deem itself as the key EU state and remains most committed to delivering EU principles. Germany's self-interest in the refugee crisis is considered indicative of how far it is willing to take risks that alienate partners. In the Ukraine crisis, Aggestam and Hyde-Price (2020) suggest that Germany's multilayered relations with Russia, the expectation of US President Obama that Germany would be involved in Foreign Policy and Security solutions and the perception of German political elite that the country needed to take a leading role after being criticised for abstaining from doing so in relation to Libya in 2011 were significant reasons for its involvement rather than dominance in EU. Germany is perceived to have led the foreign policy in two ways, to stress collaboration and shared EU leadership but rather than by means of the EU's formal Common Foreign and Security Policy (CSFP); it selected informal shared lateral cooperation with selected EU Member States, France and Poland (Aggestam & Hyde-Price, 2020); than intergovernmentalist approach to integration. During this period Merkel was the EU representative liaising with Putin, the EU and NATO and referred to as the actual leader of the EU (Cassidy, 2014). German dominance was evaluated as one of the reasons for the UK continuing focus on exiting the single market; Germany was able to accomplish considerable self-interested objectives, whilst simultaneously driving EU integration (Werbowski, 2013). A similar view was expressed by Ivanovitch (2019a, 2019b), a former OECD senior economist, who described EU as a German-run superstate that was the underlying reason for Brexit.

The case study implies that many EU policies follow Germany's economic solution, which is referred to as ordoliberalism, a socio-economic theory based on the requirement of the state intervention in a free market to ensure it optimises the outcomes that are theoretically possible (Dumont, 2018; Hein & Joerges, 2017). Ordoliberalism is described as the German form of neoliberalism and an alternative to Keynesian economics (Dumont, 2018) that relies on a set of rules and focuses on price stability. In regard to the German stance on the Eurozone debt crisis, neoliberalism emphasised EU insistence on strict budgetary commitments and fiscal responsibility by Eurozone Member States, restricting their political preferences relating to their economies, and exemplified by the introduction of the Fiscal Compact (Dumont, 2018). Managing labour markets, particularly wage restraint and erosion of the welfare state, was perceived as a major contributor to restoring Eurozone competitiveness and can be directly associated with the German model (Hein & Joerges, 2017; Wandel, 2019). Germany's insistence that Eurozone countries complied with the Stability and Growth Pact and the associated austerity measures, in contrast to other Eurozone members that preferred solidarity and Keynesian solution, is confirmed by Wandel (2019). The German economic model and its related structural reforms were increasingly referred to as a solution to European competitiveness, but Bastasin (2013) suggested that it is not. In contrast, Bastasin (2013) considers it as a potential danger to Eurozone survival, for different reasons than the surplus issue, proposing that there is no guarantee that other countries could align economic and social policies to do so. The underlying rationale for this belief was that the reforms in Germany were implemented many years before 2008 and by private companies and banks to ensure global competitiveness, rather than by government policies. In addition, Germany's export-led economy, which directed huge surpluses and allowed it to pay interest on debt, is not replicated in other Eurozone nations. Therefore, as the Euro became stronger, Germany thrived because of the decline in its labour costs, whilst other nations became increasingly less competitive.

Primary Research on German Case Study

A quantitative survey was conducted to gather the opinions of professionals on the efficacy of EU policies regarding supporting Germany to recover from the 2008 recession and whether they aligned with the Principles of Proportionality and Subsidiarity.

The following hypothesis is tested:

H1: Germany's continuously increasing authority in EU matters has been more influential in shaping its economic success than lack of domestic demand or negative spillovers from other EU Member States.

German Survey Analysis and Discussion

The 1540 participants in the German survey who disclosed their highest qualification comprised 34% with doctorate and 50% holding master's degrees and specialisms predominantly in economics and/or finance or social law. The gender mix was 77.5% males and 22.5% females with 57.5% in the age group 30–44 years.

The first question regarding Germany's participation in forming the body that was to become the European Union revealed poor understanding of the history of the single market, with 24.8% participants selecting 1952 (Bulmer, 2019), but 30.6% and 25.8% choosing 1958 and 1992 respectively (Fig. 9.7). This confusion maybe somewhat associated with German reunification not occurring until 1989 (Bulmer, 2019).

This summary of the findings focuses on the results of the hypothesis testing and includes a brief outline of responses to most important questions; the responses to all questions are attached in the Case Study Appendix.

Hypothesis Testing

The main hypothesis tested in this case was related particularly to question 11:

H1: Germany's continuously increasing authority in EU matters has been more influential in shaping its economic success than lack of domestic demand or negative spillovers from other EU Member States.

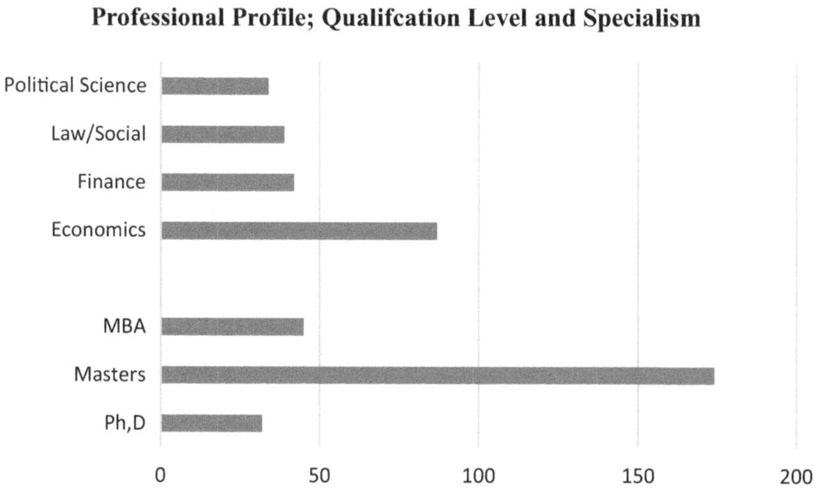

Fig. 9.7 Participant profile

The average rating for question 11 was greater than two but less than three, and all responses were statistically significant with $p<0.05$. This infers that there was overall slight disagreement with the statements. The highest agreement of German participants was with the statements: that low German domestic demand was not a factor which impacted on the economic growth of other Eurozone countries, mean 2.91; Germany's dominance in EU policy after the crisis was based on imposing monetary policies and ordoliberalism, which most aligned with its interests and neglected those southern EU states; mean 2.8. In the first case, the participants demonstrate an opinion which is contrary to economic evidence (Bernanks, 2015; Ellyatt, 2018) as is the second outcome that Northern European state favouring monetarism, which is not the preference of southern Eurozone countries (Priewe, 2017). Testing the correlations between statement 11a, 11c and 11f produced the results shown in Table 9.4.

The results demonstrate a statistically significant but very weak correlation between Germany exerting too high an influence on EU policies and EU failure to take action regarding its continuing budget surplus. The inference is that participants who consider Germany's influence in EU policy making is too strong are slightly more likely to agree that Germany's

Table 9.4 Correlations between statements

		11a Germany's influence on EU policies	*11c Germany's lack of domestic demand*	*11f The EU's failure to take action budget surplus*
11a	Pearson correlation	1	0.040	0.176**
	Sig. (2-tailed)		0.205	0.000
	N	1022	1008	875
11c	Pearson correlation	0.040	1	0.082*
	Sig. (2-tailed)	0.205		0.015
	N	1008	1043	882
11f	Pearson correlation	0.176**	0.082*	1
	Sig. (2-tailed)	0.000	0.015	
	N	875	882	931

**. Correlation is significant at the 0.01 level (2-tailed);
*. Correlation is significant at the 0.05 level (2-tailed).

lack of domestic demand is not a factor impacting on the economic growth in other Eurozone countries, and the statement regarding EU's failure to take action about Germany's continuous budget surplus cannot be considered responsible for negative spillovers to other EMU member. The overall value of the means, which is greater than 2 and is significant, demonstrates the overall disagreement with these statements. Therefore, H1 must be refuted.

The findings are not in alignment with other studies which emphasise that German influence in EU policies has enabled it to continue to make surpluses (Ivanovitch, 2019a, 2019b) and created negative spillovers in other Eurozone countries (Oxfam, 2013a, 2013b, 2013c).

The question regarding whether the EU had permitted Germany to have too much influence in the development, and implementation of EU policy since 2008, such that the Principle of Proportionality and the Principle of Subsidiarity had been compromised with regard to the benefits of membership for other Member States, resulted in a 51% yes response and 49% no. A borderline majority that somewhat acknowledges German influence, providing some alignment with Oxfam (2013a, 2013b, 2013c), Werbowski (2013), Ivanovitch (2019a, 2019b).

In regard to Germany's position in the EU prior to 2008, the participants tended to most agree with the statement that Germany was a major EU member with a strong neo-functionalist stance towards European integration and recognising the importance of a supranational body for the promotion of peace between nations (Bulmer, 2019; Bergmann & Niemann, 2015). The strongest disagreement occurred with the idea that Germany had a minor influence in the creation of the Euro whilst there was also relatively strong tendency to disagree with the statement that Substitution of the Deutsche Mark for the Euro was intended to reduce German power in Europe. These findings support the perspectives on significant German influence expressed by Werbowski (2013) and Bulmer (2019).

The questions posed to evaluate German participants' opinions about its economic position after 2008 revealed mean ratings values, which demonstrated a tendency to agree that toxic financial instruments were responsible for the crisis and that it resulted in declining German GDP owing to reduced export levels, but that quick restoration of exports reversed the GDP trend. No strong disagreements emerged but the highest mean indicates the Germans acknowledge that any lack of competitiveness was not a result of high labour rates, which is in agreement with Dustmann et al. (2014).

The final question concerned interventions for Germany to recover its stagnant GDP growth in 2020, six options were given (Table 9.5).

The most favoured action, b, is that Germany should spend its surpluses on infrastructure as this is the lowest mean indicating most agreement and it is in alignment with the ideas presented by Bernanks (2015). There is low agreement with interference with the Euro mechanism and with increasing domestic demand, options, e and f, which tends to reinforce somewhat higher agreement with continuing to aim for surpluses.

Table 9.5 Potential solutions to increasing GDP

Option	*Proposed action*	*Mean rank*
a	Germany should cease taking the dominant role in EU policy making	3,46
b	Germany should spend its surpluses on its declining transportation infrastructure	2,64
c	Wage levels should be raised to reduce Germany's competitiveness	3,11
d	Germany should continue to aim for surpluses	3,40
e	Create a balance of payments control mechanism for the Euro	4,20
f	Germany should create higher domestic demand by announcing tax incentives and encourage more imported goods for domestic consumption	4,18

These responses suggest that German citizens wish to continue current economic policies despite their acknowledged impact on other Eurozone countries (Wandel, 2019).

Case Study 3: Italy

Introduction

This case study demonstrates the marked contrast of economic and social development of Italy as a member of the Eurozone with Germany, and with the UK as an EU member not restricted by the fiscal policies and ultimate EU control after 2008. It also demonstrates Italy's involvement in creating some key EU policies, the historical reasons for the challenges it has experienced by being forced to align with EU economic and social policies, which have contributed to its incapacity to recover from the 2008 recession. Therefore, this case contains a higher level of detail of the period prior to 2008 and of the social consequences since 2008 than those of UK and Germany.

Background

One of the fundamental objectives of Italy becoming a founding member of the European Atomic Energy Community (EURATOM) in 1957 was to demonstrate its European interest rather than the negative national interest it had been attributed during World War Two, owing to the country being linked with Nazi Germany (Bindi, 2011). Italy had initiated its strategy in 1952 as a member of the European Coal and Steel Community (ECSC), which effectively delegated all decision making in coal and steel matters to a supranational body (Glockner & Rittberger, 2012), although this action was opposed by several important and influential Italian public figures (Bindi, 2011). Italy was the first member of this group to insist that the arrangement would allow free movement of people between member countries so that its surplus labour force could be exported to other member nations. The Dutch and the Germans also had excessive labour forces and favoured free movement of people, whilst the Belgian and French coal industries already employed substantial proportions of foreign workers (Maas, 2005). Therefore, the Italian government was able to obtain this concession with the support of other interested governments; it became Article 69 of the Treaty (Maas, 2005) and demonstrates application of an intergovernmentalist integration approach (Sandholtz & Sweet, 2014). Free movement was limited by an associated clause that worker immigrants from other Member States must be qualified coal or steel workers, with Member States being urged to devise a common definition of qualifications, and the condition that there was compliance with the host nation's health and safety policy. This clause meant that Member States could refuse free movement across borders to obtain employment in the industry by implementing the relevant health or public policy issue to protect jobs for domestic labour; this clause continued to be enforced (Maa 2005). The Italian negotiator, Taviani, generated a second proposal that was also historically important to the current EU stance, the creation of a higher power, a Ministry of Labour, which would set and enforce a common wage policy across the group; this was not adopted at that time (Maas, 2005). Therefore, Italy became a member of the EEC in 1958 and subsequently of the EU in 1992, when it also committed its support for European Monetary Union by signing the Maastricht Treaty.

The Economic Miracle

During the period from 1950 to 1973 Italy's gross national product increased by 6.8% annually and its per capita GDP was 4.8%, this period is referred to as Italy's Economic Miracle because it outperformed most other European countries. From 1973 Italy's GDP, exports, productivity and manufacturing output were also the highest in Europe (Tolliday2000), and it remained internationally competitive because it was able to devalue its national currency, the Lira (Lenti, 2014). State-owned enterprises (SOEs), which were not directly controlled by the government, contributed to this output because they were run by entrepreneurial independent managers, for instance at Eni and Finsider, national oil and steel companies. However, SOE general productivity declined after 1970 owing direct government intervention, increasing trade union power, political self-interest, corruption and waste, and the fact that most SOEs were in declining industrial sectors (Tolliday, 2000; EB, 2020). The Socialist Party, which had come to power, made further investments in them, including acquiring subsidiaries of private companies, that owners divested because they were relatively unprofitable but closing them was costly owing to employee compensation that was compulsory by law. This SOE intervention ultimately led to an extremely high level of redundancy payments by the state, resulting from disbanding these companies, which increased public sector debt (Tolliday, 2000; Lenti, 2014). This was made possible by the focus of government on instigating a contemporary welfare state with high levels of social benefits, instead of developing efficient economic and industrial policies (Lenti,2014). The government did not fund these new benefits with increased tax levels, so that over time the income to spending gap made a significant contribution to public debt (Antonin et al., 2019).

The Italian government perceived that state investment was more effective to stimulate investment and growth than implementation of Keynesian policies, and this approach had worked well until 1970s, because its monetary policy had been tightly controlled and budgets balanced to restrict wage and price rises, whilst boosting exports (Tolliday, 2000). The high levels of more recent direct government intervention, favoured by four or five party coalition governments dominated by socialist parties, was responsible for decline in competitiveness, since stimulation to compete had been reduced by too much state assistance and money protectionism, according to Nardozzi (2003). Budget deficits were not generally managed and by 1989 accumulated national debt was greater than the level of GDP; recession in 1991 led to a rise in budget deficit to 10% GDP, industrial production declined by 4% in 1992–1993 (EB, 2020).

The ongoing trends in Italy's average GDP growth did not compare well with that of Germany, UK, France and Spain prior to the 2008 financial crisis (Fig. 9.8); the decline began in 1995 according to Daveri (2009), when Italy was no longer able to devalue its national currency, the Lira, in

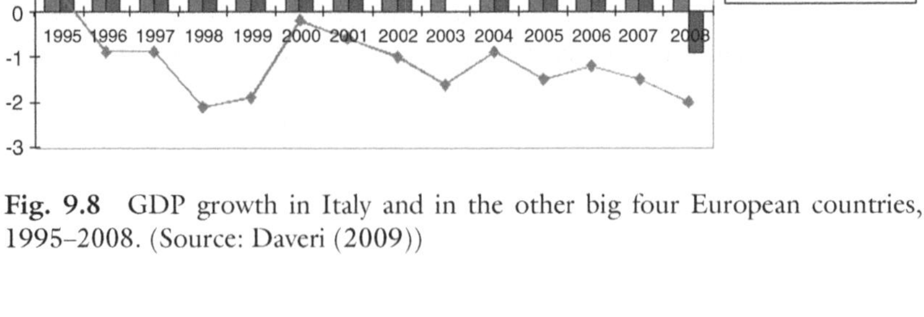

Fig. 9.8 GDP growth in Italy and in the other big four European countries, 1995–2008. (Source: Daveri (2009))

relation to the German Deutsche Mark, because fixed exchange rates were agreed in preparation for the EMU; the total comparative decline was 20% in the period concerned (Bindi, 2011; Daveri, 2009).

The average real GDP growth rates in Italy that had begun to decline in the 1980s reflecting public debt increases remained comparable to those in Germany and France, but they began to diverge in the early 2000s, when Italy's GDP continued to average less than 1% and its productivity rapidly declined compared to Germany and France (Antonin et al., 2019).

As indicated earlier, the increasing levels of government debt in relation to GDP growth began slowly from 1960s to 1980, whereas a sharp rise in the GDP growth-to-debt ratio from 54% to 117% occurred from 1980 to 1992 (Antonin et al., 2019). In 1992, the terms of the Maastricht Treaty relating to accession to the Monetary Union were discussed, with Germany favouring standard economic indicators for all members whilst Italy preferred terms to be of a similar and more dynamic nature; the German proposal was implemented (Bindi, 2011). In addition, the Italian public debt ratio exceeded the proposed 60% of GDP limit, and other conditions such as public deficit limit of 3% GDP and interest rates of no more than 1.5% above the inflation rate of the average of the three lowest Member States defined in the Treaty were of significant disadvantage to Italy. Italy negotiated a more flexible approach on the understanding that it had coalition governments that were acknowledged to cost more than a single political party governing (Bindi, 2011). However, financial spending needed to be controlled so that Italy could accede to the EMU or lose credibility in financial markets (Bindi, 2011). A change of government at this period enabled Prime Minister Amato to introduce a new budget that restricted higher spending and public debt declined to less than 100% (Antonin et al., 2019). Therefore, from almost the start of the Eurozone, Italy's economic position has been unique within the structure, with no urgent attention appearing to have been given to the gravity it would experience in the next economic downturn.

Italy Economic Trends Since 2008 Financial Crisis

The initial effect of the 2008 financial crisis on Italian GDP was a decline of 4.4% from the beginning of the fourth quarter of 2008 to the end of the first quarter of 2009, a higher contraction than the 27 EU country and Eurozone averages (Daveri, 2009). The relative impacts are summarised in Table 9.6.

Table 9.6 Comparison of initial effects of 2008 crisis

GDP growth	*Italy*	*EU 27*	*Germany*	*France*	*Spain*	*UK*	*US*
Q4 vs. Q3 2008	-21%	-1.6%	-2.1%	-1.2%	-1.0%	-1.6%	-1.6%
Q4 2008 vs. Q1 2009	-2.4%	-2.4%	-3.8%	-1.2%	-1.8%	-1.9%	-1.6%
Year on year Q1 2009 vs. Q1 2008	-5.9%	-4.5%	-6.9%	-3.2%	-2.9%	-4.1%	-2.6%

Source: Istat

Apart from Germany, Italy had the largest decline in GDP, the contraction in Germany was attributed to loss of global export trade, whilst in Italy it is more a reflection of the fact that it was already in recession prior to the crisis and had experienced 20% lower GDP growth than the other four European countries since 1995. In 2009, Italy's GDP decline aligned with the average in EU. The non-Eurozone countries in Eastern Europe had greater GDP reduction than UK and US owing to the link between their economies and German economy (Daveri, 2009). Overall, the four largest Eurozone suffered greater initial contraction than US which had caused the crisis by the collapse of toxic debt instruments. The low annual growth of 1% annually was forecast to continue by Daveri (2009) unless Italy aggressively adopted the EU reforms on labour markets, pensions and education. The trend in GDP growth from 2010 was initial weak growth of 1.69% and 0.58% in 2010 and 2011, respectively, negative growth of -2.82% and -1.73% in the following two years, with a flat and fluctuating trend between 0.11% and 1.68% until 2018 (TE, 2020). The trends in Italy's debt-to-GDP ratio are shown in Fig. 9.9.

The public sector stabilisation policies that were commenced in 1992 and had reduced Italy's public sector deficit to less than 100% by 2007 were interrupted by the 2008 recession and its impact on EU public finances as a group, so that by 2018 Italy's public sector debt had risen to 132.1% GDP. The rise in real interest rates on debt from 2008 to 2012 accompanied by low GDP growth rates, negative in the case of Italy, resulted in a high rapid debt-to-GDP ratio and when debt-to-GDP ratio is already high, very small increases in debt ratio or reductions in GDP can neutralise or lessen the austerity efforts made by governments. In the period of low inflation and central bank interest rates near to 0%, Italy required real GDP growth to recover from the recession. However, although domestic aggregate demand had contributed to GDP growth in

Fig. 9.9 Italy debt trends 1963 to 2018. (Source: Antonin et al. (2019, p.7))

Italy after the recession, public sector consumption was almost zero from 2008 to 2014, which Antonin et al. (2019) suggest was a consequence of its high GDP-to-debt ratio and the austerity measures it was forced to take by EU fiscal rules, which also prevented government investment. At the same time, the EU rules to increase unemployment benefits from 2008 had to be complied with, requiring public sector resources that were already debt driven. The EU enforced this action, despite the acknowledged issues that Italy experienced with generating revenues from tax collection owing to tax evasion, which had increased from 2005 to 2013. The fact that Italy went into recession in 2008 meant that fiscal expenditure multipliers were larger than they would have been in an economic upturn, worsened by the size of the recession, and debt-to-GDP ratio grew faster (De Nardis & Pappalardo, 2018).

As is evident elsewhere in this case study, Italy had experienced lower growth relative to other EU countries prior to the 2008 recession, which is relevant to its unique position and explained by structural differences with other large EU economies. The underlying productivity gap between Italy, with low or no GDP growth, and Germany and France is evident in Fig. 9.10.

The difference was attributed to Italy's structural performance, which relates to the efficiency gains between inputs and outputs; the relative

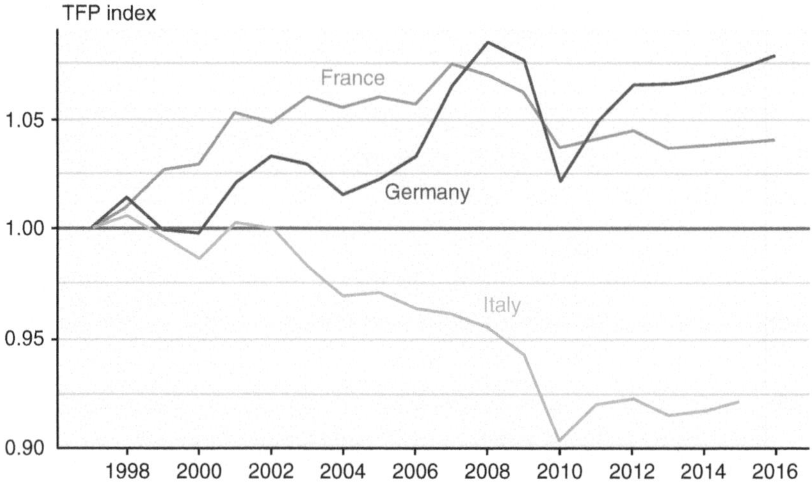

Fig. 9.10 Total factor productivity comparisons from 1998 to 2016. (Source Antonin et al. (2019, p.10))

Total Factor Productivity (TFP) for Italy declined by 7.9% in the 20-year period compared with Germany's rising to the same degree. The structural issues relate not only to traditional north-south economic divide in Italy since unification of states in 1871, but also to the prevalence of small firms that predominantly operate in low-technology sectors, inferring low technology and investment (Antonin et al., 2019). From the year 2000 onwards, these firms experienced increasing low-wage competition from firms based in Asia Pacific, especially China. The average small firm size in Italy is less than nine employees, 80% of total compared with less than 70% in EU, and Italy has very few medium- and large-sized firms. The productivity of micro firms and small firms is also lower, and while that of medium and large Italian firm is higher than EU average, at 3% of the total, there are too few of them to compensate (Fig. 9.11; Antonin et al., 2019).

This structural difference generates an aggregate effect of lower productivity compared with other EU countries. Historically small artisan firms have worked in collaboration with very large companies that are far more technologically advanced, and these artisans survive owing to their high capacity to exploit market niches. Therefore, the gap in technological investment and new learning in Italy compared to the EU average is high and widening. Another issue relates to the difficulty of expanding firm size because of the

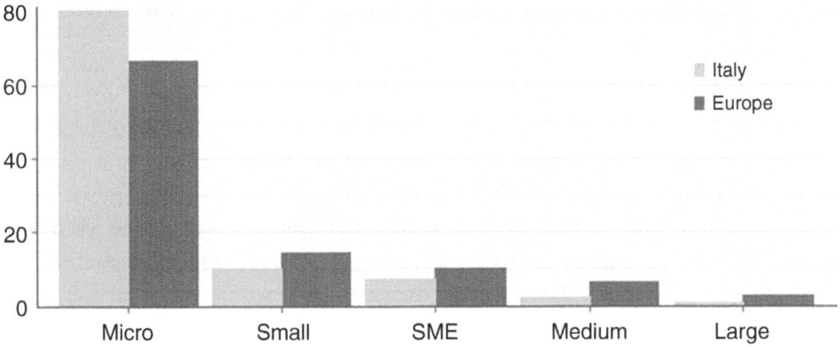

Fig. 9.11 Average labour productivity by firm size Italy versus Europe 2000–2012. (Source: Antonin et al. (2019, p. 12))

restriction on credit for micro- and small-sized companies in Italy (Antonin et al., 2019). The lack of commitment to Research and Development (R&D), to investment in innovation, is partly a consequence of Italy entering the industrial age late, mainly after 1945, and there is no tradition of government intervention in firms to innovate. The process of applying for public R&D funds is also highly bureaucratic and the funds available declined significantly in 1990s. In contrast to Germany, which invested between 2.1% and 2.5% GDP annually between 1981 and 2001, Italy invested a much lower annual sum, for instance 0.6% in 1981 and 0.8% in 2001 (Tylecote & Visintin, 2007). The added value captured in traditional manufacturing in the Italian fashion goods sector is 14% of the national added value total, compared with 3% in Germany. In contrast the contribution of innovative sectors requiring new knowledge such as ICT, pharmaceuticals and chemicals to Italian GDP is 15% compared with 21% in Germany.

The inference of these considerable structural differences between Italy and other Eurozone countries is that employing a universal approach to all Eurozone nations and later EU Member States to reverse economic downturn after 2008 did not align with justice and equity in regard to the Principle of Proportionality (Portuese, 2013). The action is also contrary to the meaning of the Principle of Subsidiarity since the later policies extended to EU claiming competence in these matters, but without considering regional/national structural differences that have historical importance (Buxbaum et al., 2011). In other words, EU focused on austerity measures to reduce public sector debt levels and budget deficits, which were not the only factors impacting on economic growth.

Major EU Policy Intervention in Italy Since 2009

The four types of interventions that impacted on Italy and other Eurozone countries from 2009 were financial reform of banking sector including monitoring process and legislative changes to levels of retained capital funding; a financial stabilisation programme to enable EU to grant funds to Member States to restart their economies and reliant on issuing of debt instruments in capital markets; extended economic governance of Member State budgets; and generation of economic growth, which impacted on employment (Barnard, 2012). The measures are summarised in Chap. 2 and discussed in more detail in Chap. 6. These policies did not have the effect intended by the EU as is evident from Italy's rising public debt-to-GDP ratio and its weak economic growth for the past 12 years. The political consequences of the policies and the growing tensions between the Italian government are described to demonstrate the current position.

In 2016 a referendum on Italian constitutional reform resulted in the pro-EU Italian Prime Minister being forced to resign and the election of a coalition government of the populist left-wing political party, the Five Star Movement and far-right wing Northern League party. The change of government reflected the electorate's dissatisfaction with EU policies on immigration, which had had a larger impact on Italy than Northern European countries, and their weariness with a flat economy (Jones & Bindi, 2018). The 'disastrous' austerity policies supported by Germany's Chancellor and her initial open door policy on immigrants in 2015 led to the substantial backlash in Italy, when the government refused to continue allowing thousands of African and Middle Eastern immigrants landing mainly in Sicily, to enter Europe by that route. Germany preached solidarity and criticised Italy for abandoning people existing in dangerous circumstances. It also formed an alliance with the French, in refusing to agree to Italy's proposed fiscal policies that were an attempt to return the economy to growth ten years after 2008 crisis, despite the fact that the policies stayed within the Eurozone budget guidelines of 3% GDP (TE, 2020). This was the first time that the EC had rejected a Member State's budget; the reason it gave was that the spending plans of the new populist government were contrary to the EC debt limit and must be revised (Ng, 2019; Guarascio, 2018). The revision was rejected a month later in December 2018 with the threat of instigating EU financial sanctions and a comment that the country was at high risk of becoming unstable without realising it would happen (DW, 2018).

The Italian Minister for Economics stressed that the budget was only moderately expansionary and amounted to 2.4% GDP; the EC suggested that the growth forecast that was submitted with the budget was unrealistic. The potential for the situation to generate a Euro debt crisis resembling that in 2012 was also considered credible (DW, 2018). A compromise agreement was reached in December 2019 for a budget representing 2.04% GDP (Tondo & Giuffrida, 2018). Italy entered recession at the end of 2018 (Ivanovitch, 2019a, 2019b) and its economy grew by 0.2% overall in 2019 although it had contracted by 0.3% in quarter four 2019, the highest decline since quarter one 2013. The forecast for the future is growth of 0.2% in quarter 1 of 2020, and 0.3% in 2021 (TE, 2020).

A report by the Centre for European Policy (Gasparotti & Kullas, 2019) compares the outcomes of Euro membership across Eurozone membership, and the analysis for the period 1999 to 2019 demonstrates that Germany has obtained the highest gains in prosperity of €1.9 billion or €23,000 per capita whilst prosperity in Italy has declined most at €74,009 per capita or a comparative loss of €4.235 billion. The study also estimated the difference in GDP in 2017 if the country had not joined the Euro, and proposed that for Italy the sum would have been an increase of €530 billion on the actual GDP generated that year; Italian per capita GDP loss is illustrated in Fig. 9.12.

The conclusion drawn by Gasparotti and Kullas (2019) was that Italy had not been able to shape policies to remain competitive within the Euro but had been competitive prior to joining the monetary union because it could devalue its currency. The authors also suggest that structural reforms were the solution to reversing the declining trend in prosperity within the Euro as Spain had proven.

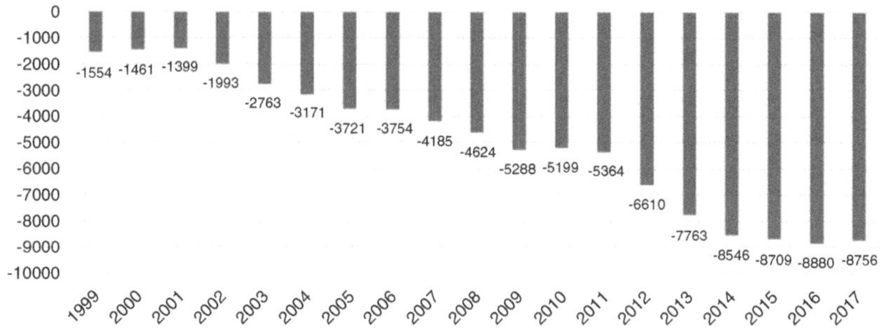

Fig. 9.12 Impact of introduction of Euro on GDP per capita Italy. (Source: Gasparotti and Kullas 2019, p.10)

A Third Italian Recession: Impact on Europe

The real threat of the third recession in Italy provoked by the austerity measures imposed on the country since 2008 is likely to have a significant impact on other European countries. A report by Storm (2019a, 2019b) suggests that the EU is devising new measures to support it, for instance by resurrecting the Italian sovereign bond programme, which was near its expiry date, and revising its GDP forecast for Italy to negative values. The impact on other EU countries is reduced trade and risk of default on large loans made by banks in other countries to Italy (Storm, 2019a, 2019b), and amounting to €450 billion (Gros, 2019), including France, Germany, Belgium and UK, which are owed €285.5 billion, € 58.78 billion, €25.2 billion and €17.48 billion respectively (Salzano et al., 2019). In addition, the EU countries hold credit commitments, guarantees and derivatives, which Storm (2019a, 2019b) suggests adds in excess of another 30% to Italian debt in France and 50% in Germany. The conundrum for the EU is allowing one its major economies to fail by not supporting its demands, or being accused of non-compliance with its commitment to the Stability and Growth pact if it does.

However, Storm's (2019a, 2019b) analysis of Italy's commitment to the EMU's conditions when combined with agreement with Antonin et al.'s (2019) description of its unique structural features of low-technology firms and substantial competition from low-wage countries such as China evokes the suggestion that Italy's loyalty to EU principles that were held as strongly by other countries such as Germany has been the major cause of its present situation. Italy complied closely with the permanent fiscal consolidation and wage-restraint strategies from 1995 to 2008 and beyond, but when these were combined with what was described as an overvalued exchange rate between the Lira and the Euro, aggregate demand fell and productive jobs and incomes were lost (Storm, 2019a, 2019b).

In order to remove the threat to the EU inferred by a third recession, it must be assisted to revive its aggregate domestic demand and export demand, and to alter its commercial structure to one based on higher proportions of medium and larger firms, higher innovation and technological focus, neither of which is possible whilst austerity and suppression of wage growth continue (Storm, 2019a, 2019b). If there was a sudden downturn in the markets and confidence in Italy's Government fell, supposingly its financing requirements would grow too fast and might result in EMU collapsing.

Primary Research on Italy Case Study

A quantitative survey was conducted to gather the opinions of professionals on the efficacy of EU policies regarding supporting Italy to recover from the 2008 recession, specifically whether they aligned with the Principles of Proportionality and Subsidiarity. The survey also intended to gather perspectives on alternative approaches that the EU might have taken to Italy as representative of Southern European Member States with substantial economic and structural differences than those in the Northern European group.

The following hypotheses are tested:

H1: Italy's increasing public sector debt level is more a consequence of its failure to reform its labour market and education system than being unable to find a specific mechanism to support its unique economic and social position in the EU.

H2: The relatively low competitiveness of Italy predominantly results from not being able to devalue the Euro rather than the fact that its economic structure comprises more low-technology micro firms than the EU average.

Italy Survey Analysis and Discussion

The descriptive statistics show that 1575 individuals participated in this survey, and their highest qualifications were 40.3% with doctorate, 45.9% with master's degree and 17.8% had an MBA; 68% participants were males and 32% females. The most common specialisation was economics (Fig. 9.13).

Italian entry to the single market concept did not occur until 1992 according to 40% participants; 26.5% correctly selected 1952. This suggests lack of knowledge of the importance of Italy as a founding member (Maas, 2005: Bindi, 2011).

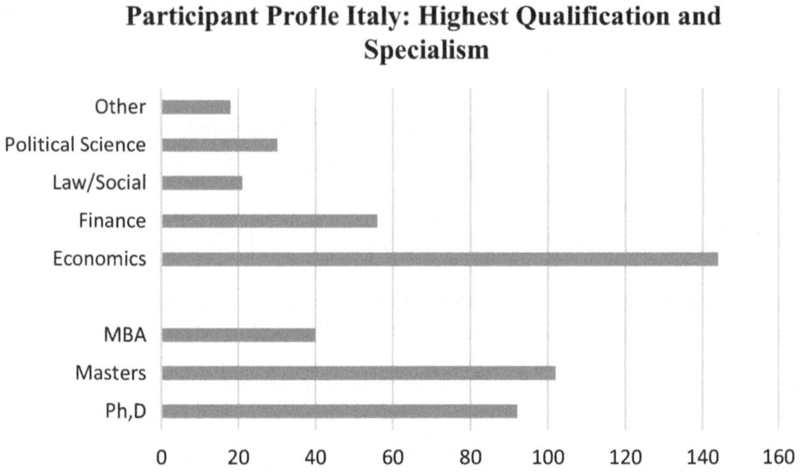

Fig. 9.13 Italy participant profile

The results of the hypothesis testing are presented first, and then the most relevant findings for this case are outlined with full details of the responses to all questions in Appendix Case Studies.

Hypothesis Testing

The main hypotheses tested in this case, H1 and H2, were related particularly to questions 10 and 12 respectively:

H1: Italy's increasing public sector debt level is more a consequence of its failure to reform its labour market and education system than being unable to find a specific mechanism to support its unique economic and social position in the EU.

In these four statements the strongest level of agreement was with 10a at a mean of 2.08, which recognises its unique social and economic position in terms of debt being primarily public debt. There is lower agreement with 10c that GDP has not grown owing to its failure to reform its labour market and education system and with 10e whose origins are in 1991.

Table 9.7 Public sector debt

Paired samples correlations

		N	*Correlation*	*Sig.*
Pair 1	10c. The major reason that the Italian GDP did not grow after 2009 was failure to reform its labour and education system. 10a Italy's debt levels relate to public sector borrowing rather than excessive private credit/loans.	1043	0.101	0.001
Pair 2	10c The major reason that the Italian GDP did not grow after 2009 was failure to reform its labour and education system. 10e Italy's high public sector debt-to-GDP issues relate to before EU foundation in 1992 not to the 2008 crisis but this was not considered relevant by EU so that no specific mechanism was implemented to support Italy's unique position.	1001	0.184	0.000
Pair 3	10c The major reason that the Italian GDP did not grow after 2009 was failure to reform its labour and education system. 10 f Applying the required EU social measures related to unemployment benefits after 2008 impacted on Italy possessing the required financial resources to reduce the public debt levels.	861	0.195	0.000

The statistical analysis of 10c with each of 10a, 10e and 10f is summarised in Table 9.7.

The correlation coefficient between c and e is high at 0.184 and significant but even higher correlation is shown between c and f at 0.195, both have significance levels of 0.000. This implies that public sector debt and specific economic conditions in 1992 are most correlated with public sector debt but that Italy was also not in a financial position to implement the reforms fully. The correlation of public debt with education and labour market reform is also significant but lower at 1.00. Hence H1 is refuted.

The responses regarding Italy's unique social and economic position related to changes in 1992 align with Bindi (2011) and Daveri (2009).

H2: The relatively low competitiveness of Italy predominantly results from not being able to devalue the Euro rather than because its economic structure comprises more low-technology micro firms than the EU average.

Table 9.8 Competitiveness

Paired samples correlations		*N*	*Correlation*	*Sig.*
Pair 1	12a Italy has a much higher than average proportion of micro-sized firms than other large European economies. 12f. Italy's products are uncompetitive in its traditional markets because of the strength of the Euro which cannot be devalued	945	-0.070	0.032
Pair 2	12c. Italy's competitiveness has traditionally been in low-tech products, which can be made more cheaply by emerging economies such as China 12f. Italy's products are uncompetitive in its traditional markets because of the strength of the Euro which cannot be devalued	945	0.124	0.000

The questions that were used to test this hypothesis were 12(f), 12 (1) and 12(c), and the descriptive statistics showed the highest participant agreement was with 12(a), where 79.5% or mean score 2.10 strongly agreed or agreed with the higher-than-average number of micro firms in Italy than EU average agreement with national competitiveness being associated with low-tech products being 2.76 and with strength of Euro 2.83 (Table 9.8).

When paired statements were tested for correlation, 12 a and 12f were negatively weakly correlated with statistical significance since $p < 0.05$ which infers that an increase in micro firms leads to a decrease in competitiveness which tends to support a relationship between firm type and competitiveness in Italy in alignment with Antonin et al. (2019; Fig. 9.8). A higher positive correlation of 0.124 was found between low-tech products associated with Italian economy and poor competitiveness owing to be unable to devalue the Euro, a stronger correlation (Antonin et al., 2019). The overall conclusion from both pairs is the more micro firms, the lower the competitiveness, and if Italian micro firms are assumed to produce mainly low-tech goods the strength of the Euro will make them uncompetitive. This tends to confirm H2. When the differences in means from these pairings were tested, the t values were high and significant in the case of the first pair $t = 13.52$, which confirms that H2 is partly proven in purely statistical terms.

These responses to the statement that the EU's universal approach to reviving the Eurozone Member State economies was in alignment with the Principle of Proportionality or the Principle of Subsidiarity were 62% yes, 38% no. These findings do not correspond to the conclusions made by Portuese (2013) and Buxbaum et al. (2011). However, a lower proportion of 52% considered that Italy had benefitted from being a member of the EU.

The final question is important since it asked for opinions regarding actions Italy should take to revive its economy. The statements are summarised in Table 9.9.

Participants most favoured the reduction of Italy's public debt by IMF/EU, which indicates that their opinion is that public debt is the core factor hindering economic growth. However, gathering global opinion and input into a recovery plan is an interesting second option, which suggests perception of EU competence and/or motivation to do so is insufficient. This aligns with higher disagreement that EU should continue its universal solution regarding the economic and social strategies for all Member States and suggests that participants have relatively low confidence that the Italian government can solve its problem without external support. Overall these suggestions correspond to the study by Storm (2019a, 2019b). Italy is threatened by a third recession and needs support to revive its domestic demand, alter its commercial structure including proportion of larger firms in the economy, which is not possible if austerity and associated wage suppression are re-imposed by EU.

One of the major limitations of this study is that the participants were all highly educated and predominantly male and economists dominated the specialism, therefore these views may not be representative of the Italian population.

Table 9.9 Economic growth proposals

Option	*Proposed EU action to revive Italian economy*	*Mean score*
a	EU and Italy should employ independent global economic and political science experts as consultants to develop an economic and social plan to meet Italy's unique structural situation	**2.48**
b	The EU/IMF should eliminate a large proportion of Italian debt	**2.35**
c	Italy should leave the Euro	**3.19**
d	EU should continue to impose the same conditions on Italy as on other Eurozone countries	**3.4**
e	EU should enable Italy more independence to find a local solution as the local expert in alignment with the Principle of Subsidiarity	**3.5**

Case Study Limitations and Outcome

The limitations of this research are time and the scope of the main thesis. As with the other case studies there is potential for an extensive study on each of the countries, which is a recommendation for further research. There is also considerable scope for in-depth research into the benefits and limitations of EU membership on the former communist states, which was not possible in this thesis.

However, these case studies have outlined the differences between EU Member States over time indicating very wide variations in economic and social trends.

Epilogue

In the first six months of 2020 a number of events have occurred that reinforce the findings of this research, which has been developed over the past five years. These mostly concern Italy, UK and to a lesser extent, Spain, and provide further evidence for Germany's dominance in EU policies, which impact on the application of the Principles of Proportionality and Subsidiarity. Since these occurrences are so recent, academic studies are not readily available to verify the interventions and the reactions to them, which have been reported in the reliable news sources utilised for this epilogue. However, a report in April 2020 by the Robert Schuman Foundation (Brehon, 2020) emphasises the absence of mutual aid during the Coronavirus crisis from EU Members States for countries such as Italy, the most affected in Europe. It comments on the EU's fundamental principle of commitment to solidarity when a crisis occurs that impacts one Member State and may affect others. This principle of solidarity published in the Treaty of Lisbon and intended for unexpected disaster situations failed to be activated by EU or the majority of Member States. Germany and France for example banned medical equipment and protective masks from being sent to other countries, retaining them for national use (Henley, 2020), and when a Coronavirus Bond was suggested to raise funding to assist the worst affected members Italy and Spain, the Northern European states including Germany firmly rejected the idea (Barigazzi, 2020).

It was China which sent medical teams and masks to Italy on 11 March not the EU, and Cuba sent a medical team on 22 March on the same day that Russian virologists arrived in the country (Brehon, 2020). The EU failed to implement the Treaty wording that it had the power to proactively intervene to enhance coordination between member countries, instead it neither proposed, organised nor financed any type of solidarity (Brehon, 2020, p.1). The lack of solidarity towards Italy during the Coronavirus crisis further alienates Italian citizens, who already consider that other Members States and the EU failed to adequately support it during the immigration crisis, and this inaction was forecast to possibly have severe political implications by Brehon (2020). The negative reaction of Italy to lack of solidarity from other Member States, and the subsequent offer of aid to Southern European states, which failed to meet what they actually required, is also stressed by Junkermann (2020). A survey conducted in March 2020 by Tecnè resulted in 67% of participants stating that being part of the EU was a disadvantage for Italy, compared with 47% in November 2018 (Johnson et al., 2020).

The political ramifications of the EU's inaction are evident from Italy's recent considerable strengthening of relations with China, such that further trade agreements with China would position Italy as the entry point for Chinese trade in EU (Junkermann, 2020). The deepening economic crisis in Italy following the Coronavirus epidemic represents a substantial opportunity for Chinese investors to acquire Italian small- and medium-sized businesses at low prices, particularly if the EU does not organise sufficient post crisis funding (Zeneli and Capriati, 2020), and without the conditions of austerity associated with many of its bailout agreements such as ESM. In addition, if such a funding solution with significant restrictive conditions was offered by the EU, the likelihood of an election and victory by left-wing political parties is mooted by Barigazzi (2020), who suggests that Italy would leave the Euro and possibly the single market. In mid-April 2020, the new president of the European Commission eventually recognised its failure to support Italy during the most severe part of the Coronavirus by making an apology on behalf of all Member States. The EU had failed to coordinate healthcare cooperation as its responsibility, even after Italy had asked for aid under the EU emergency mechanism (Henley, 2020).

By mid-December 2020, the number of Coronavirus cases reported in EU countries was 16,190,212 and deaths 403,131 (ECDC, 2020). The report on Europe's response to the pandemic (Janse & Tsanova, 2020) reiterates the inappropriate stance of Member States withholding medical supplies and closing borders but suggests that within a few weeks it had acted to reduce mortality rates, save jobs and businesses. An ECB Pandemic

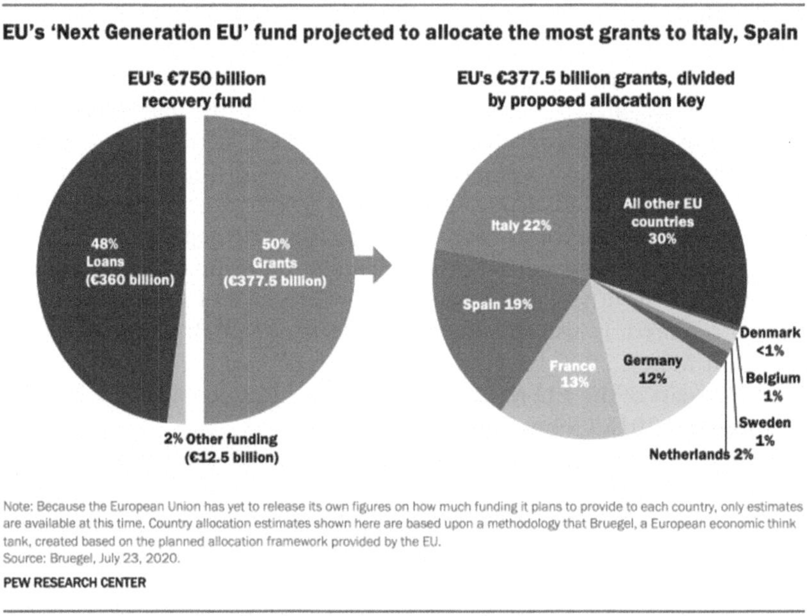

Fig. 9.14 Initial EU funding proposals. (Source: Kent (2020, p.1))

Emergency Programme was initiated to stem liquidity risk; the initial sum was €750 billion but was increased to €1.35 billion ten weeks later. This was an unprecedented initiative as poorer countries are being funded by the wealthier Member States and indicates solidarity missing earlier in the pandemic. The details of the funds and grants are shown in Fig. 9.14 and demonstrate that the big four economies will be given the largest support, in contrast to the less affected Northern European members.

In order to support businesses €540 billion was provided to develop vaccines, to assist with healthcare costs and finance employment. The funds were specifically directed at households, the self-employed and businesses, and the EU authorities adopted a more flexible approach to who could receive state aid and towards domestic fiscal rules (Janse & Tsanova, 2020). However, Horizon (2020) emphasises that the EU acted too late into the pandemic, comments on its lack of preparedness for a pandemic and its relatively slow response. The absence of any defined EU communication system that could have prevented incorrect, misleading information being spread deliberately was an additional weakness. It seems likely that the EU will use the Coronavirus pandemic to increase its powers within Europe by arguing that Member States did not have individual competence to manage the pandemic and therefore citing the Principle of Subsidiarity The inference according to Boffey (2020) was that the EU would require Member States to provide regular reports on how effective their healthcare systems were, including their capacity to cope with future crises and to produce a crisis contingency plan to be critically appraised by the relevant EU authority (Boffey, 2020).

The economic effect of the pandemic was severe, GDP declining by 11.7% between the first and second quarters, which Kent (2020) highlights as more than four times the highest quarterly contraction generated by the 2008 crisis. Some of the biggest economies were most affected, France, Italy and Spain experiencing GDP declines of 12.4%, 13.8% and 18.5% respectively. The implication is that EU survival and prosperity will be even more dependent on appropriate policy making, especially as the most affected countries are again in Southern Europe and their economies have not recovered from the earlier event. The IMF (Kammer, 2020) suggests that real GDP is forecast to rise by 4.7% in 2021, and that recovery will be a medium-term phenomenon as indicated by the implied loss of €3 trillion in comparison with the prediction made before the pandemic.

Another recent issue involved the highest court in Germany being very critical of the ECB's change in policy in 2015, which allowed Member States to financially support other Member States by means of the bond buying scheme. This strategy had first been launched in 2010 to support the value of the Euro, but the 2015 version, referred to as the Public Sector Purchase Programme (PSPP), enabled the ECB to buy a total of €2.1trillion of Member State bonds by late 2019, and another €0.5 trillion outside that scheme. The plaintiffs in the trial cite this strategy as a violation of EU Treaty (BBC, 2020), as was suggested in this thesis, the reference being Article 125 of the Treaty on the Functioning of the European Union (TFEU). The court ruled that the policy was partly contrary to the German Constitution (BBC, 2020).

The concept of proportionality is stated to be a core aspect of German Constitutional law such that government and lawmakers must ensure that the interest of all parties is considered in policy making. The Principle of Subsidiarity is also alluded to in the ruling by the comment that the EU possessed

€2 trillion stock of assets on the ECB's balance sheet constitutes a risk that encroaches on the competences of national parliaments. (Munchau, 2020, p1)

The ruling partly implicates the German Bundesbank which is the dominant party in ECB decision making. There is a possibility that the Bundesbank will need to cease any involvement in ECB bond purchases if the ECB cannot satisfy the German Court's demands for an explanation about its apparent contravention of the Treaty. The Southern European Member States, especially Italy and Spain, could be severely affected as they need ECB to purchase their bonds, owing to their level of economic difficulty resulting from the Coronavirus pandemic (BBC, 2020).

The continuing Brexit negotiations are also a matter of controversy for the EU, which is accused of attempting to subject the UK to conditions it has not imposed in agreements with other countries, in order to retain benefits of UK membership it will now lose, particularly fishing rights, which has high political importance for both EU and UK (Erlanger, 2020). In essence the UK has asked for a similar trade agreement to the ones in operation between the EU and Canada, Japan and South Korea, in which the majority of trade tariffs are eliminated and close alignment with EU rules is not mandatory. However, the EU insists that UK's adjacent geographical position precludes such a stance being taken (Sandford, 2020a). The UK is focused on a single trade agreement and additional partnerships relating to data policies, fishing and farming and security, for instance, whilst the EU's objective is to negotiate a comprehensive single agreement, with which it can demonstrate that membership of EU is more favourable than being outside of the bloc (Sandford, 2020a, 2020b, 2020c; Erlanger, 2020). A major issue is the jurisdiction of the European Court of Justice, which UK insists most to not continue to have precedence over legal decisions made in British courts; a solution must be found to how future legal issues would be arbitrated by an independent body according to UK. The EU posits that if UK were able to change regulation and taxes without consulting it, the consequence would be higher competition, which it fears, despite goods having to comply with EU standards. An impasse now appears to exist owing to lack of agreement on fishing rights and competition rules in particular. The basis on which the EU was founded as building a special relationship with neighbouring countries (Rayner, 2019) may be considered to be inoperable in this case.

Bibliography

Introduction and Epilogue

Barigazzi, J. (2020, March 18). As Italy Asks for Coronavirus Help, Its Populists Wait for the Answer. *Politico*. https://www.politico.eu/article/coronavirus-italy-populists/. Accessed 7 July 2020.

BBC. (2020, May 5). German Court Criticises European Central Bank Crisis Bond-Buying. *BBC*. https://www.bbc.com/news/world-europe-52542993#:~:text=Germany's%20top%20court%20has%20ruled,purchases%20in%20the%20coronavirus%20crisis. Accessed 7 July 2020.

Boffey, D. (2020, November 11). EU Seeks Greater Public Health Powers After Covid 'Wake-Up Call'. *The Guardian*. https://www.theguardian.com/world/2020/nov/11/eu-seeks-greater-public-health-powers-in-wake-of-covid-wake-up-call. Accessed 26 December 2020.

Brehon, N. (2020, April 6). *The European Union and the Coronavirus*. Robert Schuman Foundation. Accessed 7 July 2020. https://www.theglobaltreasurer.com/2017/05/31/eu-agrees-measures-to-revive-asset-backed-securities-market/

ECDC. (2020). *COVID-19 Situation Update for the EU/EEA and the UK, As of Week 51 2020*. ECDC. https://www.ecdc.europa.eu/en/cases-2019-ncov-eueea. Accessed 23 December 2020.

Erlanger, S. (2020, June 15). With Brexit Trade Talks at an Impasse, Boris Johnson Finally Engages. *New York Times*, Accessed 7 July 2020. https://www.nytimes.com/2020/06/15/world/europe/uk-brexit-boris-johnson.html

Henley, J. (2020, April 16). EU Offers 'Heartfelt Apology' to Italy Over Coronavirus Response. *The Guardian*. https://www.theguardian.com/world/2020/apr/16/eu-offers-heartfelt-apology-italy-coronavirus-response-herd-immunity. Accessed 7 July 2020.

Horizon. (2020). Lack of Solidarity Hampered Europe's Coronavirus Response, Research Finds. *Horizon EU Magazine*. https://horizon-magazine.eu/article/lack-solidarity-hampered-europe-s-coronavirus-response-research-finds.html. Accessed 23 Dec 2020.

Janse, K., & Tsanova, I. (2020, August 12). *What We Can Learn from Europe's Response to the COVID-19 Crisis?* World Economic Forum. https://www.weforum.org/agenda/2020/08/europe-response-covid-19-coronavirus-economic-crisis-euro-fiscal-monetary-policy-green-deal/. Accessed 23 Dec 2020.

Johnson, M., Fleming, S., & Chazan, G. (2020, April 6). Coronavirus: Is Europe Losing Italy? *Financial Times*. https://www.ft.com/content/f21cf708-759e-11ea-ad98-044200cb277f. Accessed 7 July 2020.

Junkermann, N. (2020, June 24). Betrayed by the EU, Italy Is Turning to China. *The Telegraph*. https://www.telegraph.co.uk/news/2020/06/24/betrayed-eu-italy-turning-china/. Accessed 7 July 2020.

Kammer, A. (2020). *Europe Needs to Maintain Strong Policy Support to Sustain the Recovery*. IMF. https://blogs.imf.org/2020/10/21/europe-needs-to-maintain-strong-policy-support-to-sustain-the-recovery/. Accessed 23 Dec 2020.

Kent, N. (2020, November 17). *Europeans Approved of EU's Handling of COVID-19 This Summer – But Much Has Changed Since*. Pew Research. https://www.pewresearch.org/fact-tank/. Accessed 23 Dec 2020.

Munchau, W. (2020, May 10). The European Central Bank Is Deluding Itself Over German Court Ruling. *Financial Times*. https://www.ft.com/content/fc487cac-9105-11ea-9207-ace009a12028. Accessed 7 July 2020.

Sandford, A. (2020a, February 11). Post-Brexit Guide: Where Are We Now – And How Did We Get Here? *Euronews*. https://www.euronews.com/2020/02/11/brexit-draft-deal-first-of-many-hurdles-to-a-smooth-exit. Accessed 13 Feb 2020.

Storm, S. (2019a, April 10). *How to Ruin a Country in Three Decades*. Institute for New Economic Thinking. https://www.ineteconomics.org/perspectives/blog/how-to-ruin-a-country-in-three-decades. Accessed 26 Dec 2020.

UK Parliament. (2020). *Into Europe*. UK Parliament. https://www.parliament.uk/about/living-heritage/transformingsociety/tradeindustry/importexport/overview/europe/. Accessed 26 Dec 2020.

Zeneli, V., & Capriati, M. (2020, June 4). Is Italy's Economic Crisis an Opportunity for China? As Italy reels, Chinese companies might sense an opportunity to buy up more Italian brands on the cheap. *The Diplomat* [online]. https://thediplomat.com/2020/04/is-italys-economic-crisis-an-opportunity-for-china/. Accessed 7 July 2020.

Case Study UK

BBC. (2019a, September 19). David Cameron: EU Referendum Claim Fact-Checked. *BBC News*. https://www.bbc.com/news/uk-politics-49753420. Accessed 13 Feb 2020.

BBC. (2019b). UK Referendum. *BBC News*. https://www.bbc.com/news/politics/eu_referendum/results. Accessed 13 Feb 2020.

Bulmer, S., & Quaglia, L. (2018). The Politics and Economics of Brexit. *Journal of European Public Policy, 25*(8), 1089–1098.

De Witte, B. (2011). The European Treaty Amendment for the Creation of a Financial Stability Mechanism. *European Policy Analysis, 6*, 1–8.

Engle, E. (2012a). The History of the General Principle of Proportionality. *Dartmouth Law Journal, 10*(1), 1–11.

Eubanks, W. W. (2010). *The European Union's Response to the 2007–2009 Financial Crisis*. Congressional Research Service.

Eurostat. (2020). *National Accounts and GDP*. Eurostat. https://ec.europa.eu/eurostat/statistics-explained/index.php/National_accounts_and_GDP. Accessed 14 Feb 2020.

Hooghe, L., & Marks, G. (2019). Grand theories of European Integration in the Twenty-First Century. *Journal of European Public Policy, 26*(8), 1113–1133.

Hunt, A., & Wheeler, B. (2018, July 31). Brexit: All You Need to Know About the UK Leaving the EU. *BBC News*. https://www.bbc.com/news/uk-politics-32810887. Accessed 18 Aug 2018.

Innes, D., & Tetlow, G. (2015). Delivering Fiscal Squeeze by Cutting Local Government Spending. *Fiscal Studies, 36*, 303–325.

Kassim, H., & James, S., & Heap, S. (2017). *The UK and the Eurozone Crisis: Preferences and Preference Formation in a Euro Area Out* (EMU Choices, Working Paper 2017).

Leetim, T. (2016, June 25). *Why Did Britain Vote to Leave the EU?* Vox Media. https://www.vox.com/2016/6/25/12029962/why-did-britain-leave-the-eu. Accessed 13 Feb 2020.

Liddle, R. (2019). *The Great Betrayal*. Hachette UK.

Mudge, R. (2018, July 26). *Is the Brexit Hard-Liner European Research Group Running the UK?* DW. https://www.dw.com/en/is-the-brexit-hard-liner-european-research-group-running-the-uk/a-44835382. Accessed 13 Feb 2020.

NA. (2020). *The EEC and Britain's Late Entry*. National Archives. https://www.nationalarchives.gov.uk/cabinetpapers/themes/eec-britains-late-entry.htm. Accessed 11 Feb 2020.

PCK. (2011, December 3). Eurozone Financial Crisis. *Politics.co.uk*. https://www.politics.co.uk/reference/eurozone-financial-crisis. Accessed 13 Feb 2020.

Peers, S. (2015). *The UK and the Schengen System*. Kings College UK and EU. https://ukandeu.ac.uk/the-uk-and-the-schengen-system/. Accessed 13 Feb 2020.

Pylas, P. (2020, January 23). Britain's EU Journey: When the EU Faced Its Biggest Crisis. *AP News*. https://apnews.com/5f244e0d4a4ed3d88e07ae3996020be5. Accessed 13 Feb 2020.

Raitio, J., & Raulus, H. (2017). The UK EU Referendum and the Move Towards Brexit. *Maastricht Journal of European and Comparative Law, 24*(1), 25–42.

Rayner, G. (2019, July 19). Britain's EU Contribution Rises by 20 Per cent in Year, as UK's Booming Economy Props Up Brussels' Budget. *The Telegraph*. https://www.telegraph.co.uk/politics/2019/07/19/britains-contribution-eu-rises-20-per-cent-year-uks-booming/. Accessed 29 July 2019.

Renwick, A. (2017). *The Process Of Brexit: What Comes Next?* (UCL European Institute Working Paper).

Sandford, A. (2020b, February 11). Post-Brexit Guide: Where Are We Now – And How Did We Get Here? *Euronews*. https://www.euronews.com/2020/02/11/brexit-draft-deal-first-of-many-hurdles-to-a-smooth-exit. Accessed 13 Feb 2020.

Sandford, A. (2020c, July 6). Post-Brexit Guide: Where Are We Now – And How Did We Get Here? *Euronews*. https://www.euronews.com/2020/06/11/brexit-draft-deal-first-of-many-hurdles-to-a-smooth-exit. Accessed 7 July 2020.

Thompson, H. (2017). *The Transformation of British Politics: Was It Really Caused by the 2008 Crisis?* London: LSE. https://blogs.lse.ac.uk/politicsandpolicy/british-politics-after-the-2008-crash/. Accessed 13 Feb 2020.

Timothy, N. (2019, July 28). Varadkar Can Blame Britain All He Likes – But He Is the Real Threat to Peace. *The Telegraph*. https://www.telegraph.co.uk/politics/2019/07/28/varadkar-can-blame-britain-likes-real-threat-peace/. Accessed 29 July 2019.

Walker, N. (2019, May 23). *Brexit Timeline: Events Leading to the UK's Exit from the European Union* (House of Commons Briefing Paper Number 7960).

Young, J. W. (1989). The Parting of the Ways'?: Britain, the Messina Conference and the Spaak Committee, June–December 1955. In M. Dockrill & J. W. Young (Eds.), *British Foreign Policy, 1945–56* (pp. 197–224). Palgrave Macmillan.

Case Study Germany

Aggestam, L., & Hyde-Price, A. (2020). Learning to Lead? Germany and the Leadership Paradox in EU Foreign Policy. *German Politics, 29*(1), 8–24.

Anderson, C. (2009, January 22). *IMF Survey: Germany Faces Extended Downturn Despite Stimulus*. IMF. https://www.imf.org/en/News/Articles/2015/09/28/04/53/socar012209a. Accessed 16 Feb 2020.

Bastasin, C. (2013). *Germany: A Global Miracle and a European Challenge* (Brookings Institute Global Economy & Development Working Paper 62).

Bergmann, J, & Niemann, A. (2015). *Theories of European Integration* (E. Knud, A. Jorgensen, K. Aarstad, E. Drieskens, K. Laatikainen, & B. Tonra, Ed., pp.166–182). The SAGE Handbook of European Foreign Policy.

Bernanks, B. (2015, April 3). *Germany's Trade Surplus Is a Problem*. Brookings Institute. https://www.brookings.edu/blog/ben-bernanke/2015/04/03/germanys-trade-surplus-is-a-problem/. Accessed 3 Feb 2020.

Boeri, T. (2011). Institutional Reforms and Dualism in European Labor Markets. In A. Orley & D. Card (Eds.), *Handbook of Labor Economics, Volume 4A and 4B* (pp. 1173–1236). Elsevier.

Bulmer, S. (2019). *Germany and the European Union*. Oxford Research Encyclopaedia. https://oxfordre.com/politics/view/10.1093/acrefore/9780190228637.001.0001/acrefore-9780190228637-e-1063. Accessed 14 Feb 2020.

Cassidy, J. (2014, March 3). Ukraine Crisis; Keep Your Eyes on Angela Merkel. *The New Yorker*. https://www.newyorker.com/news/john-cassidy/ukraine-crisis-keep-your-eyes-on-angela-merkel. Accessed 16 Feb 2020.

Destatis. (2018, January 11). *Press Release No. 011 of 11 January 2018*. Destatis. https://www.destatis.de/EN/Press/2018/01/PE18_011_811.html. Accessed 16 Feb 2020.

Deutsche Bank. (2010). *German Balance of Payments in 2009*. Deutsche Bank.

Dumont, J. (2018, May 10). *The Other Neoliberalism: German Ordoliberalism After the Euro Crisis*. London School of Economics. https://blogs.lse.ac.uk/government/2018/05/29/the-other-neoliberalism-german-ordoliberalism-after-the-euro-crisis/. Accessed 16 Feb 2020.

Dustmann, C., Fitzenberger, B., Schönberg, U., & Spitz-Oener, A. (2014). From Sick Man of Europe to Economic Superstar: Germany's Resurgent Economy. *Journal of Economic Perspectives, 28*(1), 167–188.

DW. (2019, September 10). *Germany Falls in Global Competitiveness Ranking*. DW. https://www.dw.com/en/germany-falls-in-global-competitiveness-ranking/a-50745071. Accessed 16 Feb 2020.

DW. (2020, January 15). *German Economic Growth Saw Major Drop in 2019*. DW. https://www.dw.com/en/german-economic-growth-saw-major-drop-in-2019/a-52008522. Accessed 16 Feb 2020.

EC. (2008). *Communication from the Commission to the European Council: A European Economic Recovery Plan*. European Commission.

Economist. (2019, November 14). Are the Black Zero's Days Numbered? Why Germany Sticks to Strict Budget Rules Despite a Slowdown. *The Economist*. https://www.economist.com/europe/2019/11/14/why-germany-sticks-to-strict-budget-rules-despite-a-slowdown. Accessed 14 Feb 2020.

Ellyatt, H. (2018, July 4). *Germany's Massive Trade Surplus 'Is Becoming Toxic,' IFO Director Says*. CNBC. https://www.cnbc.com/2018/07/04/germanys-massive-trade-surplus-is-becoming-toxic-ifo-director-says.html. Accessed 17 Feb 2020.

Engle, E. (2012b). The History of the General Principle of Proportionality. *Dartmouth Law Journal, 10*(1), 1–11.

Haran, D. (2014, February 26). *Recession and Recovery: the German Experience*. House of Commons Library. https://commonslibrary.parliament.uk/economy-business/economy-economy/recession-and-recovery-the-german-experience/. Accessed 14 Feb 2020.

Hein, J., & Joerges, C. (2017). *Ordoliberalism, Law and the Rule of Economics*. Hart Publishing.

Ivanovitch, M. (2019a, February 4). *Brexit Is a Revolt Against a German-Run European Super-State*. CNBC. https://www.cnbc.com/2019/02/04/brexit-is-a-revolt-against-german-run-europe-super-state%2D%2D-commentary.html. Accessed 14 Feb 2020.

Janning, J., & Moller, A. (2016). *Leading From The Centre: Germany's New Role In Europe*. European Council on Foreign Relations.

Macrotrends. (2020, March 14). *Germany GDP Growth Rate 1971–2020*. Macrotrends. https://www.macrotrends.net/countries/DEU/germany/gdp-growth-rate. Accessed 16 Feb 2020.

Moravcsik, A. (1993). Preferences and Power in the European Community. A Liberal Intergovernmentalist Approach. *Journal of Common Market Studies, 31*(4), 473–524.

Oxfam. (2013a). *The True Cost of Austerity and Inequality; Portugal Case Study*. Oxfam.

Oxfam. (2013b). *The True Cost of Austerity and Inequality: Italy Case Study*. Oxfam.

Oxfam. (2013c). *The True Cost of Austerity and Inequality; Germany Case Study*. Oxfam.

Priewe, J. (2017). *A Time Bomb for the Euro? Understanding Germany's Current Account Surplus* (Macroeconomic Policy Institute (IMK) IMK Study, No. 59).

Rudd, K. (2009). The Global Financial Crisis. *The Monthly, 13*(42), 14.

Walker, S. (2020, January 15). German Economy Sees Weakest Growth Since 2013. *BBC*. https://www.bbc.com/news/world-asia-51122215. Accessed 16 Feb 2020.

Wandel, J. (2019). Prospects for an Ordoliberal Reform of the European Union. *Economic Affairs, 39*, 28–43.

Werbowski, M. (2013, March 14). *Germany's Dominant Role in the European Union*. Global Research. https://www.globalresearch.ca/germanys-dominant-role-in-the-european-union/5326785. Accessed 14 Feb 2020.

Wolf, M. (2001). Authority: Delegation. In S. N. Bates & P. (Eds.), *International Encyclopedia of the Social & Behavioral Sciences* (pp. 972–978). Elsevier.

Case Study Italy

Antonin, C., Guerini, M., Napoletano, M., & Vona, F. (2019). *Italy: Escaping the High-Debt and Low-Growth Trap* (Sciences Po OFCE Working Paper No. 07/2019).

Barnard, C. (2012). The Financial Crisis and the Euro Plus Pact: A Labour Lawyer's Perspective. *Industrial Law Journal, 41*(1), 98–114.

Bindi, F. (2011). *Italy and the European Union*. Brookings Institution.

Buxbaum, R., Hertig, G., Hirsch, A., & Hopt, K. (2011). *European Economic and Business Law: Legal and Economic Analyses on Integration and Harmonization*. De Gruyter.

Daveri, F. (2009, June 5). *Italy, Before and After Lehman Brothers*. CEPR/Voxeu. https://voxeu.org/article/italy-and-after-lehman-brothers. Accessed 18 Feb 2020.

De Nardis, S., & Pappalardo, C. (2018). *Fiscal Multipliers in Abnormal Times: the Case of a Model of the Italian Economy* (Ufficio Parlamentare di Bilancio, Working Paper 1).

DW. (2018, November 21). *EU Shoots Down Italy's Budget Plans, Again.* DW. https://www.dw.com/en/eu-shoots-down-italys-budget-plans-again/a-46388939. Accessed 27 Feb 2020.

EB. (2020). *The Economic Miracle and Industrial Growth.* Britannica. https://www.britannica.com/place/Italy/Italy-from-the-1960s. Accessed 29 Feb 2020.

Gasparotti, A., & Kullas, M. (2019). *20 Years of the Euro: Winners and Losers An Empirical Study.* Centre for European Policy.

Glockner, I., & Rittberger, B. (2012). The European Coal and Steel Community (ECSC) and European Defence Community (EDC) Treaties. In F. Laursen (Ed.), *Designing the European Union* (pp. 16–47). Palgrave Macmillan.

Gros, D. 2019. *Who Holds Italian Government Debt? A Primer* (CEPS Policy Insights No 2019–11).

Guarascio, F. (2018, October 11). Factbox: Key Dates If EU Moves to Reject Italy's Budget. *Reuters.* http://reuters.com/article/us-italy-budget-eu-factbox/factbox-key-dates-if-eu-moves-to-reject-italys-budget-idUSKCN1ML2AH. Accessed 27 Feb 2020.

Ivanovitch, M. (2019b, February 4). *Brexit Is a Revolt Against a German-Run European Super-State.* CNBC. https://www.cnbc.com/2019/02/04/brexit-is-a-revolt-against-german-run-europe-super-state%2D%2D-commentary.html. Accessed 14 Feb 2020.

Jones, E., & Bindi, F. (2018, July 31). *Will Italy's Divided Politics Cripple Europe's Economy – or Worse?* University of Philadelphia Wharton School Knowledge Wharton. https://knowledge.wharton.upenn.edu/article/instability-italy-crisis-will-impact-europe/. Accessed 18 Jan 2010.

Lenti, R. T. (2014). The Italian Economy 1961–2010: From Economic "Miracle" to Decline. In S. Beretta, F. Rugge, & A. Berkofsky (Eds.), *Italy and Japan: How Similar Are They?: A Comparative Analysis of Politics, Economics, and International Relations* (pp. 185–204). Springer.

Maas, W. (2005). The Genesis of European Rights. *JCMS, 43*(5), 1009–1025.

Nardozzi, G. (2003). The Italian "Economic Miracle". *Rivista di storia economica, 2,* 130–180.

Ng, N. (2019, February 25). *CEP Study: Germany Gains Most from Euro Introduction.* DW. https://www.dw.com/en/cep-study-germany-gains-most-from-euro-introduction/a-47675856. Accessed 27 Feb 2020.

Portuese, A. (2013). Principle of Proportionality as Principle of Economic Efficiency. *European Law Journal, 19*(5), 612–635.

Salzano, G., Pogkas, D., & Sills, B. (2019, February 4). *Why Italy's Debts Are Europe's Big Problem.* Bloomberg. https://www.bloomberg.com/graphics/2019-italian-banks/. Accessed 29 Feb 2020.

Sandholtz, W., & Sweet, A. (2014). Neo-functionalism and Supranational Governance. In E. Jones, A. Menon, & S. Weatherill (Eds.), *The Oxford Handbook of the European Union* (pp. 18–33). Oxford University Press.

Storm, S. (2019b, April 10). *How to Ruin a Country in Three Decades*. Institute for New Economic Thinking. https://www.ineteconomics.org/perspectives/blog/how-to-ruin-a-country-in-three-decades. Accessed 26 Dec 2020.

TE. (2020). *Italy GDP Growth Rate*. Trading Economics. https://tradingeconomics.com/italy/gdp-growth. Accessed 187 Feb 2020.

Tolliday, S. (2000). Enterprise and State in the Italian "Economic Miracle". *Enterprise and Society, 1*, 241–248.

Tondo, L., & Giuffrida, A. (2018, December 19). Italy Avoids EU Sanctions After Reaching 2019 Budget Agreement. *The Guardian*. https://www.theguardian.com/world/2018/dec/19/italy-avoids-eu-sanctions-after-reaching-2019-budget-agreement. Accessed 18 Feb 2020.

Tylecote, A., & Visintin, F. (2007). *Corporate Governance, Finance and the Technological Advantage of Nations*. Routledge.

Case Study Appendices

UK Questionnaire and Analysis

Questionnaire: European Union Management of 2008 Financial Crisis

The purpose of this research is to critically evaluate the extent to which the European Commission (EC), which is the part of the European Union responsible for single market, economic and monetary union issues, has upheld the principles for which it was founded as it attempted to resolve the impact of the 2008 global financial crisis on Member States. The desired outcomes being minimum impact on the development of each Member State and on the group as a whole.

This Survey Concerns the Member State United Kingdom (UK)
Thank you for agreeing to participate in this research by completing this questionnaire. Please provide your personal perspectives when answering the questions, there are no correct or incorrect responses. Any comments you make remain confidential, and the subsequent report will not reveal the identity of any individual. Please answer ALL questions. The questionnaire should take no longer than 30 minutes. You can withdraw from this research at any time.

S. Weißschnur, *The Proportionality of State Intervention*,
https://doi.org/10.1007/978-3-030-75676-5

I have read the confidentiality statement and am happy to take part in this survey:

Yes
No

Are you?

Male
Female

To which age group do you belong?

18–25
26–35
36–45
46–55
Over 55

Please indicate your highest qualification

Doctorate
Master's degree
Bachelor degree
Professional qualification
Secondary school education

Which specialist subject is your major interest?

Economics
Finance
Social Justice
Political Science
Other

SECTION TWO: MAIN QUESTIONNAIRE

Question 6: When did UK join the single market?

1992 as member of European Union (EU) under the Maastricht Treaty
1973 by application after several refusals
1957 as member of EUROATOM in 1957
1958 as member of the European Economic Community (EEC)
1952 as part of European Coal and Steel Community (ECSC)

Question 7: This question relates to UK's position in the single market prior to 2008. Please indicate the extent of your agreement or disagreement with each of the statements in the grid—for EACH statement choose ONE option which is nearest to your opinion.

	Statement	*Agree strongly*	*Agree*	*Neither agree nor disagree*	*Disagree*	*Strongly disagree*
a	The UK's prime motive for joining the EU was its fear that its economy was falling behind that of member states					
b	The UK has always believed in the neofunctionlist model of integration rather than the intergovernmentalist approach					
c	The UK held a referendum to leave the EU in 1973					
d	Historically UK has had strong ties with its Commonwealth countries, which were more important than being part of the single market					
e	Aspects of the EU membership such as free movement of people and money were of little benefit to the UK prior to 2008					
f	Margaret Thatcher, UK Prime Minister from 1975 to 1990, was in favour of the idea of the supranational state					
g	Strong links between UK and US were not a factor in EU decision to delay its entry to the single market					

Question 8: This question relates to the UK's capacity to recover from the 2008 crisis as a Member State of the EU Single Market after 2008. Please indicate the extent of your agreement or disagreement with each statement—for EACH statement choose ONE option which is nearest to your opinion.

	Statement	*Agree strongly*	*Agree*	*Neither agree nor disagree*	*Disagree*	*Strongly disagree*
a	The UK focused on supporting the EU with the euro crisis after 2008 rather than on protecting City of London and national interests					
b	Initial austerity measures instigated by the UK government were not as effective as those selected by the EU as a universal solution to reviving GDP growth					
c	The UK was hindered from recovering from the 2008 economic crisis because of the level of bad debt and bank failure					
d	UK's closed decision-making stance in relation to economic recovery illustrates its liberal intergovernmental preference for integration and cherry-picking attitude to EU membership					
d	As a non-Eurozone Member State, UK was at a disadvantage in managing economic recovery because it had no access to EU bailout mechanisms					
e	The UK recovered more slowly from the 2008 recession than the EU average because it was not subject to the EU rules that would have accelerated GDP growth					
f	A major factor in UK recovery was its capacity to recapitalise its banks quickly, avoiding the long-term issues that would have been generated by Eurozone membership					

Question 9: This concerns EU relations with UK before Brexit negotiations. Please indicate the extent of your agreement or disagreement with each statement—for EACH statement choose ONE option which is nearest to your opinion.

	Statement	*Agree strongly*	*Agree*	*Neither agree nor disagree*	*Disagree*	*Strongly disagree*
a	UK opinion that the EU has neither acted quickly enough to manage the crisis nor appropriately in the case of Member States such as Greece was not a reasonable deduction					
b	UK was totally opposed to EU plans to increase its supranational power over non-Eurozone members with regard to single market financial services regulation, which would have involved it using UK taxpayers' money to bailout EU banks					
c	The UK was opposed to a European banking agency because it would lessen the power of the City of London and the government's influence on decisions because it was not a Eurozone member					
d	Euroscepticism in the UK from the late 1990s was a strong driver in the 2016 referendum result to exit the EU					
e	UK conflict with EU over the proposed change to Article 122(2) was a ruse to gain later advantage over EU rather than a genuine objection to an alleged controversial change in the original Treaty of Functioning of the European Union, which allowed Member State bailouts only for natural disasters					
f	The UK has not benefitted greatly from EU membership since joining the group					
g	Whist the EU makes a very large contribution to the EU budget its position is weakened by not belonging to the Eurozone					

(*continued*)

(continued)

	Statement	*Agree strongly*	*Agree*	*Neither agree nor disagree*	*Disagree*	*Strongly disagree*
h	The EU has had a negative attitude to close relationships between US and UK, which have caused it to punish the UK in terms of UK-EU trade relationships, since the formation of the single market					

Question 10: This focuses on the major reasons that UK population voted to leave the EU

	Statement	*Agree strongly*	*Agree*	*Neither agree nor disagree*	*Disagree*	*Strongly disagree*
a	Low EU economic growth over a relatively long period was a major factor for vote leave					
b	Excessive free movement, internal immigration, was not a major reason for the decision to leave					
c	Increasing EU regulation in every aspect of trade and life was considered unacceptable to UK population					
d	The continuous enlargement of the EU was regarded as indicating its preference for increasing its power rather than the economic growth and prosperity principles of the original EEC					
e	British voters were tired of being subject to inappropriate legislation passed by EU bureaucrats that had not been elected by them					
f	Many UK voters were totally opposed to leaving the EU predominantly because of the loss of free movement					

Question 11: In your opinion what were the three main factors that resulted in the UK population voting to leave the EU?

1. ....
2. ....
3. ....

Question 12: This concerns the Brexit negotiations between UK and EU

Option	*Proposed EU action to revive Italian economy*	*Agree strongly*	*Agree*	*Neither agree nor disagree*	*Disagree*	*Strongly disagree*
a	The UK has been deliberately obstinate during the Withdrawal Agreement negotiations despite EU effort to reach a reasonable agreement					
b	The value of UK import trade to other EU members is not being considered seriously enough in the obstinate stance the EU has to the talks					
c	The EU has no mechanism for a country to withdraw from the group and fears UK exit will provoke further requests to leave and weaken its power					
d	UK exit is being deliberately hindered to retain its budget payments for as long as possible					
e	The EU does not fear UK's ability to sign substantial trade agreements with US and former UK Commonwealth countries					
f	The UK will leave the EU without a trade deal and become subject to World Trade Organisation rules					

Question 13

(a) **Please answer Yes or NO to the statement regarding the EU's management**
STATEMENT: The EU's approach to UK's exit is in alignment with the Principle of Proportionality or the Principle of Subsidiarity.
Yes
No

(b) **Please provide an explanation for your choice of answer to part (a)**

Question 14: Please make any further comments you wish about the relationships between the UK and the EU policies from 2008 onwards

....

THANK YOU FOR TAKING THE TIME TO COMPLETE THIS QUESTIONNAIRE

UK Frequencies and Descriptives

q0001 I have read the confidentiality statement and am happy to take part in this survey

		Frequency	*Per cent*	*Valid per cent*	*Cumulative per cent*
Valid	1 Yes!	1624	99	99	99
	2 No.	14	0.9	0.9	100
	Total	1638	100	100	

Frequency Tables

q0002_0001 Please indicate your highest qualification and your area of expertise!

		Frequency	*Per cent*	*Valid per cent*	*Cumulative per cent*
Valid	1 Ph.D./ Doctorate	448	27.4	100	100
Missing	System	1190	72.6		
Total		1638	100		

q0002_0002 Please indicate your highest qualification and your area of expertise!

		Frequency	*Per cent*	*Valid per cent*	*Cumulative per cent*
Valid	1 Master's Degree	994	60.7	100	100
Missing	System	644	39.3		
Total		1638	100		

q0002_0003 Please indicate your highest qualification and your area of expertise!

		Frequency	*Per cent*	*Valid per cent*	*Cumulative per cent*
Valid	1 MBA / Master of Business Administration	511	31.2	100	100
Missing	System	1127	68.8		
Total		1638	100		

q0002_0004 Please indicate your highest qualification and your area of expertise!

		Frequency	*Per cent*	*Valid per cent*	*Cumulative per cent*
Valid	1 Economics	728	44.4	100	100
Missing	System	910	55.6		
Total		1638	100		

q0002_0005 Please indicate your highest qualification and your area of expertise!

		Frequency	*Per cent*	*Valid per cent*	*Cumulative per cent*
Valid	1 Finance	609	37.2	100	100
Missing	System	1029	62.8		
Total		1638	100		

q0002_0006 Please indicate your highest qualification and your area of expertise!

		Frequency	*Per cent*	*Valid per cent*	*Cumulative per cent*
Valid	1 Social law	77	4.7	100	100
Missing	System	1561	95.3		
Total		1638	100		

q0002_0007 Please indicate your highest qualification and your area of expertise!

		Frequency	Per cent	Valid per cent	Cumulative per cent
Valid	1 Political science	175	10.7	100	100
Missing	System	1463	89.3		
Total		1638	100		

q0002_0008 Please indicate your highest qualification and your area of expertise!

		Frequency	Per cent
Missing	System	1638	100

q0002_other Other (please specify):

		Frequency	Per cent	Valid per cent	Cumulative per cent
Valid		1519	92.7	92.7	92.7
	ACMA	7	0.4	0.4	93.2
	Bachelor degree Economics/ accounting	7	0.4	0.4	93.6
	Bookkeeping and accountancy	7	0.4	0.4	94.0
	city planning	7	0.4	0.4	94.4
	ECONOMICS	7	0.4	0.4	94.9
	Economist	7	0.4	0.4	95.3
	Education	7	0.4	0.4	95.7
	Geography	7	0.4	0.4	96.2
	HND administration	7	0.4	0.4	96.6
	Information management	7	0.4	0.4	97.0
	International relations	7	0.4	0.4	97.4
	Manufacturing	7	0.4	0.4	97.9
	MCIPS	7	0.4	0.4	98.3
	No	7	0.4	0.4	98.7
	PGC project management	7	0.4	0.4	99.1
	Telecommunications	7	0.4	0.4	99.6
	Yes	7	0.4	0.4	100
	Total	1638	100	100	

q0003 When did UK join the EU Single Market?

		Frequency	*Per cent*	*Valid per cent*	*Cumulative per cent*
Valid	1 1952 as part of European Coal and Steel Community (ECSC)	126	7.7	10.3	10.3
	2 1957 as member of EUROATOM	91	5.6	7.4	17.7
	3 1958 as member of the European Economic Community (EEC)	203	12.4	16.6	34.3
	4 1973 by application after several refusals	588	35.9	48.0	82.3
	5 1992 as member of European Union (EU) under the Maastricht Treaty	217	13.2	17.7	100
	Total	1225	74.8	100	
Missing	System	413	25.2		
Total		1638	100		

Descriptives

Question 7: This question relates to UK's position in the single market prior to 2008.

Descriptive statistics

	N	*Minimum*	*Maximum*	*Mean*	*Std. deviation*
q0004_0001 a. The UK's prime motive for joining the EU was its fear that its economy was falling behind that of member states.	1204	1	5	2.37	1.106
q0004_0002 b. The UK has always believed in the neofunctionlist model of integration rather than the intergovernmentalist approach.	1169	1	5	2.38	0.874
q0004_0003 c. The UK held a referendum to leave the EU in 1973.	1155	1	5	3.30	1.253
q0004_0004 d. Historically UK has had strong ties with its Commonwealth countries, which were more important than being part of the Single Market.	1162	1	5	2.29	1.007

(*continued*)

(continued)

	N	*Minimum*	*Maximum*	*Mean*	*Std. deviation*
q0004_0005 e. Aspects of the EU membership such as free movement of people and money were of little benefit to the UK prior to 2008.	1190	1	5	2.88	1.229
q0004_0006 f. Margaret Thatcher, UK Prime Minister from 1975 to 1990 was in favour the idea of the supranational state.	1148	1	5	2.90	1.241
q0004_0007 g. Strong links between UK and US were not a factor in EU decision to delay its entry to the single market.	1162	1	5	2.85	1.028
Valid N (listwise)	1001				

Descriptives

Question 8: This question relates to the UK's capacity to recover from the 2008 crisis as a Member State of the EU Single Market after 2008.

Descriptive statistics

	N	*Minimum*	*Maximum*	*Mean*	*Std. deviation*
q0005_0001 a. The UK focused on supporting the EU with the euro crisis after 2008 rather than on protecting City of London and national interests.	1190	1	5	2.67	1.188
q0005_0002 b. Initial austerity measures instigated by the UK government were not as effective as those selected by the EU as a universal solution to reviving GDP growth.	1204	1	5	2.67	1.084
q0005_0003 c. The UK was hindered from recovering from the 2008 economic crisis because of the level of bad debt and bank failure.	1183	1	5	2.44	0.966
q0005_0004 d. UK's closed decision-making stance in relation to economic recovery illustrates its liberal intergovernmental preference for integration and cherry-picking attitude to EU membership.	1169	1	5	2.63	1.063

(continued)

(continued)

	N	*Minimum*	*Maximum*	*Mean*	*Std. deviation*
q0005_0005 e. As a non-Eurozone Member State, UK was at a disadvantage in managing economic recovery because it had no access to EU bailout mechanisms.	1190	1	5	2.98	1.300
q0005_0006 f. The UK recovered more slowly from the 2008 recession than the EU average because it was not subject to the EU rules that would have accelerated GDP growth.	1141	1	5	2.98	1.191
q0005_0007 g. A major factor in UK recovery was its capacity to recapitalise its banks quickly, avoiding the long-term issues that would have been generated by Eurozone membership.	1148	1	5	2.37	1.020
Valid N (listwise)	1029				

Descriptives

Question 9 concerns EU relations with UK before Brexit negotiations.

Descriptive statistics

	N	*Minimum*	*Maximum*	*Mean*	*Std. Deviation*
q0006_0001 a. UK opinion that the EU has neither acted quickly enough to manage the crisis nor appropriately in the case of Member States such as Greece was not a reasonable deduction.	1190	1	5	2.49	1.160
q0006_0002 b. UK was total opposed to EU plans to increase its supranational power over non Eurozone members with regard to single market financial services regulation, which would have involved it using UK taxpayers' money to bail out EU banks.	1190	1	5	2.24	0.960

(*continued*)

(continued)

	N	*Minimum*	*Maximum*	*Mean*	*Std. Deviation*
q0006_0003 c. The UK was opposed to a European Banking Agency because it would lessen the power of the City of London and the Governments influence on decisions because it was not a Eurozone member.	1197	1	5	2.36	0.996
q0006_0004 d. Euroscepticism in the UK from the late 1990s was a strong driver in the 2016 referendum result to exit the EU.	1169	1	5	2.37	1.092
q0006_0005 e. UK conflict with EU over the proposed change to Article 122(2) was a ruse to gain later advantage over EU rather than a genuine objection to an alleged controversial change in the original Treaty of Functioning of the European Union, which allowed Membe	1169	1	5	2.83	1.095
q0006_0006 f. The UK has not benefited greatly from EU membership since joining the group.	1127	1	5	2.89	1.327
q0006_0007 g. Whist the EU makes a very large contribution to the EU budget its position is weakened by not belonging to the Eurozone.	1120	1	5	2.83	1.099
q0006_0008 h. The EU has had a negative attitude to close relationships between US and UK, which have caused it to punish the UK in terms of UK-EU trade relationships, since the formation of the single market.	1113	1	5	2.49	1.075
Valid N (listwise)	1043				

Descriptives

Question 10: This question focuses on the major reasons that UK population voted to leave the EU

Descriptive statistics

	N	*Minimum*	*Maximum*	*Mean*	*Std. Deviation*
q0007_0001 a. Low EU economic growth over a relatively long period was a major factor for vote leave.	1204	1	5	2.55	1.217
q0007_0002 b. Excessive free movement, internal immigration was not a major reason for the decision to leave.	1204	1	5	3.05	1..276
q0007_0003 c. Increasing EU regulation in every aspect of trade and life was considered unacceptable to UK population.	1204	1	5	2.34	1.069
q0007_0004 d. The continuous enlargement of the EU was regarded as indicating its preference for increasing its power rather than the economic growth and prosperity principles of the original EEC.	1197	1	5	2.42	1.076
q0007_0005 e. British voters were tired of being subject to inappropriate legislation passed by EU bureaucrats that had not been elected by them.	1211	1	5	2.44	1.279
q0007_0006 f. Many UK voters were totally opposed to leaving the EU predominantly because of the loss of free movement.	1148	1	5	2.53	1.177
Valid N (listwise)	1050				

Descriptives

Question 12: This question concerns the Brexit negotiations between UK and EU

Descriptive statistics

	N	*Minimum*	*Maximum*	*Mean*	*Std. Deviation*
q0009_0001 a. The UK has been deliberately obstinate during the Withdrawal Agreement negotiations despite EU effort to reach a reasonable agreement.	1197	1	5	2.54	1.326

(*continued*)

(continued)

	N	*Minimum*	*Maximum*	*Mean*	*Std. Deviation*
q0009_0002 b. The value of UK import trade to other EU members is not being considered seriously enough in the obstinate stance the EU has to the talks.	1183	1	5	2.54	1.126
q0009_0003 c. The EU has no mechanism for a country to withdraw from the group and fears UK exit will provoke further requests to leave and weaken its power.	1190	1	5	2.25	1.080
q0009_0004 d. UK exit is being deliberately hindered to retain its budget payments for as long as possible.	1197	1	5	2.68	1.178
q0009_0005 e. The EU does not fear UK's ability to sign substantial trade agreements with US and former UK Commonwealth countries.	1204	1	5	2.83	1.226
q0009_0006 f. The UK will leave the EU without a trade deals and become subject to World Trade Organisation rules.	1155	1	5	2.43	1.097
Valid N (listwise)	1043				

Frequencies

Frequency Table

q0010 Please answer the following statement regarding the EU's management of EU: "The EU's approach to UK's exit is in alignment with the Principle of Proportionality or the Principle of Subsidiarity".

		Frequency	*Percent*	*Valid Percent*	*Cumulative Percent*
Valid	1 Yes!	735	44.9	60	60
	2 No!	490	29.9	40	100
	Total	1225	74.8	100	
Missing	System	413	25.2		
Total		1638	100		

q0012 LEGACY—Alter

		Frequency	*Per cent*	*Valid per cent*	*Cumulative per cent*
Valid	2 18–29	63	3.8	23.1	23.1
	3 30–44	126	7.7	46.2	69.2
	4 45–60	49	3.0	17.9	87.2
	5 Über 60	35	2.1	12.8	100
	Total	273	16.7	100	
Missing	System	1365	83.3		
Total		1638	100		

q0013 LEGACY—Geschlecht

		Frequency	*Per cent*	*Valid per cent*	*Cumulative per cent*
Valid	1 Männlich	175	10.7	64.1	64.1
	2 Weiblich	98	6	35.9	100
	Total	273	16.7	100	
Missing	System	1365	83.3		
Total		1638	100		

Tests for the UK Sample

The descriptive statistics for the whole of question 10 are also requested—in other words the average/mean level of agreement with each of the statements.

Custom Tables

	1 Agree strongly	*2 Agree*	*3 Neither agree nor disagree*	*4 Disagree*	*5 Strongly disagree*
	Row N %	*Row N %*	*Row N %*	*Row N %*	*Row N %*
q0007_0001 a. Low EU economic growth over a relatively long period was a major factor for vote leave.	20.9%	36.6%	16.9%	18.0%	7.6%
q0007_0002 b. Excessive free movement, internal immigration, was not a major reason for the decision to leave.	10.5%	30.8%	19.2%	22.7%	16.9%

(*continued*)

(continued)

	1 Agree strongly	*2 Agree*	*3 Neither agree nor disagree*	*4 Disagree*	*5 Strongly disagree*
	Row N %	*Row N %*	*Row N %*	*Row N %*	*Row N %*
q0007_0003 c. Increasing EU regulation in every aspect of trade and life was considered unacceptable to UK population.	24.4%	34.3%	29.1%	7.6%	4.7%
q0007_0004 d. The continuous enlargement of the EU was regarded as indicating its preference for increasing its power rather than the economic growth and prosperity principles of the original EEC.	19.3%	41.5%	21.1%	14.0%	4.1%
q0007_0005 e. British voters were tired of being subject to inappropriate legislation passed by EU bureaucrats that had not been elected by them.	26.6%	35.3%	16.2%	11.6%	10.4%
q0007_0006 f. Many UK voters were totally opposed to leaving the EU predominantly because of the loss of free movement.	18.3%	40.2%	20.1%	12.8%	8.5%

H1: UK citizens were increasingly more dissatisfied with the perceived disadvantages of EU membership (e.g. EU power, influence) so that its advantages were less likely to be valued (such as freedom of movement).

T-Test—Part 1: 10c, d, e Versus 10b

Reference Q 10 (test 10c, 10d and 10e against 10b, 10f)—a lower mean means more agreement!

Paired samples statistics

		Mean	*N*	*Std. Deviation*	*Std. Error Mean*
Pair 1 <u>higher</u> lower	q0007_0002 b. Excessive free movement, internal immigration was not a major reason for the decision to leave. – low agreement	3.07	1183	1.267	0.037
	q0007_0003 c. Increasing EU regulation in every aspect of trade and life was considered unacceptable to UK population.- high agreement	2.33	1183	1.075	0.031

(continued)

		Mean	*N*	*Std. Deviation*	*Std. Error Mean*
Pair 2	q0007_0002 b. Excessive free movement, internal immigration was not a major reason for the decision to leave. low	3.04	1176	1.275	0.037
	q0007_0004 d. The continuous enlargement of the EU was regarded as indicating its preference for increasing its power rather than the economic growth and prosperity principles of the original EEC.high	2.40	1176	1.071	0.031
Pair 3 higher lower	q0007_0002 b. Excessive free movement, internal immigration was not a major reason for the decision to leave. low	3.05	1190	1.278	0.037
	q0007_0005 e. British voters were tired of being subject to inappropriate legislation passed by EU bureaucrats that had not been elected by them. High	2.40	1190	1.253	0.036

Paired samples correlations

		N	*Correlation*	*Sig.*
Pair 1 Significant!	q0007_0002 b. Excessive free movement, internal immigration was not a major reason for the decision to leave. & q0007_0003 c. Increasing EU regulation in every aspect of trade and life was considered unacceptable to UK population.	1183	-0.060	0.038
Pair 2 Not significant!	q0007_0002 b. Excessive free movement, internal immigration was not a major reason for the decision to leave. & q0007_0004 d. The continuous enlargement of the EU was regarded as indicating its preference for increasing its power rather than the economic growth and prosperity principles of the original EEC.	1176	-0.008	0.784
Pair 3 Significant!	q0007_0002 b. Excessive free movement, internal immigration was not a major reason for the decision to leave. & q0007_0005 e. British voters were tired of being subject to inappropriate legislation passed by EU bureaucrats that had not been elected by them.	1190	-0.177	0.000

Paired samples test

		Paired Differences					*t*	*df*	*Sig. (2-tailed)*
		Mean	*Std. Deviation*	*Std. Error Mean*	*95% Confidence Interval of the Difference*				
					Lower	*Upper*			
Pair 1 **Significant!**	q0007_0002 b. Excessive free movement, internal immigration was not a major reason for the decision to leave. – q0007_0003 c. Increasing EU regulation in every aspect of trade and life was considered unacceptable to UK population.	0.746	1.711	0.050	0.648	0.843	14.99	1182	0.000
Pair 2 **Significant!**	q0007_0002 b. Excessive free movement, internal immigration was not a major reason for the decision to leave. – q0007_0004 d. The continuous enlargement of the EU was regarded as indicating its preference for increasing its power rather than the economic growth and prosperity principles of the original EEC.	0.637	1.671	0.049	0.541	0.733	13.07	1175	0.000

Pair 3 **Significant!**	q0007_0002 b. Excessive free movement, internal immigration was not a major reason for the decision to leave. – q0007_0005 e. British voters were tired of being subject to inappropriate legislation passed by EU bureaucrats that had not been elected by them.	0.647	1.942	0.056	0.537	0.758	11.49	1189	0.000

T-Test Part 2: 10c, d, e Versus 10f

Reference Q 10 (test 10c, 10d and 10e against 10b, 10f)—a lower mean means more agreement!

Paired samples statistics

		Mean	*N*	*Std. Deviation*	*Std. Error Mean*
Pair 1 higher lower	q0007_0006 f. Many UK voters were totally opposed to leaving the EU predominantly because of the loss of free movement.	2.48	1127	1.138	0.034
	q0007_0003 c. Increasing EU regulation in every aspect of trade and life was considered unacceptable to UK population.	2.30	1127	1.064	0.032
Pair 2 higher lower	q0007_0006 f. Many UK voters were totally opposed to leaving the EU predominantly because of the loss of free movement.	2.53	1120	1.173	0.035
	q0007_0004 d. The continuous enlargement of the EU was regarded as indicating its preference for increasing its power rather than the economic growth and prosperity principles of the original EEC.	2.37	1120	1.059	0.032
Pair 3 higher lower	q0007_0006 f. Many UK voters were totally opposed to leaving the EU predominantly because of the loss of free movement.	2.52	1134	1.178	0.035
	q0007_0005 e. British voters were tired of being subject to inappropriate legislation passed by EU bureaucrats that had not been elected by them.	2.38	1134	1.203	0.036

Test the correlation between 10c and 10f and whether this correlation between 10c and 10f is statistically significant.

No, this correlation is not significant

Paired samples correlations

		N	*Correlation*	*Sig.*
Pair 1 **NOT** SIGNIFICANT!	q0007_0006 f. Many UK voters were totally opposed to leaving the EU predominantly because of the loss of free movement. & q0007_0003 c. Increasing EU regulation in every aspect of trade and life was considered unacceptable to UK population.	1127	-0.019	0.520
Pair 2	q0007_0006 f. Many UK voters were totally opposed to leaving the EU predominantly because of the loss of free movement. & q0007_0004 d. The continuous enlargement of the EU was regarded as indicating its preference for increasing its power rather than the economic growth and prosperity principles of the original EEC.	1120	0.040	0.176
Pair 3	q0007_0006 f. Many UK voters were totally opposed to leaving the EU predominantly because of the loss of free movement. & q0007_0005 e. British voters were tired of being subject to inappropriate legislation passed by EU bureaucrats that had not been elected by them.	1134	0.030	0.315

Paired samples test

All differences are significant		*Paired Differences*					*t*	*df*	
		Mean	*Std. Deviation*	*Std. Error Mean*	*95% Confidence Interval of the Difference*				*Sig. (2-tailed)*
					Lower	*Upper*			
Pair 1	q0007_0006 f. Many UK voters were totally opposed to leaving the EU predominantly because of the loss of free movement. – q0007_0003 c. Increasing EU regulation in every aspect of trade and life was considered unacceptable to UK population.	0.180	1.573	0.047	0.088	0.272	3.845	1126	0.000
Pair 2	q0007_0006 f. Many UK voters were totally opposed to leaving the EU predominantly because of the loss of free movement. – q0007_0004 d. The continuous enlargement of the EU was regarded as indicating its preference for increasing its power rather than the economic growth and prosperity principles of the original EEC.	0.156	1.548	0.046	0.065	0.247	3.378	1119	0.001
Pair 3	q0007_0006 f. Many UK voters were totally opposed to leaving the EU predominantly because of the loss of free movement. – q0007_0005 e. British voters were tired of being subject to inappropriate legislation passed by EU bureaucrats that had not been elected by them.	0.136	1.658	0.049	0.039	0.232	2.758	1133	0.006

The descriptive statistics for the whole of question 12 are also requested—in other words the average/mean level of agreement with each of the statements.

Custom Tables

	1 Agree strongly	*2 Agree*	*3 Neither agree nor disagree*	*4 Disagree*	*5 Strongly disagree*
	Row N %	*Row N %*	*Row N %*	*Row N %*	*Row N %*
q0009_0001 a. The UK has been deliberately obstinate during the Withdrawal Agreement negotiations despite EU effort to reach a reasonable agreement.	25.1%	32.2%	19.3%	9.9%	13.5%
q0009_0002 b. The value of UK import trade to other EU members is not being considered seriously enough in the obstinate stance the EU has to the talks.	17.2%	37.9%	25.4%	12.4%	7.1%
q0009_0003 c. The EU has no mechanism for a country to withdraw from the group and fears UK exit will provoke further requests to leave and weaken its power.	27.6%	36.5%	22.9%	8.8%	4.1%
q0009_0004 d. UK exit is being deliberately hindered to retain its budget payments for as long as possible.	17.0%	30.4%	28.7%	15.2%	8.8%
q0009_0005 e. The EU does not fear UK's ability to sign substantial trade agreements with US and former UK Commonwealth countries.	14.0%	31.4%	23.8%	19.2%	11.6%
q0009_0006 f. The UK will leave the EU without a trade deals and become subject to World Trade Organisation rules.	22.4%	33.3%	27.3%	12.7%	4.2%

T-Test

All differences are significant—a lower mean means more agreement!
Paired samples statistics

		Mean	*N*	*Std. Deviation*	*Std. Error Mean*
Pair 1 <u>**lower**</u> **higher**	q0009_0002 b. The value of UK import trade to other EU members is not being considered seriously enough in the obstinate stance the EU has to the talks.	2.55	1162	1.134	0.033
	q0009_0005 e. The EU does not fear UK's ability to sign substantial trade agreements with US and former UK Commonwealth countries.	2.81	1162	1.226	0.036
Pair 2 <u>**lower**</u> **higher**	q0009_0003 c. The EU has no mechanism for a country to withdraw from the group and fears UK exit will provoke further requests to leave and weaken its power.	2.23	1176	1.064	0.031
	q0009_0005 e. The EU does not fear UK's ability to sign substantial trade agreements with US and former UK Commonwealth countries.	2.83	1176	1.235	0.036

Reference Q12 Test 12b, 12c against 12e

H 2: The EU had stronger reasons to dissuade the UK from withdrawing from the single market (e.g. budget contribution and weakening the EU's position with the remaining 27 states) than its fear that UK trade focus would move to its former commonwealth countries and US. Test the correlation between 12b and 12e and whether this correlation between 12d and 12e is statistically significant

Paired samples correlations

		N	Correlation	Sig.
Pair 1 **significant**	q0009_0002 b. The value of UK import trade to other EU members is not being considered seriously enough in the obstinate stance the EU has to the talks. & q0009_0005 e. The EU does not fear UK's ability to sign substantial trade agreements with US and former UK Commonwealth countries.	1162	-0.082	0.005
Pair 2 **NOT significant**	q0009_0003 c. The EU has no mechanism for a country to withdraw from the group and fears UK exit will provoke further requests to leave and weaken its power. & q0009_0005 e. The EU does not fear UK's ability to sign substantial trade agreements with US and former UK Commonwealth countries.	1176	-0.006	0.844

Paired samples test

All differences are significant		*Paired Differences*					*t*	*df*	*Sig. (2-tailed)*
		Mean	*Std. Deviation*	*Std. Error Mean*	*95% Confidence Interval of the Difference*				
					Lower	*Upper*			
Pair 1	q0009_0002 b. The value of UK import trade to other EU members is not being considered seriously enough in the obstinate stance the EU has to the talks. – q0009_0005 e. The EU does not fear UK's ability to sign substantial trade agreements with US and former UK Commonwealth countries.	-0.265	1.737	0.051	-0.365	-0.165	-5.202	1161	0.000
Pair 2	q0009_0003 c. The EU has no mechanism for a country to withdraw from the group and fears UK exit will provoke further requests to leave and weaken its power. – q0009_0005 e. The EU does not fear UK's ability to sign substantial trade agreements with US and former UK Commonwealth countries.	-0.595	1.635	0.048	-0.689	-0.502	-12.488	1175	0.000

Germany Questionnaire and Analysis

Questionnaire: European Union Management of 2008 Financial Crisis

The purpose of this research is to critically evaluate the extent to which the European Commission, EC, which is the part of the European Union responsible for single market, economic and monetary union issues, has upheld the principles for which it was founded as it attempted to resolve the impact of the 2008 global financial crisis on Member States. The desired outcomes being minimum impact on the development of each Member State and on the group as a whole.

This Survey Concerns the Member State Germany

Thank you for agreeing to participate in this research by completing this questionnaire. Please provide your personal perspectives when answering the questions, there are no correct or incorrect responses. Any comments you make remain confidential, and the subsequent report will not reveal the identity of any individual. Please answer ALL questions. The questionnaire should take no longer than 30 minutes. You can withdraw from this research at any time.

I have read the confidentiality statement and am happy to take part in this survey:

Yes
No

Are you?

Male
Female

To which age group do you belong?

18–25
26–35
36–45
46–55
over 55

Please indicate your highest qualification

Doctorate
Master's degree
Bachelor degree
Professional qualification
Secondary school education

Which specialist subject is your major interest?

Economics
Finance
Social Justice
Political Science
Other

SECTION TWO: MAIN QUESTIONNAIRE
Question 6: When did Germany join the single market?

1957 as member of EUROATOM in 1957
1989 on unification
1958 as member of the European Economic Community (EEC)
1952 as part of European Coal and Steel Community (ECSC)
1992 as member of European Union (EU) under the Maastricht Treaty

Question 7: This question relates to Germany's position in the single market prior to 2008. Please indicate the extent of your agreement or disagreement with each of the statements in the grid—for EACH statement choose ONE option which is nearest to your opinion.

	Statement	*Agree strongly*	*Agree*	*Neither agree nor disagree*	*Disagree*	*Strongly disagree*
a	Germany was a major EU member with a strong neofunctionalist stance towards European integration, believing that two or more states could exist in harmony supported by a supranational body					
b	Germany's GDP output prior to 2008 was relatively volatile					

(*continued*)

(continued)

	Statement	*Agree strongly*	*Agree*	*Neither agree nor disagree*	*Disagree*	*Strongly disagree*
c	Germany had a relatively minor influence in the creation of the Euro					
d	Germany's objective for joining the European group was political, to denounce its Nazi principles for European unity					
e	German GDP was traditionally export led with low domestic consumption					
f	Substitution of the Deutsche Mark for the Euro was intended to reduce German power in Europe					

Question 8: This question relates to German economic trends immediately after the 2008 crisis. Please indicate the extent of your agreement or disagreement with each statement—for EACH statement choose ONE option which is nearest to your opinion.

	Statement	*Agree strongly*	*Agree*	*Neither agree nor disagree*	*Disagree*	*Strongly disagree*
a	German GDP decline during the 2008 crisis was a consequence of toxic financial debt instruments, as was the issues in US and UK					
b	The major GDP issue for Germany during and just after the 2008 recession was sharp decline in exports, which severely restricted growth					
c	In contrast to UK and US, German unemployment fell from 2008 to 2010					
d	GDP growth was restored quickly in Germany despite a short deep recession in 2008, owing to restoration of its export market					
d	Germany was able to restore GDP growth quickly because it injected a very large sum into the economy rather than by following EU policy					

(*continued*)

(continued)

	Statement	*Agree strongly*	*Agree*	*Neither agree nor disagree*	*Disagree*	*Strongly disagree*
e	Germany's labour market policies after 2008 resulted in severe social divide					
f	After 2012 the effects of Eurozone country debt had little effect on German exports or GDP growth					
g	Germany's economic recovery was faster than other Eurozone countries because its productivity was higher, and its wages were lower					
h	German competitiveness after the recession was negatively impacted by high labour rates in Germany					
i	Germany's decentralised labour laws were important to retaining market competitiveness					
j	Low public sector debt-to-GDP growth is the major reason for Germany's quick recovery immediately after 2008					

Question 10: This question appraises the decline in German GDP growth from 2013 onwards. Please indicate the extent of your agreement or disagreement with each statement—for EACH statement choose ONE option which is nearest to your opinion.

	Statement	*Agree strongly*	*Agree*	*Neither agree nor disagree*	*Disagree*	*Strongly disagree*
a	German GDP growth has been relatively flat and volatile since 2013 reflecting low EU GDP growth generally					
b	The lower German GDP growth trend is a result of its lower competitiveness					
c	Balanced budget policy in Germany is relatively unimportant in explaining its continuing GDP growth trend					

(*continued*)

(continued)

	Statement	*Agree strongly*	*Agree*	*Neither agree nor disagree*	*Disagree*	*Strongly disagree*
d	German's continuous budget surpluses directly impact on other Eurozone nations' domestic and export markets and their capacity to rebalance their economies					

Question 11: This question is specifically concerned with the influence that Germany has on EU policies and the benefits it has accrued from membership

	Statement	*Agree strongly*	*Agree*	*Neither agree nor disagree*	*Disagree*	*Strongly disagree*
a	Germany has too much influence on EU policies					
b	Germany is the EU Member State that benefitted most from membership					
c	Germany's lack of domestic demand is not a factor that impacts on the economic growth in other Eurozone countries					
d	Germany's dominance in EU policy after the crisis was based on imposing monetary policies and ordoliberalism, which most aligned with its interests and neglected those southern EU states					
e	The transfer to the Euro benefitted German economy considerably as it represented a devaluation of the Mark and boosted exports					
f	The EU's failure to take action about Germany's continuous budget surplus cannot be considered responsible for negative spillovers to other EMU members					

(*continued*)

(continued)

	Statement	*Agree strongly*	*Agree*	*Neither agree nor disagree*	*Disagree*	*Strongly disagree*
g	The failure of EU to integrate balance of payments control mechanism for the Euro is not a significant factor in Germany's continuing ability to create surpluses					
h	Germany's stance that other Eurozone countries have failed to recover GDP growth is a consequence of not following EU rules on reducing their deficits is a valid notion					
i	Germany's lead on foreign policy and security policies as pseudo EU spokesperson is not acceptable under the terms of EU principles					

Question 12:

(a) **Please answer Yes or NO to the statement regarding the EU's management of Germany's economic prosperity since 2008**

STATEMENT: The EU has allowed Germany to have too much influence in the development, and implementation of EU policy since 2008, such that the Principle of Proportionality and the Principle of Subsidiarity have been compromised with regard to the benefits of membership for other Member States

Yes

No

(b) **Please provide an explanation for your choice of answer to part (a)**

Question 13: Potential solutions to Germany's surplus situation

In 2020, twelve years after the recession, Germany's surplus appears to be preventing return to prosperity, so that several recommendations have been made to reduce it, in order to support more balanced EU economic performance

Please rank **ALL** options **in order of importance;** 1 is the most important and 5 is the least important

Option	*Proposed action to support more balanced EU recovery*	*RANK (1–5; 1 is the most important)*
a	Germany should cease taking the dominant role in EU policy making	
b	Germany should spend its surpluses on its declining transportation infrastructure	
c	Wage levels should be raised to reduce Germany's competitiveness	
d	Germany should continue to aim for surpluses	
e	Create a balance of payments control mechanism for the Euro	
f	Germany should create higher domestic demand by announcing tax incentives and encourage more imported goods for domestic consumption	

Question 14: Please make any further comments you wish about Germany's position in the EU and the effects of the stance it takes to other EU Member State economies

....

THANK YOU FOR TAKING THE TIME TO COMPLETE THIS QUESTIONNAIRE

Frequencies and Descriptives Germany

Frequency Tables

q0001 Ich habe die Vertraulichkeitserklärung gelesen und nehme gerne an dieser Umfrage teil.I have read the confidentiality statement and am happy to take part in this survey.

		Frequency	*Per cent*	*Valid per cent*	*Cumulative per cent*
Valid	1 Ja! // Yes!	1540	100.0	100.0	100.0

q0002_0001 Geschlecht und Alter // Gender and age

		Frequency	*Per cent*	*Valid per cent*	*Cumulative per cent*
Valid	1 zwischen 23–30 Jahre alt // between 23–30 years old	280	18.2	100.0	100.0
Missing	System	1260	81.8		

		Frequency	*Per cent*	*Valid per cent*	*Cumulative per cent*
Total		1540	100.0		

q0002_0002 Geschlecht und Alter // Gender and age

		Frequency	*Per cent*	*Valid per cent*	*Cumulative per cent*
Valid	1 zwischen 31–40 Jahre alt // between 31–40 years old	567	36.8	100.0	100.0
Missing	System	973	63.2		
Total		1540	100.0		

q0002_0003 Geschlecht und Alter // Gender and age

		Frequency	*Per cent*	*Valid per cent*	*Cumulative per cent*
Valid	1 zwischen 41–50 Jahre alt // between 41–50 years old	392	25.5	100.0	100.0
Missing	System	1148	74.5		
Total		1540	100.0		

q0002_0004 Geschlecht und Alter // Gender and age

		Frequency	*Per cent*	*Valid per cent*	*Cumulative per cent*
Valid	1 zwischen 51–60 Jahre alt // between 51–60 years old	175	11.4	100.0	100.0
Missing	System	1365	88.6		
Total		1540	100.0		

q0002_0005 Geschlecht und Alter // Gender and age

		Frequency	*Per cent*	*Valid per cent*	*Cumulative per cent*
Valid	1 über 61 Jahre alt // over 61 years old	182	11.8	100.0	100.0

(continued)

		Frequency	Per cent	Valid per cent	Cumulative per cent
Missing	System	1358	88.2		
Total		1540	100.0		

q0002_0006 Geschlecht und Alter // Gender and age

		Frequency	Per cent	Valid per cent	Cumulative per cent
Valid	1 männlich // male	945	61.4	100.0	100.0
Missing	System	595	38.6		
Total		1540	100.0		

q0002_0007 Geschlecht und Alter // Gender and age

		Frequency	Per cent	Valid per cent	Cumulative per cent
Valid	1 weiblich // female	567	36.8	100.0	100.0
Missing	System	973	63.2		
Total		1540	100.0		

q0002_other Sonstiges Geschlecht (bitte angeben): // Other gender (please specify):

		Frequency	Per cent	Valid per cent	Cumulative per cent
Valid		1491	96.8	96.8	96.8
	–	7	0.5	0.5	97.3
	1. u. 2. juristisches Staatsexamen mit Schwerpunkt Wirtschaft u. Wettbewerb	7	0.5	0.5	97.7
	Funk	7	0.5	0.5	98.2
	Keins	7	0.5	0.5	98.6
	Me gusta mucho	7	0.5	0.5	99.1
	Nein	7	0.5	0.5	99.5
	Steuerberater	7	0.5	0.5	100.0
	Total	1540	100.0	100.0	

q0004 Wann ist Deutschland dem EU-Binnenmarkt beigetreten? // When did Germany join the EU Single Market?

		Frequency	*Per cent*	*Valid per cent*	*Cumulative per cent*
Valid	1 1952 als Teil der Europäischen Gemeinschaft für Kohle und Stahl (EGKS) // 1952 as part of European Coal and Steel Community	273	17.7	24.8	24.8
	2 1957 als EUROATOM-Mitglied im Jahr 1957 // 1957 as member of EUROATOM in 1957	147	9.5	13.4	38.2
	3 1958 als Mitglied der Europäischen Wirtschaftsgemeinschaft (EWG) // 1958 as member of the European Economic Community	336	21.8	30.6	68.8
	4 1989 durch die Wiedervereinigung // 1989 on unification	49	3.2	4.5	73.2
	5 1992 als Mitglied der Europäischen Union (EU) nach dem Vertrag von Maastricht // 1992 as member of European Union (EU)	294	19.1	26.8	100.0
	Total	1099	71.4	100.0	
Missing	System	441	28.6		
Total		1540	100.0		

Descriptives

Question 7: This question relates to Germany's position in the single market prior to 2008.

Descriptive statistics

	N	*Minimum*	*Maximum*	*Mean*	*Std. deviation*
q0005_0001 a. Deutschland war ein wichtiges EU-Mitglied mit einer starken neofunktionalistischen Haltung gegenüber der europäischen Integration und glaubte, dass zwei oder mehr Staaten in Harmonie existieren könnten, unterstützt durch ein supranationales Gremium.	1029	1	5	1.96	0.996

(*continued*)

(continued)

	N	*Minimum*	*Maximum*	*Mean*	*Std. deviation*
q0005_0002 b. Das deutsche Bruttoinlandsprodukt (BIP) vor 2008 war relativ volatil. // Germany's GDP output prior to 2008 was relatively volatile.	1071	1	5	2.63	1.120
q0005_0003 c. Deutschlands Einfluss auf die Schaffung des Euro war gering. // Germany had a relatively minor influence in the creation of the Euro.	1078	1	5	3.33	1.275
q0005_0004 d. Deutschlands Beitritt zur Europäischen Union war vor allem politisch motiviert, um offenkundig entgegen nationalistischer Grundsätze (z.B. aus dem 3. Reich) zu agieren. // Germany's objective for joining the European group was political, to act overtly against nationalist principles (e.g. from the 3rd Reich).	1043	1	5	2.54	1.185
q0005_0005 e. Das deutsche BIP war traditionell exportorientiert mit geringem Inlandsverbrauch. // German GDP was traditionally export led with low domestic consumption.	1064	1	5	2.53	1.176
q0005_0006 f. Der Ersatz des Euro durch die Deutsche Mark sollte die deutsche Macht in Europa reduzieren. // Substitution of the Deutsche Mark for the Euro was intended to reduce German power in Europe.	1015	1	5	2.93	1.275
Valid N (listwise)	805				

Descriptives

Question 8: This question relates to German economic trends immediately after the 2008 crisis.

Descriptive statistics

	N	*Minimum*	*Maximum*	*Mean*	*Std. deviation*
q0006_0001 a. Der Rückgang des deutschen BIP während der Finanzkrise 2008 war eine Folge toxischer Finanzinstrumente, ebenso wie der Probleme in den USA und in Großbritannien. // German GDP decline during the 2008 financial crisis was a consequence of toxic financial debt instruments, as was the issues in US and UK	994	1	5	2.01	0.924
q0006_0002 b. Das größte Problem mit dem BIP hatte Deutschland während und kurz nach der Rezession in 2008 durch einen starken Rückgang der Exporte, der das Wachstum stark hemmte. // The major GDP issue for Germany during and just after the 2008 recession was sharp decline in exports, which severely restricted growth.	1008	1	5	2.21	0.889
q0006_0003 c. Im Gegensatz zu Großbritannien und den USA ging die Arbeitslosigkeit in D zwischen 20082010 zurück. // In contrast to UK and US, German unemployment fell from 2008 to 2010.	1008	1	5	2.60	1.069
q0006_0004 d. Deutschlands BIP wuchs nach einer kurzen starken Rezession im Jahr 2008 wieder stärker, da der Export von Gütern wieder anstieg. // GDP growth was restored quickly in Germany despite a short deep recession in 2008, owing to restoration of its export market.	1036	1	5	2.36	1.021
q0006_0005 e. Deutschland verfügte schnell wieder über ein wachsendes BIP, da der Bundeshaushalt der Wirtschaft hohe Förderungen zuführte, anstatt eine EU-bezogene Politik zu verfolgen. // Germany was able to restore GDP growth quickly because it injected a very large sum into the economy rather than by following EU policy.	1001	1	5	2.66	1.212

(*continued*)

(continued)

	N	*Minimum*	*Maximum*	*Mean*	*Std. deviation*
q0006_0006 f. Die deutsche Arbeitsmarktpolitik nach 2008 führte zu einer starken sozialen Kluft. // Germany's labour market policies after 2008 resulted in severe social divide.	931	1	5	2.56	1.166
q0006_0007 g. Nach 2012 hatten die Auswirkungen der Staatsverschuldung der Eurozone nur geringe Auswirkungen auf die deutschen Exporte oder das BIPWachstum. // After 2012 the effects of Eurozone country debt had little effect on German exports or GDP growth.	903	1	5	2.46	1.004
q0006_0008 h. Die wirtschaftliche Erholung Deutschlands war schneller als in anderen Ländern der Eurozone, da die Produktivität höher und die Löhne niedriger waren. // Germany's economic recovery was faster than other Eurozone countries because its productivity was higher, and its wages were lower.	868	1	5	2.38	0.956
q0006_0009 i. Die Wettbewerbsfähigkeit Deutschlands nach der Rezession wurde durch die hohen Arbeitsquoten in Deutschland negativ beeinflusst. // German competitiveness after the recession was negatively impacted by high labour rates in Germany.	868	1	5	2.96	1.043
q0006_0010 j. Deutschlands dezentrales Arbeitsrecht war wichtig, um die Wettbewerbsfähigkeit des Marktes zu erhalten. // Germany's decentralised labour laws were important to retaining market competitiveness.	868	1	5	2.55	1.035

(*continued*)

(continued)

	N	*Minimum*	*Maximum*	*Mean*	*Std. deviation*
q0006_0011 k. Die geringe Verschuldung des öffentlichen Sektors gegenüber dem BIP-Wachstum ist der Hauptgrund für die rasche Erholung Deutschlands unmittelbar nach 2008. // Low public sector debt-to-GDP growth is the major reason for Germany's quick recovery immediately after 2008.	882	1	5	2.48	0.990
Valid N (listwise)	784				

Descriptives

Question 10 appraises the decline in German GDP growth from 2013 onwards.

Descriptive statistics

	N	*Minimum*	*Maximum*	*Mean*	*Std. deviation*
q0007_0001 a. Das deutsche BIP-Wachstum ist seit 2013 relativ flach und volatil, was auf das allgemein niedrige BIP-Wachstum der EU zurückzuführen ist. // German GDP growth has been relatively flat and volatile since 2013 reflecting low EU GDP growth generally.	1099	1	5	2.57	1.119
q0007_0002 b. Der geringe deutsche BIP-Wachstumstrend ist auf die rückläufige Wettbewerbsfähigkeit zurückzuführen. // The lower German GDP growth trend is a result of its lower competitiveness.	1099	1	5	2.69	1.100
q0007_0003 c. Eine ausgewogene Haushaltspolitik in Deutschland ist für die Erklärung des anhaltenden BIP-Wachstumstrends relativ unwichtig. // Balanced budget policy in Germany is relatively unimportant in explaining its continuing GDP growth trend.	1099	1	5	2.88	1.091

(continued)

(continued)

	N	*Minimum*	*Maximum*	*Mean*	*Std. deviation*
q0007_0004 d. Die kontinuierlichen Haushaltsüberschüsse Deutschlands wirken sich direkt auf die Inlands- und Exportmärkte anderer Länder der Eurozone und auf deren Fähigkeit aus, ihre Volkswirtschaften wieder ins Gleichgewicht zu bringen. // German's continuous budget surpluses directly impact on other Eurozone nations' domestic and export markets and their capacity to rebalance their economies.	1099	1	5	2.59	1.107
Valid N (listwise)	1099				

Descriptives

Question 11: This question is specifically concerned with the influence that Germany has on EU policies and the benefits it has accrued from membership

Descriptive statistics

	N	*Minimum*	*Maximum*	*Mean*	*Std. deviation*
q0008_0001 a. Deutschland hat zu viel Einfluss auf die EU-Politik. // Germany has too much influence on EU policies.	1022	1	5	2.58	1.254
q0008_0002 b. Germany is the EU member state that benefitted most from membership. // Deutschland ist der EU-Mitgliedstaat, der am meisten von der Mitgliedschaft profitiert hat.	1015	1	5	2.59	1.099

(*continued*)

(continued)

	N	*Minimum*	*Maximum*	*Mean*	*Std. deviation*
q0008_0003 c. Der Mangel an Inlandsnachfrage in Deutschland ist kein Faktor, der das Wirtschaftswachstum in anderen Ländern der Eurozone beeinflusst. // Germany's lack of domestic demand is not a factor that impacts on the economic growth in other Eurozone countries.	1043	1	5	2.91	1.068
q0008_0004 d. Die Dominanz Deutschlands in der EU-Politik nach der Krise beruhte auf der Einführung von Geldpolitik und Ordoliberalismus, die am ehesten mit seinen Interessen übereinstimmten und diese südlichen EU-Staaten vernachlässigten. // Germany's dominance in EU policy after the crisis was based on imposing monetary policies and ordoliberalism, which most aligned with its interests and neglected those southern EU states.	1029	1	5	2.80	1.088
q0008_0005 e. Die Übertragung auf den Euro kam der deutschen Wirtschaft erheblich zugute, da sie eine Abwertung der Mark darstellte und die Exporte ankurbelte. // The transfer to the euro benefitted German economy considerably as it represented a devaluation of the Mark and boosted exports.	1050	1	5	2.67	1.279
q0008_0006 f. Das Versäumnis der EU, Maßnahmen gegen den kontinuierlichen Haushaltsüberschuss Deutschlands zu ergreifen, kann nicht als verantwortlich für negative Auswirkungen auf andere WWU-Mitglieder angesehen werden. // The EU's failure to take action about Germany's continuous budget surplus cannot be considered responsible for negative spillovers to other EMU members.	931	1	5	2.57	1.079

(*continued*)

(continued)

	N	*Minimum*	*Maximum*	*Mean*	*Std. deviation*
q0008_0007 g. Das Versäumnis der EU, den Mechanismus zur Kontrolle der Zahlungsbilanz für den Euro zu integrieren, ist kein wesentlicher Faktor für die anhaltende Fähigkeit Deutschlands, Überschüsse zu erzielen. // The failure of EU to integrate balance of payments control mechanism for the Euro is not a significant factor in Germany's continuing ability to create surpluses.	875	1	5	2.60	1.089
q0008_0008 h. Die Haltung Deutschlands, dass andere Länder der Eurozone das BIP-Wachstum nicht wiedererlangt haben, ist eine Folge der Nichteinhaltung der EU-Vorschriften zur Reduzierung ihrer Defizite. // Germany's stance that other Eurozone countries have failed to recover GDP growth is a consequence of not following EU rules on reducing their deficits is a valid notion.	896	1	5	2.55	0.991
q0008_0009 i. Deutschlands außen- und sicherheitspolitischer Vorsprung als Pseudo-EU-Sprecher ist nach den EU-Grundsätzen nicht akzeptabel. // Germany's lead on foreign policy and security policies as pseudo EU spokesperson is not acceptable under the terms of EU principles	875	1	5	2.75	1.049
Valid N (listwise)	784				

Frequencies

q0009 Bitte antworten Sie mit Ja oder NEIN auf die nachfolgende Erklärung. ERKLÄRUNG: "Die EU hat Deutschland seit 2008 zu viel Einfluss auf die Entwicklung und Umsetzung der EU-Politik eingeräumt, so dass das Prinzip der Verhältnismäßigkeit und das Prinzip der Subsidiarität in Bezug auf die Vorteile einer Mitgliedschaft für andere Mitgliedsstaaten beeinträchtigt wurden."

(continued)

		Frequency	Per cent	Valid per cent	Cumulative per cent
Valid	1 Ja // Yes	560	36.4	51.0	51.0
	2 Nein // No	539	35.0	49.0	100.0
	Total	1099	71.4	100.0	
Missing	System	441	28.6		
Total		1540	100.0		

Descriptives

Proposed action to support more balanced EU recovery

Please rank **ALL** options **in order of importance;** 1 is the most important and 5 the least important

Descriptive statistics

	N	Minimum	Maximum	Mean	Std. deviation
q0010_0001 Deutschland sollte aufhören, die dominierende Rolle in der Politikgestaltung der EU zu übernehmen. // Germany should cease taking the dominant role in EU policy making.	1099	1	6	3.46	2.015
q0010_0002 Deutschland sollte seine Überschüsse für seine rückläufige Verkehrsinfrastruktur ausgeben. // Germany should spend its surpluses on its declining transportation infrastructure.	1099	1	6	2.64	1.415
q0010_0003 Das Lohnniveau sollte angehoben werden, um die Wettbewerbsfähigkeit Deutschlands zu verringern. // Wage levels should be raised to reduce Germany's competitiveness.	1099	1	6	3.11	1.631
q0010_0004 Deutschland sollte weiterhin Überschüsse anstreben. // Germany should continue to aim for surpluses.	1099	1	6	3.40	1.405
q0010_0005 Schaffung eines Zahlungs bilanzkontrollmechanismus für den Euro. // Create a balance of payments control mechanism for the Euro.	1099	1	6	4.20	1.372

(*continued*)

(continued)

	N	*Minimum*	*Maximum*	*Mean*	*Std. deviation*
q0010_0006 Deutschland sollte durch die Ankündigung von Steueranreizen eine höhere Inlandsnachfrage schaffen und mehr importierte Waren für den Inlandsverbrauch fördern. // Germany should create higher domestic demand by announcing tax incentives and encourage more imported goods for domestic consumption	1099	1	6	4.18	1.755
Valid N (listwise)	1099				

Frequency Tables

q0011 LEGACY—Alter

		Frequency	*Per cent*	*Valid per cent*	*Cumulative per cent*
Valid	2.00 18 – 29	49	3.3	17.5	17.5
	3.00 30 – 44	161	10.7	57.5	75.0
	4.00 45 – 60	49	3.3	17.5	92.5
	5.00 Über 60	21	1.4	7.5	100.0
	Total	280	18.7	100.0	
Missing	System	1218	81.3		
Total		1498	100.0		

q0012 LEGACY—Geschlecht

		Frequency	*Per cent*	*Valid per cent*	*Cumulative per cent*
Valid	1.00 Männlich	217	14.5	77.5	77.5
	2.00 Weiblich	63	4.2	22.5	100.0
	Total	280	18.7	100.0	
Missing	System	1218	81.3		
Total		1498	100.0		

Italy Questionnaire and Analysis

Questionnaire: European Union Management of 2008 Financial Crisis

The purpose of this research is to critically evaluate the extent to which the European Commission, EC, which is the part of the European Union responsible for single market, economic and monetary union issues, has upheld the principles for which it was founded as it attempted to resolve the impact of the 2008 global financial crisis on Member States. The desired outcomes being minimum impact on the development of each Member State and on the group as a whole.

This Survey Concerns the Member State Italy

Thank you for agreeing to participate in this research by completing this questionnaire. Please provide your personal perspectives when answering the questions, there are no correct or incorrect responses. Any comments you make remain confidential, and the subsequent report will not reveal the identity of any individual. Please answer ALL questions. The questionnaire should take no longer than 30 minutes. You can withdraw from this research at any time.

I have read the confidentiality statement and am happy to take part in this survey:

Yes
No

Are you?

Male
Female

To which age group do you belong?

18–25
26–35
36–45
46–55
over 55

Please indicate your highest qualification

Doctorate
Master's degree
Bachelor degree
Professional qualification
Secondary school education

Which specialist subject is your major interest?

Economics
Finance
Social Justice
Political Science
Other

SECTION TWO: MAIN QUESTIONNAIRE

Question 6: When did Italy join the single market?

1992 as member of European Union (EU) under the Maastricht Treaty
1957 as member of EUROATOM in 1957
1958 as member of the European Economic Community (EEC)
1952 as part of European Coal and Steel Community (ECSC)
1973 by application

Question 7: This question relates to Italy's position in the single market prior to 2008. Please indicate the extent of your agreement or disagreement with each of the statements in the grid—for EACH statement choose ONE option which is nearest to your opinion.

	Statement	*Agree strongly*	*Agree*	*Neither agree nor disagree*	*Disagree*	*Strongly disagree*
a	Italy's purpose in joining the European group was to indicate a political stance of being European after World War Two					
b	Italy was instigator of free movement of workers across borders					
c	Italy was opposed to common labour and wage policies					

(*continued*)

(continued)

	Statement	Agree strongly	Agree	Neither agree nor disagree	Disagree	Strongly disagree
d	The Italian public sector debt and current account deficit began in the 2000s					
e	Italy had a successful economy until 1992					
f	The structure of Italy's economy was dominated by large public sector firms					
g	Italy did not favour intergovernmentalist integration					
h	Italy's public sector debt problem resulted from its generous welfare system and inadequate taxation to fund it					
i	Italy was already in recession prior to the 2008 crisis but had received insufficient assistance from the EC to prepare it for a downturn					
i	Italy's competitiveness fell in 1970s and 1980s owing to excessive socialist party state intervention in state-run firms					

Question 8: This question relates to the initial effects of joining the Euro on Italy's position in the single market prior to 2008. Please indicate the extent of your agreement or disagreement with each statement—for EACH statement choose ONE option which is nearest to your opinion.

Italy and the Euro

	Statement	Agree strongly	Agree	Neither agree nor disagree	Disagree	Strongly disagree
a	The introduction of the eEuro in Italy was at too high an exchange rate					
b	Italy has shown high alignment with wage restraint and permanent fiscal consolidation principles of the European Monetary Union (EMU)					

(continued)

(continued)

	Statement	*Agree strongly*	*Agree*	*Neither agree nor disagree*	*Disagree*	*Strongly disagree*
c	Italy's EMU membership has decreased its competitiveness					
d	The barrier to Italy's economic recovery is its inability to devalue its currency as had been effective prior to joining the Euro					
d	Germany's domination of the decision on Eurozone standard EMU terms had a highly negative effect on the Italian economy					
e	From the time of joining the Euro, Italy's GDP levels were much lower than those of other major European Member State economies					

Question 9: Please make any comments you wish regarding Italy's economic and political situation related to its performance within the single market prior to 2008, especially those that you feel are particularly relevant to its political, economic or social position in 2020

....

Questions 10 to 15 concern Italy's position within the EU for the period from 2008 onwards

Question 10: This question concerns Italy's public sector debt-to-GDP ratio. Please indicate the extent of your agreement or disagreement with each statement—for EACH statement choose ONE option which is nearest to your opinion.

	Statement	*Agree strongly*	*Agree*	*Neither agree nor disagree*	*Disagree*	*Strongly disagree*
a	Italy's debt levels relate to public sector borrowing rather than excessive private credit/loans					
b	Italy has managed its debt-to-GDP ratio strictly since 1995					
c	The major reason that the Italian GDP did not grow after 2009 was failure to reform its labour markets and education system					

(*continued*)

(continued)

	Statement	*Agree strongly*	*Agree*	*Neither agree nor disagree*	*Disagree*	*Strongly disagree*
d	The public sector debt-to-GDP growth in Italy after 2008 was not simply a matter of continued excessive borrowing					
e	Italy's high public sector debt-to-GDP issues relate to before EU foundation in 1992 not to the 2008 crisis but this was not considered relevant by EU so that no specific mechanism was implemented to support Italy's unique position					
e	Applying the required EU social measures related to unemployment benefits after 2008 impacted on Italy possessing the required financial resources to reduce the public debt levels					
f	Lack of public sector aggregate demand was an important factor in the lack of growth of Italian GDP from 2008					
g	Public sector aggregated demand to support GDP growth was not hindered by the EU requirement to implement social benefits for the unemployed and other measures					

Question 11: Please indicate your explanation of why Italy's GDP-\ with fiscal consolidation and wage restraint according to EMU conditions. Choose ONE answer only.

GDP was negative in 2008

Italian government continued to borrow

Multiplier effect had higher impact because there was an economic downturn and Italian recession was deep

None of these

GDP rates were insufficient to service the debt levels

Question 12: This question focuses on structural issues in Italy that influence its capacity to increase GDP growth by means of the formula that the EU considers suitable.

	Statement	*Agree strongly*	*Agree*	*Neither agree nor disagree*	*Disagree*	*Strongly disagree*
a	Italy has a much higher than average proportion of micro-sized firms than other large European economies					
b	The Italian government has traditionally supported innovation by its economic interventions					
c	Italy's competitiveness has traditionally been in low-tech products, which can be made more cheaply by emerging economies such as China					
d	Italian micro firms are highly focused on technology					
	Overall productivity rates in Italian companies are lower than the European average because of the high proportion of large firms					
e	Italy's products are uncompetitive in its traditional markets because of the strength of the Euro which cannot be devalued					

Question 13:

(a) **Please answer Yes or NO to the statement regarding the EU's management of Italy's economic problems arising since 2008**

STATEMENT: The EU's universal approach to reviving the Eurozone Member State economies was in alignment with the Principle of Proportionality or the Principle of Subsidiarity.

Yes

No

(b) **Please provide an explanation for your choice of answer to part (a)**

Question 14

In your opinion has Italy benefitted from membership of the EU?

Yes
No

Question 15: Potential solutions to Italy's GDP growth challenges

In 2020, twelve years after the recession, Italy has the lowest GDP growth and highest debt levels in the Eurozone, which of the following do you consider would most assist Italy to recover and participate fully in Europe as it did prior to 1995. Please rank **ALL** options **in order of importance.** 1 is the most important and 5 is the least important

Option	*Proposed EU action to revive Italian economy*	*RANK (1 to 5; 1 is the most important)*
a	EU and Italy should employ independent global economic and political science experts as consultants to develop an economic and social plan to meet Italy's unique structural situation	
b	The EU/IMF should eliminate a large proportion of Italian debt	
c	Italy should leave the Euro	
d	EU should continue to impose the same conditions on Italy as on other Eurozone countries	
e	EU should enable Italy more independence to find a local solution as the local expert in alignment with the Principle of Subsidiarity	

Question 16: Please make any further comments you wish about the suitability of EU policies to support GDP growth and prosperity in Italy

...

THANK YOU FOR TAKING THE TIME TO COMPLETE THIS QUESTIONNAIRE

Frequencies and Descriptives Italy

Frequency Tables

q0001 Ho letto la dichiarazione di riservatezza e sono felice di prendere parte a questo sondaggio:// I have read the confidentiality statement and am happy to take part in this survey.

(continued)

		Frequency	Per cent	Valid per cent	Cumulative per cent
Valid	1 Sì! // Yes!	1547	98.2	98.2	98.2
	2 No.	28	1.8	1.8	100.0
	Total	1575	100.0	100.0	

q0002_0001 Indica la tua qualifica più alta:// Please indicate your highest qualification and your area of expertise!

		Frequency	Per cent	Valid per cent	Cumulative per cent
Valid	1 Ph.D./Doctorate	644	40.9	100.0	100.0
Missing	System	931	59.1		
Total		1575	100.0		

q0002_0002 Indica la tua qualifica più alta:// Please indicate your highest qualification and your area of expertise!

		Frequency	Per cent	Valid per cent	Cumulative per cent
Valid	1 Master's degree	714	45.3	100.0	100.0
Missing	System	861	54.7		
Total		1575	100.0		

q0002_0003 Indica la tua qualifica più alta:// Please indicate your highest qualification and your area of expertise!

		Frequency	Per cent	Valid per cent	Cumulative per cent
Valid	1 MBA/ Master of Business Administration	280	17.8	100.0	100.0
Missing	System	1295	82.2		
Total		1575	100.0		

q0002_0004 Indica la tua qualifica più alta:// Please indicate your highest qualification and your area of expertise!

		Frequency	*Per cent*	*Valid per cent*	*Cumulative per cent*
Valid	1 Economia // Economics	1008	64.0	100.0	100.0
Missing	System	567	36.0		
Total		1575	100.0		

q0002_0005 Indica la tua qualifica più alta:// Please indicate your highest qualification and your area of expertise!

		Frequency	*Per cent*	*Valid per cent*	*Cumulative per cent*
Valid	1,0 Finanza // Finance	392	24.9	100.0	100.0
Missing	System	1183	75.1		
Total		1575	100.0		

q0002_0006 Indica la tua qualifica più alta:// Please indicate your highest qualification and your area of expertise!

		Frequency	*Per cent*	*Valid per cent*	*Cumulative per cent*
Valid	1 Diritto sociale // Social law	147	9.3	100.0	100.0
Missing	System	1428	90.7		
Total		1575	100.0		

q0002_0007 Indica la tua qualifica più alta:// Please indicate your highest qualification and your area of expertise!

		Frequency	*Per cent*	*Valid per cent*	*Cumulative per cent*
Valid	1 Scienze Politiche // Political science	210	13.3	100.0	100.0
Missing	System	1365	86.7		
Total		1575	100.0		

q0002_other Altro (prego specificare:) // Other (please specify):

		Frequency	*Per cent*	*Valid per cent*	*Cumulative per cent*
Valid		1449	92.0	92.0	92.0
	Alimentazione	7	0.4	0.4	92.4
	Bbb	7	0.4	0.4	92.9
	Cc	7	0.4	0.4	93.3
	Contabilità	7	0.4	0.4	93.8
	Degree	7	0.4	0.4	94.2
	Diploma ragioniere e perito commerciale	7	0.4	0.4	94.7
	Dottorato	7	0.4	0.4	95.1
	Dottore	7	0.4	0.4	95.6
	Economics	7	0.4	0.4	96.0
	Employee	7	0.4	0.4	96.4
	Esperto Pari Opportunità	7	0.4	0.4	96.9
	Finance	7	0.4	0.4	97.3
	Immobili	7	0.4	0.4	97.8
	laurea	7	0.4	0.4	98.2
	Licenza media	7	0.4	0.4	98.7
	Master	7	0.4	0.4	99.1
	No	7	0.4	0.4	99.6
	Sporta	7	0.4	0.4	100.0
	Total	1575	100.0	100.0	

Question 6: When did Italy join the single market?

q0003 Quando ha aderito l'Italia al mercato unico?// When did Italy join the EU Single Market?

		Frequency	*Per cent*	*Valid per cent*	*Cumulative per cent*
Valid	1 1952 come parte della Comunità europea del carbone e dell'acciaio (CECA) // 1952 as part of European Coal and Steel Community	336	21.3	26.5	26.5
	2 1957 come membro di EUROATOM nel 1957 // 1957 as member of EUROATOM	112	7.1	8.8	35.4
	3 1958 come membro della Comunità economica europea (CEE) // 1958 as member of the European Economic Community (EEC)	266	16.9	21.0	56.4
	4 1973 per applicazione // 1973 by application	42	2.7	3.3	59.7
	5 1992 come membro dell'Unione Europea (UE) ai sensi del Trattato di Maastricht // 1992 as member of European Union (EU) under the Maastricht Treaty	511	32.4	40.3	100.0
	Total	1267	80.4	100.0	
Missing	System	308	19.6		
Total		1575	100.0		

Descriptives

Question 7: This question relates to Italy's position in the single market prior to 2008

Descriptive statistics

	N	*Minimum*	*Maximum*	*Mean*	*Std. deviation*
q0004_0001 a. L'obiettivo dell'Italia di entrare a far parte del gruppo europeo era quello di indicare una posizione politica di essere europea dopo la seconda guerra mondiale. // Italy's purpose in joining the European group was to indicate a political stance of being European after World War Two.	1155	1	5	2.13	1.036
q0004_0002 b. L'Italia è stata istigatrice della libera circolazione dei lavoratori attraverso le frontiere. // Italy was instigator of free movement of workers across borders.	1183	1	5	2.36	0.988
q0004_0003 c. L'Italia era contraria alle politiche comuni in materia di lavoro e salari. // Italy was opposed to common labour and wage policies.	1183	1	5	3.08	1.018
q0004_0004 d. Il debito del settore pubblico italiano e il disavanzo delle partite correnti sono iniziati negli anni 2000. // The Italian public sector debt and current account deficit began in the 2000s.	1099	1	5	3.10	1.313
q0004_0005 e. L'Italia ha avuto un'economia di successo fino al 1992. // Italy had a successful economy until 1992.	1120	1	5	2.64	1.192
q0004_0006 f. La struttura dell'economia italiana era dominata da grandi aziende del settore pubblico. // The structure of Italy's economy was dominated by large public sector firms.	1071	1	5	2.40	1.105

(*continued*)

(continued)

	N	*Minimum*	*Maximum*	*Mean*	*Std. deviation*
q0004_0007 g. L'Italia non ha favorito l'integrazione intergovernativa. // Italy did not favour intergovernmentalist integration.	1029	1	5	3.01	1.092
q0004_0008 h. Il problema del debito del settore pubblico in Italia è derivato dal suo generoso sistema di welfare e dall'insufficiente tassazione per finanziarlo. // Italy's public sector debt problem resulted from its generous welfare system and inadequate taxation to fund it.	1057	1	5	2.75	1.180
q0004_0009 i. L'Italia era già in recessione prima della crisi del 2008 ma aveva ricevuto assistenza insufficiente dalla CE per prepararla a una recessione. // Italy was already in recession prior to the 2008 crisis but had received insufficient assistance from the EC to prepare it for a downturn.	1036	1	5	2.55	1.080
q0004_0010 j. La competitività dell'Italia è diminuita negli anni '70 e '80 a causa dell'eccessivo intervento statale dei partiti socialisti nelle imprese statali. // Italy's competitiveness fell in 1970s and 1980s owing to excessive socialist party state intervention in state-run firms	1022	1	5	2.57	1.098
Valid N (listwise)	903				

Descriptives

Question 8: This question relates to the initial effects of joining the Euro on Italy's position in the single market prior to 2008

Descriptive statistics

	N	*Minimum*	*Maximum*	*Mean*	*Std. deviation*
q0005_0001 a. L'introduzione dell'euro in Italia ha avuto un tasso di cambio troppo elevato. // The introduction of the eEuro in Italy was at too high an exchange rate.	1239	1	5	1.95	1.065
q0005_0002 b. L'Italia ha mostrato un elevato allineamento con la restrizione salariale e i principi di consolidamento fiscale permanente dell'Unione Monetaria Europea (UEM). // Italy has shown high alignment with wage restraint and permanent fiscal consolidation.	1211	1	5	2.47	1.057
q0005_0003 c. L'adesione all'UEM in Italia ha diminuito la sua competitività. // Italy's EMU membership has decreased its competitiveness.	1218	1	5	2.49	1.103
q0005_0004 d. La barriera alla ripresa economica dell'Italia è la sua incapacità di svalutare la sua valuta come era stata efficace prima dell'adesione all'euro. // The barrier to Italy's economic recovery is its inability to devalue its currency as had been effective prior to joining the Euro.	1204	1	5	2.70	1.146
q0005_0005 e. Il dominio tedesco della decisione sulle condizioni UEM standard dell'Eurozona ha avuto un effetto fortemente negativo sull'economia italiana. // Germany's domination of the decision on Eurozone standard EMU terms had a highly negative effect on the Italian economy	1239	1	5	2.33	1.283

(*continued*)

(continued)

	N	*Minimum*	*Maximum*	*Mean*	*Std. deviation*
q0005_0006 f. Dal momento dell'adesione all'euro, i livelli del PIL italiano erano molto più bassi di quelli delle altre maggiori economie degli Stati membri europei. // From the time of joining the Euro, Italy's GDP levels were much lower than those of other than those of other major European Member State economies	1148	1	5	2.63	1.144
Valid N (listwise)	924				

Descriptives

Question 10: This question concerns Italy's public sector debt-to-GDP ratio.

Descriptive statistics

	N	*Minimum*	*Maximum*	*Mean*	*Std. deviation*
q0007_0001 a. I livelli di debito dell'Italia si riferiscono ai prestiti del settore pubblico piuttosto che a prestiti / prestiti privati eccessivi. // Italy's debt levels relate to public sector borrowing rather than excessive private credit/loans.	1071	1	5	2.08	0.990
q0007_0002 b. L'Italia ha gestito il proprio rapporto debito / PIL rigorosamente dal 1995. // Italy has managed its debt-to-GDP ratio strictly since 1995.	1050	1	5	2.84	1.115
q0007_0003 c. La ragione principale per cui il PIL italiano non è cresciuto dopo il 2009 è stata la mancata riforma dei mercati del lavoro e del sistema educativo. // The major reason that the Italian GDP did not grow after 2009 was failure to reform its labour	1078	1	5	2.65	1.017

(*continued*)

(continued)

	N	*Minimum*	*Maximum*	*Mean*	*Std. deviation*
q0007_0004 d. Il debito del settore pubblico nei confronti della crescita del PIL in Italia dopo il 2008 non era semplicemente una questione di continui prestiti eccessivi. // The public sector debt-to-GDP growth in Italy after 2008 was not simply a matter of continued excessive borrowing	1064	1	5	2.63	1.032
q0007_0005 e. L'elevato debito pubblico italiano nei confronti del PIL si riferisce alla prima fondazione dell'UE nel 1992, non alla crisi del 2008, ma ciò non è stato ritenuto pertinente dall'UE, pertanto non è stato attuato alcun meccanismo specifico a sostegno	1029	1	5	2.84	1.217
q0007_0006 f. L'applicazione delle necessarie misure sociali dell'UE relative alle indennità di disoccupazione dopo il 2008 ha avuto un impatto sull'Italia che possiede le risorse finanziarie necessarie per ridurre i livelli di debito pubblico. // Applying required EU social measures related to unemployment benefits after 2008 impacted on Italy possessing the required financial resources to reduce the public debt levels	889	1	5	2.55	0.954
q0007_0007 g. La mancanza di domanda aggregata del settore pubblico è stata un fattore importante nella mancanza di crescita del PIL italiano dal 2008. // Lack of public sector aggregate demand was an important factor in the lack of growth of Italian GDP from 2008	917	1	5	2.64	0.950

(*continued*)

(continued)

	N	*Minimum*	*Maximum*	*Mean*	*Std. deviation*
q0007_0008 h. La domanda aggregata del settore pubblico a sostegno della crescita del PIL non è stata ostacolata dall'obbligo dell'UE di attuare le prestazioni sociali per i disoccupati e altre misure. // Public sector aggregated demand to support GDP growth was not hindered by the EU requirement to implement social benefits for the unemployed and other measures	868	1	5	2.75	1.022
Valid N (listwise)	791				

Frequencies

Question 11: Please indicate your explanation of why Italy's GDP-to-debt ratio grew so rapidly after 2008 despite Italy's compliance with fiscal consolidation and wage restraint according to EMU conditions. Choose ONE answer only

q0008 Indica la tua spiegazione del perché il rapporto tra PIL e debito italiano è cresciuto così rapidamente dopo il 2008, nonostante la conformità dell'Italia con il consolidamento fiscale e la limitazione dei salari in base alle condizioni dell'UEM. Scegl

		Frequency	*Per cent*	*Valid per cent*	*Cumulative per cent*
Valid	1 Il PIL è stato negativo nel 2008. // GDP was negative in 2008.	154	9.8	13.8	13.8
	2 Il governo italiano ha continuato a prendere in prestito. // Italian government continued to borrow.	378	24.0	33.8	47.5
	3 L'effetto moltiplicatore ha avuto un impatto maggiore perché si è verificata una recessione economica e la recessione	357	22.7	31.9	79.4
	4 I tassi del PIL erano insufficienti per soddisfare i livelli del debito. // GDP rates were insufficient to service the debt levels	154	9.8	13.8	93.1
	5 Nessuna di queste. // None of these.	77	4.9	6.9	100.0
	Total	1120	71.1	100.0	

(*continued*)

(continued)

		Frequency	*Per cent*	*Valid per cent*	*Cumulative per cent*
Missing	System	455	28.9		
Total		1575	100.0		

Descriptives

Question 12: This question focuses on structural issues in Italy that influence its capacity to increase GDP growth by means of the formula that the EU considers suitable.

Descriptive statistics

	N	*Minimum*	*Maximum*	*Mean*	*Std. deviation*
q0009_0001 a. L'Italia ha una percentuale molto più alta della media di microimprese rispetto ad altre grandi economie europee. // Italy has a much higher than average proportion of micro-sized firms than other large European economies.	1057	1	5	2.03	.924
q0009_0002 b. Il governo italiano ha tradizionalmente sostenuto l'innovazione con i suoi interventi economici. // The Italian government has traditionally supported innovation by its economic interventions.	1106	1	5	2.96	1.268
q0009_0003 c. La competitività dell'Italia è stata tradizionalmente nei prodotti a bassa tecnologia, che possono essere resi più economici dalle economie emergenti come la Cina. // Italy's competitiveness has traditionally been in low-tech products, which can be made more cheaply by emerging economies such as China.	1057	1	5	2.76	1.097

(*continued*)

(continued)

	N	*Minimum*	*Maximum*	*Mean*	*Std. deviation*
q0009_0004 d. Le microimprese italiane sono fortemente focalizzate sulla tecnologia. // Italian micro firms are highly focused on technology.	1099	1	5	3.06	1.049
q0009_0005 e. I tassi di produttività complessivi nelle aziende italiane sono inferiori alla media europea a causa dell'alta percentuale di grandi aziende. // Overall productivity rates in Italian companies are lower than the European average because of the high proportion of large firms	1071	1	5	3.09	1.180
q0009_0006 f. I prodotti italiani non sono competitivi nei suoi mercati tradizionali a causa della forza dell'euro che non può essere svalutata. // Italy's products are uncompetitive in its traditional markets because of the strength of the Euro which cannot be devalued.	1008	1	5	2.83	1.204
Valid N (listwise)	798				

Frequencies

q0010 Rispondere Sì o NO alla dichiarazione relativa alla gestione dell'UE dei problemi economici dell'Italia che si presentano dal 2008:DICHIA RAZIONE: L'approccio universale dell'UE per rilanciare le economie degli Stati membri dell'Eurozona era in linea con i

(continued)

		Frequency	Per cent	Valid per cent	Cumulative per cent
Valid	1 Si! // Yes!	707	44.9	63.1	63.1
	2 No!	413	26.2	36.9	100.0
	Total	1120	71.1	100.0	
Missing	System	455	28.9		
Total		1575	100.0		

Descriptives

Question 15: Potential solutions to Italy's GDP growth challenges

Descriptive statistics

	N	Minimum	Maximum	Mean	Std. deviation
q0012_0001 L'UE e l'Italia dovrebbero impiegare esperti di scienze economiche e politiche globali indipendenti come consulenti per sviluppare un piano economico e sociale per far fronte alla singolare situazione strutturale dell'Italia. // EU and Italy should employ independent global economic and political science experts as consultants to develop an economic and social plan to meet Italy's unique structural situation.	1120	1	5	2.48	1.388
q0012_0002 L'UE / FMI dovrebbe eliminare gran parte del debito italiano. // The EU/ IMF should eliminate a large proportion of Italian debt.	1120	1	5	2.35	1.305
q0012_0003 L'Italia dovrebbe lasciare l'euro. // Italy should leave the Euro.	1120	1	5	3.19	1.416
q0012_0004 L'UE dovrebbe continuare a imporre le stesse condizioni in Italia degli altri paesi della zona euro. // EU should continue to impose the same conditions on Italy as on other Eurozone countries.	1120	1	5	3.40	1.142

(*continued*)

(continued)

	N	Minimum	Maximum	Mean	Std. deviation
q0012_0005 L'UE dovrebbe consentire all'Italia maggiore indipendenza nel trovare una soluzione locale, come un esperto locale in linea con il principio di sussidiarietà. // EU should enable Italy more independence to find a local solution as the local expert in alignment with the Principle of Subsidiarity.	1120	1	5	3.58	1.358
Valid N (listwise)	1120				

	2 No!	*469*	*29.8*	*41.9*	*100.0*
	Total	*1120*	*71.1*	*100.0*	
Missing	System	455	28.9		
Total		1575	100.0		

q0014 LEGACY—Alter

		Frequency	Per cent	Valid per cent	Cumulative per cent
Valid	2 18–29	70	4.4	22.2	22.2
	3 30–44	133	8.4	42.2	64.4
	4 45–60	98	6.2	31.1	95.6
	5 Über 60	14	0.9	4.4	100.0
	Total	315	20.0	100.0	
Missing	System	1260	80.0		
Total		1575	100.0		

q0015 LEGACY—Geschlecht

		Frequency	Per cent	Valid per cent	Cumulative per cent
Valid	1 Männlich	196	12.4	62.2	62.2
	2 Weiblich	119	7.6	37.8	100.0
	Total	315	20.0	100.0	
Missing	System	1260	80.0		
Total		1575	100.0		

q0016 LEGACY—Gerätetyp

		Frequency	*Per cent*	*Valid per cent*	*Cumulative per cent*
Valid	1 iOS-Smartphone/-Tablet	35	2.2	11.1	11.1
	2 Android-Smartphone/-Tablet	126	8.0	40.0	51.1
	4 Windows-Desktop/-Laptop	147	9.3	46.7	97.8
	6 Sonstiges	7	0.4	2.2	100.0
	Total	315	20.0	100.0	
Missing	System	1260	80.0		
Total		1575	100.0		

Custom Tables

Question 10: This question concerns Italy's public sector debt-to-GDP ratio.

Note: "1" means strong agreement; "5" means strong disagreement!

	1 Concordo fortemente // Agree strongly	*2 Essere d'accordo // Agree*	*3 Nè d'accordo né in disaccordo // Neither agree nor disagree*	*4 Disaccordo // Disagree*	*5 Fortemente in disaccordo // Strongly disagree*
	Row N %	*Row N %*	*Row N %*	*Row N %*	*Row N %*
q0007_0001 a. I livelli di debito dell'Italia si riferiscono ai prestiti del settore pubblico piuttosto che a prestiti / prestiti privati eccessivi. // Italy's debt levels relate to public sector borrowing rather than excessive private credit/ loans.	32.0%	37.9%	22.2%	5.2%	2.6%

(*continued*)

(continued)

	1 Concordo fortemente // Agree strongly	*2 Essere d'accordo // Agree*	*3 Nè d'accordo né in disaccordo // Neither agree nor disagree*	*4 Disaccordo // Disagree*	*5 Fortemente in disaccordo // Strongly disagree*
	Row N %	*Row N %*	*Row N %*	*Row N %*	*Row N %*
q0007_0002 b. L'Italia ha gestito il proprio rapporto debito / PIL rigorosamente dal 1995. // Italy has managed its debt-to-GDP ratio strictly since 1995.	10.7%	30.7%	31.3%	18.7%	8.7%
q0007_0003 c. La ragione principale per cui il PIL italiano non è cresciuto dopo il 2009 è stata la mancata riforma dei mercati del lavoro e del sistema educativo. // The major reason that the Italian GDP did not grow after 2009 was failure to reform its labour.	14.3%	29.2%	37.0%	16.2%	3.2%
q0007_0004 d. Il debito del settore pubblico nei confronti della crescita del PIL in Italia dopo il 2008 non era semplicemente una questione di continui prestiti eccessivi. // The public sector debt-to-GDP growth in Italy after 2008 was not simply a matter of continued excessive borrowing	13.2%	36.8%	27.0%	20.4%	2.6%

(*continued*)

(continued)

	1 Concordo fortemente // Agree strongly	*2 Essere d'accordo // Agree*	*3 Nè d'accordo né in disaccordo // Neither agree nor disagree*	*4 Disaccordo // Disagree*	*5 Fortemente in disaccordo // Strongly disagree*
	Row N %	*Row N %*	*Row N %*	*Row N %*	*Row N %*
q0007_0005 e. L'elevato debito pubblico italiano nei confronti del PIL si riferisce alla prima fondazione dell'UE nel 1992, non alla crisi del 2008, ma ciò non è stato ritenuto pertinente dall'UE, pertanto non è stato attuato alcun meccanismo specifico a sostegno	12.9%	29.3%	33.3%	9.5%	15.0%
q0007_0006 f. L'applicazione delle necessarie misure sociali dell'UE relative alle indennità di disoccupazione dopo il 2008 ha avuto un impatto sull'Italia che possiede le risorse finanziarie necessarie per ridurre i livelli di debito pubblico. // Applying the r required EU social measures related to unemployment benefits after 2008 impacted on Italy possessing the required financial resources to reduce the public debt levels	15.0%	30.7%	40.9%	11.0%	2.4%

(*continued*)

(continued)

	1 Concordo fortemente // Agree strongly	*2 Essere d'accordo // Agree*	*3 Nè d'accordo né in disaccordo // Neither agree nor disagree*	*4 Disaccordo // Disagree*	*5 Fortemente in disaccordo // Strongly disagree*
	Row N %	*Row N %*	*Row N %*	*Row N %*	*Row N %*
q0007_0007 g. La mancanza di domanda aggregata del settore pubblico è stata un fattore importante nella mancanza di crescita del PIL italiano dal 2008. // Lack of public sector aggregate demand was an important factor in the lack of growth of Italian GDP from 20	9.9%	36.6%	35.9%	14.5%	3.1%
q0007_0008 h. La domanda aggregata del settore pubblico a sostegno della crescita del PIL non è stata ostacolata dall'obbligo dell'UE di attuare le prestazioni sociali per i disoccupati e altre misure. // Public sector aggregated demand to support GDP growth was not hindered by the EU requirement to implement social benefits for the unemployed and other measures	10.5%	32.3%	33.1%	20.2%	4.0%

(*continued*)

Descriptives

Descriptive statistics

	N	*Minimum*	*Maximum*	*Mean*	*Std. deviation*
q0007_0001 a. I livelli di debito dell'Italia si riferiscono ai prestiti del settore pubblico piuttosto che a prestiti / prestiti privati eccessivi. // Italy's debt levels relate to public sector borrowing rather than excessive private credit/ loans.	1071	1	5	2.08	0.990
q0007_0002 b. L'Italia ha gestito il proprio rapporto debito / PIL rigorosamente dal 1995. // Italy has managed its debt-to-GDP ratio strictly since 1995.	1050	1	5	2.84	1.115

(*continued*)

(continued)

	N	*Minimum*	*Maximum*	*Mean*	*Std. deviation*
q0007_0003 c. La ragione principale per cui il PIL italiano non è cresciuto dopo il 2009 è stata la mancata riforma dei mercati del lavoro e del sistema educativo. // The major reason that the Italian GDP did not grow after 2009 was failure to reform its labour.	1078	1	5	2.65	1.017
q0007_0004 d. Il debito del settore pubblico nei confronti della crescita del PIL in Italia dopo il 2008 non era semplicemente una questione di continui prestiti eccessivi. // The public sector debt-to-GDP growth in Italy after 2008 was not simply a matter of continued excessive borrowing.	1064	1	5	2.63	1.032

(continued)

(continued)

	N	*Minimum*	*Maximum*	*Mean*	*Std. deviation*
q0007_0005 e. L'elevato debito pubblico italiano nei confronti del PIL si riferisce alla prima fondazione dell'UE nel 1992, non alla crisi del 2008, ma ciò non è stato ritenuto pertinente dall'UE, pertanto non è stato attuato alcun meccanismo specifico a sostegno	1029	1	5	2.84	1.217

(*continued*)

(continued)

	N	*Minimum*	*Maximum*	*Mean*	*Std. deviation*
q0007_0006 f. L'applicazione delle necessarie misure sociali dell'UE relative alle indennità di disoccupazione dopo il 2008 ha avuto un impatto sull'Italia che possiede le risorse finanziarie necessarie per ridurre i livelli di debito pubblico. // Applying the r required EU social measures related to unemployment benefits after 2008 impacted on Italy possessing the required financial resources to reduce the public debt levels.	889	1	5	2.55	0.954

(*continued*)

(continued)

	N	*Minimum*	*Maximum*	*Mean*	*Std. deviation*
q0007_0007 g. La mancanza di domanda aggregata del settore pubblico è stata un fattore importante nella mancanza di crescita del PIL italiano dal 2008. // Lack of public sector aggregate demand was an important factor in the lack of growth of Italian GDP from 2008.	917	1	5	2.64	.950

(*continued*)

(continued)

	N	*Minimum*	*Maximum*	*Mean*	*Std. deviation*
q0007_0008 h. La domanda aggregata del settore pubblico a sostegno della crescita del PIL non è stata ostacolata dall'obbligo dell'UE di attuare le prestazioni sociali per i disoccupati e altre misure. // Public sector aggregated demand to support GDP growth was not hindered by the EU requirement to implement social benefits for the unemployed and other measures.	868	1	5	2.75	1.022
Valid N (listwise)	791				

(*continued*)

T-Test

Paired samples statistics

		Mean	*N*	*Std. deviation*	*Std. error mean*
Pair 1	q0007_0003 c. La ragione principale per cui il PIL italiano non è cresciuto dopo il 2009 è stata la mancata riforma dei mercati del lavoro e del sistema educativo. // The major reason that the Italian GDP did not grow after 2009 was failure to reform its labour.	2.66	1043	1.016	0.031
	q0007_0001 a. I livelli di debito dell'Italia si riferiscono ai prestiti del settore pubblico piuttosto che a prestiti / prestiti privati eccessivi. // Italy's debt levels relate to public sector borrowing rather than excessive private credit/loans.	2.07	1043	0.963	0.030

(continued)

		Mean	*N*	*Std. deviation*	*Std. error mean*
Pair 2	q0007_0003 c. La ragione principale per cui il PIL italiano non è cresciuto dopo il 2009 è stata la mancata riforma dei mercati del lavoro e del sistema educativo. // The major reason that the Italian GDP did not grow after 2009 was failure to reform its labour.	2.57	1001	0.986	0.031
	q0007_0005 e. L'elevato debito pubblico italiano nei confronti del PIL si riferisce alla prima fondazione dell'UE nel 1992, non alla crisi del 2008, ma ciò non è stato ritenuto pertinente dall'UE, pertanto non è stato attuato alcun meccanismo specifico a sostegno	2.84	1001	1.205	0.038

(*continued*)

(continued)

		Mean	*N*	*Std. deviation*	*Std. error mean*
Pair 3	q0007_0003 c. La ragione principale per cui il PIL italiano non è cresciuto dopo il 2009 è stata la mancata riforma dei mercati del lavoro e del sistema educativo. // The major reason that the Italian GDP did not grow after 2009 was failure to reform its labour.	2.54	861	1.031	0.035
	q0007_0006 f. L'applicazione delle necessarie misure sociali dell'UE relative alle indennità di disoccupazione dopo il 2008 ha avuto un impatto sull'Italia che possiede le risorse finanziarie necessarie per ridurre i livelli di debito pubblico. // Applying the required EU social measures related to unemployment benefits after 2008 impacted on Italy possessing the required financial resources to reduce the public debt levels	2.54	861	0.931	0.032

(*continued*)

The t-Test (next page) shows: The level of Q10c is significantly higher than Q10a—the agreement is lower!

Also The level of Q10c is significantly lower than Q10e—the agreement is higher!

There is no difference between Q10c and Q10f.

Correlations

Q 10 c/a, c/e and c/f are correlated low, but significant. If the one is lower or higher, the others may be too.

Paired samples correlations

		N	*Correlation*	*Sig.*
Pair 1	q0007_0003 c. La ragione principale per cui il PIL italiano non è cresciuto dopo il 2009 è stata la mancata riforma dei mercati del lavoro e del sistema educativo. // The major reason that the Italian GDP did not grow after 2009 was failure to reform its labour & q0007_0001 a. I livelli di debito dell'Italia si riferiscono ai prestiti del settore pubblico piuttosto che a prestiti / prestiti privati eccessivi. // Italy's debt levels relate to public sector borrowing rather than excessive private credit/loans.	1043	0.101	0.001
Pair 2	q0007_0003 c. La ragione principale per cui il PIL italiano non è cresciuto dopo il 2009 è stata la mancata riforma dei mercati del lavoro e del sistema educativo. // The major reason that the Italian GDP did not grow after 2009 was failure to reform its labour & q0007_0005 e. L'elevato debito pubblico italiano nei confronti del PIL si riferisce alla prima fondazione dell'UE nel 1992, non alla crisi del 2008, ma ciò non è stato ritenuto pertinente dall'UE, pertanto non è stato attuato alcun meccanismo specifico a sostegno	1001	0.184	0.000

(*continued*)

(continued)

		N	*Correlation*	*Sig.*
Pair 3	q0007_0003 c. La ragione principale per cui il PIL italiano non è cresciuto dopo il 2009 è stata la mancata riforma dei mercati del lavoro e del sistema educativo. // The major reason that the Italian GDP did not grow after 2009 was failure to reform its labour & q0007_0006 f. L'applicazione delle necessarie misure sociali dell'UE relative alle indennità di disoccupazione dopo il 2008 ha avuto un impatto sull'Italia che possiede le risorse finanziarie necessarie per ridurre i livelli di debito pubblico. // Applying the required EU social measures related to unemployment benefits after 2008 impacted on Italy possessing the required financial resources to reduce the public debt levels.	861	0.195	0.000

Test of levels of answers Q 10 c/a; c/e and c/f

Paired samples test

		Paired differences					*t*	*df*	*Sig. (2-tailed)*
		Mean	*Std. deviation*	*Std. error mean*	*95% confidence interval of the difference*				
					Lower	*Upper*			
Pair 1	q0007_0003 c. La ragione principale per cui il PIL italiano non è cresciuto dopo il 2009 è stata la mancata riforma dei mercati del lavoro e del sistema educativo. // The major reason that the Italian GDP did not grow after 2009 was failure to reform its labour – q0007_0001 a. I livelli di debito dell'Italia si riferiscono ai prestiti del settore pubblico piuttosto che a prestiti / prestiti privati eccessivi. // Italy's debt levels relate to public sector borrowing rather than excessive private credit/loans.	0.584	1.327	0.041	0.503	0.665	14.21	1042	0.000

(*continued*)

(continued)

		Paired differences					*t*	*df*	*Sig. (2-tailed)*
		Mean	*Std. deviation*	*Std. error mean*	*95% confidence interval of the difference*				
					Lower	*Upper*			
Pair 2	q0007_0003 c. La ragione principale per cui il PIL italiano non è cresciuto dopo il 2009 è stata la mancata riforma dei mercati del lavoro e del sistema educativo. // The major reason that the Italian GDP did not grow after 2009 was failure to reform its labour – q0007_0005 e. L'elevato debito pubblico italiano nei confronti del PIL si riferisce alla prima fondazione dell'UE nel 1992, non alla crisi del 2008, ma ciò non è stato ritenuto pertinente dall'UE, pertanto non è stato attuato alcun meccanismo specifico a sostegno	-0.266	1.410	0.045	-0.353	-0.178	-5.96	1000	0.000

(*continued*)

(continued)

		Paired differences					*t*	*df*	*Sig. (2-tailed)*
		Mean	*Std. deviation*	*Std. error mean*	*95% confidence interval of the difference*				
					Lower	*Upper*			
Pair 3	q0007_0003 c. La ragione principale per cui il PIL italiano non è cresciuto dopo il 2009 è stata la mancata riforma dei mercati del lavoro e del sistema educativo. // The major reason that the Italian GDP did not grow after 2009 was failure to reform its labour – q0007_0006 f. L'applicazione delle necessarie misure sociali dell'UE relative alle indennità di disoccupazione dopo il 2008 ha avuto un impatto sull'Italia che possiede le risorse finanziarie necessarie per ridurre i livelli di debito pubblico. // Applying the required EU social measures related to unemployment benefits after 2008 impacted on Italy possessing the required financial resources to reduce the public debt levels	0.008	1.247	0.042	-0.075	0.092	0.191	860	0.848

Custom Tables

Question 12: This question focuses on structural issues in Italy that influence its capacity to increase GDP growth by means of the formula that the EU considers suitable.

Note: "1" means strong agreement; "5" means strong disagreement!

	1 Concordo fortemente // Agree strongly	*2 Essere d'accordo // Agree*	*3 Nè d'accordo né in disaccordo // Neither agree nor disagree*	*4 Disaccordo // Disagree*	*5 Fortemente in disaccordo // Strongly disagree*
	Row N %	*Row N %*	*Row N %*	*Row N %*	*Row N %*
q0009_0001 a. L'Italia ha una percentuale molto più alta della media di microimprese rispetto ad altre grandi economie europee. // Italy has a much higher than average proportion of micro-sized firms than other large European economies.	33.1%	36.4%	26.5%	2.0%	2.0%
q0009_0002 b. Il governo italiano ha tradizionalmente sostenuto l'innovazione con i suoi interventi economici. // The Italian government has traditionally supported innovation by its economic interventions.	15.8%	22.8%	22.8%	26.6%	12.0%

(*continued*)

(continued)

	1 Concordo fortemente // Agree strongly	*2 Essere d'accordo // Agree*	*3 Nè d'accordo né in disaccordo // Neither agree nor disagree*	*4 Disaccordo // Disagree*	*5 Fortemente in disaccordo // Strongly disagree*
	Row N %	*Row N %*	*Row N %*	*Row N %*	*Row N %*
q0009_0003 c. La competitività dell'Italia è stata tradizionalmente nei prodotti a bassa tecnologia, che possono essere resi più economici dalle economie emergenti come la Cina. // Italy's competitiveness has traditionally been in low-tech products, which can be made more cheaply by emerging economies such as China.	13.2%	27.2%	37.7%	13.9%	7.9%
q0009_0004 d. Le microimprese italiane sono fortemente focalizzate sulla tecnologia. // Italian micro firms are highly focused on technology.	8.3%	21.0%	33.8%	30.6%	6.4%

(*continued*)

(continued)

	1 Concordo fortemente // Agree strongly	*2 Essere d'accordo // Agree*	*3 Nè d'accordo né in disaccordo // Neither agree nor disagree*	*4 Disaccordo // Disagree*	*5 Fortemente in disaccordo // Strongly disagree*
	Row N %	*Row N %*	*Row N %*	*Row N %*	*Row N %*
q0009_0005 e. I tassi di produttività complessivi nelle aziende italiane sono inferiori alla media europea a causa dell'alta percentuale di grandi aziende. // Overall productivity rates in Italian companies are lower than the European average because of the high proportion of large firms	10.5%	21.6%	28.8%	26.8%	12.4%
q0009_0006 f. I prodotti italiani non sono competitivi nei suoi mercati tradizionali a causa della forza dell'euro che non può essere svalutata. // Italy's products are uncompetitive in its traditional markets because of the strength of the euro which cannot be devalued	16.0%	24.3%	31.3%	18.1%	10.4%

(*continued*)

Descriptives

Descriptive statistics

	N	*Minimum*	*Maximum*	*Mean*	*Std. seviation*
q0009_0001 a. L'Italia ha una percentuale molto più alta della media di microimprese rispetto ad altre grandi economie europee. // Italy has a much higher than average proportion of micro-sized firms than other large European economies.	1057	1	5	2.03	0.924
q0009_0002 b. Il governo italiano ha tradizionalmente sostenuto l'innovazione con i suoi interventi economici. // The Italian government has traditionally supported innovation by its economic interventions.	1106	1	5	2.96	1.268

(*continued*)

(continued)

	N	*Minimum*	*Maximum*	*Mean*	*Std. seviation*
q0009_0003 c. La competitività dell'Italia è stata tradizionalmente nei prodotti a bassa tecnologia, che possono essere resi più economici dalle economie emergenti come la Cina. // Italy's competitiveness has traditionally been in low-tech products, which can be made more cheaply by emerging economies such as China.	1057	1	5	2.76	1.097
q0009_0004 d. Le microimprese italiane sono fortemente focalizzate sulla tecnologia. // Italian micro firms are highly focused on technology.	1099	1	5	3.06	1.049

(*continued*)

(continued)

	N	*Minimum*	*Maximum*	*Mean*	*Std. seviation*
q0009_0005 e. I tassi di produttività complessivi nelle aziende italiane sono inferiori alla media europea a causa dell'alta percentuale di grandi aziende. // Overall productivity rates in Italian companies are lower than the European average because of the high proportion of large firms	1071	1	5	3.09	1.180
q0009_0006 f. I prodotti italiani non sono competitivi nei suoi mercati tradizionali a causa della forza dell'euro che non può essere svalutata. // Italy's products are uncompetitive in its traditional markets because of the strength of the Euro which cannot be devalued.	1008	1	5	2.83	1.204
Valid N (listwise)	798				

(*continued*)

T-Test

Paired samples statistics

		Mean	*N*	*Std. deviation*	*Std. error mean*
Pair 1	q0009_0001 a. L'Italia ha una percentuale molto più alta della media di microimprese rispetto ad altre grandi economie europee. // Italy has a much higher than average proportion of micro-sized firms than other large European economies.	2.10	945	0.934	0.030
	q0009_0006 f. I prodotti italiani non sono competitivi nei suoi mercati tradizionali a causa della forza dell'euro che non può essere svalutata. // Italy's products are uncompetitive in its traditional markets because of the strength of the Euro which cannot be devalued.	2.76	945	1.131	0.037
Pair 2	q0009_0003 c. La competitività dell'Italia è stata tradizionalmente nei prodotti a bassa tecnologia, che possono essere resi più economici dalle economie emergenti come la Cina. // Italy's competitiveness has traditionally been in low-tech products. which can be made more cheaply by emerging economies such as China.	2.77	945	1.102	0.036
	q0009_0006 f. I prodotti italiani non sono competitivi nei suoi mercati tradizionali a causa della forza dell'euro che non può essere svalutata. // Italy's products are uncompetitive in its traditional markets because of the strength of the eEuro which cannot be devalued.	2.80	945	1.179	0.038

Correlations: Q12f is correlated low, but significant with Q12a (negative!) and with Q12c.

Paired samples correlations

		N	*Correlation*	*Sig.*
Pair 1	q0009_0001 a. L'Italia ha una percentuale molto più alta della media di microimprese rispetto ad altre grandi economie europee. // Italy has a much higher than average proportion of micro-sized firms than other large European economies. & q0009_0006 f. I prodotti italiani non sono competitivi nei suoi mercati tradizionali a causa della forza dell'euro che non può essere svalutata. // Italy's products are uncompetitive in its traditional markets because of the strength of the eEuro which cannot be devalued	945	-0.070	0.032
Pair 2	q0009_0003 c. La competitività dell'Italia è stata tradizionalmente nei prodotti a bassa tecnologia, che possono essere resi più economici dalle economie emergenti come la Cina. // Italy's competitiveness has traditionally been in low-tech products, which can be made more cheaply by emerging economies such as China. & q0009_0006 f. I prodotti italiani non sono competitivi nei suoi mercati tradizionali a causa della forza dell'euro che non può essere svalutata. // Italy's products are uncompetitive in its traditional markets because of the strength of the Euro which cannot be devalued	945	0.124	0.000

Test of levels of answers Q12 f/a and f/c

There is a significant difference between Q12f and Q12a; Q12f is answered with less agreement.

Paired samples test

		Paired differences					*t*	*df*	*Sig. (2-tailed)*
		Mean	*Std. dev.*	*Std. error mean*	*95% confidence interval of the difference*				
					Lower	*Upper*			
Pair 1	q0009_0001 a. L'Italia ha una percentuale molto più alta della media di microimprese rispetto ad altre grandi economie europee. // Italy has a much higher than average proportion of micro-sized firms than other large European economies. & q0009_0006 f. I prodotti italiani non sono competitivi nei suoi mercati tradizionali a causa della forza dell'euro che non può essere svalutata. // Italy's products are uncompetitive in its traditional markets because of the strength of the Euro which cannot be devalued	-0.667	1.516	0.049	-0.763	-0.570	-13.52	944	0.000

(*continued*)

(continued)

		Paired differences					*t*	*df*	*Sig. (2-tailed)*
		Mean	*Std. dev.*	*Std. error mean*	*95% confidence interval of the difference*				
					Lower	*Upper*			
Pair 2	q0009_0003 c. La competitività dell'Italia è stata tradizionalmente nei prodotti a bassa tecnologia, che possono essere resi più economici dalle economie emergenti come la Cina. // Italy's competitiveness has traditionally been in low-tech products, which can be made more cheaply by emerging economies such as China & q0009_0006 f. I prodotti italiani non sono competitivi nei suoi mercati tradizionali a causa della forza dell'euro che non può essere svalutata. // Italy's products are uncompetitive in its traditional markets because of the strength of the Euro which cannot be devalued.	-0.030	1.511	0.049	-0.126	0.067	-0.603	944	0.547

(continued)

Test of levels of answers Q12 f/a and f/c

There is a significant difference between Q12f and Q12a; Q12f is answered with less agreement.

Paired samples test

		Paired differences					*t*	*df*	*Sig. (2-tailed)*
		Mean	*Std. dev.*	*Std. error mean*	*95% confidence interval of the difference*				
					Lower	*Upper*			
Pair 1	q0009_0001 a. L'Italia ha una percentuale molto più alta della media di microimprese rispetto ad altre grandi economie europee. // Italy has a much higher than average proportion of micro-sized firms than other large European economies. & q0009_0006 f. I prodotti italiani non sono competitivi nei suoi mercati tradizionali a causa della forza dell'euro che non può essere svalutata. // Italy's products are uncompetitive in its traditional markets because of the strength of the Euro which cannot be devalued	-0.667	1.516	0.049	-0.763	-0.570	-13.52	944	0.000

(*continued*)

(continued)

		Paired differences					*t*	*df*	*Sig. (2-tailed)*
		Mean	*Std. dev.*	*Std. error mean*	*95% confidence interval of the difference*				
					Lower	*Upper*			
Pair 2	q0009_0003 c. La competitività dell'Italia è stata tradizionalmente nei prodotti a bassa tecnologia, che possono essere resi più economici dalle economie emergenti come la Cina. // Italy's competitiveness has traditionally been in low-tech products, which can be made more cheaply by emerging economies such as China & q0009_0006 f. I prodotti italiani non sono competitivi nei suoi mercati tradizionali a causa della forza dell'euro che non può essere svalutata. // Italy's products are uncompetitive in its traditional markets because of the strength of the Euro which cannot be devalued.	-0.030	1.511	0.049	-0.126	0.067	-0.603	944	0.547

Index

S. Weißschnur, *The Proportionality of State Intervention*,
https://doi.org/10.1007/978-3-030-75676-5

Q

The manufacturer's authorised representative in the EU is Springer Nature Customer Service Centre GmbH, Europaplatz 3, 69115 Heidelberg, Germany. If you have any concerns regarding our products, please contact ProductSafety@springernature.com

Printed and bound by CPI Group (UK) Ltd, Croydon, CR0 4YY
30/09/2026
02225701-0018